MW00800168

BEIJING'S
POWER
and CHINA'S
BORDERS

A publication of the Northeast Asia Seminar

Rediscovering Russia in Asia
Siberia and the Russian Far East
Edited by Stephen Kotkin and David Wolff

Mongolia in the Twentieth Century
Landlocked Cosmopolitan
Edited by Stephen Kotkin and Bruce A. Elleman

Korea at the Center
Dynamics of Regionalism in Northeast Asia
Edited by Charles K. Armstrong, Gilbert Rozman,
Samuel S. Kim, and Stephen Kotkin

Manchurian Railways and the Opening of China
An International History
Edited by Bruce A. Elleman and Stephen Kotkin

Beijing's Power and China's Borders
Twenty Neighbors in Asia
Edited by Bruce A. Elleman, Stephen Kotkin,
and Clive Schofield

BEIJING'S POWER

and CHINA'S BORDERS

Twenty Neighbors in Asia

Edited by
Bruce A. Elleman, Stephen Kotkin,
and Clive Schofield

M.E.Sharpe
Armonk, New York
London, England

Copyright © 2013 by M.E. Sharpe, Inc.

All rights reserved. No part of this book may be reproduced in any form
without written permission from the publisher, M.E. Sharpe, Inc.,
80 Business Park Drive, Armonk, New York 10504.

The EuroSlavic fonts used to create this work are © 1986–2012 Payne Loving Trust.
EuroSlavic is available from Linguist's Software, Inc.,
www.linguistsoftware.com, P.O. Box 580, Edmonds, WA 98020-0580 USA
tel (425) 775-1130.

Library of Congress Cataloging-in-Publication Data

Beijing's power and China's borders : twenty neighbors in Asia / edited by Bruce A. Elleman,
Stephen Kotkin, and Clive Schofield.
    p. cm.
"A publication of the Northeast Asia Seminar"—P. facing t.p.
Includes bibliographical references and index.

ISBN 978-0-7656-2763-6 (hardcover : alk. paper) — ISBN 978-0-7656–2764-3 (pbk. : alk. paper)
    1. China—Foreign relations—Asia. 2. Asia—Foreign relations—China. 3. China—
Boundaries. I. Elleman, Bruce A., 1959– II. Kotkin, Stephen. III. Schofield, Clive H., 1969–

DS33.4.C5B45 2012
327.5105—dc23   2012014912

Printed in the United States of America

The paper used in this publication meets the minimum requirements of
American National Standard for Information Sciences
Permanence of Paper for Printed Library Materials,
ANSI Z 39.48-1984.

IBT (c)   10   9   8   7   6   5   4   3   2   1
IBT (p)   10   9   8   7   6   5   4   3   2   1

For Allen S. Whiting, Regents' Professor of Political Science, University of Arizona, for his contributions to the study of China's border relations with Russia.

Contents

Acknowledgments   ix

Series Editor's Preface *Stephen Kotkin*   xi

Abbreviations   xvi

List of Maps   xvii

Introduction
   Bruce A. Elleman and Clive Schofield   3

1. Sino-Afghani Border Relations   13
    Artemy M. Kalinovsky

2. Bhutan-China Border Disputes and Their Geopolitical Implications   23
    Paul J. Smith

3. Brunei's Contested Sea Border with China   37
    Ian Storey

4. India's Intractable Border Dispute with China   47
    Brahma Chellaney

5. Indonesia's "Invisible" Border with China   61
    I Made Andi Arsana and Clive Schofield

6. Sino-Japanese Territorial and Maritime Disputes   81
    June Teufel Dreyer

7. Kazakhstan's Border Relations with China   97
    Stephen Blank

8. Sino-Korean Border Relations   111
    Charles K. Armstrong

9. Kyrgyzstan: China's Regional Playground?   127
    Erica Marat

10. The China-Laos Boundary: Lan Xang Meets the Middle Kingdom   143
    Ian Townsend-Gault

11. Malaysia and China: Economic Growth Overshadows
    Sovereignty Dispute   155
    Vivian Louis Forbes

12. Sino-Mongol Border: From Conflict to Precarious Resolution   169
    Morris Rossabi

13. The Sino-Myanmar Border   191
    Brendan Whyte

14. China-Nepal Border: Potential Hot Spot?   205
    Chitra K. Tiwari

15. The Sino-Pakistan Border: Stability in an Unstable Region   219
    Christopher Tang

16. Philippine-China Border Relations: Cautious Engagement
    Amid Tensions   235
    Lowell Bautista and Clive Schofield

17. Sino-Russian Border Resolution   251
    Mark Galeotti

18. PRC Disputes with the ROC on Taiwan   267
    Bruce A. Elleman

19. Tajikistan-China Border Normalization   283
    Gregory Gleason

20. Sino-Vietnamese Border Disputes   295
    Ramses Amer

Conclusions   311
    Bruce A. Elleman, Stephen Kotkin, and Clive Schofield

Selected Bibliography   331

Index   341

About the Editors and Contributors   365

Acknowledgments

Our thanks to Professor Chen Jian at Cornell University; Valarie Russell for her research assistance at the George C. Marshall Center; James Person of the Woodrow Wilson International Center for Scholars; Professor Kim Dong-gil of Peking University; Dr. N. Altantsetseg, Director of the School of Foreign Service of the National University of Mongolia; Mr. J. Enkhsaikhan, former Ambassador of Mongolia to the United Nations and current Ambassador of Mongolia to Austria; Dr. Dan Dzurek, Geographer, formerly of the U.S. State Department; Antonio Giustozzi, Visiting Professor at King's College, London; Mr. Graeme Rymill, librarian of the University of Western Australia; Dr. Mohan Malik at the Asia-Pacific Center for Security Studies, Honolulu; and Christopher Jasparro, Associate Professor, National Security Affairs Department, U.S. Naval War College.

Most of the maps that appear in this book have been significantly amended or redrawn from existing sources to match them to the specific chapters. In some instances, the changes have been less extensive. Special thanks to I Made Andi Arsana for redrafting the majority of the maps appearing in this volume. Particular thanks also to Miss Kabita Ghimire for meticulously preparing the map of the Sino-Nepalese border. The map on India-China territorial disputes has been adapted from Brahma Chellaney, *Water: Asia's New Battleground* (Georgetown University Press, 2011). Maps 5.1, 11.1, 16.1, and 20.1 have been adapted from Figure 2, and Map 6 has been adapted from Figure 1, in Clive Schofield, et al., *From Disputed Waters to Seas of Opportunity: Overcoming Barriers to Maritime Cooperation in East and Southeast Asia* (National Bureau of Asian Research Special Report No. 30, July 2011). Map 20.3 was adapted from Ramses Amer, *The Sino-Vietnamese Approach to Managing Boundary Disputes*, Maritime Briefing 3, no. 5 (Durham: International Boundaries Research Unit, University of Durham, 2002). We are also indebted to Brendan Whyte for providing Map 13 of the Myanmar-China border.

Profound thanks to Allen Whiting, who, in addition to writing such classics as *China Crosses the Yalu*, during the 1950s "discovered" the Columbia University copy of the original Karakhan manifesto that promised the return of the Chinese Eastern Railway to China without compensation, thus helping to inspire a whole generation of students researching Sino-Soviet diplomatic and border relations.

Patricia Kolb of M.E. Sharpe has maintained a strong interest in our series over many years. Along with the able Kimberly Giambattisto and Ana Erlic at M.E. Sharpe, Pat provided invaluable editorial assistance on the current volume.

Finally, the editors would like to thank their spouses, Sarah C.M. Paine (Elleman) Soyoung Lee (Kotkin), and Sandra Carruthers (Schofield) for their support.

Series Editor's Preface

Stephen Kotkin

Publications and commentaries continue to proclaim China as the world's newest superpower, though fewer analysts evince similar passion for elucidating the many limits to Beijing's great power ambitions. Fewer still take account of the unique circumstance that China borders on 20 countries—more than any other state. Unlike the United States, which abuts Canada and Mexico as well as the Atlantic and Pacific Oceans, China has perhaps the world's most strategically complex geography. China has twelve land and six maritime neighbors, together with two neighbors—Korea and Vietnam—with which it shares both land and sea boundaries. This circumstance provides China with a source of enormous leverage, but also equally monumental challenges.

Beijing has made significant progress in forging diplomatic and economic links with its neighbors, and in resolving many territorial disputes, but China and its neighbors disagree over a significant number of overlapping territorial and maritime claims, including disputes over what lies under the ground and under the sea. The present volume of twenty essays addresses China's neighborhood and boundaries with Afghanistan, Bhutan, Brunei, Indonesia, India, Japan, Kazakhstan, Korea, Kyrgyzstan, Laos, Malaysia, Mongolia, Myanmar, Nepal, Pakistan, the Philippines, Russia, Taiwan, Tajikistan, and Vietnam. In doing so, we offer a very different vantage point on China's rise as a great power—the perspective of its 20 neighbors.

Beijing's Power and China's Borders: Twenty Neighbors in Asia constitutes the fifth volume in a series on Northeast Asia that I launched with colleagues and the publisher M.E. Sharpe—*Rediscovering Russia in Asia: Siberia and the Russian Far East* (1995); *Mongolia in the Twentieth Century: Landlocked Cosmopolitan* (1999); *Korea at the Center: Dynamics of Regionalism in Northeast Asia* (2005); and *Manchurian Railways and the Opening of China: An International History* (2009). The first three of the four books were based on scholarly conferences. All pursue a form of international history that is rooted in specific places but transcends current national boundaries. Here, we confront the borders themselves.

We are hardly the first to do so. In *Strong Borders, Secure Nation: Cooperation and Conflict in China's Territorial Disputes* (2008), the MIT-based political scientist M. Taylor Fravel underscored Beijing's practical willingness to compromise, alongside its rhetorical inflexibility, in territorial disputes over decades. Fravel argued that China's behavior did not reflect the external balance of power—a neighbor's manifest weakness did not elicit a forward Chinese policy.

Nor in Fravel's telling did Beijing's conciliatory behavior in territorial matters reflect a supposed internalization of international norms, a favorite notion of those who see China bending to the American-centric global order. Rather, according to Fravel, China's willingness to compromise in frontier disputes derived from perceptions of its own domestic vulnerabilities: when the regime in Beijing has felt threatened internally, it has sought compromise externally.

Fravel noted that some disputes that China considers as wholly internal its neighbors view as external—notably Taiwan (the last of the three "homeland" disputes, after the absorption of Hong Kong and Macao). Still, he depicted China (before 2008, the publication date of his book) as a status quo power, concerned about domestic separatists and long-term modernization, favoring stability, and therefore measured in its foreign policy rather than prone to expansionism or provocative international behavior. If true, and enduring, this would offer a comforting vision for a lot of countries. Fravel allowed, however, that the converse of his main point held as well: when China has felt secure internally, it has not hesitated to use force in international territorial disputes.

Numerous analysts, not all of them wielding the depth of Fravel's painstaking case-study research, in effect turn Fravel on his head, putting forth what is his key explanatory factor for external moderation—internal political difficulties—as an explanation for what they perceive to be China's increasing aggressiveness. In this overall less benign view of China's external behavior, analysts also single out, among other factors, Chinese nationalism, factions in the opaque Chinese leadership (especially the military), and the allegedly inexorable conflict dynamic generated by rising powers as drivers of assertiveness. This is hardly a view limited to Americans. Masako Ikegami, a Stockholm-based Japanese scholar, has likened current Chinese policy in Northeast and Southeast Asia to imperial Japan's forcible intervention to create the puppet state of Manchukuo on Chinese territory in the 1930s (*Tamkang Journal of International Affairs*, April 2011). And yet, even many hawkish analysts of China have often felt constrained to admit that Beijing has generally tended to be more moderate than many people (i.e., themselves) predicted. Of course, past performance is no guarantee of future performance, as we hear after every market crash.

But one thing we do know for certain is that despite the far-reaching globalization of the world order, state sovereignty remains enshrined at the core of the international system and, as a result, border issues in Asia will continue to present challenges and opportunities for everyone there, America included. To be sure, the United States and China do not share a formal state border, but given mutual and competing economic interests, as well as rival military projections, they might as well: U.S. and Chinese interests seem to converge much more outside the Asia-Pacific region than within it. The larger point, though, is that in an interconnected world, China's international behavior will not be determined by China alone.

Chinese officials, for their part, frequently claim their country is a victim and is merely in the process of overcoming indisputable legacies of unequal treaties. By contrast, China's neighbors, even powerful ones such as Japan, see contemporary China throwing its weight around, on such issues as the disputed Diaoyu/Senkaku islands. Both these views are true. China's external behavior, such as the efforts to extend its naval power far beyond its territorial waters (described in China as a move from "coastal defense" to "far sea defense"), can fairly be interpreted as either aggressive or as a natural (and expensive) outgrowth of its export-led growth and insatiable demand for commodities, crops, and other resources, and a desire to ensure open sea lanes. Both explanations are inseparable. But what really stands out—independent of Beijing's motives, or of regime type—is the inherent difficulty that *any* Chinese state would face in managing borders with 20 different neighbors.

Consider that even though China's international water disputes have been numerous, as the essays that follow show, no less consequentially China is the source of cross-border river flows into Russia, Kazakhstan, India, Bangladesh, Myanmar, North Korea, Indochina—overall, into the largest number of countries in the world. (Tibetan sources alone supply water to 11 countries.) China's construction of dams within its borders ipso facto affects hundreds of millions of people—outside China. (China also builds more dams overseas than any other country.) Sharing so many critically important rivers with so many neighbors is a source of power for China, but it is also a burden, arousing suspicion and anger, especially when China makes decisions it regards as vital for its own internal development and national interests that can fundamentally alter daily life and development patterns in other countries.

Innumerable examples in the essays below will be seen of China's decisions being fraught. This should not be taken in the least to vindicate (or impugn) China's positions in territorial disputes, but rather highlights how no other state is challenged by the balancing act China faces.

Ultimately, any book on China's borders must acknowledge that China is not just a regional, but also a global power, whose state and private companies pursue foreign direct investment and trade far beyond its borders, with Europe, Africa, the Middle East, South and North America. Beijing's treasury and sovereign wealth fund enable it to purchase large amounts of foreign debt, while accumulating huge foreign currency reserves, and China's own currency, the *renminbi*, appears on a trajectory to become a global reserve currency in its own right. China's expanding numbers of submarines and the acquisition of a retrofitted Ukrainian aircraft carrier (the U.S. Navy has eleven carrier groups) has underscored a desire to deploy a blue-water navy. Chinese construction firms have become ubiquitous as China's huge infrastructure build-out extends far beyond East Asia. For all these global matters, however, China's neighborhood and border disputes remain absolutely fundamental.

Consider the strategic trade routes from China to Europe. Currently, these run predominantly through the South China Sea and Indian Ocean via the Malacca and Singapore Straits and Suez Canal. A largely ice-free route through the Arctic could prove revolutionary, though that proposition remains to be seen. Alternative routes on land currently proceed by means of the Trans-Siberian Railroad, from Harbin, or across Central Asia, the Caspian, and the Black Sea. East Asian goods going through Suez into the Mediterranean reach European ports in approximately 45 days; rail across Russia could, in theory, deliver those same goods to Finland in a third of that time. But Russia's ability to rebuild infrastructure across vast distances and inhospitable terrain including natural swamps, as well as across its domestic bureaucratic bog, have so far brought that proposition no nearer. Moscow and Vladivostok lie 5,753 miles (9,259 km) apart; Moscow and Pyongyang, 6,380 miles (10,267 km). Russia's dream of extending the Trans-Siberian through the Korean peninsula has gotten nowhere, undermined by severe underinvestment in upgrading Russian railroads as well as geopolitics.

In the meantime, eight different countries—China, Mongolia, Afghanistan, Uzbekistan, Kazakhstan, Turkmenistan, Tajikistan, and Kyrgyzstan—have been cooperating on a multi-billion dollar effort to upgrade the patchwork transit system in Central Asia. Drawing on multicountry expertise, labor, and financing, the group has envisioned up to eight rail and road corridors across the trails of the Silk Road, the 19th century name for the ancient route. The west-east land corridors would lead to Turkey, and possibly to southwestern Russia, from China's far west. (In addition, the Central Asians have been eager to reinforce their north-south routes, down to South Asia and the Middle East.) But even though China has completed an internal rail link to Lhasa, China's far west continues to suffer social and political unrest (in Xinjiang as well as Tibet), while China lacks an integrated domestic trucking system inland; visions of building dozens of airports in western regions—a "Silk Road in the sky"—have met skepticism about overcapacity. With so many states in Central Asia, maintaining such cooperation is not a given. The upshot has been that China has been investing far more in infrastructure along the sea route to Europe. In doing so, the border story is inescapable.

China has no California—that is, its western frontier does not border on an ocean. But Chinese-funded infrastructure projects across neighboring Myanmar and on that country's coast could afford Beijing strategic access to the Bay of Bengal and to the

Indian Ocean. The largest and most important projects, as of 2012, have been an oil pipeline and a hydroelectric dam. The dam on the Irrawaddy River had been intended to deliver 90 percent of the power it generates to China, while leaving Myanmar with many of the side effects, such as forcibly resettled villagers. Here, the Chinese squeeze appears to have induced the Myanmar junta to seek the balancing power of the United States. In January 2012, the junta released a slate of political prisoners, signed a tentative cease-fire with Karen ethnic rebels, and promised to permit elections—and the United States reopened its embassy and planned to send an ambassador for the first time in two decades. The U.S. Secretary of State followed with the first such visit to Myanmar in 50 years. The elections took place, delivering impressive success for the opposition. The Myanmar authorities also promptly sent a high-level delegation to Beijing to soothe the impact. The U.S. attention span in Southeast Asia remains to be seen. China is in for the long haul, and its currency, mobile phone networks, and companies and laborers continue to spread over Myanmar. The oil pipeline, from a deep sea port on the Bay of Bengal, is going forward with more generous attention (schools, hospitals) to those affected.

On China's eastern frontiers, a similarly strategic area for Beijing, China eyes ports on the northern Pacific. Beijing's North Korean policy perplexes American policy makers, particularly when the North Korean regime appears to surprise and buck its Chinese patron. But the prospect of a collapse-unification enabling American military bases to move into North Korea may be making Beijing more indulgent. Meanwhile, Chinese-funded development projects in North Korea could potentially compensate for Russia's seizure of the Amur Basin in the 19th century, and afford China better positioning on the Pacific than does the Liaodong peninsula alone. To be sure, China already enjoys freedom of navigation on the river system leading to the Pacific, as well as on the ocean itself. Nonetheless, for China's northern regions a Chinese infrastructure build-out in North Korea could someday deliver improved access from the Pacific coastline, including northward to the Arctic Ocean. South Korea, for its part, looks warily upon the prospect of Chinese investment and infrastructure in North Korea. China's border with the Korean peninsula remains highly unpredictable.

In the end, relations with neighbors support not only China's regional position in East Asia but its global position. Knowing more about the territorial issues between China and its 20 neighbors is tantamount to a deeper understanding of the possibilities and limits of Chinese power.

Abbreviations

ADB Asian Development Bank
AMM ASEAN Ministerial Meeting
ASEAN Association of Southeast Asian Nations
ASEAN+3 The ASEAN nations plus Japan, Korea, and China
CBM Confidence Building Measures
CCP Chinese Communist Party
CENTO Central Treaty Organization
CER Chinese Eastern Railway
CIA Central Intelligence Agency
COMECON Council for Mutual Economic Assistance
CPV Chinese People's Volunteer troops
CSTO Collective Security Treaty Organization
CU Customs Union
DoC ASEAN-China Declaration on the Conduct of Parties in the South China Sea
DPRK Democratic People's Republic of Korea
DVFO Far Eastern Federal District
EEZ Exclusive Economic Zone
EoL Exchange of Letters
GNH Gross National Happiness
GTI Greater Tumen Initiative
GWOT Global War on Terror
IAEA International Atomic Energy Agency
ICRC International Committee of the Red Cross
IMF International Monetary Fund
IRPT Islamic Revival Party
ISAF International Security Assistance Force
JMSU Joint Marine Seismic Undertaking Tripartite Agreement
KIG Kalayaan Island Group
KKH Karakoram Highway
KMT Kuomintang
KPA Korean People's Army
KVA Korean Volunteer Army
LAO PDR Lao People's Democratic Republic
LDP Liberal Democratic Party

MFTC Malaysian Friendship and Trade Centre
MMAF Ministry of Marine Affairs and Fisheries
MNDAA Kokang Myanmar National Democratic Alliance Army
MOU Memoranda of Understanding
MPR Mongolian People's Republic
MPRP Mongolian People's Revolutionary Party
NSG Nuclear Suppliers Group
PLA People's Liberation Army
PLAN People's Liberation Army Navy
PMZ Provisional Measures Zone
PoK Pakistani-occupied Kashmir
PRC People's Republic of China
QDII Qualified Domestic Institutional Investor
RATS Regional Anti-Terrorism Structure
RFE Russian Far East
ROC Republic of China
ROK Republic of Korea
ROV Republic of Vietnam
SAARC South Asian Association for Regional Cooperation
SAR Special Administrative Region
SCO Shanghai Cooperation Organization
SEATO Southeast Asian Treaty Organization
SEZ Special Economic Zone
SRBM Short Range Ballistic Missile
TAR Tibet Autonomous Region
TRADP Tumen River Area Development Project
TZ Transitional Zones
UNCLCS United Nations Commission on the Limits of the Continental Shelf
UNCLOS United Nations Convention on the Law of the Sea, 1982
UNESCO United Nations Educational, Scientific and Cultural Organization
UNHCR United Nations High Commissioner for Refugees
WTO World Trade Organization
XUAR Xinjiang Uyghur Autonomous Region

List of Maps

China and Its Neighbors 2
Map 1: Afghanistan's Border with China 12
Map 2: Bhutan's Border with China 22
Map 3: Overlapping Maritime Claims in the Southern South China Sea 36
Map 4: India's Disputed Border with China 46
Map 5.1: Competing Maritime Claims in the South China Sea 60
Map 5.2: Maritime Claims in the Southwestern South China Sea 65
Map 6: Competing Maritime Claims in the East China Sea 80
Map 7: Kazakhstan's Border with China 96
Map 8.1: Korea's Land Border with China 110
Map 8.2: Maritime Claims and Joint Arrangements in the Yellow Sea 120
Map 9: Kyrgyzstan's Border with China 126
Map 10: The China-Laos Border 142
Map 11.1: Competing Maritime Claims in the South China Sea 154
Map 11.2: Overlapping Maritime Claims in the Southern South China Sea 161
Map 12: Mongolia's Border with China 168
Map 13: Myanmar's Border with China 190
Map 14: Nepal's Border with China 204
Map 15: Pakistan's Border with China 218
Map 16.1: Competing Maritime Claims in the South China Sea 234
Map 16.2: The Philippine Treaty Limits and the KIG 239
Map 17.1: Russia's Far Eastern Borders with China 250
Map 17.2: Russia's Absorption of Chinese Territory 255
Map 18.1: Chinese Maritime Claims in the South China Sea 266
Map 18.2: Taiwan's Straight Baseline and Maritime Claims 275
Map 18.3: 1927 Nationalist Map with "Former Borders" Outer Black Line 278
Map 19: Tajikistan's Border with China 282
Map 20.1: Competing Maritime Claims in the South China Sea 294
Map 20.2: Vietnam's Land Border with China 299
Map 20.3: Gulf of Tonkin Maritime Delimitation and Fishery Arrangements 302
China and Its Neighbors (by Region) 310

BEIJING'S POWER and CHINA'S BORDERS

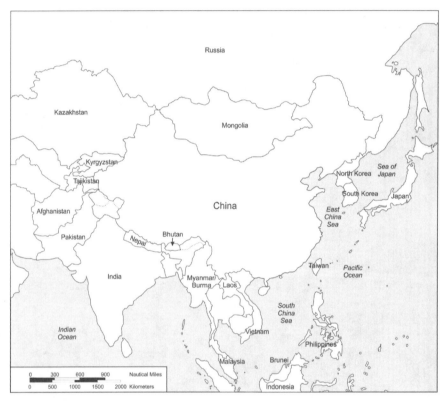

China and Its Neighbors

Introduction

Bruce A. Elleman and Clive Schofield

A virtual avalanche of books has been published in recent years proclaiming China to be the world's newest superpower. Some even argue that China will soon catch up to, and then surpass, the United States. But few discuss the limits to China's great power ambitions. The majority of the 20 countries neighboring on the People's Republic of China (PRC) have had a long history of border conflicts with China both on land and, increasingly, at sea.

The PRC has undoubtedly made significant, and arguably remarkable, progress over the past two decades and more in terms of both transforming its bilateral relationships with its neighbors and formally settling its international boundaries. From being a supporter of fraternal communist movements and insurgencies beyond its borders, and thus a direct threat to the stability of numerous of its neighboring states, China has established diplomatic relations and represents a major and increasingly important economic partner for many if not all of its neighbors. Despite this substantial progress in enhancing transboundary ties and settling salient territorial problems, however, many of China's neighbors have yet to settle completely their mutual international boundaries with the Beijing government. Further, the vast majority of its potential maritime boundaries remain unsettled.

Even when formally settled, China's boundaries provide an important interface with neighboring states and the wider international community. Opportunities for transboundary cooperation as well as friction, disputes, and conflict abound along China's borders. Countries that have formally settled their borders are not always sure these settlements will endure China's ongoing "great power" rise. For example, in many cases the treaties delimiting boundaries were secret, and so the exact terms of the border accords are still not known, much less understood, by the citizens of that country. These suspicions concerning the longevity of border agreements signed with China linger despite the privileged position of boundary agreements in international law.[1]

Each chapter in this book will offer a fresh perspective on the creation of that country's land or sea border with China by detailing historical conflicts, providing critical analysis of contemporary issues and tensions, and discussing how these conflicts have been resolved, in those cases where they have been settled. Equally important, each chapter will examine how transnational interactions—trade, resource exploitation, environmental issues, population movements—have been managed (or not, as the case may be) with the Beijing government.

The twenty case studies have been arranged in alphabetical order. When evaluating the Sino-Afghan border, Artemy M. Kalinovsky explains how the PRC and Afghanistan share a short 40 mile (57 km) border, which has been formally settled. The border is located in Afghanistan's Northeast, on the frontier of an area known as the "Wakhan corridor," and in the PRC on the Tashkurgan Tajik Autonomous County, part of Kashgar district in the province of Xinjiang. The Sino-Afghan border was delimited as part of a secret treaty dating to November 1963, so the terms have never been published. In December 2009, the PRC newspaper *Huanqiu Shibao* did call for China to take control of the Wakhan corridor, and China has also been developing infrastructure on its side of the border, including a 47-mile long road being built only six miles from the Sino-Afghan border funded by the Chinese Ministry of Defense. Beijing, however, seems unlikely to press for opening the Sino-Afghan border to trade so long as Afghanistan remains unstable, and so long as there are other more dependable land and air routes that can be used to conduct trade and to expedite military deployments in the region.

Paul Smith addresses how the Kingdom of Bhutan has unresolved border disputes with the PRC, mainly due to Sino-Indian reluctance to negotiate the western and eastern trijunctions where the three countries meet. When the PRC consolidated its control over Tibet in late 1950 and 1951, this region lost its previous position as a semi-autonomous nation and a buffer state. As relations between India and China began to sour, the pressure on Bhutan to take sides began to rise. While Bhutan and China have recently completed lengthy negotiations on their mutual border, the full and final resolution of this border dispute will probably need to wait for a parallel Sino-Indian agreement.

As for Brunei, Ian Storey discusses how its contested maritime claims with the PRC could cover an area of 12,600 nm^2 (43,272 km^2). Although China recognized Brunei following its independence from the United Kingdom in 1984, it was not until 1991 that formal ties were established. Brunei and China's maritime claims remain ambiguous to this day, although both countries appear to claim sovereignty, or at the very least jurisdiction, over Louisa Reef in the Spratlys. Because Brunei's political and economic relations with China are overshadowed by those with the other members of the Association of Southeast Asian Nations (ASEAN), this territorial dispute has received only passing attention in the press. Meanwhile, trade links between the two countries remain modest—around $300 million in 2008—despite China's seemingly insatiable thirst for Brunei's energy resources.

India and China's competing territorial claims represent China's, and arguably the world's, largest outstanding border dispute in terms of area. Brahma Chellaney argues that virtually the entire 2,521 mile (4,057 km) border is unsettled, with the size of the disputed territory perhaps topping 52,125 square miles (135,000 km^2). As China and India both grow economically, how these two countries face up to this border dispute will have an important bearing on Asian geopolitics, international security, and globalization. Sharp disagreement over the status of Tibet remains at the heart of the India-China divide, since Tibet ceased to be a political buffer when China annexed it more than six decades ago. Only when Tibet becomes a political bridge between China and India will there be any hope of resolving this conflict.

Indonesia is the only country in this study that claims not to border on China, but I Made Andi Arsana and Clive Schofield examine how Beijing has argued that overlaps do exist between the maritime claims of the two states in the southern South China Sea. Mainland China and Indonesia are separated by almost 800 nm (1,482 km) from Hainan Island to Indonesia's Natuna Island Group, but the maritime space potentially under dispute could be on the order of 28,500 nm^2 (98,000 km^2). In particular, the offshore energy fields adjacent to the Natuna islands are estimated to contain 46 trillion cubic feet of recoverable reserves of natural gas, and thus accessing the resources within the disputed areas may require delimiting a maritime boundary. To date, Indonesia has rejected all Chinese overtures to engage in bilateral delimitation talks, but a series of recent spats over illegal Chinese fishing activities in the South China Sea and Natuna Sea may ultimately force Indonesia and China to the negotiating table.

Japan's maritime frictions with the PRC are well known, and June Teufel Dreyer outlines the ongoing maritime delimitation dispute and contention over the Chunxiao/Shirakaba gas fields in the East China Sea, Japan's contested control over the Diaoyu/Senkaku islands, and arguments over the status of Okinotori, a tiny formation that Japan claims is an island capable of generating extended maritime claims while China says it is only a rock that cannot do so. Joint development in a specified area and cooperative development of one of the valuable underwater gas and oil fields in the East China Sea was agreed to in principle in 2008, but progress on implementation has been slow. Meanwhile, Beijing's dispute with Japan over its exclusive economic zone (EEZ) surrounding the Diaoyu/Senkaku islands could add up to as much as 20,000 nm^2 (68,686 km^2). China also contests Japan's claim to an EEZ surrounding Okinotori encompassing an area estimated at 116,472 nm^2 (400,000 km^2). While legal considerations remain important, the long-term trend in East Asia is that China is growing larger, and Japan is at best stagnant, so China's salami tactics—advancing its claims in small, carefully measured increments—may become ever more difficult for Tokyo to respond to.

As Stephen Blank explains, when the USSR collapsed in 1991 the PRC and Kazakhstan shared a 1,056 mile (1,700 km) border, along which 365 square miles

(944 km^2) remained in dispute. In a series of agreements dating to 1994 and 1998, the border was changed by only 72 square miles (187 km^2), with China securing just over 43 percent of the land still under dispute while Kazakhstan confirmed title over just under 57 percent. While this resolution appears on the surface to show Beijing's willingness to compromise, relative to the total size of their territories China was still arguably the winner. Moreover, as recently as 2009 Beijing requested that Kazakhstan lease almost 4,000 square miles (one million hectares) of land to Chinese farmers to grow soya beans and rapeseed, which has created new concerns throughout Central Asia over a policy of gradual Chinese encroachment.

Charles Armstrong discusses how China's 880 mile (1,415 km) land border with North Korea was established by means of an as-yet secret Sino-DPRK treaty in 1963. While this border is formally undisputed, a number of issues regarding control of the waterways, ports, islands, and mountain territories in the border region have emerged since the 1950s and continue to be unresolved to this day. China's biggest fear is arguably being flooded by North Korean refugees in the event of the collapse of the DRPK government. This possibility perhaps even explains Beijing's continued support for the Kim dynasty. In particular, should the two Koreas ever merge under the aegis of South Korea, the validity of the current Sino-Korean border might be challenged by the leaders of a newly reunified Korea. There are also outstanding maritime disputes between China and South Korea, though the two states have sought to manage their competing maritime claims and friction over access to valuable marine resources by their rival fishing fleets through the establishment of a joint fishing zone in the Yellow Sea.

According to Erica Marat, during 1999 China and Kyrgyzstan settled their dispute along their 533 mile (858 km) border, with Bishkek ceding almost 480 square miles (1,240 km^2) of land to Beijing. Two years later, rumors surfaced claiming that Kyrgyzstan President Askar Akayev had reaped personal financial gains from the deal and on 17 March 2002, Akayev ordered police to quell protesters, leaving six demonstrators dead. The incident provoked an uproar in Kyrgyzstan and energized the opposition movement, forcing Akayev to flee the country in 2005. Kyrgyzstan's economic relations with Beijing have grown quickly, and Beijing's 2001 creation of the Shanghai Cooperation Organization (SCO) appears to be pulling the country away from its traditional ties to Moscow. But Russia has tried to limit China's influence in Kyrgyzstan through regional organizations such as the Collective Security Treaty Organization (CSTO). In 2011, in particular, Russia tried hard to lure Kyrgyzstan back into its orbit by agreeing to expand the Moscow-led Customs Union to include Kyrgyzstan, which could potentially weaken Bishkek's commercial relations with Beijing.

As Ian Townsend-Gault explains, the undisputed border between Laos and China is only 263 miles (423 km) long. Nevertheless, Laos is strategically well-placed to constitute one or more east-west land bridges linking northern Myanmar and Thailand to ports on the South China Sea, as well as allowing the development of north-south trade routes from Yunnan Province. The extent to which Laos can retain full sovereign control over its territory along the Sino-Lao border remains to be seen, however, in particular with the growth of Chinese-owned and operated factories, plus a large Chinese casino located in the Laotian border town of Boten. According to some press reports, Chinese owners have apparently refused to even allow local Laotian officials to inspect these commercial developments, much less to regulate their activities, which is a worrying trend for the Laotian government to contend with.

Sino-Malaysia border relations are examined by Vivian Forbes, who emphasizes the importance of the contested sovereignty claims over small islands and overlapping claims to maritime jurisdiction in the South China Sea. These disputes are almost all awaiting resolution, and China appears reluctant to move quickly to settle the dispute relating to sovereignty claims over the Spratly islands. The current Malaysian government has demonstrated great reluctance toward joint development of the Spratly islands. Instead, Malaysia is actively exploiting marine resources in the disputed area on its own, even while trying to enhance its claim over the area through military presence and commercial development. Most importantly, Malaysia's 2009 decision to make a joint continental submission with Vietnam to the UN Commission on the Limits of the Continental Shelf cannot help but interfere with China's claim to almost the entire South China Sea.

Mongolia has one of the longest borders with China, but as Morris Rossabi explains these borders were clarified on 25 December 1962, when China and the Mongolian People's Republic (MPR) signed an agreement officially delimiting the Sino-Mongolian border; later, in 1988, a second treaty settled the remaining disputes along the 2,886 mile (4,645 km) border. Rather, China's enormous economic growth has given Beijing considerable economic leverage over Mongolia, making any Chinese attempt to take additional border territory or annex Mongolia outright highly unlikely. If Mongolia hopes to avert Chinese domination and to guarantee its border and its territorial integrity, it will need to adopt duties on foreign goods and begin to regulate foreign, specifically Chinese, capital, thereby permitting Mongolia to avoid becoming merely an economic satellite of China.

As Brendan Whyte points out, Myanmar's 1,367 mile (2,200 km) boundary with China is still not fully settled, since defining the trijunction with India is contingent on the resolution of the Sino-Indian dispute. A Sino-Burmese boundary treaty delimiting the bulk of their mutual border was signed on 1 October 1960, and was ratified a year afterwards, whereby China secured approximately 44 square miles (114 km^2) of disputed territory. While most of the Sino-Myanmar border remains unchanged to this day, the "provisional western extremity" still awaits the settlement of the Sino-Indian boundary. Meanwhile, domestic rebellion in the Han Chinese-dominated Kokang region of Myanmar has led to recent border tensions between the PRC and Myanmar, as approximately 50,000 ethnic Han Chinese have fled to China during the past ten years. During 2010, the People's Liberation Army (PLA) was even forced to deploy additional troops to this tense border region to halt the further flow of refugees.

Chitra K. Tiwari discusses how boundary delimitation and demarcation between Nepal and China began during October 1961, but the as-yet unfinished boundary line between China and Nepal extends for 881.6 miles (1,414.8 km), with seven Nepalese counties bordering on Tibet. Most importantly, the two trijunctions— where the Nepalese, Chinese, and Indian territories meet—have yet to be negotiated on both the western and eastern ends of Nepal as a consequence of the Sino-Indian dispute. Meanwhile, there have been a number of bilateral disputes between the PRC and Nepal, including over the exact ownership of Mount Everest.

Pakistan is one of China's only firm allies along its southern border, and Christopher Tang emphasizes how Sino-Pakistani relations are dominated by the notion of "special relationship" or "entente cordiale." Since settling their shared 325 mile (523 km) border through secret negotiations in 1963, the two allies have avoided any major boundary disputes. The Sino-Pakistani relationship has proven "remarkably durable" during the past fifty years, including Beijing's decision to provide Pakistan with nuclear technology, and Pakistan's assistance to Beijing in furthering the PRC's presence in the Indian Ocean via the deep-water port at Gwadar. The challenge of transnational terrorism and Islamic fundamentalism has posed a threat to Sino-Pakistani border diplomacy since the mid-1990s, but Beijing's pipeline plans and anticipated linkage with the Karakoram Highway denote even greater cooperation, making the Sino-Pakistani border a beacon of stability in an otherwise unstable region.

As discussed by Lowell Bautista and Clive Schofield, undelimited maritime boundaries and overlapping maritime claims are an enduring source of tension between the Philippines and China, despite rapidly expanding economic ties and talk of a "golden age of partnership" in bilateral relations. In particular, the dispute over the South China Sea tends to dominate their interactions. China asserts territorial sovereignty over numerous islands in the southern South China Sea, especially the Spratly islands, on historic grounds. Meanwhile, the Philippines claims sovereignty over several of the same islands, which it refers to as the Kalayaan Island Group (KIG). The Philippines and China also contest sovereignty over Scarborough Shoal (or Reef), located in the northeast of the South China Sea. Philippine relations with China, while increasingly strong, especially in economic terms, can in political and diplomatic terms be characterized largely as cautious at best, and even hostile at times.

Despite being formally settled, Russia's 2,672 mile (4,300 km) border with China is potentially dangerous. Mark Galeotti explains that the Sino-Russian border demarcation in 2008 represented a massive economic opportunity to many, but also a potential future threat. Moscow's relationship with Beijing remains both a foundation stone of Russia's geopolitical architecture and also a vital economic partnership. This is tempered, however, by a deep unease about the sustainability of the border in the face of a rising China, which has in effect made Russia the front line of Europe versus Asia; a new political generation in Beijing may be willing to reopen the question of historical iniquities and the legitimacy of the 19th century treaties, in which huge territories were seized by Russia. In sharp contrast to Moscow's wariness, however, to many Russians living in the Russian Far East (RFE) China represents the future, a source of labor, investment, goods, and opportunities to develop eastern Siberia's and the Russian Far East's 65 percent of Russia's prospective petroleum reserves, 85 percent of its natural gas reserves, almost all its diamonds, 70 percent of its gold, and large reserves of coal, timber, and other valuable resources.

China and Taiwan's border dispute is complex, and Bruce Elleman shows how for much of its post-1949 history the Republic of China (ROC) on Taiwan claimed all of mainland China plus Mongolia as its sovereign territory. Gradually Taipei's expectations of retaking the mainland diminished, but it still has territorial claims and exerts actual control over a number of small islands off the coast of China, including Jinmen (formerly Quemoy) and Mazu islands, as well as the Pratas islands to the southwest. It also retains control over the largest island in the Spratlys, Itu Aba (Taiping Island). By contrast, the PRC claims not only all of the offshore islands controlled by Taiwan, but all of the islands that make up the ROC proper, such as the Penghu (formerly the Pescadores), Green (Lü Dao), and Orchid (Lan Yu) islands. The two governments do agree with each other, however, on many South China Sea territorial and maritime claims against other Asian nations. Indeed Beijing and Taipei have cooperated in the past against other claimants in the South China Sea. Further, it was, in fact, the ROC that first published a map in 1947 including the infamous eleven-dashed line claiming the majority of the South China Sea, a claim that the PRC later adopted in its nine-dashed line map.

Gregory Gleason discusses how when the Tajikistan legislature in January 2011 ratified an agreement with China concerning the roughly 250 mile (400 km) border, it brought an end to more than a decade of negotiation and well over a century of dispute. The normalization of the Tajik-China border in 1999 specified that Tajikistan cede to China 77 square miles (200 km^2), and in 2002 a second agreement increased this to 433 square miles (1,122 km^2), mainly in the Pamir mountains. Tajikistan's chief negotiator, Foreign Minister Hamrokhon Zarifi, heralded it as a great success, explaining that it was far less territory (only about 5 percent) than the 10,811 square miles (28,000 km^2) that had previously been in dispute. The Tajikistan government's political opponents saw it differently, since this equaled .78 percent of Tajikistan's entire territory of 55,212 square miles (143,100 km^2). If current economic trends continue, however, the resolution of the Tajik-China border issues will prove to be of comparatively small significance in comparison with the ever-growing importance of Chinese political and economic influence in Tajikistan.

Vietnam's border relations with the PRC include both land and sea boundaries. Ramses Amer begins his examination with Beijing's and Hanoi's full normalization of bilateral relations in 1991. The major land dispute along the two countries' mutual border included 88 square miles (227 km^2). In 1999, the two countries agreed to split these areas, with Vietnam receiving just under 44 square miles (113 km^2) and the PRC just over 44 square miles (114 km^2). The sea disputes encompass both maritime areas in the Gulf of Tonkin and competing sovereignty claims over the Paracel and Spratly archipelagos in the South China Sea. While an agreement dividing the Gulf of Tonkin was reached in 2000, and a joint-fishing zone was established, disputes on these other maritime issues remained unresolved. Furthermore, China's claim within the so-called nine-dashed lines in the South China Sea overlap with Vietnam's claims to EEZ and continental shelf areas immediately to the east of Vietnam's coastline. During 2009-2011, bilateral tensions have periodically increased due to actions in and relating to the South China Sea.

The Conclusions will attempt to draw relevant contemporary lessons from the book's case studies by examining the history of settling the Chinese borders, the way in which Beijing has sought to acquire "new" maritime boundaries—mainly as a result of evolutions in the international law of the sea allowing for the extension of maritime jurisdictional claims further offshore—the type and intensity of China's border conflicts with her neighbors, successful and unsuccessful efforts to delimit official borders, and possible areas where future border disputes might arise. We will use these findings to discuss the likelihood and character of future border conflicts so as to address this book's central question: can China truly become a global power, much less the world's next superpower, if the Chinese government has to worry about so many boundary disputes on both land and at sea?

Notes

The thoughts and opinions expressed in this publication are those of the author and are not necessarily those of the U.S. government, the U.S. Navy Department, or the Naval War College.

1. Article 62(2)(a) of the Vienna Convention in the Law of Treaties states that boundary treaties are not subject to change even in the case of "subsequent fundamental change of circumstances." See, Vienna Convention on the Law of Treaties, 23 May 1969 1155 UNTS 331 (entered into force 27 January 1980).

Map 1: Afghanistan's Border with China

1

Sino-Afghani Border Relations

Artemy M. Kalinovsky

The People's Republic of China (hereafter PRC) and the Islamic Republic of Afghanistan share a short, undisputed 40 mile (57 km) border. It is located in Afghanistan's Northeast, on the frontier of an area known as the "Wakhan corridor" or "panhandle." On the Chinese side of the border is Tashkurgan Tajik Autonomous County, part of Kashgar district in the province of Xinjiang. Depending on your perspective, the corridor resembles a limb or branch extending from Badakshan Province into East Asia. The Sino-Afghan border was delimited in a secret treaty signed during November 1963.

The corridor shares a border with Pakistan to its south and Tajikistan to its north. The border follows the crestline of the Little Pamir mountains, then continues across the Wakhir River Valley, and its southern section runs along the mountain crestline of Murkushi.[1] The Wakhan corridor historically represented a portion of the Silk Road. Although the more important routes passed north or south of the corridor, the Wakhir Pass did serve to connect Afghanistan with China. Traders from Badakshan and elsewhere in northern Afghanistan took items such as cumin seed, furs, pelts, and spices to Kashgar, bringing back carpets, chinaware, silks and cotton material, utensils, and other goods. The significance of the route declined with the opening of sea routes between Europe and China, but local trade continued well into the 20th century.

The Wakhan corridor has a small population of some 9,000 Wakhis, who practice agriculture in the valleys, and 2,000 Kyrgyz pastoralists, who move with their flocks at higher elevations. The Wakhi, who refer to themselves as Khik, are Shiite Ismailis; the Kyrgyz are Sunni Muslims. The Wakhi language (*khik zik*) is an eastern Iranian language related to Tajik, and still does not exist in a written form, though various phonetic notation systems have been created. The Wakhi and Kyrgyz rarely acted as traders, although they were hired by merchants passing through the area; Uyghur traders also sold goods required by the Wakhi and Kyrgyz. The Kyrgyz apparently were more active traders than the Wakhi, and thus served as intermediaries for them. Trade through the area also served as a main source of revenue for the Mir of Wakhan, prior to the area's absorption into Afghanistan.[2] Overall there are some 50,000 Wakhis living in Xinjiang, Tajikistan,

Afghanistan, and Pakistan.[3] Roughly the same number of Kyrgyz live in the area, although they are very much the minority within the Wakhan corridor itself.

The Making of the Sino-Afghan Political Borders

The Sino-Afghan boundary, as well as the creation of the Wakhan corridor itself, is a 19th century product of the Great Game. British contacts with Afghanistan dated from the late 1830s, when the Afghan kings appealed to the British and Russians for help in extending their control and fending off Persian and Sikh advances. Afghanistan's foreign policy was increasingly defined by this Anglo-Russian rivalry. It was Russia's expansion in Central Asia that most concerned the British, and only timely and careful diplomacy helped avoid a clash between the countries. A series of diplomatic agreements were used to contain the ambitions of both sides, but parts of the frontier, still poorly mapped and even less well understood, remained contested. By the early 1890s, Russian-British rivalry and diplomacy focused on the Pamir region.

The first attempt to delimit the borders in the area was an agreement reached in 1873; this established the Amu Darya River as the dividing line between Russian and British spheres of influence. From the conquest of Khokand in 1875-1876, Russian exploration pushed into the Pamirs. Rumors of Russian designs on Wakhan in 1891 led to new worries on the part of the British and a flurry of activity to secure the area as part of the Afghanistan buffer. First, however, Amir Abdur Rahman had to be convinced to take on the responsibility of governing the territory in question. In 1893, Sir Mortimer Durand came to Kabul to discuss Afghanistan's northern boundaries in preparation for British talks with Russia. The Amir was far from enthusiastic about adding new territory to his realm. It was too remote, too difficult to govern, and could prove too tempting to all three of the empires in the vicinity. Durand recorded that "he [the Amir] says he had a hand cut off at Somatash the other day, and he is not going to stretch out a long arm along the Hindu Kush to have that shorn off also."[4] Finally, he was persuaded to add Wakhan to his realm and awarded 5,000 pounds a year to help pay for its administration.[5]

Although this agreement extended Russia's territory, it was also important for the British, since it created a boundary and a buffer between their empire and Imperial Russia. In the late summer of 1895, the British team on the Pamir Boundary Commission, assigned to demarcate the border between Afghanistan and Russia, left their camp and proceeded east toward Chinese territory. The British officials had been unable to reach an agreement with their Russian counterparts, and while both sides consulted their respective governments, the British party decided to move out on its own. At the beginning of September they returned to their camp, where they learned that the British government had decided to accept the proposed Russian line. But complete demarcation was impossible. The Russian team had placed its last pillar on the Sarikol range but could go no further; the "Durand Line," agreed to two years previously and delimiting the border between Afghanistan and British India, was some 23 miles to the south, and 15 miles to the east was a Chinese outpost. The British team wrote in their report: "Here, amidst a solitary wilderness 20,000 feet above sea level, absolutely inaccessible to man and within the ken of no living creatures except the Pamir eagles, the three great Empires actually meet. No more fitting trijunction could possibly be found."[6]

China had briefly taken control of the Pamirs during the Tang dynasty and again in the 18th century, but its 20th-century claims stem mostly from 19th-century conflicts. During the late 1860s, Yakub Beg, an adventurer from Khokand who established a kingdom centered in Kashgar, extended his influence into the Pamirs; the Mir of Wakhan fought as part of Beg's forces. After the Qing government pacified the region, the Chinese insisted that those lands that had belonged to Yakub Beg were now legally part of China. The British at first tried to convince the Chinese to extend a corridor through the Pamirs up to Yashil Kul, thus bordering Afghanistan and creating a buffer separating British interests from Russia. But the Chinese remained uninterested in such proposals, understandably concerned that occupation of indefensible territory could simply lead to clashes with Russia.[7]

While the drawing of the Durand Line and the outlines of the Wakhan corridor had limited effects on the ethnic groups living in this area, the Russian revolutions in 1917, and later developments in China, greatly restricted both their mobility and trade. Some 250 Kyrgyz households had migrated to the area in the wake of the Russian revolution and the consolidation of Soviet power in Central Asia, and many more Kyrgyz and Kazakhs moved to Chinese Turkestan. Well into the 1930s the Kyrgyz were allowed to migrate back and forth across the Soviet borders in exchange for a pasturage fee of "one animal for every ten of the same type." In the 1930s the border was closed, however, and the Kyrgyz were no longer able to move to Soviet territory; in addition, Soviet forces reportedly raided Kyrgyz camps on a number of occasions in the 1930s and early 1941, taking livestock, personal possessions, and prisoners.[8] After 1949 the Chinese closed their border with Afghanistan as well, and China's near isolation continued for the first two decades of the Cold War.

The Sino-Afghan Border in the Cold War

Sino-Afghan relations in the decades after the 1949 Chinese revolution developed in the shadow of the growing Sino-Soviet split and China's increasingly close relationship with Pakistan and its rivalry with India. Afghanistan was not a top priority for China, but it was arguably more important to Pakistan and the Soviet Union. Thus, while China provided interest free loans, advisers, and aid to Afghanistan in the 1960s and 1970s, its support paled by comparison with that of the Soviet Union or even the United States. However, China's involvement did help draw some Afghan intellectuals to Maoism, leading to the creation of a Maoist organization, which later spawned splinter organizations and heavily influenced the student union at Kabul University.[9] The actual importance of these groups in Afghan politics was probably less than the paranoia they caused among Soviet officials, as evidenced by dispatches from the Kabul embassy.[10]

Due to these Cold War tensions, it was not until 1963 that China and Afghanistan formally agreed to demarcate their mutual border. Afghanistan had recognized the PRC during January 1950, but formal diplomatic relations were not established until 1955. China and Afghanistan announced their decision to negotiate a "boundary existing between their two countries" on 2 March 1963, and a secret boundary agreement was signed in November of that year. Although it was never stated publicly, the agreement effectively confirmed the boundary existing as a result of the Russian-British negotiations. A joint boundary commission went to work the next year to demarcate the border.[11]

Sino-Afghan relations remained rocky. Beijing was suspicious of the pro-Soviet communists that came to power after the Saur revolution in 1978, and, not surprisingly, was highly critical of the Soviet intervention in December 1979. In its wake, the Soviet ambassador in Beijing was told that "Afghanistan is China's neighbour . . . and therefore the Soviet armed invasion of that country poses a threat to China's security. This cannot but arouse the grave concern of the Chinese people."[12] Chinese leaders viewed the Afghan intervention as part of more general encirclement by the Soviet Union and its allies. The USSR's 1979 action took place soon after the end of the PRC's short war with Vietnam, only recently a Chinese ally but at that time tilting heavily toward the Soviet Union. The Soviet presence in Afghanistan was part of a more broadly menacing policy, with Deng Xiaoping stating: "In seeking hegemony against China, the Soviet Union had not only stationed 1,000,000 troops along the Sino–Soviet border, but had dispatched troops to invade Afghanistan."[13]

Although Afghanistan's short border with China was not particularly important in and of itself, the Wakhan corridor was critical, since it bordered Pakistan to the south and the USSR to the north. With Pakistan the single most important source of arms and infiltration of mujahideen into Afghanistan, border control was a constant—though ultimately frustrating—priority of Soviet forces. Thus, from mid-1980, Soviet forces became increasingly involved in the Wakhan, reportedly building all-weather roads and sending its troops to occupy the area. There were also reports that Soviet troops had established a signal intelligence post and missile sites. Then, in June 1981, the Soviet Union and the Democratic Republic of Afghanistan signed a border agreement reconfirming their mutual Wakhan borders. China dismissed the treaty, calling it "illegal and invalid."[14]

In subsequent years the PRC became a supporter and sponsor of a number of armed opposition groups fighting the Kabul regime and Soviet troops. These included Maoist groups within Afghanistan, but more importantly also Pakistan-based Islamist groups, which were funded by the Central Intelligence Agency (CIA). Chinese aid included $400 million worth of weapons, among them surface-to-air missiles, launchers, rockets, mines, and anti-aircraft guns. Moscow also claimed that the Chinese trained 30,000 revolutionaries in Pakistan and in various camps in Xinjiang between 1980 and 1985.[15] However, it was the route through Chitral, on the Pakistani-Afghan border, that was employed.[16]

While Chinese officials frequently lashed out at the Soviet Union for its "hegemonic impulse," they rarely mentioned the border as such, nor did the Soviets.[17] The Soviet presence in Afghanistan was often cited as one of the "three obstacles" to normalization of Sino-Soviet relations. As noted by the geographer Hermann Kreutzmann, border closings and near constant political turmoil had a significant impact on this region:

> The standards of living, mobility and levels of political and commercial participation were modified by social-political systems which significantly influenced lifestyles, levels of educational attainment and survival conditions in remote mountain locations such as the Pamirs. The "Cold War" created hermetically closed frontiers and stifled exchange across borders. Separate societies with affiliated cultural expressions and economic options came into being.[18]

The Soviets ultimately withdrew their troops from the area in the summer of 1988, as part of the first phase of a withdrawal of its troops from Afghanistan that began in May 1988 and was completed on 15 February 1989. These changes corresponded with the weakening of the Soviet empire and the end of the Cold War.

Contemporary Issues

The difficulty of the terrain along the 40-mile Sino-Afghan border means that relatively few issues are directly connected with that boundary. There is perennial concern on Beijing's part, however, about the effect that events in Afghanistan might have on its own restive Uyghur population. Although some sources indicated that the Taliban had gained a foothold in the Wakhan corridor after taking power in Kabul in 1996, Taliban officials denied this, and they also categorically rejected the possibility of helping Uyghur separatists.[19]

Opium trafficking is another example of a typical border problem that largely bypasses the Sino-Afghan border. Although opium farming does take place in Wakhan, and Afghan heroin does find its way to China, it is almost impossible for it to do so over the Sino-Afghan border. A trafficker would first have to bring the opium up to the Wakhir Pass. The trafficker would then have to follow a road along the Tajik border that is mostly accessible only by 4-wheel drive vehicles to Sard-e Wakhan, then follow a series of paths along the river. This is difficult but not impossible, and in fact is similar to the way that bulk deliveries of opium into and throughout Wakhan are made. But the Wakhir path itself is considered impassable half the year and very difficult the other half; a trafficker would have to make the journey with pack animals or on foot. There are much easier routes through neighboring Tajikistan.[20]

Since 2001, China has played only a limited role in Afghanistan, investing in the country while staying aloof from the international stabilization and assistance effort. But developments in Afghanistan are of interest to China for several reasons: 1) it stands to be affected by any deterioration in regional stability, as it also shares a border with Pakistan and India, as well as Tajikistan; 2) it seeks to avoid the export of extremism into Xinjiang, where the Muslim Uyghur population has been restive; and finally; 3) it seeks to take advantage of the considerable mineral resources said to lie beneath Afghanistan's soil that are crucial for China's resource-hungry factories. To date, China Metallurgical Group Corporation has invested $3.4 billion to develop copper deposits near the village of Aynak. The site was initially explored by Soviet geologists, but decades of war and targeted attacks on Soviet and Afghan installations there made any development of the site impossible. In 2008, Beijing signed a 30-year lease, promising revenues that would make up a substantial proportion of Afghanistan's annual state budget.[21]

The PRC has also made some direct aid contributions. Following calls for funds issued at the United Nations conference on aid and assistance to Afghanistan in London in January 2010, Beijing pledged an additional $75 million, bringing its total contribution from 2001 to $1 billion, a substantial sum but one that is still at a level far inferior to that of major donors, including Japan, which pledged $5 billion over five years.[22] But China has largely rebuffed any requests by the U.S. and its allies in Afghanistan to commit itself to stabilization efforts. Chinese officials, newspaper reporters, and commentators have consistently rejected the possibility of China sending a stabilization force, despite occasional rumors to the contrary. When British Prime Minister Gordon Brown suggested that China should contribute troops to the International Security Assistance Forces (ISAF) in 2008, a Chinese Foreign

Ministry Spokesman replied: "Except for the UN peace-keeping missions approved by the UN Security Council, China never sends a single troop abroad. It's [*sic*] out of the question to send Chinese troops to ISAF in Afghanistan."[23]

Although efforts to convince Beijing to commit to the stabilization program in Afghanistan have been half-hearted at best, China's potential role there became more important following Kyrgyzstan President Kurmanbek Bakiyev's threat to force U.S. forces from their Manas airbase, a crucial resupply point for forces in Afghanistan. The U.S. then proposed that China open a resupply route for northern Afghanistan, but nothing came of this, and the issue became less acute after Bakiyev backed off from his threat and Russia also agreed to help supply ISAF forces.[24] There were apparently some expectations among American diplomats that China was preparing to take a more active role in Afghanistan, but again, nothing appears to have materialized.[25]

Conclusions

Although the Sino-Afghan border is small compared to China's border with its other neighbors, Beijing does seem to be taking more of an interest in this border region as a result of constant concerns about instability in Xinjiang. In December 2009, the newspaper *Huanqiu Shibao* published an article calling for China to take control of the Wakhan corridor; there have also been comments from military officials about their increasing willingness to deploy Chinese troops in Central Asia to combat terrorism from "East Turkestan."[26]

In case of conflict in this region, China has also been developing infrastructure on its side of the border. Recent projects include a 47 mile (75 km) road being built only six miles (10 km) from the Sino-Afghan border, which is funded by the Chinese Ministry of Defense. A supply depot has been built to raise the quality of food for police forces guarding the frontier. Finally, a mobile communications center has been established to improve command-and-control.[27]

Any long-term effect of this border region on warming Sino-Afghan relations is likely to be limited, however. In April 2011, the *Wall Street Journal* reported that the Pakistani Prime Minister Yousuf Raza Gilani had tried to convince Afghan President Hamid Karzai to reorient the country away from the U.S. and more toward China and Pakistan.[28] Albeit unlikely, even if this reorientation were to take place the border itself would probably play only a limited role. Beijing seems unwilling to open the Sino-Afghan border to trade so long as there is instability in Afghanistan and in Xinjiang, and so long as there are other more dependable land and air routes to use for trade and military deployments.

Notes

1. M.D. Stephens, "The Sino-Afghanistan boundary," *Contemporary Review,* Vol. 213, No. 1230 (July 1968), 19.

2. M. Nazif Mohib Shahrani, *The Kirghiz and Wakhi of Afghanistan: Adaptation to Closed Frontiers* (Seattle: University of Washington, Press, 1979), 38, 41-42.

3. Hermann Kreutzmann, "Ethnic minorities and marginality in the Pamirian knot: survival of Wakhi and Kirghiz in a harsh environment and global contexts," *Geographic Journal,* Vol. 169, No. 3 (September 2003), 218.

4. Quoted in Percy Sykes, *A History of Afghanistan* (London: Macmillan, 1940), 175.

5. W.K. Fraser-Tytler, *Afghanistan: A Study of Political Developments in Central and Southern Asia* (London: Oxford University Press, 1953), 168-170.

6. Ibid., 329-330. See also "Report on the proceedings of the Pamir Boundary Commission," http://digitalcommons.unl.edu/afghanenglish/159/ [Accessed on 30 May 2011].

7. John W. Garver, "The Sino-Soviet Dispute in the Pamir Mountain Region," *China Quarterly,* No. 85 (1981), 111-114.

8. Shahrani, 39-41.

9. Hafizullah Emadi, "China's politics and developments in Afghanistan," *Journal of Asian and African Studies,* Vol. 28, Nos. 1/2 (January 1993), 108-112.

10. For examples, see "Peking's policies with regard to the DRA," 19 September 1982, Russian State Archive of Contemporary History, Fond 5, opis 88, delo 945.

11. "Afghanistan–China boundary," *International Boundary Study No. 89,* 1 May 1969 (Washington, DC: US Department of State, Office of Intelligence and Research), http://www.law.fsu.edu/library/collection/LimitsinSeas/IBS089.pdf.

12. A.Z. Hilali, "China's response to the Soviet invasion of Afghanistan," *Central Asian Survey,* Vol. 20 (2001), 326-27.

13. Ibid., 327.

14. Ibid., 330.

15. Emadi, 115.

16. Hilali, 339.

17. Gerald Segal, "China and Afghanistan," *Asian Survey,* Vol. 21, No. 11 (1981), 1165-1166.

18. Kreutzmann, 216-218.

19. "Taliban denies Xinjiang aid allegations," *Asia Times,* 29 April 1997.

20. Jacob Townsend, *China and the Afghan Opiates: Assessing the Risk* (Washington, DC: Central Asia-Caucasus Institute Silk Road Studies Program, 2005), 37-38.

21. "Afghanistan copper deposits worth $88 billion attract Chinese investors," *Times,* 15 May 2008.

22. Congressional Research Service, "Afghanistan: Post-Taliban Governance, Security, and U.S. Policy," 20 April 2010.

23. "China builds closer ties to Afghanistan through Wakhan Corridor," *Jamestown Foundation: China Brief,* Vol. 10, No. 1 (7 January 2010).

24. CRS Report RL33001, *U.S.-China Counterterrorism Cooperation: Issues for U.S. Policy,* 31.

25. Congressional Research Service, "Afghanistan," 59-60.

26. CRS Report RL33001, 1.

27. "China builds closer ties," *Jamestown Foundation: China Brief.*

28. "Karzai told to dump U.S.," *Wall Street Journal,* 27 April 2011.

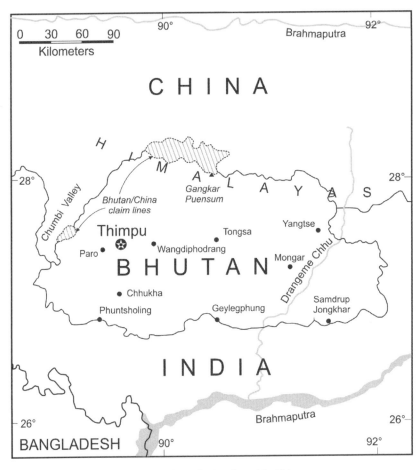

Map 2: Bhutan's Border with China

2

Bhutan-China Border Disputes and Their Geopolitical Implications

Paul J. Smith

The Kingdom of Bhutan is one of China's neighbors with which Beijing officially has unresolved border disputes, mainly due to China's and India's political inability to negotiate the western and eastern trijunctions where the three countries meet. Nestled in the Himalayan mountains between China and India, Bhutan, with a population of 708,000, is one of the smallest countries in the world in terms of population size.[1] Its territorial space, approximately 14,824 square miles (38,394 km^2)—or about the size of the American state of Maryland—features rough and mountainous topographical features. Given its geographical position, it is not surprising that Bhutan has, until fairly recently, successfully resisted outside influence and pressure.

Equally notable is Bhutan's geopolitical position, lodged between two of Asia's most significant economic and political powers—China and India. Despite cultural and religious ties to Tibet, Bhutan has maintained a much closer relationship with British India before 1947, and with India today. In 1865, Bhutan and Britain signed the Treaty of Sinchula, under which the British agreed to provide Bhutan an annual subsidy in return for ceding a portion of its border territory to British India.[2] In 1910, Bhutan entered into a second major treaty with Britain, which gave the British responsibility for handling Bhutan's external affairs; in exchange, Bhutan was assured that Britain would not interfere in the kingdom's internal affairs.[3] This arrangement would be continued in another form between Bhutan and India, following the latter's independence from Britain in 1947.

On 1 October 1949, Mao Zedong declared the establishment of the People's Republic of China (PRC) in Beijing. During the early years of their respective governments, India looked toward China as a natural ally and friend. Indian Prime Minister Jawaharlal Nehru campaigned extensively in 1950 to have Communist China seated in the United Nations. However, in late 1950 and 1951, China used military force to consolidate its rule over Tibet, which had traditionally enjoyed a semi-autonomous status and which India had traditionally viewed as a buffer state. As relations between India and China began to sour, the pressure on Bhutan began to rise. These dynamics would define Bhutan's border disputes with China for the next six decades.

Bhutan and the Growing Tibetan Maelstrom

On 8 August 1949, Bhutan signed a treaty with India known as the Perpetual Peace and Friendship Agreement, which acknowledged Bhutan's de jure sovereignty, but simultaneous dependence on India with regard to external matters. This treaty mirrored, in many respects, its 1910 antecedent, signed by Bhutan and Britain. Under Article 2 of the 1949 treaty, India undertook "to exercise no interference in the internal administration of Bhutan."[4] For its part, the government of Bhutan agreed to be "guided by the advice of the Government of India with regard to its external relations."[5] By assuming responsibility over Bhutan's external relations, India demonstrated its intent to "exclude all foreign influences and intrigues from this area."[6] India also promised to provide Bhutan with an annual subsidy.

Bhutan's other neighbor, China, initially appeared to accept the new arrangement between Bhutan and India. At the same time, however, Beijing was keen to leverage Bhutan's quasi-independent status as a way of gaining influence within the kingdom. In 1953, the Chinese government sent gifts to Bhutan's King, and, in 1955, Chinese officers in Lhasa began issuing visas directly to Bhutanese citizens. Despite these initiatives, Bhutan remained "cautious if not suspicious" with regard to Chinese intentions.[7]

As conditions in Tibet deteriorated in the 1950s, however, Chinese attitudes toward Bhutan would begin to harden. This highlights a fact that is critical to understanding future China-Bhutan relations, including border controversies: Tibet's fate would ultimately shape Bhutan's calculations about its security and the parameters of its border negotiation efforts. In 1950, China deployed forces of the People's Liberation Army (PLA) to Tibet, which in turn "liberated" the region. The Chinese government insisted on negotiations with the Tibetan authorities and eventually a Tibetan delegation traveled to Beijing and signed a "Seventeen Point Agreement for the Peaceful Liberation of Tibet" in 1951. This agreement, seemingly negotiated on the basis of parity between the two parties, gave Beijing license to assert its sovereignty over Tibet, while the Tibetans were granted the privilege of maintaining the Dalai Lama and Tibet's traditional political and economic system.[8]

For Bhutan, China's deployment of troops in Tibet—which shared a common cultural and religious tradition with Bhutan—generated alarm among the political elite, particularly as it became evident in subsequent years that Chinese authorities were reneging on their assurances that Tibet would be allowed to maintain its independence and that the Dalai Lama would be allowed to continue exercising his authority. The period from 1951-1959 was characterized by "increasing discord between the traditional Tibetan government, Chinese officials in Tibet, and after 1955-1956, a growing rebel force in the countryside."[9] Many Tibetans complained that Beijing had failed to live up to its side of the "Seventeen Point Agreement," which might have been attributed to the fact that Chinese leaders viewed their obligations to respect and maintain Tibet's political, social, and monarchic system as "conditional" and "provisional."[10]

For various reasons, following the imposition of PRC governance over Tibet, living standards in Tibet declined precipitously and massive food shortages resulted in the deaths of more than 65,000 Tibetans.[11] It was during this period that Prime Minister Nehru traveled to Bhutan in 1958 in hopes of convincing the government that it should end its isolationist policy. At a speech delivered in Bhutan, Nehru assured his audience that India's only wish was that Bhutan "should remain an independent country, choosing [its] own way of life and taking the path of progress according to [its] will."[12]

The following year, 1959, would emerge as a turning point not only for Tibet, but also for geopolitical trends in South Asia. On 10 March 1959, thousands of Tibetans began to congregate around the Dalai Lama's summer palace, Norbulingka, because of a rumor that Chinese officials were planning to kidnap him and remove him from Tibet. By the middle of the day, what had begun as a relatively quiet demonstration gradually deteriorated into a "large-scale popular revolt" in which certain high-ranking PLA officers were either injured or stoned to death. Although under orders to proceed with restraint, an errant Chinese police officer fired two artillery rounds, which exploded near Norbulingka. The Dalai Lama, who had been reluctant to leave Tibet, perceived that he was in immediate danger; thus, he and his followers fled the Tibetan capital on 17 March 1959 and they would eventually escape to India. Historic records suggest that Mao Zedong was unconcerned with the Dalai Lama's escape from Tibet. He reportedly wrote: "If the Dalai Lama and his entourage flee [the Tibetan capital] . . . our troops should not try to stop them. Whether [the Tibetans] are heading to southern Tibet or India, just let them go." With the Dalai Lama out of the picture, the Chinese government on 20 March 1959 issued the order to launch a "comprehensive counteroffensive" in Tibet.[13]

China's crackdown in 1959 would affect Bhutan in several ways. First, it significantly exacerbated tensions between China and India, Bhutan's protector. During this period, Indian leaders had never really recovered from the shock of the early 1950s related to Beijing's decision to occupy Tibet by force. As Chen Jian observes: "Throughout the 1950s, even during the heyday of Sino-Indian friendship, Beijing and New Delhi were never able to escape the shadow of the

Tibet issue." China was particularly indignant that India had granted political asylum to the Dalai Lama and his followers in 1959. Moreover, the Chinese government accused Prime Minister Nehru and the Indian government of being "deeply involved in the rebellion in Lhasa." Beijing began publicly criticizing India, describing New Delhi as "expansionist" and asserting that India "had adopted the British colonial traditions." This would lead to a precipitous decline in the relationship between the two countries, establishing the basis for a future border war in 1962 and other tensions, including low-level skirmishes, which persist to the present day.[14]

Secondly, China's 1959 crackdown in Tibet sent shockwaves through blissfully isolationist Bhutan. Bhutanese officials were horrified by stories relayed to them by Tibetan refugees describing Chinese atrocities against Tibetan people, their culture, and religion. Bhutan also discovered that the PRC had blocked the normal conduct of trade between Tibet and Bhutan. Feeling overwhelmed by refugees and seeking to isolate itself from turmoil, Bhutan shut off its border with Tibet in 1960.[15] Yet this did not stop Chinese border guards from making small incursions into Bhutanese territory. Overall, a palpable state of fear had begun to permeate Bhutan's political elites. Bhutan's Prime Minister told a newspaper: "If they [the Chinese] try to take over Bhutan we will stand and fight. But who has the strength, in this area, to oppose the Chinese? We do not know who would help us."[16] In response, Prime Minister Nehru announced on 26 August 1959 that India would defend Bhutan or the state of Sikkim if either was attacked by a foreign power.[17]

Bhutan's response was to end its isolation and turn politically and economically toward India. First, the two governments entered into an economic aid agreement, in which both parties agreed to build a road connecting Bhutan and India. India also began training Bhutan's army in 1961. A year later, Bhutan's linkage with India would be solidified as a border conflict erupted between China and India. Initially, Bhutan attempted to maintain its neutrality, out of fear that its linkages to India might make it a vulnerable target for the Chinese. But in October 1962, Bhutan called up all males 16 years or older to military service.[18] Following the Sino-Indian conflict, Bhutan nudged closer and closer to India, although its confidence in India's ability to defend it was badly shaken by China's victory over Indian forces; such confidence would not be restored until 1971, following India's victory over Pakistan.[19]

Sino-Bhutan Border Troubles Emerge

Throughout the 1950s and 1960s, Bhutan was consistently anxious about an underlying theme that emanated from Chinese propaganda, which implied or stated outright that Bhutan was a natural part of Tibet and that it ultimately should be reunited with China. In August 1959, Prime Minister Nehru announced that he had heard of Chinese reports claiming that Bhutanese, Sikkimese, and Ladakhis "must once again be made a united family under China."[20] One metaphor proposed by the noted British journalist Desmond Doig posited that Bhutan was one of the "fingers" of the "hand" of Tibet with the other "fingers" including Sikkim, Assam, Nepal, and Ladakh. "Now that the hand has been restored to China . . . the fingers should also go with it."[21] Reports also circulated that Chinese troops were pursuing Tibetan refugees up to Bhutan's border, but had not crossed it.[22]

What made Bhutanese leaders particularly nervous was the fact that Chinese propaganda was at least partially grounded in truth. Indeed, Bhutan and Tibet had enjoyed or endured various interactions, including invasions, war, intermarriage, and shared religious institutions, since the early 8th century. Tibet even considered Bhutan a vassal, a role Bhutanese pretended to accept as a way of diminishing British influence. At the same time, however, Bhutan sought to maintain its independence from Tibet. One sign of this was Bhutan's prohibition of any monastic institution associated with the Dalai Lama's Gelugpa sect.[23]

In 1959, the Chinese government handed an 11,000 word document to the Indian Embassy in Beijing that reiterated Chinese claims on nearly 50,000 square miles of Indian territory, including more than 300 square miles of Bhutan's territory. Characterizing the Chinese claims as "cartographical aggression," Bhutan's Prime Minister Jigme Dorje stated that "Bhutan does not recognize any Chinese claim on Bhutanese territory."[24] Bhutan issued a protest via its Indian representatives, who handled Bhutan's foreign policy matters during this period, since Bhutan had never had diplomatic relations with China.

On 26 September 1959, Prime Minister Nehru sent a letter to the Chinese Premier in which he raised the issue of "errors" on the part of Chinese maps that showed large areas of Bhutan as being part of Tibet. The letter also stated that the government of India was the only "competent authority to take up with other governments matters concerning Bhutan's external relations," which also included border negotiations.[25] However, in an effort to circumvent India's influence over Tibet, Premier Zhou Enlai sent a letter in September 1959 directly to Bhutan's King expressing hopes that both countries could engage in bilateral talks about the border problem, indicating a desire to separate the China-Bhutan border discussions from China-India border talks.[26] In fact, China was so keen to exclude India from any Sino-Bhutan border negotiations that the issue was omitted from the agenda of the Sino-Indian border discussions held in 1961.[27]

Throughout this period, China continued to insinuate that it was not finished with its own interpretation regarding Bhutan's status. In 1961, reports began circulating

China was claiming Bhutan as an "integral part of Tibet."[28] That same year, China reportedly reached out to Bhutan, offering "unconditional aid" if Bhutan would engage in direct negotiations to settle their mutual border dispute. Bhutan's King, who was in New Delhi when the offer was made, reportedly "ignored these overtures."[29] In 1966, Bhutan accused China of allowing four "intrusions" into its territory by Chinese nationals. In one case, a Bhutanese patrol found "five Tibetans with 300 yaks camped two miles south of the same pass [in which a previous intrusion had occurred]."[30] Bhutan's complaints were conveyed to China via India, per the two countries' arrangement. Ironically, however, Bhutan occasionally expressed consternation at discovering Indian maps showing parts of Bhutanese territory as belonging to India. In 1966, Bhutan's King Jigme Dorji Wangchuck met with Prime Minister Indira Gandhi and expressed "dismay at finding [Bhutan's] territory shown as part of India in some widely distributed Indian maps."[31]

Prior to 1959, the issue of border demarcation with China was not the highest priority for Bhutan. After 1959, periodic disputes and clashes, primarily between Tibetan and Bhutanese herders, gave the issue greater salience.[32] However, direct border talks were stymied by tensions in the Sino-Indian relationship. In addition, Bhutan's lack of diplomatic relations with China and its treaty obligations with India—which stipulated that India had responsibility for handling Thimpu's foreign relations—prevented any direct negotiations during this period. Consequently, Bhutan essentially maintained its role as a de facto buffer state, which was subject to the currents and countercurrents of Sino-Indian relations.[33]

During the 1970s, Bhutan gradually began asserting its independence as a sovereign state. In 1970, Bhutan applied for UN membership and, with the support of India, Bhutan was admitted as a member of the United Nations on 21 September 1971. In his letter requesting membership, Bhutan's King Jigme Dorji Wangchuck stated that his country had become "acutely aware of the proven value of the United Nations organization to small and developing nations."[34] Not only did UN membership boost Bhutan's confidence as a sovereign state, it also gave the country access to UN development and technical assistance and funding.[35] Moreover, with its UN membership secured, Bhutan began to distance itself from its traditional reliance on India. In some international meetings, Bhutan voted for certain initiatives that were contrary to India's position; simultaneously, Bhutan voted for a number of positions favorable to China, including the critical vote in 1971 to give the China seat in the UN to the PRC. In addition, Bhutan renamed its mission in New Delhi the "Royal Bhutan Embassy."[36]

Formal Border Negotiations Begin

Beginning in 1984, Bhutan's relations with the PRC experienced a fundamental breakthrough as the countries embarked upon direct negotiations over their border disagreements and related matters. In April 1984, the two countries established formal boundary discussions in Beijing. The first five rounds of negotiations—held between 1984 and 1988—were cautious, as both sides sought to establish the parameters of their discussions. Bhutan's negotiating team was headed by its ambassador in New Delhi, while China's team was led by a Vice Foreign Minister.[37]

During the 6th round of talks in 1989, both sides upgraded the diplomatic level of their dialogue. The Bhutanese government assigned its Foreign Minister to be its negotiating team leader; China's team would be led by a Senior Vice Foreign Minister.[38] By the late 1980s, both sides had narrowed their border disagreements to two general areas: the north-central area and the western sector (see Map 2). Chinese leaders were particularly vigilant in pushing their claims in the western sector, since Beijing viewed the western sector, at the trijunction of India, Bhutan, and China, as strategically more important.[39] During the 11th round of talks held in Beijing in 1996, Bhutan raised concerns about Chinese road construction and logging activities in disputed areas, which were discovered as a result of a 1996 survey of the country.[40]

In 1998, the two countries achieved a new milestone at their 12th round of talks by signing the "Agreement on the Maintenance of Peace and Tranquility along the Sino-Bhutan Border Areas." This was the first formal agreement between the Chinese and Bhutan governments.[41] The treaty was designed to instill a spirit of amicability during the negotiation phase, while specific border details were being negotiated. The signing of this treaty was particularly notable because Bhutanese lawmakers have consistently referred to it when they criticize inappropriate Chinese behavior, such as road construction in disputed areas or various types of border intrusions.

In 1999, China changed the pace and tenor of the bilateral negotiations by offering a "package" that included a series of concessions to the demands submitted by Bhutan. China was hoping to bundle border talks with the much larger objective of establishing diplomatic relations and expanding trade between the two sides.[42] The following year, Bhutan indicated to China that it was not yet prepared to accept the package offer and, instead, invoked the spirit of friendliness that had been developed between the two countries to seek greater Chinese flexibility in accommodating Bhutan's territorial requests, particularly as it was— according to Bhutanese officials—a matter of national survival. In 2000, Bhutan expanded its claims, by including Doklam, Chharithang, Sinchulumpa, Dramana, and Gieu (in the western sector of the country) along the disputed border "as these pasture lands were important for the people living in the highlands of western Bhutan who mainly depended on livestock for their livelihood." Bhutan also contended that its citizens had been using these lands "since time immemorial."[43]

In 2001, the two countries held their 15th round of negotiations, in which they were able to concentrate on the three sectors of Doklam, Sinchulumba, and Dramana.[44] Notwithstanding the absence of formal diplomatic relations, Bhutan and China engaged in cultural exchanges that year, including the visit to China by Bhutan's second highest-ranking Buddhist leader.[45] In July 2002, a new issue emerged when Bhutan was presented with apparent Chinese documentary evidence proving its ownership of certain disputed sections of land. Bhutan's strategy was to continue invoking the spirit of good-neighborliness from China, although China reportedly replied that it "could not afford to be generous with one particular neighbor" since it also has 25 other neighbors.[46] This larger number of "neighbors" may include the five "fingers," mentioned above.

Key Trends in Border Negotiations

As border negotiations have proceeded, a number of trends can be discerned. First, during the negotiation phase beginning in 1984, Bhutan has gradually raised its international and diplomatic profile and, in so doing, has increasingly asserted a more independent streak in its foreign policy. In April 2010, Bhutan successfully hosted the sixteenth South Asian Association for Regional Cooperation (SAARC) Summit in Thimpu. Bhutan also transitioned from an absolute monarchy to a constitutional monarchy, having held elections in both houses of parliament—the National Council and National Assembly—in 2007 and 2008, respectively.[47] In addition, Bhutan has attracted international attention with its introduction of the "Gross National Happiness" (GNH) concept, which was first proposed by King Jigme Singye Wangchuck. Under this paradigm, a government evaluates potential social policies or economic plans on the basis of whether and how much they contribute to the overall happiness of the country. In 2008, the Secretary of the Gross Happiness Commission, Karma Tsheetem, stated that GNH means "there has to be a better balance between the spiritual and the material."[48]

Second, Bhutan recognizes that the China of 2012 is quite different from the China of 1984. China now has the second largest economy in the world and, with its ambitious military modernization goals, is emerging as a leading military power. Bhutan has attempted to leverage its international position—and particularly its position within the United Nations body—to cultivate good relations with Beijing. China acknowledges and appreciates Bhutan's support on key questions, including Thimpu's pro-Beijing votes on human rights questions and questions related to the status of Taiwan. At the same time, China recognizes that successful resolution of the border question, in a manner that is fair and equitable to both sides, is a precondition to any formal diplomatic and economic relations between the two countries.[49]

Third, India remains a key factor in the border negotiations, notwithstanding Bhutan's attempt to increase diplomatic distance between the two countries during the past three decades. Bhutanese leaders have realized that Sino-Bhutan border negotiations also impinge on Indian interests. In 2005, India expressed alarm by a decision by Bhutan to adjust its claim line in its negotiations with China. India was worried that Bhutan had conceded too much, possibly to India's detriment. India immediately dispatched top military leaders to Bhutan to explain the strategic significance of the western sector, particularly the areas north of the Torsa River where, in the past, "any move to cede territory in this zone has traditionally been considered detrimental to Indian security."[50]

Moreover, India is concerned that Chinese pressure on Bhutan to grant additional land in the Chumbi Valley would put more pressure on India. According to one Indian strategic analyst: "India's Achilles heel in this area has been the severing of the Siliguri corridor through the Chumbi Valley." When China claimed the Doklam plateau in western Bhutan in 1993, Indian military analysts saw this as a gambit by Beijing to gain closer access to the Siliguri corridor.[51] Thus, from a geopolitical perspective, Bhutan's western region is far more strategically significant that the central region, which may explain why Beijing has proposed giving up its claims in the center in exchange for Thimpu's concessions in the western sector, in particular the disputed territory in the Doklam area.

Fourth, Bhutanese leaders recognize that even if border negotiations are successfully concluded, as current trends suggest, there will be residual problems that will require constant negotiation and dialogue with Beijing. For example, Bhutan has lodged numerous complaints and protests regarding Chinese encroachment on its territory. In June 2005, Bhutan's parliament was informed that Chinese entities were building roads "across the international border and into Bhutanese territory."[52] This recent round of road construction activities allegedly began in 2004. A Bhutanese lawmaker from Haa district (in the west) told the country's official newspaper, *Kuensel*, that "the Chinese government did not adhere to the 1998 understanding signed between Bhutan and China by constructing several roads in our territory."[53]

China responded that the lawmakers' complaints reflected Bhutan's "overreaction" and that the roads in questions were "legitimately constructed" as part of a larger Chinese plan to develop Tibet.[54] Nevertheless, in 2009, Bhutan's

National Council learned that China had once again engaged in road construction in disputed land, this time adding more than 900 meters of road.[55] This was despite Bhutan having lodged five different protests, in which the government asked China to halt construction "on the basis of [the] 1998 agreement on the maintenance of peace and tranquility in Bhutan-China border areas."[56]

More ominous are reports of Chinese soldiers crossing into Bhutanese territory. In 2009, Bhutan's Secretary for International Boundaries, Dasho Pema Wangchuck, told the country's parliament that "Chinese soldiers had intruded into Bhutanese territory as many as seventeen times in 2009 alone."[57] Another Bhutanese official provided the National Council (upper house) with further details: in 2008, 21 members of China's PLA had intruded into Bhutanese territory, while in 2009 the number was 17 members. He further characterized the events as a "serious security concern."[58]

Poaching is another major worry for Bhutan. Hundreds of Tibetans enter Bhutan every year to collect a medicinal mushroom known as *cordyceps sinensis* and other medicinal herbs. In some cases, Chinese nationals have crossed the border into Bhutan and harassed yak herders, including, in some extreme cases, actually slaughtering yaks.[59] Such concerns are likely to persist, even after an agreement is reached. A related concern for Bhutan is that if borders are successfully negotiated, then cross-border activities—both legal and illegal—will continue unless the borders are actually enforced or physically demarcated in some manner, an unlikely proposition given Bhutan's rugged and mountainous terrain. Melting glaciers, stimulated by climate change, may actually increase the porosity of the borders by allowing new openings where Tibetans can enter Bhutan illegally.[60]

Finally, there is a palpable fear among some leaders that Bhutan, by virtue of its small size compared to China, will end up with a less than satisfactory outcome when the borders are finally settled. One lawmaker stated: "Even if we lose a small area it would be a big problem for our future generations."[61] For this reason, some Bhutanese officials have attempted to invoke China's sense of benevolence. A lawmaker from Haa Dzongkhag [Haa District] stated that "China was admired based on its area, population and economy not only in Asia but world over." Consequently, he hoped that China "would keep in view its global image" by setting a good example by not "indulging in disputes with a country like Bhutan over a tiny piece of land."[62]

Conclusions

After 27 years of border negotiations, it would appear that both sides are perhaps nearing a final agreement on their mutual boundary. In January 2010, the head of the Chinese delegation to the 19th round of border talks, Hu Zhengyue, stated that the "majority of the work is completed. What's left is minor."[63] However, even if border discussions are successfully concluded, they will have served merely as a prelude to the much more geopolitically complex relationship that will likely develop among Bhutan, China, and India in the decades ahead, which includes determining the trijunctions where the three neighbors meet.

Thus, Sino-Bhutan border negotiations have never been solely about real estate or territory; they also reflect the larger geopolitical dynamics of South Asia, which ultimately is driven by Sino-Indian competition. Moreover, the negotiations also reflect Bhutan's rise as an independent and democratic country in the international system, just as they reflect China's ascendancy as an economic behemoth, second only to the United States.

Once Bhutan and China achieve their goal of demarcating their borders, then they can turn to other outstanding transboundary problems, including poaching, smuggling, etc. However, they will still need to manage their nascent relationship and "geographic marriage" so as to avoid the fallout that may occur in the context of occasional Sino-Indian antagonisms.

Notes

1. Bhutan, "Background," https://www.cia.gov/library/publications/the-world-factbook/geos/bt.html [Accessed on 27 October 2011].

2. Ibid.

3. Ibid.

4. T.T. Poulose, "Bhutan's External Relations and India," *The International and Comparative Law Quarterly,* Vol. 20, No. 2 (April 1971), 199.

5. Ibid.

6. Ibid.

7. Thierry Mathou, "Bhutan-China Relations: Towards a New Step in Himalayan Politics," 393, http://www.bhutanstudies.org.bt/?page_id=74 [Accessed on 26 April 2011].

8. Melvyn C. Goldstein and Cynthia M. Beall, "The Impact of China's Reform Policy on the Nomads of Western Tibet," *Asian Survey,* Vol. 29, No. 6 (June 1989), 621.

9. Ibid.

10. Chen Jian, "The Tibetan Rebellion of 1959 and China's Changing Relations with India and the Soviet Union," *Journal of Cold War Studies,* Vol. 8, No. 3 (Summer 2006), 61.

11. Guangqiu Xu, "The United States and the Tibet Issue," *Asian Survey,* Vol. 37, No. 11 (November 1997), 1064.

12. "Nehru Assures Bhutan of Non-Interference," *New York Times,* 24 September 1958, 4.

13. As quoted by Chen, 71-77.

14. Ibid., 80-85.

15. By 1973, Bhutan had received over 6,300 refugees from Tibet, 2,300 of whom would eventually choose to become Bhutanese citizens; the remainder moved to India or to various Western countries. Mathou, 398.

16. Henry S. Bradsher, "Bhutan Ends Isolation as Reds Apply Squeeze," *Washington Post and Times-Herald,* 24 August 1959, A4.

17. "Nehru Asserts India Has Duty to Defend Bhutan and Sikkim," *New York Times,* 26 August 1959, 1.

18. "Bhutan Calls Males over 16 to Service," *Washington Post and Times-Herald,* 27 October 1962, A11.

19. L.K. Choudhary, et al., "Indo-Bhutan Relationship: a Unique Example of Bilateral Friendship in South Asia," *India Quarterly,* Vol. LXI, No. 2 (1 April 2005), 213-229.

20. "India to Protect Border States," *Washington Post and Times-Herald,* 26 August 1959, A4.

21. "Bhutan Bolsters Army to Counter Chinese," *Washington Post and Times-Herald,* 22 August 1959, A6; "India to Protect Border States," *Washington Post and Times-Herald,* 26 August 1959, A4.

22. Henry S. Bradsher, "Bhutan ends isolation as Reds apply squeeze," *Washington Post and Times-Herald,* 24 August 1959, A4.

23. Mathou, 390-391.

24. "Bhutan Sends a Protest to Red China on Border," *New York Times,* 17 March 1960, 14; Ajit K. Das, "Bhutan Peers Warily at Border 'Discrepancy,'" *Christian Science Monitor,* 1 April 1990, 3.

25. Poulose, 201.

26. 刘建 [Liu Jian], "不丹的对外关系 [Bhutan's Foreign Relations]," 南亚研究 [South Asia Studies], 2006 年第2 期 [2006, No. 2]: 54-55.

27. Mathou, 395.

28. "China Reported Claiming Bhutan," *Washington Post and Times-Herald,* 17 February 1961, A12.

29. "Offer of Peking Aid to Bhutan Reported," *Christian Science Monitor,* 25 January 1961, 3.

30. "China Said to Intrude into Bhutan," *Washington Post and Times-Herald,* 4 October 1966, A20.

31. "India Talks Cheer King of Bhutan," *Washington Post and Times-Herald,* 4 May 1966, A26.

32. Mathou, 397.

33. Syed Aziz-al Ahsan and Bhumitra Chakma, "Bhutan's Foreign Policy: Cautious Self-Assertion?" *Asian Survey,* Vol. 33, No. 11 (November 1993), 1047.

34. Kathleen Teltsch, "Bhutan Is Seeking U.N. Membership," *New York Times,* 26 December 1970, 20.

35. "1971—Bhutan Joins the U.N.," http://www.bhutan2008.bt/en/node/224 [Accessed on 26 April 2011].

36. Mohan Ram, "Tiny Bhutan Stands Up to Big Neighbor," *Christian Science Monitor,* 18 September 1979, 6.

37. Mathou, 400.

38. Ibid.

39. Dr. S. Chandrasekharan, *Bhutan's Northern Border: China's Bullying and Teasing Tactics: Update No. 82* (New Delhi: South Asia Analysis, 14 January 2010).

40. Mathou, 400.

41. Ibid.

42. Chandrasekharan, *Bhutan's Northern Border.*

43. Official transcript of Resolutions (Translation) of the 4th Session of the National Council of Bhutan, 23 November 2009, 25, www.nationalcouncil.bt/wp-content/uploads/.../4th_Session_Res_eng.pdf.

44. Thierry Mathou, "Bhutan in 2001: at the Crossroad," *Asian Survey*, Vol. 42, No. 1 (January/February 2002): 196.

45. Ibid.

46. Mathou, "Bhutan-China Relations," 402.

47. "U.S. Congratulates Bhutan on Vote," *BBC News,* 25 March 2008, http://news.bbc.co.uk/2/hi/south_asia/7311958.stm [Accessed on 27 April 2011].

48. Chris Morris, "Bhutan Experiments with democracy," *BBC News,* 25 March 2008, http://news.bbc.co.uk/2/hi/south_asia/7313325.stm [Accessed on 27 April 2011].

49. Liu, "Bhutan's Foreign Policy," 54-55.

50. Pranab Dhal Samanta, "Thimphu-Beijing Border Talks Has Delhi Worried," *Indian Express* [Internet Version], 28 July 2005, OSC#SAP20050729000014.

51. Pravin Sawhney, "Chinese Whispers," New Delhi *Force*, 1 January 2008, OSC# SAP20080106342011.

52. "Assembly Members Alarmed by Road Construction across Northern Boundary," *Kuensel Online*, 8 June 2005.

53. Zarir Hussain, "AFP: Lawmakers Accuse China of Encroaching on Bhutan Territory," *AFP* [Hong Kong], 30 November 2005, OSC# CPP20051130062058.

54. Ibid.

55. Official transcript of Resolutions, 25.

56. Kalsang Rinchen, "Bhutan Reports 17 Border Intrusions by China in 2009," Dharamsala *Phayul.com* [in English], 9 December 2009, OSC#CPP2009120953 3028.

57. *Ibid.*

58. Official transcript of Resolutions, 32.

59. Rinjzin Wangchuk and Ygyen Penjore, "Bhutan Parliament updated on status of China border issues," *Kuensel Online*, 7 December 2009, OSC# SAP20091207950 071.

60. Hussain, "AFP: Lawmakers Accuse China of Encroaching on Bhutan Territory."

61. Ibid.

62. Official transcript of Resolutions, 27.

63. "Chinese Official Says only 'Minor' Issues Left in Bhutan Border Talks," Thimpu *Kuensel Online*, 12 January 2010, OSC#SAP20100112950021.

36

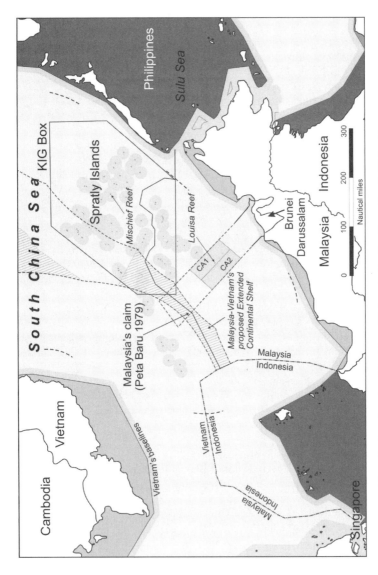

Map 3: Overlapping Maritime Claims in the Southern South China Sea

3
Brunei's Contested Sea Border with China

Ian Storey

Among China's 20 neighbors under examination in this volume, Brunei Darussalam, the hydrocarbon-rich Sultanate situated on the northeast coast of Borneo, is one of China's most distant "neighbors." In fact it is only because of China's expansive claims in the South China Sea that the two countries can be regarded as neighbors at all. The exact nature of their respective sovereignty claims remains unclear, but could be as much as 12,600 nm^2 (43,272 km^2). However, given the absence of tensions between Brunei and China over islands and sovereign rights in the South China Sea, the issue has received only passing scholarly attention.

Geographically, a thousand miles of water separates Sanya, the capital of Hainan Province, and the Bruneian capital Bandar Seri Bagawan. Politically and economically, Brunei's relations with Beijing are less extensive than most of the other members of the Association of Southeast Asian Nations (ASEAN).[1] Although China recognized Brunei following its independence from the United Kingdom in 1984, it was not until 1991 that formal ties were established, a delay caused in part by the limited number of Bruneian diplomats, but also because of lingering apprehensions among the country's ruling elite concerning China's intentions in Southeast Asia.[2] Trade links between the two countries remain modest—around $300 million in 2008—despite China's thirst for Brunei's energy resources.[3]

Recent agreements between Brunei and Malaysia have served to shed some light on the positions of the various claimants, and seem to have removed Kuala Lumpur from the equation vis-à-vis the dispute over Louisa Reef in the Spratly archipelago. Although Brunei and Vietnam may still have overlapping claims in the Spratlys, Brunei's South China Sea dispute is principally with the PRC. Yet as neither country has clarified its maritime claims, including for example by lodging a full submission with the United Nations Commission on the Limits of the Continental Shelf (CLCS), a complete picture still eludes us. The purpose of this chapter is to examine Brunei's claims in the South China Sea to date, how Malaysia and Brunei moved to resolve their differences, and what the implications of their agreement might be for Sino-Bruneian relations.

Brunei's Claims in the South China Sea

Following independence from the UK in 1984, the Brunei government issued a series of maps in the late 1980s outlining the country's maritime claims: *Map Showing Territorial Waters of Brunei Darussalam* (1987); *Maps Showing Continental Shelf of Brunei Darussalam* (1988); and *Maps Showing Fishery Limits of Brunei Darussalam* (1988).[4] These maps indicate a rectangular exclusive economic zone (EEZ) stretching 200 nautical miles (nm) from Brunei's coast. Contained within Brunei's EEZ claim are two geographical features generally considered to be part of the Spratly islands: Louisa Reef (Terumbu Semarang Barat Kecil in Malay and Nan Tong Jiao in Chinese) and Rifleman Bank (Bai Vung May in Vietnamese, Nanwei Tan in Chinese).[5] As China claims indisputable sovereignty over the Spratlys, these two reefs form the basis of the Sino-Bruneian dispute.

Louisa Reef is approximately 120 nm north-northwest of the Bruneian town of Kuala Belait. The reef is approximately 1.24 miles long east to west and 0.6 miles wide from north to south.[6] Louisa Reef can best be described as a low-tide elevation that is above the water at low tide but submerged at high tide. As Louisa Reef lies well beyond 12 nm from the nearest above high tide feature, in accordance with Article 13 of the United Nations Convention on the Law of the Sea (UNCLOS), it is therefore incapable of generating a maritime zone of its own, including a 12 nm territorial sea, let alone a 200 nm EEZ. Moreover, it has been observed that under international law it remains unclear whether low-tide elevations can be considered as territory subject to a claim of sovereignty.[7] In fact, Brunei has never formally lodged a claim to Louisa Reef. Indeed in January 1992 *The Borneo Bulletin* reported that Foreign Minister Prince Mohamed Bolkiah had stated that Brunei was only claiming the seas surrounding Louisa Reef, and not the feature itself.[8] However, according to officials from the Ministry of Foreign Affairs, Brunei does claim sovereignty over Louisa Reef.[9] To date, this claim has yet to be formalized.

Brunei is the only South China Sea claimant not to have occupied or garrisoned any of the Spratlys. Various observers have stated that Malaysia "occupied" Louisa Reef in 1983 and constructed a lighthouse, and that in 1988 China planted a marker on the reef that was subsequently removed by Malaysia.[10] The word "occupation" is clearly erroneous as no Malaysian troops have ever been stationed on the reef. Nor is there any evidence of a Malaysian-constructed lighthouse. A diving group based in Brunei has, however, published a photograph of an obelisk on Louisa Reef, though who planted it and when remain unclear.[11]

Brunei's claim to Rifleman Bank, a submerged feature, stems from its extended continental shelf submission. According to Brunei's preliminary submission to the CLCS on 12 May 2009, the country's continental shelf extends beyond the 200 nm EEZ and will be the subject of Brunei's full submission.[12] Brunei's full submission, which at the time of writing had yet to be made, is likely to encompass Rifleman Bank. Some reports suggest the reef was "occupied" by Vietnam in 1983, but there is no evidence that Hanoi has tried to consolidate its claims by building a structure on the reef.[13]

Brunei, Malaysia, and the South China Sea Dispute

In order to gain a better understanding of Brunei's claims in the South China Sea it is necessary to review developments in Malaysia-Brunei relations over the past few years. This includes several very specific bilateral agreements that appear to have a direct impact on the sovereignty dispute.

In 1979, the Malaysian government published the *Map Showing the Territorial Waters and Continental Shelf Boundaries of Malaysia*, usually referred to as the *Peta Baru* [*Peta Menunjukkan Sempadan Perairan dan Pelantar Benua Malaysia*] or "New Map." The map indicated that Malaysia claimed 12 features in the Spratlys, including Louisa Reef. Malaysia subsequently occupied five of those features: Swallow Reef (1983), Mariveles Reef (1986), Ardasier Reef (1986), Erica Reef (1999), and Investigator Shoal (1999). As noted earlier, it has been suggested that Malaysia also occupied Louisa Reef sometime in the 1980s, but that this is almost certainly inaccurate. In 1980, the UK, acting on behalf of Brunei, protested the *Peta Baru* on the basis that Louisa Reef fell within the 1958 delimitation of Brunei's continental shelf.[14] It was not until 1995, however, that Malaysia and Brunei agreed to hold talks to resolve their territorial and maritime boundary claims. One of the most contentious issues under discussion was Brunei's claim to Limbang, an area of Sarawak that was annexed by Rajah Charles Brooke in 1890 and which became part of Malaysian territory in 1963. Limbang splits Brunei into two non-contiguous territories; Brunei has always disputed the annexation.

Bilateral talks made little progress, but a flare up in tensions between Malaysia and Brunei in 2003 provided a catalyst for a resolution. In 2000, Brunei had awarded exploration contracts to a consortium led by Shell and Total for Blocks J and K in the country's claimed EEZ. In 2003, Malaysia awarded concessions to state-owned energy company Petronas and its partner U.S.-based Murphy Oil for two blocks in almost exactly the same area, labeled Blocks L and M by Kuala Lumpur.[15] In 2003, however, all exploration work was halted following two incidents at sea: in March a Bruneian patrol boat intercepted a drilling ship owned by Murphy Oil, and in April two Malaysian warships prevented a Total chartered vessel from carrying out survey work in the concession area. Both countries claimed the oil companies licensed by the other state were working illegally in their EEZ.[16] But with oil and gas reserves in both Brunei and Malaysia falling, the naval standoffs brought into sharp relief that it was in no one's interests to allow the dispute to persist. Bilateral talks were thus given fresh impetus.

The culmination of 39 rounds of talks was the Exchange of Letters (EoL) signed by Malaysian Prime Minister Abdullah Badawi and Brunei's Sultan Hassanal Bolkiah on 16 March 2009. Due to sensitivities in both countries, the exact contents of the EoL remained secret. However, contemporary press reports suggested that the two countries had reached agreement on four key points. First, the final settlement of maritime boundaries. Second, joint development of offshore energy resources. Third, agreement on the modalities of resolving their land frontiers. And fourth, the right of movement by Malaysian ships in Bruneian waters.[17]

Controversy erupted immediately when Prime Minister Abdullah claimed that by signing the EoL Brunei had dropped its claim to Limbang, an assertion rejected by Brunei, on the grounds that the agreement made no explicit mention of the contested territory.[18] Brunei did concede, however, that the Limbang Question would be settled once the border between the two countries had been finally delimited.[19] Political observers concluded that Brunei would drop its claim to Limbang in return for Malaysian recognition of its EEZ, and that both countries would jointly develop resources in Blocks J and K (or L and M). However, on 6 May 2009, Malaysia and Vietnam made a joint submission to the CLCS with respect to an area of seabed in the southern central South China Sea that apparently ignores Brunei's EEZ claim.[20] China protested the joint submission, but curiously Brunei has yet to do so.

Controversy over the contents of the EoL quickly blew over but resurfaced in 2010, providing greater clarity to the contents of the agreement. On 21 April, Murphy Oil issued a statement announcing the termination of its contracts for Blocks L and M because they were "no longer part of Malaysia."[21] On 29 April, writing in his blog, former Prime Minister Mahathir Mohamad made the accusation that by signing the EoL, his successor, Abdullah Badawi, had caused Malaysia to lose $100 billion worth of oil and gas revenues.[22] In a statement to the media, Abdullah countered that the EoL was "not a loss for Malaysia" as both countries had agreed to develop jointly the energy resources through the establishment of a Commercial Arrangement Area. Abdullah also acknowledged for the first time that Brunei had "sovereign rights" to the two blocks and that Malaysia and Brunei had agreed to "establish a final and permanent sea boundary" and, further, that once the land demarcation process had been completed "there will be no longer any land boundary dispute between Malaysia and Brunei as a whole."[23]

A press statement issued by Malaysia's Ministry of Foreign Affairs a few days later confirmed Abdullah's press release, and added that the EoL had:

> established the final delimitation of territorial sea, continental shelf and exclusive economic zone of both States. Malaysia's oil

concession Blocks L and M which coincided with Brunei Darussalam's Blocks J and K are recognised under the Exchange of Letters as being situated within Brunei Darussalam's maritime areas, over which Brunei Darussalam is entitled to exercise sovereign rights under the relevant provisions of the United Nations Convention on the Law of the Sea 1982 (UNCLOS).[24]

It was subsequently revealed that Production Sharing Agreements between Malaysia and Brunei had been signed in September and December 2010 for Blocks CA1 and CA2 (the renamed Blocks J/L and K/M) by which Petronas would have a 10 percent interest in the former and Murphy Oil a 30 percent stake in the latter.[25] Drilling in Block CA1 was slated to begin in the third quarter of 2011.[26] The Joint Malaysia-Brunei Darussalam Land Boundary Technical Committee was due to begin demarcation and survey activities in early 2011 and was expected to complete its work within 18 months.[27]

Brunei, China, and the South China Sea Dispute

As noted above, by means of the 2009 EoL Malaysia recognizes Brunei's EEZ and its sovereign rights therein. Essentially, therefore, the Malaysian government has dropped its claim to Louisa Reef. Vietnam, on the other hand, may still covet Louisa Reef. Hanoi maintains "indisputable sovereignty" over the Spratly islands as a whole, but it has never provided a clear geographical definition of the archipelago. Brunei has also not commented on Vietnam's claims and vice versa. As such, the main problem for Brunei lies with PRC claims in the South China Sea.

China also maintains that it has "indisputable sovereignty over the islands in the South China Sea and the adjacent waters, and enjoys sovereign rights and jurisdiction over the relevant waters as well as the seabed and subsoil thereof."[28] Attached to China's protest note in response to the joint Vietnam-Malaysia submission to the CLCS in May 2009 was a map containing the infamous nine-dashed line stretching from Taiwan to the Paracel islands.[29] However, China has yet to clarify what the nine segments mean or their justification under UNCLOS. If the fifth and sixth segments are joined together, the line comes within approximately 40 miles of Brunei's coastline. This suggests that China does not recognize Brunei's EEZ claim and that it claims both Louisa Reef and Rifleman Bank. Interestingly, however, China did not make a formal response to the 2009 EoL, presumably because the agreement is not in the public domain.[30] China, in an analogous fashion to Brunei, has also made a preliminary submission to the CLCS. While this preliminary submission largely concerns the East China Sea, China has reserved the right to make further submissions in relation to "other sea areas," presumably meaning to parts of the South China Sea.

As mentioned earlier, Malaysia and Brunei have agreed to exploit jointly the energy resources in Blocks CA1 and CA2 contained within the latter's EEZ. Yet according to a joint statement released by both countries in September 2010, they have held out the possibility of future cooperation beyond the two blocks with a "third country"—but whether this is a reference to the PRC remains unclear.[31] In the past, China's leaders have raised the issue of shelving sovereignty claims and engaging in joint exploitation of maritime resources in the South China Sea with their Bruneian counterparts. On the sidelines of the 2006 ASEAN-China Summit in Nanning, for instance, Chinese Premier Wen Jiabao reiterated the utility of this formula to Sultan Hassanal Bolkiah.[32] Interestingly, however, Brunei has remained silent on the possibility of joint exploration with the PRC in the disputed waters of the South China Sea.

Brunei's approach to the South China Sea puts a strong accent on diplomacy. Brunei has sent representatives to participate in the Indonesian sponsored workshops on the South China Sea since their inception in the early 1990s. In 1992, Brunei supported the ASEAN Declaration on the South China Sea and, in 1995, it closed ranks with its ASEAN partners when the organization issued a statement of "serious concern" following China's occupation of Philippine-claimed Mischief Reef.[33] Brunei is also a signatory to the November 2002 *ASEAN-China Declaration on the Conduct of Parties in the South China Sea* (DoC). The DoC is designed to manage rather than resolve the South China Sea problem and reduce tensions and build trust through the implementation of cooperative confidence building measures (CBMs). Yet, since the DoC was signed, not a single CBM has been effectively operationalized. Negotiations on implementation guidelines became stymied in 2009 because China opposed inclusion of a clause stating that the ASEAN members would consult among themselves prior to meeting with PRC officials. The impasse was finally broken in July 2011 when ASEAN conceded to Beijing's demand to drop formal reference to the member states caucusing on the South China Sea. In early 2012 the two sides began discussions on implementing joint cooperative projects in the South China Sea, as well as drawing up guiding principles for a formal code of conduct. As a member of ASEAN, Brunei is a participant in these talks. Prior to the July 2011 "breakthrough," officially it made no comment on the lack of progress, though privately Bruneian officials expressed their frustration.[34]

Given the shortcomings of the current diplomatic process in better managing the dispute, several Southeast Asian claimants, most notably Vietnam, have accelerated their military modernization programs as a hedge against a more assertive China. If Brunei wanted to pursue a similar strategy, however, it would face considerable manpower and technical restraints. Although the country's most recent defense policy document, *Shaping the Force Today: Defence White Paper Update 2007*, does not explicitly mention the South China Sea dispute, it does highlight the vital importance of offshore maritime resources for the country's continued prosperity. It is in this context that the defense policy update notes the Royal Brunei Armed Forces' (RBAF) critical role in exercising control over the country's "border and adjacent maritime areas."[35]

As part of Ministry of Defence efforts to modernize the RBAF, the white paper update outlined plans to replace existing maritime patrol craft with new small and medium-sized patrol boats able to operate more effectively "out to the limits" of the country's EEZ.[36] In 2010-2011 the Royal Brunei Navy (RBN) commissioned three Darussalam-class offshore patrol boats and four Ijhtihad-class fast attack boats.[37] However, at just over 1,000 personnel operating 16 vessels, the RBN is a veritable minnow by regional standards and does not pose a credible deterrent to the rapidly modernizing People's Liberation Army Navy (PLAN) should Beijing choose to press its claims more forcefully. Brunei does, however, maintain close defense links with Singapore, the UK, Australia, and the United States, which provide the country with valuable hedging options vis-à-vis the PRC.

Conclusions

Brunei and China inhabit the same neighborhood, and consequently have shared interests in preserving a peaceful and stable environment conducive to strengthening bilateral economic linkages. They are also neighbors in the sense that they have conflicting territorial and sovereignty claims in the South China Sea. Pending full submissions to the CLCS and clarification of China's apparent historic claims, Brunei and China's maritime claims remain ambiguous and open to interpretation. In this context it should be noted that the CLCS, as a scientific and technical body, is unable to resolve competing claims to extended continental shelf areas. However, it may be concluded that both countries claim sovereignty or, at the least, jurisdiction over Louisa Reef in the Spratlys. Unlike some of the other countries in Southeast Asia, however, the South China Sea dispute does not occupy center stage in Sino-Bruneian relations.

Looking to the future, Brunei might be amenable to joint development of offshore energy resources with the PRC in a manner analogous to its resolution of its disputes with Malaysia. Since the Sultanate seldom takes the lead on matters pertaining to the South China Sea, however, this would likely be contingent on consensus among the Southeast Asian claimants or ASEAN as a group.

For the foreseeable future, Brunei remains committed to diplomatic mechanisms as a means to better manage the dispute with a view to a final political or possibly even legal resolution. As the 2009 EoL between Brunei and Malaysia demonstrates, such a resolution is not beyond the realm of possibility, despite the significant hurdles the claimant countries would have to overcome.

Notes

1. ASEAN is comprised of 10 members: Brunei, Cambodia, Indonesia, Laos, Malaysia, Myanmar, the Philippines, Singapore, Thailand, and Vietnam.
2. For a full account of the development of Brunei-China relations, see Chapter 13 in Ian Storey, *Southeast Asia and the Rise of China: The Search for Security* (Abingdon, Oxon: Routledge, 2011), 268-273.
3. Ibid., 271.
4. Asri Salleh, Che Hamdan Che Mohd Razali, and Kamaruzman Jusoff, "Malaysia's policy towards its 1963-2008 territorial disputes," *Journal of Law and Conflict Resolution,* Vol. 1, No. 5 (October 2009), 111.
5. Mark J. Valencia, Jon M. Van Dyke, and Noel A. Ludwig, *Sharing the Resources of the South China Sea* (Honolulu: University of Hawai'i Press, 1997), 232.
6. Panaga Divers website, http://www.panagadivers.com/Diving/Reefs.htm [Accessed on 27 October 2011].
7. Robert C. Beckman and Clive Schofield, "Moving beyond disputes over island sovereignty: ICJ decision sets stage for maritime boundary delimitation in the Singapore Strait," *Ocean Development and International Law*, Vol. 40, No. 1 (2009), 1-35.
8. "Brunei seeks security network," *The Borneo Bulletin*, 27 January 1992.
9. Interviews with senior officials at the Ministry of Foreign Affairs, Brunei, 6-7 April 2011.
10. Greg Austin, *China's Ocean Frontier: International Law, Military Force and National Development* (St. Leonards, NSW: Allen & Unwin, 1998), 155; Valencia, et al., 231.
11. Panaga Divers website.
12. Brunei Darussalam's Preliminary Submission concerning the Outer Limits of its Continental Shelf, 12 May 2009, http://www.un.org/Depts/los/clcs_new/submissions_files/preliminary/brn2009preliminaryinformation.pdf.
13. Valencia, et al., 232.
14. Beckman and Davenport.
15. Hadi DP Mahmud, "Is Brunei's offshore Block J area really ours or Malaysia's?" *The Brunei Times*, 19 December 2007.
16. Ibid.
17. "Brunei drops claim over Limbang district, says Abdullah," *The Star Online*, 17 March 2009.
18. "Brunei denies Limbang story," *The Borneo Bulletin*, 18 March 2009.
19. "Limbang border to be set," *The Star Online*, 20 March 2009.
20. Joint submission by Malaysia and Viet Nam—in the southern part of the South China Sea, 6 May 2009, http://www.un.org/Depts/los/clcs_new/

submissions_files/submission_mysvnm_33_2009.htm [Accessed on 14 November 2011].

21. "Murphy Oil Corporation Announces Termination of Production Sharing Contracts For Blocks L and M in Malaysia," 21 April 2010, http://www.murphyoilcorp.com/ir/modal.aspx?ID=836&Year=2010 [Accessed on 15 November 2011].

22. Mahathir Mohamad, "Malaysia's generosity," 29 April 2010, http://mahathir-mohamad.blogspot.com/2010_05_01_archive.html [Accessed on 27 October 2011].

23. Abdullah Ahmad Badawi, "The exchange of letters between Malaysia and Brunei," *The Malaysian Insider*, 1 May 2010.

24. Press Statement, Ministry of Foreign Affairs, Malaysia, 3 May 2010, http://www.kln.gov.my/web/guest/pr2010/-/asset_publisher/X9Nx/content/press-release-:-the-exchange-of-letters-between-yab-dato'-seri-abdullah-haji-ahmad-badawi-prime-minister-of-malaysia-and-his-majesty-sultan-haji-hassanal-bolkiah-mu'izzaddin-waddaulah-english-version-only?redirect=%2Fweb%2Fguest%2Fpr2010 [Accessed on 27 October 2011].

25. "Drilling in CA1, CA2," *The Brunei Times*, 4 March 2011.

26. "Bright future ahead with CA1, CA2," *The Brunei Times*, 24 March 2011.

27. Joint Statement on the 14th Annual Leaders Consultation between Malaysia and Brunei Darussalam, 21 September 2010, http://bruneiembassy.be/joint-statement-on-the-14th-annual-leaders%E2%80%99-consultation-between-malaysia-and-brunei-darussalam/[Accessed on 27 October 2011].

28. Submission to the CLCS, 7 May 2009, http://www.un.org/Depts/los/clcs_new/submissions_files/mysvnm33_09/chn_2009re_mys_vnm_e.pdf.

29. Ibid.

30. Interviews with senior officials at the Ministry of Foreign Affairs, Brunei, 6-7 April 2011.

31. Joint Statement on the 14th Annual Leaders Consultation between Malaysia and Brunei Darussalam, 21 September 2010, http://bruneiembassy.be/joint-statement-on-the-14th-annual-leaders%E2%80%99-consultation-between-malaysia-and-brunei-darussalam/ [Accessed on 31 October 2011].

32. "Brunei, China eye trade boost," *The Borneo Bulletin*, 1 November 2006.

33. "ASEAN ministers express concern over Spratlys," *Reuters News Service*, 18 March 1995.

34. Interviews with senior officials at the Ministry of Foreign Affairs, Brunei, 6-7 April 2011.

35. *Shaping the Force Today: Defence White Paper Update 2007* (Brunei: Ministry of Defence, 2007), http://www.mindef.gov.bn/new_home/whitepaper2007/english.pdf.

36. Ibid.

37. "New sea power for Brunei," *The Borneo Bulletin,* 8 January 2011.

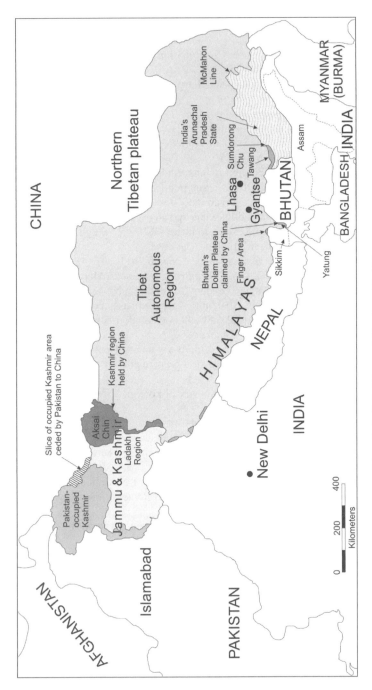

Map 4: India's Disputed Border with China

4

India's Intractable Border Dispute with China

Brahma Chellaney

As geopolitical rivals, India and China face each other over a highly disputed border. Virtually the entire 2,521 mile (4,057 km) border—one of the longest in the world—is in dispute, without a mutually agreed line of control in the Himalayas separating the two countries. The amount of land under dispute tops 52,125 square miles (135,000 km^2), or approximately the size of Costa Rica or the U.S. state of Alabama. It is apparent that in comparison with China's territorial disputes with other neighbors now or in the past, the PRC's land disputes with India stand out both for their sheer size and for their importance to the region.

Both China and India seek to play a pivotal global role by reclaiming the glory they enjoyed before they went into decline from the 18th century onward and fell prey to the machinations of colonialist invaders. They see their rise not as a challenge to the presently dominant countries, but as ushering in a return to the normal state of affairs in history when they were preeminent. Even though neither country is in a position to dominate the other, yet each views the other as a potential geopolitical rival.

As China and India gain economic heft, they are drawing ever more international attention at a time of an ongoing global shift of power to Asia. Their underlying strategic dissonance and rivalry, however, usually attracts less notice. The two giants represent competing political and social models of development. In fact, China and India are more than just nation-states; they are large ancient civilizations that together represent nearly two-fifths of humanity. How the intricate and fluid relationship between these two great countries of markedly different histories, identities, and cultures evolves will have an important bearing on Asian geopolitics, international security, and globalization.

Origins of the Sino-Indian Border Dispute

While it has become fashionable to pair and compare China and India, as if they were joined at the hip, it is often forgotten that the two are—comparatively speaking—new neighbors.[1] The huge Tibetan plateau, measuring almost two-thirds the size of the entire European continent, separated the two civilizations, thereby limiting interaction to sporadic cultural and religious contacts, with political relations absent. It was only after Tibet's annexation in 1951 that Han Chinese troops appeared for the first time in large numbers on India's Himalayan frontiers.

As new neighbors, India and China have been on a steep learning curve. Their 32-day war in 1962 did not settle matters, because China's dramatic triumph only sowed the seeds of greater rivalry and India's own political rise. Today, China and India represent two separate cultural and political blocks, each with its own distinct set of values. India, which sees itself as a bridge between the West and the East, shares basic values more with Europe than with China. Politically, the Chinese and Indian societies remain polar-opposite in terms of their systems, with one under an authoritarian regime that rules by instilling fear and the other governed by a raucous democracy.

Paradoxically, after the Communists came to power in China in 1949, India was one of the first countries to embrace the Mao Zedong-led regime. Yet in one of his first actions after seizing power, Mao confided to Soviet dictator Joseph Stalin that Chinese forces were "preparing for an attack on Tibet," and he inquired whether the Soviet Air Force could help transport supplies to them.[2] Even as the new Communist state annexed the large historical buffer state of Tibet—an action that eliminated India's outer line of defense—the Indian government continued to court China, seeing it as a benign neighbor that had, like India, only recently emerged from the ravages of colonialism. New Delhi even opposed a discussion in the United Nations General Assembly in November 1950 on the then-independent Tibet's appeal for international help against Chinese aggression.

The Indian government, led by a romantic politician, Jawaharlal Nehru, was taken largely unawares by the start of the Chinese military attack on Tibet in October 1950, when global attention was focused on the Korean War. The PLA's rapid success in seizing eastern Tibet emboldened China to intervene in the Korean War. Nehru later admitted that he had not anticipated the swiftness and callousness with which China took over Tibet because he had been "led to believe by the Chinese Foreign Office that the Chinese would settle the future of Tibet in a peaceful manner by direct negotiation with the representatives of Tibet."[3]

Indeed, as proof of his strategic naïveté, Nehru recorded the following note in July 1949 to close an internal debate on Tibet within the Indian government, when a Communist victory appeared imminent in China:

> Whatever may be the ultimate fate of Tibet in relation to China, I
> think there is practically no chance of any military danger to India
> arising from any change in Tibet. Geographically, this is very

difficult and practically it would be a foolish adventure. If India is
to be influenced or an attempt made to bring pressure on her,
Tibet is not the route for it. I do not think there is any necessity
for our Defence Ministry, or any part of it, to consider possible
military repercussions on the India-Tibetan frontier. The event is
remote and may not arise at all.[4]

What Nehru credulously saw as a "foolish adventure" was mounted within a
matter of months by Mao's regime, which gobbled up Tibet and gained control of
its strategic crossroads, and then soon afterwards began exerting direct military
pressure on India. What Nehru averred was geographically impractical all too soon
became a geopolitical reality that has affected Indian security like no other
development. It also helped create a common land corridor between the PRC and
Pakistan, which helped to nurture the Sino-Pakistan strategic axis. Tibet's
annexation also gave China, for the first time under Han Chinese rule, a contiguous
border with India, Bhutan, and Nepal.

Yet Nehru remained such an incorrigible idealist that he even rejected the U.S.
and Soviet proposal that India take China's vacant seat in the United Nations
Security Council. The officially-blessed selected works of Nehru quote the then
Indian prime minister as stating: "Informally, suggestions have been made by the
U.S. that China should be taken into the UN but not in the Security Council and that
India should take her place in the Council. We cannot, of course, accept this as it
means falling out with China and it would be very unfair for a great country like
China not to be in the Council."[5]

Another blunder that virtually guaranteed the festering of the Sino-Indian border
dispute occurred in 1954, when Nehru signed a largely one-sided pact with Beijing.
This pact ostensibly established India-China friendship under the rubric of
"Panchsheel," or "five principles," of peaceful coexistence. The Panchsheel
Agreement, as it became popularly known, incorporated a formal Indian recognition
of the new Chinese control over Tibet, with India formally forfeiting all the
extraterritorial rights and privileges it had enjoyed in Tibet until the Chinese
invasion.[6] This accord recorded India's agreement both to withdraw fully within six
months its "military escorts now stationed at Yatung and Gyantse" in the "Tibet
Region of China," as well as "to hand over to the Government of China at a
reasonable price the postal, telegraph and public telephone services together with
their equipment operated by the Government of India in Tibet Region of China." Up
through the 1950 invasion, China had maintained a diplomatic mission in Lhasa,
just as India did, underscoring Tibet's autonomous status.[7]

India's formal acceptance of the Chinese claim over Tibet came without extracting a reciprocal Chinese acceptance of the then prevailing Indo-Tibetan border, including the McMahon line in the east that was agreed upon in 1914 between the British Indian government and the then-autonomous Tibetan government. Indeed, Nehru misconstrued the mention of specific border-trade mountain passes and posts in the 1954 accord as Chinese acknowledgement of where the Tibetan frontier with India lay. To make matters worse, he refused to pay heed to Beijing's statements that it had signed a border-trade accord and not a border-settlement accord with India. In fact, no sooner had the Panchsheel Agreement been signed than China laid claim to some Indian frontier areas and then furtively intruded south of two mountain passes specified as border points in that accord. Before long, China began building a highway through India's Ladakh region to link Tibet with another vast, occupied region, Xinjiang, home to Turkic-speaking Muslim ethnic groups.[8]

In the years after the Panchsheel Agreement, Sino-Indian relations became tense, with Chinese cross-border encroachments culminating in a full-fledged Chinese military attack in 1962. Just as Mao began his invasion of Tibet while the world was occupied with the Korean War, he chose a perfect time for invading India: the beginning of the attack, spread over two separate rounds, coincided with a major international crisis that brought the United States and the Soviet Union within a whisker of nuclear war over the stealthy deployment of Soviet medium-range ballistic missiles in Cuba. A little over a month after launching the invasion of India, Mao announced a unilateral ceasefire that, significantly, coincided with America's formal termination of Cuba's quarantine.

Mao's premier, Zhou Enlai, publicly admitted that the war was intended "to teach India a lesson." As for Nehru, after having reposed his implicit faith in China, he cried foul when Beijing deceived him. The day the Chinese invaded, a shattered Nehru confessed to the nation in the following words: "Perhaps there are not many instances in history where one country has gone out of her way to be friendly and cooperative with the government and people of another country and to plead their cause in the councils of the world, and then that country returns evil for good."[9]

Renewed Frontier Tensions and Disputes

India did not restore full diplomatic relations with China—broken by the 1962 war—until after Mao's death in September 1976. In 1981, India and China agreed to open negotiations on finding ways to resolve their border disputes. More than three decades later, those negotiations are still continuing, with little progress in settling those disputes. This despite the fact that the two sides have signed three vaunted border-related accords: 1) a 1993 agreement to maintain "peace and tranquility along the Line of Actual Control" (although there is no mutually agreed line of control, let alone an *actual* line of control); 2) a 1996 accord on "confidence-building measures in the military field"; and 3) a 2005 agreement identifying six "guiding principles" for a settlement of the frontier disputes. But no sooner had the border-related principles been unveiled in 2005 with great fanfare than Beijing jettisoned one key element—the do-not-disturb-the-settled-populations principle—to buttress its claims on additional Indian areas. In recent years, the broadening of the Sino-Indian border talks into an all-encompassing strategic dialogue has been an unmistakable reminder that the negotiations stand deadlocked. Yet neither side wants to abandon the apparently fruitless process.

In the period since the border negotiations began in the early 1980s, the world has changed fundamentally. Indeed, with its rapidly accumulating military and economic power, China has emerged as a rising power in the making. The longer the negotiating process continues without yielding results, the greater the opportunity Beijing will have to mount strategic pressure on India and leverage its position. After all, China already holds the military advantage on the ground. Its forces control the heights along the long Himalayan frontier. Furthermore, by building new railroads, airports, and highways in Tibet, China is now in a position to move additional forces to the border rapidly, potentially giving it the ability to strike at India at a time of its choosing.

Diplomatically, China is a contented party, having occupied what it wanted—the Aksai Chin plateau, which is the size of Switzerland and provides the only accessible Tibet-Xinjiang route through the Karakoram passes of the Kunlun mountains. Yet China chooses to press claims on additional Indian territories, arguably as part of a grand strategy to gain leverage in bilateral relations and, more importantly, to keep India under military and diplomatic pressure. The authoritative *People's Daily*—the Chinese Communist Party mouthpiece that reflects official thinking—made this clear in an 11 June 2009 editorial: "China won't make any compromises in its border disputes with India."[10] That reflects the Chinese position in the negotiations.

At the core of China's strategy is an apparent resolve to hold off indefinitely on a border settlement with India through an overt refusal to accept the territorial status quo. In addition to disputed borderlands, China occupies 16,672 square miles (43,180 km^2) of the original princely state of Jammu and Kashmir—the so-called western sector in the Sino-Indian context—including 2,000 square miles (5,180 km^2) ceded to it by Islamabad under the Sino-Pakistan boundary agreement of 1963. It also covets some 34,750 square miles (90,000 km^2) of territory under Indian administration in the eastern sector, where Tibet shares a 640 mile (1,030 km) border with India's remote Arunachal Pradesh state, which is almost three times as large as the island of Taiwan. In addition, several small but strategic tracts of land are in dispute in the central sector and in India's Ladakh region.

In not hiding its intent to further redraw the Himalayan frontiers, Beijing only helps highlight the futility of the ongoing process of political negotiations with India. After all, the territorial status quo can be changed, on the scale sought by China, not by political talks but by further military conquest. Yet, paradoxically, the political process remains important both for Beijing and New Delhi to provide the façade of bilateral engagement. China's assertive resurrection of its claims to Arunachal Pradesh in recent years could undermine this façade.

Sino-Indian Tensions over Arunachal Pradesh

Since 2006, China has publicly raked up the issue of Arunachal Pradesh, the northeastern Indian state that Beijing calls "southern Tibet" and which it claims largely as its own. Indian defense officials have reported a rising number of Chinese military incursions across the entire Himalayan border in recent years. That the Tibet issue remains at the core of the India-China divide is being underlined by Beijing itself by laying claim to additional Indian territories on the basis of alleged Tibetan ecclesial or tutelary links to them, not to any professed Han Chinese links.

China originally fashioned its claim to Arunachal Pradesh as a bargaining chip to compel India to recognize its occupation of the Aksai Chin plateau, in the Ladakh region of the original princely state of Jammu and Kashmir. For this reason, China withdrew from the Arunachal Pradesh areas it invaded during the 32-day war with India in 1962, but retained its territorial gains in Aksai Chin. Chinese leader Deng Xiaoping in 1979 even broached the exploratory idea of a package settlement: New Delhi would accept the Chinese control over Aksai Chin and Beijing would drop its claim on Arunachal, subject to "minor readjustments" along the line of control.

The PRC's more recent resurrection of its long-dormant claim to Arunachal Pradesh has largely coincided with Beijing eyeing that state's rich water resources. In fact, Beijing has recently unveiled the plan to build a dam near the Tibet-Arunachal border that would be more than twice as large as the Three Gorges Dam—the 38-gigawatt Motuo Dam. China's resource-driven claim to Arunachal closely parallels the way it became covetous of the Japanese-controlled Senkaku islands—the Diaoyu islands—only after the issue of developing petroleum resources on the continental shelf of the East China Sea came up at in the 1970s.

The resurrected claim to Arunachal Pradesh is linked with Beijing's successful strategy of getting India to accept gradually Tibet as part of China. Whatever leverage India still had on the Tibet issue was surrendered in 2003 when it shifted its position from Tibet being an "autonomous" region within China to it being "part of the territory of the People's Republic of China." This has simply strengthened

China's long-standing negotiating stance: what it occupies is Chinese territory, and what it claims must be shared—or as it puts it in reasonably sounding terms—through a settlement based on mutual accommodation and mutual understanding.

So, while publicly laying claim to the whole of Arunachal Pradesh, China in private has asked India to cede that state's strategic Tawang Valley—a critical corridor between Lhasa and Assam of immense military importance because it overlooks the so-called chicken-neck that connects India's northeast with the rest of the country. In fact, with the Dalai Lama having publicly repudiated Chinese claims that Arunachal Pradesh, or even just Tawang, were historically part of Tibet, a discomfited Beijing has sought to argue in the now-suspended dialogue process with his envoys that for any larger political deal to emerge, the Tibetan government-in-exile must support China's position that Arunachal has always been part of traditional Tibet. The plain fact is that with China's own claim to Tibet being historically dubious, its claims to Indian territories are doubly suspect.

Sino-Indian Trade Relations

Significantly, despite the cross-border incursions and tensions, China and India have consciously sought to downplay the border friction and instead put prime emphasis on their fast-growing trade. For example, when Chinese Premier Wen Jiabao visited India in late 2010 the two countries decided to kick all contentious issues down the road and expand bilateral trade by two-thirds over the next five years. However, increased trade is no panacea for the sharpening geopolitical rivalry. First of all, while trade may benefit both sides, the perception in India is that China gains more. India's trade deficit with China is ballooning, and it largely exports raw materials to China and imports finished products.

The focus on trade, even as political disputes fester, plays into the Chinese agenda to secure new markets in India while continuing with a strategy to contain that country within the South Asian region. There has recently been a national outcry in India over attempts to undermine Indian brands through exports from China of fake pharmaceutical products labeled "Made in India." After Nigerian authorities seized a large consignment of fake anti-malarial drugs that had arrived from China with the "Made in India" stamp, Beijing promised to crack down on Chinese companies conducting such exports. However, perpetuating such an asymmetrical trade relationship indeed gives Beijing little incentive to bridge the political divide.

Nevertheless, from 2000 to 2010, Sino-Indian bilateral trade rose 20-fold, making it the only area where relations have thrived. But far from helping to turn the page on old rifts, this commerce has been accompanied by greater Sino-Indian geopolitical rivalry and military tensions. New Delhi's warming relationship with

Washington has only emboldened Beijing to up the ante through border provocations, resurrection of its claim to Arunachal Pradesh, and other diplomatic needling. Beijing had initially sought to improve ties with New Delhi so that it could dissuade it from moving closer to Washington. But after the United States and India cemented a civilian nuclear deal in mid-2005, China appears to have adopted a more coercive policy toward its southern neighbor, even adopting a type of psychological warfare.

Beijing's Psychological War on New Delhi

During 2009, Sino-Indian relations sank to their lowest political point in more than two decades when Beijing unleashed a psychological war upon New Delhi, employing its state-run media and nationalistic websites to warn of another armed conflict. It was a throwback to the coarse rhetoric China had used in the buildup to the war in 1962. The *People's Daily*, for example, berated India for "recklessness and arrogance" and asked it to weigh "the consequences of a potential confrontation with China."[11] Ignoring the lesson that booming trade by itself is no guarantee of moderation or restraint between states, China and India have left their political rows to future generations to clear up, with Wen Jiabao bluntly stating that sorting out the Himalayan border disputes "will take a fairly long period of time."[12]

Even as these old rifts remain, new problems have arisen, roiling relations further. China—which occupies one-fifth of the original princely state of Jammu and Kashmir—has started a troubling three-pronged policy to build pressure on New Delhi over Kashmir, where the disputed borders of India, Pakistan, and China converge. It has enlarged its footprint in Pakistani-occupied Kashmir (PoK) through new strategic projects and PLA deployment there, including sending from 7,000-11,000 PLA troops in 2010; it has attempted to question India's sovereignty over the Indian-controlled part of Kashmir; and it has officially shortened the length of the Himalayan border it shares with India by eliminating the 992 mile (1,597 km) line separating Indian Kashmir from Chinese-held Kashmir.

Furthermore, Chinese strategic projects around India, including ports in Sri Lanka and Pakistan and new transportation links with Myanmar, Nepal, and Pakistan, have been seriously unnerving India. The Chinese military presence in Pakistani-held Kashmir means that India faces Chinese troops on both flanks of its portion of Kashmir. The deepening China-Pakistan nexus also threatens to present India with a two-front theater in the event of a war with either country.

As a result of the renewed tensions, the India-China frontier has become more "hot" than the India-Pakistan border, but without rival troops trading fire. Indeed, Sino-Indian border tensions now are the most serious since the 1986-1987 local military skirmishes that were triggered by the PLA moving south of a rivulet marking the line of control in Sumdorong Chu sector in Arunachal Pradesh. Those skirmishes brought war clouds before the two countries moved quickly to defuse the crisis. Today, the PLA's forays into Indian territory are occurring even in the only area where Beijing does not dispute the frontier—Sikkim's 128 mile (206 km) border with Tibet. Chinese troops repeatedly have attempted to gain control of Sikkim's evocatively named Finger Area, a tiny but key salient.

In response, India has been beefing up its defensive deployments in Arunachal Pradesh, Sikkim, and Ladakh to prevent any Chinese land-grab. Besides bringing in tanks to reinforce its defenses in mountainous Sikkim, it is deploying two additional army mountain divisions and two squadrons of the advanced SU-30 MKI bomber-aircraft in its northeastern state of Assam, backed by three Airborne Warning and Control Systems. It also has launched a crash program to improve its logistical capabilities through new roads, airstrips, and advanced landing stations along the Himalayas. None of these steps, however, can materially alter the fact that China holds the military advantage on the ground.

Sino-Indian Geopolitical Tensions

Recent strains in Sino-Indian relations also have resulted from sharpening geopolitical rivalry. This was evident from China's botched 2008 move to stymie the U.S.-India nuclear deal by seeking to block the Nuclear Suppliers Group (NSG) from opening civilian nuclear trade with New Delhi. In the NSG, China landed itself in a position it tries to avoid in any international body—as the last holdout. The unsettled border, however, remains at the center of the bilateral tensions. China's increasing territorial assertiveness found expression in Beijing's unusual effort in 2009 to hold up approval of the Asian Development Bank's (ADB) $2.9-billion loan assistance plan for India because it included a flood-management project in Arunachal Pradesh. When the ADB eventually overrode the Chinese objections, Beijing expressed "strong dissatisfaction," saying approval could not change the "immense territorial disputes" with India.[13]

So, even as China has emerged as India's largest trading partner, the Sino-Indian strategic dissonance and border disputes have become more pronounced. New Delhi has sought to retaliate against Beijing's growing antagonism by banning Chinese toys and cell phones that do not meet international standards. But such modest trade actions can do little to persuade Beijing to abandon its moves to encircle and squeeze India strategically by employing China's rising clout in Pakistan, Myanmar, Bangladesh, Sri Lanka, and Nepal. In fact, the harsh truth is that India is staring at the harvest of a mismanagement of relations with China over decades by successive governments that chose propitiation to leverage building. New Delhi unwittingly helped create the context to embolden Beijing to be assertive and bellicose.

Yet another question relates to China's intentions. In muscling up to India, is China seeking to intimidate India or actually fashioning an option to wage war? The present situation, in several key aspects, is similar to the one that prevailed in the run-up to the 1962 invasion of India. Consider the following parallels:

• Like in the pre-1962 war period, it has become commonplace internationally to speak of India and China in the same breadth. The aim of "Mao's India war" in 1962, as Harvard scholar Roderick MacFarquhar has called it, was large political: To cut India down to size by demolishing what it represented—a democratic alternative to the Chinese autocracy.[14] The swiftness and force with which Mao Zedong defeated India helped discredit the Indian model, boost China's international image and consolidate Mao's internal power. The return of the China-India pairing decades later is something Beijing viscerally detests.

• Just as the Dalai Lama's flight to India in 1959—and the ready sanctuary he got there—set the stage for the Chinese military attack, the exiled Tibetan leader, more than 50 years after his escape, stands as a bigger challenge than ever for China, as underscored by Beijing's stepped-up vilification campaign against him and its admission that it is now locked in a "life and death struggle" over Tibet. With Beijing now treating the Dalai Lama as its Enemy No. 1, India has come under greater Chinese pressure to curb his activities and those of his government-in-exile. The continuing security clampdown in Tibet since the March 2008 Tibetan uprising parallels the harsh Chinese crackdown in Tibet during 1959-1962.

• The present pattern of cross-frontier incursions and other border incidents as well as new force deployments and mutual recriminations is redolent of the situation that prevailed before the 1962 war. When in 1950, the PLA marched hundreds of miles south to occupy the then-independent Tibet and later nibble at Indian territories, this supposedly was neither an expansionist strategy nor a forward policy. But when the ill-equipped and short-staffed Indian army belatedly sought to set up posts along India's unmanned Himalayan frontier to try and stop further Chinese encroachments, Beijing and its friends elsewhere dubbed it a provocative "forward policy." In the same vein, the present Indian efforts to beef up defenses in the face of growing PLA cross-border forays are being labeled "new forward policy" by Beijing.

• The 1962 war occurred against the backdrop of China instigating and arming insurgents in India's northeast. Although such Chinese activities ceased after Mao's death, China has come full circle today, with Chinese-made arms increasingly flowing into guerrilla ranks in northeastern India, including via front organizations in Myanmar. India says it has taken up this matter with Beijing. While a continuing 14-year-old ceasefire has brought peace to Nagaland, some other Indian states like

Assam and Manipur are wracked by multiple insurgencies, allowing Beijing to fish in troubled waters. In fact, Pakistan-based terrorists targeting India now rely largely on Chinese arms—from the AK-56 assault rifles to the Type 86 grenades made by China's state-owned Norinco firm.

• Just as India had retreated to a defensive position in the border negotiations with Beijing in the early 1960s after having undermined its leverage through a formal acceptance of the "Tibet region of China," New Delhi similarly has been left in the unenviable position today of having to fend off ever greater Chinese territorial demands. Little surprise, therefore, the spotlight now is on China's Tibet-linked claim to Arunachal Pradesh rather than on Tibet's status itself.

Internationally, there are at least a couple of factors contributing to China's greater assertiveness toward India as part of an apparent strategy to prevent the rise of a peer rival in Asia. First, India's growing strategic ties with the United States are more than offset by America's own rising interdependence with China, to the extent that U.S. policy gives Beijing a pass on its human-rights abuses and frenetic military buildup at home and reckless strategic opportunism abroad. America's Asia policy is no longer guided by an overarching geopolitical framework as it had been under George W. Bush; rather it is becoming Sino-centric. That may explain why President Barack Obama's administration has kept mum on the Sino-Indian border tensions, instead of cautioning Beijing against any attempt to forcibly change existing frontiers. A second factor is the weakening of China's Pakistan card against India. Pakistan's descent into a jihadist dungeon has robbed China of its premier surrogate instrument against India, necessitating the exercise of direct pressure.

Conclusions

Against this geopolitical background, India can expect no respite from Chinese pressure. Whether Beijing actually sets out to teach India "the final lesson" by launching a 1962-style surprise war will depend on several factors, including India's defense preparedness to repel such an attack, domestic factors within China—such as economic and social unrest threatening the Communist hold on power—and the availability of a propitious international timing of the type the Cuban missile crisis had provided in 1962. But if India is not to be caught napping again, it has to inject greater realism into its China policy by shedding self-deluding shibboleths, shoring up its deterrent capabilities, and putting premium on leveraged diplomacy.

In a historical revisit to Nehru's slogan, *Hindi-Chini bhai bhai* (Indians and Chinese are brothers), today there are those who trumpet the "Chindia" concept, which—disregarding all historic and current rivalries and antagonisms—attempts to blend the two rising powers together into one. However, the deterioration in China-

India relations in recent years demonstrates that rapidly expanding trade cannot be a true measure of progress in bilateral relations. Unless estranged neighbors fix their political relations, economics alone will not be enough to create goodwill or stabilize their relationship. Yet, while openly unwilling to accept the territorial status quo, China has pushed for a free-trade agreement with India. With Western and Japanese markets wracked by economic troubles, the Chinese export juggernaut needs a larger market share in India, the world's second fastest-growing economy.

The problems that divide India and China extend far beyond territorial and trade disputes to include environmental concerns and limited natural resources. Water is becoming a key security issue in Sino-Indian relations and a potential source of enduring discord. China is now pursuing major interbasin and interriver water transfer projects on the Tibetan plateau that threaten to diminish international river flows into India and other co-riparian states. The most dangerous idea China is toying with is the northward rerouting of the Brahmaputra, the world's highest river and also one of the fastest-flowing. Diversion of the Brahmaputra's water to the parched Yellow River is a project that China rarely discusses in public, because the project implies environmental devastation of India's northeastern plains and eastern Bangladesh, and would thus be akin to a declaration of water war on India and Bangladesh.[15] Nevertheless, an officially blessed book published in 2005, *Tibet's Waters Will Save China*, openly championed the northward rerouting of the Brahmaputra.[16]

All of these territorial, trade, political, environmental, and natural resource issues are a striking reminder that Tibet remains at the heart of the India-China divide. For centuries, Tibet acted as a buffer state averting potential Sino-Indian tensions. However, Tibet ceased to be a political buffer when China annexed it more than six decades ago. But Tibet can still turn into a political bridge between China and India. For that to happen, two things are needed—a China-initiated process of reconciliation and healing in Tibet, and a more cooperative Sino-Indian relationship.

Notes

1. Peter Engardio, ed., *Chindia: How China and India Are Revolutionizing Global Business* (New York: McGraw-Hill, 2006); Jagdish N. Sheth, *Chindia Rising: How China and India Will Benefit Your Business* (New York: McGraw-Hill, 2008); and Jairam Ramesh, *Making Sense of Chindia: Reflections on China and India* (New Delhi: India Research Press, 2006).

2. Jung Chang and Jon Halliday, *Mao: The Unknown Story* (London: Jonathan Cape, 2005). According to this book, Mao thought he could depend on Stalin, since the Soviet strongman had played an important role in Mao's own rise to power.

3. Cited in Brahma Chellaney, "Fatal Attraction," *The Hindustan Times*, 22 August 2001.

4. Ibid.

5. H.Y. Sharada Prasad, A.K. Damodaran, and Sarvepalli Gopal, eds., *Selected Works of Jawaharlal Nehru, Second Series, Vol. 29, 1 June-31 August 1955* (New Delhi: Oxford University Press, 2005). This volume, which claims to be "an indispensable reference for research into modern India," shows on page 231 that when Nehru met with Soviet Premier Marshal Nikolai Aleksandrovich Bulganin in Moscow on 22 June 1955, he told Bulganin that India did not want a seat on the UN Security Council: "Perhaps Bulganin knows that some people in USA have suggested that India should replace China in the Security Council. This is to create trouble between us and China. We are, of course, wholly opposed to it. Further, we are opposed to pushing ourselves forward to occupy certain positions because that may itself create difficulties, and India might itself become a subject of controversy. If India is to be admitted to the Security Council it raises the question of the revision of the Charter of the UN. We feel that this should not be done till the question of China's admission and possibly of others is first solved. I feel that we should first concentrate on getting China admitted."

6. Officially called the "Agreement between the Republic of India and the People's Republic of China on Trade and Intercourse between Tibet Region of China and India." Signed on 29 April 1954 in Beijing; ratified on 17 August 1954.

7. Item Nos. 1 and 2 in the "Notes Exchanged" concurrently with the Agreement between the Republic of India and the People's Republic of China on Trade and Intercourse between Tibet Region of China and India.

8. Claude Arpi, *Born in Sin: The Panchsheel Agreement—The Sacrifice of Tibet* (New Delhi: Mittal, 2004).

9. Address to the Nation on All India Radio, 22 October 1962, in *Jawaharlal Nehru's Speeches, September 1957-April 1963*, Vol. 4 (New Delhi: Ministry of Information and Broadcasting, 1964), 226-30.

10. *People's Day*, 11 June 2009.

11. *People's Daily*, Editorial, 14 October 2009.

12. Chinese Premier Wen Jiabao, "Working Together for New Glories of the Oriental Civilization," Speech at the Indian Council of World Affairs, New Delhi, 16 December 2010, http://www.icwa.in/pdfs/Chinapm_Lecture.pdf.

13. Chinese Foreign Affairs Ministry, "Foreign Ministry Spokesperson Qin Gang's Remarks on Asian Development Bank's Executive Board Adopting a Document Involving Disputed Territories Between China and India," Official Statement, 18 June 2009. http://www.fmcoprc.gov.mo/eng/gsxwfb/fyrth /t568306.htm [Accessed on 27 October 2011].

14. Roderick MacFarquhar, *The Origins of the Cultural Revolution*, Vol. 3: *The Coming of the Cataclysm 1961-1966* (New York: Oxford University Press, 1997).

15. Edward Wong, "Ambitious Plan for *China's Water* Crisis Spurs Concern," *New York Times*, 2 June 2011.

16. Li Ling, *Xizang Zhi Shui Jiu Zhongguo: Da Xi Xian Zai Zao Zhongguo Zhan Lue Nei Mu Xiang Lu* (Tibet's Waters Will Save China), in Chinese (Beijing: Zhongguo chang'an chubanshe, 2005).

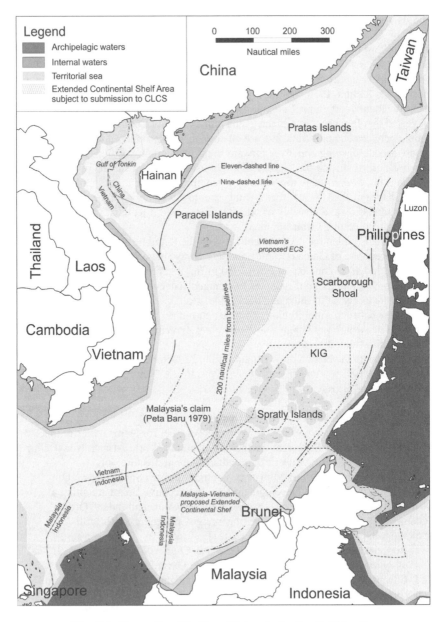

Map 5.1: Competing Maritime Claims in the South China Sea

5

Indonesia's "Invisible" Border with China

I Made Andi Arsana and Clive Schofield

Some uncertainty exists as to whether China actually shares a boundary with Indonesia. Only one of these two states appears to believe that there is a boundary line to draw, hence the, for one side at least, "invisible" character of this maritime border. It is China that has suggested that overlaps exist between the maritime claims of the two states in the southern South China Sea, and that, consequently, a maritime boundary delimitation is required. If there is an overlap, it could cover an area of approximately 28,500 nm^2 (98,000 km^2). For its part, although Indonesia officially recognizes ten neighboring states, China is not among them.[1]

While it is certainly the case that mainland China and Indonesia are remote from one another, separated by almost 800 nm (1,482 km) from Hainan Island to Indonesia's Natuna Island group, both states have, or have claims to, numerous islands and other insular features in the southern part of the South China Sea. In particular, Indonesia possesses uncontested sovereignty over the Natuna islands, an archipelago of more than 200 islands located in Riau Province about 800 nm north of Jakarta. Indonesia's maritime claims extend northeast from baselines defined around the Natuna islands into the South China Sea. The offshore energy fields adjacent to the Natuna islands are estimated to contain 46 trillion cubic feet of recoverable reserves of natural gas, and are therefore of considerably economic and energy security significance to Indonesia.[2] China meanwhile claims sovereignty, together with multiple other claimants, over the group of features scattered across the southern South China Sea collectively known as the Spratly islands (Nansha islands to China).

If Chinese sovereignty over the Spratly islands were to be confirmed, the PRC's maritime entitlements measured from these features would likely overlap Indonesian maritime claims, thus requiring delimitation with a maritime boundary. However, rather than dealing with China, Indonesia has instead opted to conclude maritime boundary agreements with Malaysia and Vietnam in precisely these same areas. China has not publicly protested these agreements. Given the ambiguous nature of China's maritime claims in the South China Sea, in particular the unclear meaning of China's so-called nine-dashed line, it is difficult to discuss the question of a potential Sino-Indonesia maritime boundary with certainty. The existence of such a maritime boundary runs counter to the generally held perception of Indonesia as not being a party to, and thus largely aloof from, the South China Sea islands disputes. While it is certainly the case that Indonesia is not a claimant state to any of the disputed South China Sea islands, it is undoubtedly a South China Sea littoral state with maritime claims in the southwestern part of the South China Sea. To date, Indonesia has rejected all Chinese overtures to engage in bilateral maritime delimitation negotiations.

Indonesia's Maritime Claims

The history of Indonesia's claims to maritime space goes back to the late 1930s, when Indonesia was still under the control of the Netherlands as the Dutch East Indies. Following a series of efforts to claim and regulate maritime areas, a definitive claim was made through the *Territoriale Zee en Maritieme Kringen Ordonnantie 1939,* or Ordinance of Territorial Sea and Maritime Environment 1939.[3]

On independence, Indonesia recognized that a 3 nm territorial sea, measured from the low-water mark, was highly disadvantageous for Indonesia in that it "could not contain the archipelago within a single jurisdictional blanket."[4] This led Indonesia to advocate the concept of an archipelagic state, following its so-called Djoeanda Declaration of 13 December 1957.[5] Through this declaration, Indonesia defined archipelagic baselines for the whole archipelago, and claims a 12 nm territorial sea measured from the archipelagic baselines.[6]

Indonesia, as the world's largest archipelagic state, was heavily involved in negotiations leading to what became the United Nations Convention on the Law of the Sea (UNCLOS) of 1982.[7] Indonesia successfully achieved a key aim in the drafting of this Convention—recognition for and codification of the archipelagic state concept—something Indonesia had long advocated. Indonesia signed UNCLOS in 1985 and became a party in 1986.[8] Indonesia established its first archipelagic baselines in 1960 through the Law No. 4/Prp/1960, which encloses the Natuna islands in the South China Sea. The 1960 law also established Indonesia's claim to a 12 nautical mile territorial sea measured from its archipelagic baselines. Indonesia's archipelagic baselines have, however, been progressively modified over the years, notably through the promulgation of the Law No. 6 of 1996 on Indonesian Waters, coupled with Government Regulation No. 61 of 1998 which provides a partial list of geographical coordinates for Indonesia's archipelagic baselines in the Natuna Sea. Further revision is through Government Regulation No. 38 of 2002, subsequently revised through Government Regulation No. 37 of 2008.[9]

The latest version of Indonesia's archipelagic baselines was deposited with the United Nations Secretary-General on 11 March 2009, accompanied by a map illustrating the baselines connecting points.[10] From the archipelagic baselines around the Natuna islands, Indonesia's maritime claims project to the north and east. While continental shelf entitlements have been delimited with Malaysia and Vietnam (see below), EEZs have yet to be delimited and any potential overlap with the claims of China—or indeed other claimants—on behalf of the Spratly islands have yet to be addressed.

In 2010 Indonesia issued an official map of the Republic of Indonesia.[11] Further, Indonesia defined a Fisheries Management Area through the Ministry of Marine Affairs and Fisheries (MMAF)'s Regulation No. 1 of 2009, which is also known as *Wilayah Pengelolaan Perikanan* (WPP).[12] The outer limits of the WPP, as shown on the accompanying map, coincide with Indonesia's official map of 2010.[13] Maritime areas in the South China Sea are included in that part of the Fisheries Management Area termed WPP-711, encompassing maritime areas in the vicinity of the Singapore Strait extending north-eastward into the southern South China Sea.[14]

Indonesia's official 2010 map and the WPP Map make it clear that Indonesia's unilateral EEZ claim extends well to the north and east of its agreed continental shelf boundaries with Malaysia and Vietnam in the vicinity of the Natuna islands. This can be viewed as Indonesia's forward position regarding maritime boundaries in the South China Sea. Accordingly, Indonesia's maritime claims, and particularly its exclusive economic zone (EEZ) claims, are located substantially seawards of Indonesia's agreed seabed boundary lines, in anticipation of future delimitation negotiations with its neighbors.

China's Maritime Claims

China has traditionally been viewed as a continental state. Despite a long coastline, China's maritime claims are limited by the presence of island chains off its coasts under the sovereignty of other states, for example islands belonging to Japan and the Philippines on the eastern margins of the East China Sea. Nonetheless, China signed UNCLOS in 1982 and became a party in 1996.[15]

China claimed straight baselines in 1992 and partially defined them in 1996. However, these straight baselines predominantly front China's mainland coast, though some were also defined around the Paracel islands, sovereignty over which is disputed with Vietnam. However, China has yet to define straight baselines around any of its claimed features in the Spratly islands. While China claims zones of maritime jurisdiction that are consistent with UNCLOS at least in terms of their spatial extent, notably a 12 nm breadth territorial sea, a 24 nm contiguous zone, and an EEZ out to 200 nm, it also appears to claim large portions of the South China Sea on a historic basis, although this issue remains shrouded in uncertainty.

By means of a map that has become generally known as China's nine-dashed map, China appears to claim substantial maritime areas in the South China Sea. China's claim to this area began as early as the 1930s, leading to the publication in 1947 of a map showing a broken line consisting of eleven-dashed segments by the Geography Department of the Republic of China's Ministry of Internal Affairs called *The Location Map of the South China Sea Islands* or *Nanhai zhudao weizhi tu* in Chinese.[16] The maritime spaces encompassed by the dashed lines include areas relatively close to Indonesia's Natuna islands. This map was adopted by the PRC in 1949. Since the early 1950s, however, Chinese maps have consistently shown a nine rather than eleven-dashed line in the South China Sea, though in slightly different locations (see Map 5.1). By connecting the dashed segments, the line forms what has been variously termed a "U shape" or "cow tongue," though it should be stressed that the PRC has never officially depicted the line as continuous (see Map 5.2).

Since this map's publication, there have been hotly contested debates about the true meaning of the nine-dashed line on the Chinese map. While it is certain that China claims sovereignty over small insular features in the region, including the Pratas islands, the Paracel islands, the Spratly islands, and Macclesfield Bank, the unanswered question is whether the line also signifies maritime areas in the South China Sea.[17] Some opine that the line only indicates claims to land territory—that is, to the disputed islands—while others state that China is also claiming the water column encompassed by the nine-dashed line, or that the dashed lines are indicative of a unilateral maritime boundary claim. One notable survey of the views of Chinese scholars regarding this map concludes that the nine-dashed line "had a dual nature"—to define Chinese sovereignty over the islands in the South China Sea and to serve as Chinese maritime boundary in the South China Sea.[18]

Recent events have served to shed some light on Chinese claims. In response to an extended continental shelf submission by Vietnam alone, as well as one by Malaysia and Vietnam jointly, Beijing issued protests to the U.N. Secretary-General, stating that it held sovereignty over the disputed islands of the South China Sea and their "adjacent waters" and that it also "enjoys sovereign rights and jurisdiction over the relevant waters as well as the seabed and subsoil thereof."[19] This language appears to be consistent with claims to territorial sea, EEZ, and continental shelf rights made from the disputed islands, as opposed to a claim to historic waters within the nine-dashed line, as has been speculated.[20] However, the fact that Beijing included a copy of the nine-dashed line map with its protests served to distract attention from this potential clarification in China's maritime claims.

65

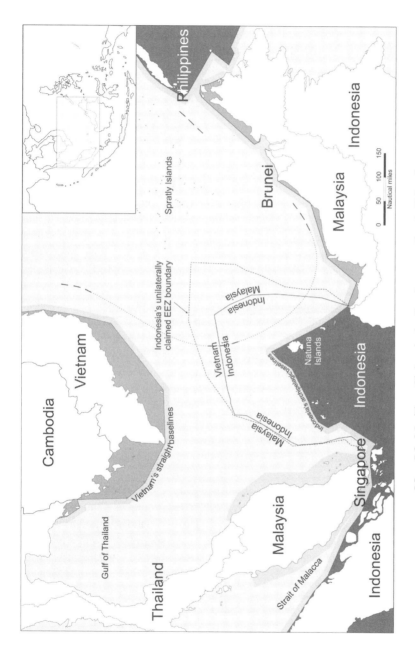

Map 5.2: Maritime Claims in the Southwestern South China Sea

Meanwhile, even though Indonesia does not claim any of the features among the Spratly islands, and has long played an active role in establishing confidence building measures among the claimant states, Indonesia issued a note of its own in respect to China's nine-dashed line. Indonesia's note of 8 July 2010 asserted that the nine-dashed lines map of China "lack[s] international basis" and therefore its purpose is "tantamount to upset[ting]" the 1982 UNCLOS.[21] At the time of writing, China had yet to respond to Indonesia's strong objections to its nine-dashed line map.[22]

Indonesia's Maritime Boundaries

Indonesia has been active in the delimitation of its maritime boundaries with neighboring states. Indeed, at the time of writing, Indonesia had concluded seventeen maritime boundary agreements, only one of which had yet to enter into force. Indonesia delimited two maritime boundaries in the vicinity of the Natuna islands—first with Malaysia and more recently with Vietnam. Both agreements serve to delimit the continental self. However, water column and EEZ boundaries between these states remain unresolved.

Indonesia's first ever maritime boundary agreement was related to seabed boundary delimitation with Malaysia in the strait of Malacca and South China Sea, signed on 27 October 1969.[23] As well as defining the Indonesia-Malaysia continental shelf boundary between their opposite coasts in the Malacca Strait, the 1969 agreement also defined two lateral boundary lines in the South China Sea—a western one between peninsula Malaysia and (largely) the Natuna islands, and an eastern one between Malaysian territories on Borneo and Indonesian possessions, including the Natuna islands. The northernmost terminal points of these boundaries stop at two locations in the South China Sea.[24] The two boundary lines were connected to each other in 2003 by a continental shelf boundary line between Indonesia and Vietnam.

The Indonesia-Vietnam continental shelf boundary was signed on 26 June 2003 and was ratified by Indonesia on 15 March 2007 through Act No. 18 of 2007.[25] The 2003 agreement took a long time to conclude. The negotiations started as early as 1978 and were finally concluded 25 years later.[26] Like several of the other maritime boundaries settled by Indonesia and its neighbors, the 2003 Indonesia-Vietnam agreement applies only to the seabed. Accordingly, Indonesia and Vietnam have yet to settle their EEZ boundaries in the South China Sea. As noted above, Indonesia has made unilateral EEZ claims in the South China Sea, which do not coincide with the 2003 seabed boundary. This scenario raises the seemingly complex prospect of different boundaries being defined for continental shelf and EEZ rights, such that Vietnam might have sovereign rights over areas of seabed, but the water column overlying the seabed could be under the jurisdiction of Indonesia. Should this proposal be agreed to by Indonesia and Vietnam, the ocean resource management in the area will not be as easy as if the seabed and EEZ boundaries are coincident. However, this option is not impossible and has, in fact, been successfully applied by Australia and Indonesia to deal with maritime rights in the Timor Sea where seabed boundaries do not coincide with EEZ boundaries.[27]

With regard to Indonesia's maritime boundary delimitations with Malaysia and Vietnam in the South China Sea, even though these seabed delimitations partly took place within China's apparent claim enclosed by the nine-dashed line, no protests or diplomatic notes have been issued by China with regard to the delimitation. If one assumes that the nine-dashed line is intended to claim maritime areas—something that is not abundantly clear—there exist substantial overlapping claims for both continental shelf and EEZ in the South China Sea. A preliminary geospatial analysis reveals that the overlap between the maritime spaces encompassed by the nine-dashed line and Indonesia's claimed maritime spaces are approximately 28,500 nm^2 (98,000 km^2).[28] However, this finding is based on a number of assumptions. In particular, it is valid only if the nine dashes are joined into a continuous line.[29] As stated above, Indonesia, in its official note of 8 July 2010, did not recognize China's claim over maritime area enclosed in the nine-dashed line.[30]

Even if the nine-dashed line does not in fact represent a claim to maritime space on the part of China, the potential for an overlap between Chinese and Indonesian maritime claims remains. China may well make claims to extended maritime zones, that is, to continental shelf and EEZ rights, from those of the Spratly islands that are above water at high tide. Indeed, China asserted in April 2011 that the disputed South China Sea islands are capable of generating EEZ and continental shelf rights.[31] Considerable uncertainty exists, however, regarding precisely how many of the features that make up the Spratly islands in fact rise above the high tide mark. Additionally, even if a number of these small features do rise above the high tide mark, it is highly questionable whether they should be capable of generating extended maritime claims or be accorded full weight in the delimitation of maritime boundaries.[32]

Increasingly Visible Disputes over an "Invisible" Boundary

As mentioned above, in Indonesia's official view there is no maritime boundary and therefore no dispute between Indonesia and China, hence references to an "invisible" border. However, it has long been known that China appears to have made extensive maritime claims in the South China Sea by issuing a map depicting a nine-dashed line. In addition, China's claims over land territory in the region need to be considered in analyzing potential maritime disputes between Indonesia and China. Indonesia's maritime claims and activities in the South China Sea and incidents involving China and Indonesia are also worth considering.

Despite these differing perspectives on maritime issues in the South China Sea, politically, Indonesia and China have developed a relatively close bilateral relationship. In April 2010, the two states celebrated the 60th anniversary of their diplomatic ties, which were opened on 13 April 1950.[33] Although diplomatic ties were temporarily severed on 30 October 1967—due to concerns over the spread of communism to Indonesia—relations were reestablished on 8 August 1990. This event was marked by Indonesia's Foreign Minister Ali Alatas's visit to China, and by the signing of a Memorandum of Understanding on the Resumption of Diplomatic Relations.

Since this diplomatic reengagement, the China-Indonesia relationship has developed positively to become a deepening strategic partnership, as indicated by, among other things, frequent high-level exchanges. While Chinese diplomats have not to date disputed Indonesian sovereignty over any of the Natuna islands themselves, a map produced by the Chinese delegation at a workshop in 1993 showed the country's "historic waters" overlapping with the Natuna islands' EEZ. This suggested that Indonesia was being "drawn into the fray" so that Indonesia, since then, has been considered by the PRC to be a party to South China Sea dispute.[34]

In response, Indonesia, through Foreign Minister Ali Alatas, sent a protest note to Beijing immediately after the Surabaya workshop. Indonesia subsequently in April 1995 asked the Chinese government to clarify its claim, and was informed that Beijing had "no problem"[35] with Jakarta and supported a "negotiated settlement."[36] However, Jakarta rejected China's call to negotiate the issue and in 1996 conducted a major military exercise in the Natuna islands, an action apparently designed to send a clear message to China that it was committed to defending its sovereignty and sovereign rights. Indonesia has subsequently tended to downplay the issue so as not to be perceived as giving legitimacy to China's maritime claims in the South China Sea.[37] As Alatas stated, "repetition of an untruth will eventually make it appear as truth."[38]

Despite Indonesia's steadfast refusal to acknowledge China's maritime claims in the South China Sea, on 20 June 2009 this dispute suddenly reemerged when eight vessels and 75 fishermen from China were detained by an Indonesian patrol vessel.[39] The vessels were seized at coordinates of 5° north and 109° east, around 112 km northeast of Indonesia's Pulau Sekatung (part of the Natuna islands group).[40] According to an Indonesian official, the Chinese fishermen were detained after they were caught fishing in the Indonesian EEZ in the South China Sea, and they were on their way to the office of the West Kalimantan Fishery and Ocean

Agency.[41] The location of the incident was in WPP-711, pursuant to Indonesia's Fisheries Management Area. However, China regards the incident as having taken place in China's traditional fishing grounds off the Spratly islands in the South China Sea.[42]

In response, China expressed its strong dissatisfaction and "demanded the immediate release of the fishermen and their boats."[43] After bilateral talks were opened, Indonesia agreed to release 59 of the 75 fishermen and allowed them to depart for China on 10 July 2009.[44] Perceived as an important diplomatic event for China, the fishermen were greeted by Chinese officials when they returned home on 11 July 2009.[45] Meanwhile, 16 of the apprehended fishermen, the ones considered to be responsible for the infringement, remained in detention for further legal processing in Indonesia.[46] The Indonesian Ambassador to China even asserted that Indonesia could impose appropriate punishments on the Chinese fishermen for illegal fishing in Indonesia's EEZ.[47]

While it can be argued that Indonesia asserted its legal position with regard to Chinese maritime claims in the South China Sea and, notwithstanding the need for prompt release in such cases, the decision to detain only 16 fishermen, not all 75, gave the appearance of a compromise in the interests of their bilateral relationship. It is worth noting that Chinese government officials had previously referred to Indonesia as a "strategic partner."[48] Indeed, the two states even signed a "strategic partnership agreement" in 2005 to strengthen their relationship.[49] This agreement was considered to be "the first such agreement between China and a Southeast Asian state."[50] It led to various types of agreements, including defense cooperation in 2007 and an extradition agreement in 2009.[51] However, these bilateral agreements might also be interpreted as levers by which the Chinese government can apply pressure over an incident that "has the potential to provide long-term advantage, and then release that pressure while retaining the moral high ground."[52]

It has been suggested that the absence of any further official reports on the 2009 fishing incident case involving Indonesia and China may indicate "that it has been quietly dropped rather than upset[ting] China."[53] However, other fishing incidents in the South China Sea involving Indonesia and China occurred during 2010, one on 15 May 2010 and another on 22 June 2010.[54] The captains of the patrol vessels *Hiu* 04 and *Hiu* 10 explained the chronology and location of the first incident. The first incident took place around the coordinates of 05° 38' 10" north and 110° 19' 05" east, and the second one, in the vicinity of 05° 00' 00" north and 109° 00' 00" east, both of which are well within Indonesia's claimed EEZ or WPP-711 pursuant to Indonesia's Fisheries Management Area. Two of the three Chinese fishing vessels were seized, but when MMAF officials were about to investigate the vessels a Chinese patrol vessel arrived on the scene and demanded that the two vessels be released. Furthermore, according to the captains of the Indonesian patrol boats, the Chinese patrol boat threatened Indonesia's vessels by aiming weapons at them. Realizing they were out-gunned, the Indonesians apparently decided to release the two vessels.[55]

The second incident occurred on 22 June 2010 and was similar in nature. The same Chinese patrol vessel appeared when Indonesian officials seized Chinese fishing vessels, which were caught allegedly fishing illegally in Indonesia's EEZ. The Chinese patrol vessel, which was also called a "Chinese fishery administration vessel," once again demanded the fishing vessels and their crews be released.[56] Unconfirmed reports indicate that, having realized that their boat was outmatched by the Chinese patrol vessel, the Indonesian officials once again decided to free the fishing vessels.

These incidents arguably represent a worrying trend, consistent with arguments that China's posture in the South China Sea and willingness to protect what it perceives to be its rights is growing more assertive. Following these events, a former Indonesian envoy to China stated that Indonesia and China needed to clarify their respective maritime borders.[57] Another more specific proposal by Indonesia's Navy Chief of Staff, Agus Suhartono, was that Indonesia and China should settle their maritime boundaries in the overlapping EEZ in the South China Sea.[58] These two statements implied that overlapping maritime claims do exist between Indonesia and China in the South China Sea and that a maritime boundary would be required. Even though they might not reflect the Indonesian government's official view, these statements perhaps indicate how Indonesia's perspective on its overlapping maritime boundaries with China in the South China Sea is evolving over time.

Opportunities and Challenges

Indonesia faces many opportunities and challenges in its relations with China, which represents an ever more important economic partner. Since the resumption of diplomatic relations, the volume of bilateral trade has risen significantly from $1.18 billion in 1990 to $7.464 billion in 2000. Due to the global economic slowdown at that time, the bilateral trade volume in 2001 decreased slightly to $6.725 billion, but increased again during the first half of 2002. For Indonesia, China is the 5th largest trade partner while Indonesia is the 17th of China.[59] With regard to the products exchanged, China exports manufactured goods to Indonesia such as toys, machinery, computers, and food products. Meanwhile, Indonesia exports mainly natural resources, such as coal and nickel, to China. It appears that Chinese businesses are also interested in operating in Indonesia and many of them have opened manufacturing plants there.[60]

Boundary tensions and disputes over maritime resources threaten to undermine warming Sino-Indonesian economic relations. The fundamental starting point for settling China and Indonesia's maritime disputes is to clarify their claims. China's maritime claims remain unclear. Without further details from Beijing, it is difficult, if not impossible, to identify whether or not there are overlapping maritime claims or entitlements between Indonesia and China.

However, a number of the Spratly islands are within 400 nm of the Natuna islands. The extent of such a potential overlap is, however, uncertain for a number of reasons. First, it is unclear whether many of the Spratly islands in question are capable of generating claims to continental shelf and EEZ rights. The vast majority of the Spratly "islands" are, in fact, not islands in international law terms and are instead low-tide elevations and even sub-surface features with strictly limited or no capacity to generate maritime claims.[61] Second, even if some of the Spratly islands are above water at high tide and could therefore be considered to be subject to the "regime of islands" in accordance with UNCLOS,[62] many of these features might most appropriately be classified as mere "rocks" and therefore could not be used to generate continental shelf and EEZ claims.[63] Third, even if some of these disputed features located in the southwestern part of the Spratly islands, such as Spratly Island itself, are substantial enough to generate EEZ and continental shelf rights,[64] it is questionable what weight they might have in the delimitation of a maritime boundary with neighboring and much longer coasts such as those of the surrounding mainland coasts and the Natuna islands. All of these factors would serve to minimize or eliminate any potential overlap in maritime claims between China and Indonesia. It is impossible at present to state with certainty whether an overlap exists and how large it may ultimately prove to be.

A related and equally important issue to address is whether or not the two states acknowledge each other's maritime claims in the South China Sea. An important point to note in this context is that, even though the eleven-dashed map was first published during 1947, and adopted by the PRC as a nine-dashed map from the early 1950s, China has not yet made any comment or response to the maritime boundary delimitation agreements made between Indonesia and Malaysia in 1969 or between Indonesia and Vietnam in 2003. As previously mentioned, part of these delimitations took place in South China Sea maritime areas described by the nine-dashed line. But Beijing's silence does not necessarily mean acquiescence.

By contrast, Indonesia's maritime claims in the South China Sea have become progressively clearer since 1960. Agreed seabed boundaries with Malaysia and Vietnam also added to this clarity. The 2009 promulgation of MMAF's Regulation on Fisheries Management Area further clarified Indonesia's position. Similarly, Indonesia's official map, which depicts, among other things, Indonesia's unilateral

EEZ claim in the South China Sea, has not yet attracted any official protests from neighboring states, including from China, though not too much significance should be placed on this.

The main question, therefore, is whether there are any overlapping maritime claims that require delimitation? To answer this, Indonesia and China need to communicate their official positions. Unfortunately, China has yet to respond to Indonesia's request to clarify its position. Meanwhile, the Indonesian government appears to want to side-step this whole issue, since to even discuss it could be perceived as acknowledging the legitimacy of China's maritime claims in the South China Sea.[65] It is worth repeating Minister Alatas's strong statement in 1995 that: "On Natuna, there is no claim from China and there has never been a problem between China and Indonesia. So there is no question to be discussed."[66]

Notwithstanding Indonesia's stated position with regard to Chinese maritime claims in the South China Sea, the presence of Chinese fishermen in waters around the Natuna islands guarded by armed Chinese fishery administration vessels may encourage Indonesia to reconsider its views. Should maritime delimitation be contemplated between China and Indonesia, however, this will necessarily also involve Malaysia and Vietnam, as these states have maritime claims, as well as agreed boundaries with Indonesia.[67] Vietnam, in particular, has rejected China's nine-dashed line, which Hanoi terms "null and void."[68] Both Malaysia and Vietnam contest Chinese sovereignty claims over some or all of the Spratly islands.[69] Moreover, through their extended continental shelf submissions both Malaysia and Vietnam have implied that they regard the disputed South China Sea islands as being incapable of generating continental shelf and EEZ claims.

Conclusions

Indonesia's official position is that it has only ten neighbors with which maritime boundaries need to be settled, and that the PRC government is not one of them. This position has been explicitly expressed since the 1990s. Furthermore, Indonesia's maritime activities, including seabed delimitation with Malaysia in 1969 and Vietnam in 2003 in the South China Sea, have not been protested by Beijing. However, China has made it apparent that it claims not only sovereignty over land territory in the South China Sea, but also over adjacent waters, seabed, and subsoil. The PRC government has in the past also intimated that maritime delimitation with Indonesia is necessary.

For Indonesia there is no such thing as "China-Indonesia maritime boundaries," but China views things differently. The presence of its fishermen in maritime areas around the Natuna islands guarded by Chinese fisheries administration vessels, and the confrontations between Chinese and Indonesian maritime patrol vessels, clearly demonstrate that a dispute exists. Ultimately, to resolve this dispute, Indonesia and China must first clarify each other's maritime claims in the South China Sea. For its part, Indonesia has largely made its claims public. But Beijing has yet to explain the exact meaning of the nine-dashed line map, which has been consistently rejected by neighboring states.

While it appears highly unlikely that Indonesia and China will enter into negotiations to delimit a maritime boundary in the foreseeable future, the possibility of escalating maritime incidents still needs to be addressed. In this respect there have been recent indications of progress, with Indonesian Defence Minister Purnomo Yusgiantoro acknowledging that a committee has been established with the PRC to discuss combined patrols.[70] Increasing Sino-Indonesian tensions, especially with regard to fishing activities in the South China Sea and the Natuna Sea, are becoming increasingly pressing issues for Indonesia and China. While it is understandable that Indonesia will maintain its position that no overlapping maritime claims exist with China, this position is coming under pressure and arguably cannot persist indefinitely.

Having said this, the main question facing Indonesia and China might not concern maritime boundary delimitation, but about how any future maritime tensions, especially over resources, should be handled so as to optimize the use of natural resources therein for the good of all concerned parties. In particular, Indonesia and China need to manage their bilateral relations cooperatively so as to avoid over-stressing marine resources vulnerable to overexploitation. As noted by Nien-Tsu Alfred Hu about the South China Sea in general, it is primarily "political will" that is the key to turning the South China Sea into "sea of opportunities" instead of remaining "troubled waters."[71]

Notes

1. Indonesia considers itself to have ten maritime neighbors, and China is not one of them. From west to east are India, Thailand, Malaysia, Singapore, Vietnam, the Philippines, Palau, Papua New Guinea, Australia, and Timor-Leste. Among those ten neighbors, land boundaries are shared with three of them, including Malaysia in Borneo, Timor-Leste in Timor Island, and Papua New Guinea on the island of New Guinea. A. H. Oegroseno, "Indonesia's Maritime Boundaries," in Robert Cribb and Michele Ford, *Indonesia beyond the water's edge- Managing an archipelagic state* (Indonesian Update Series, RSPAS Australian National University, ISEAS, Singapore, 2009), 49-58.

2. U.S. Energy Information Administration, http://www.eia.gov/countries /regions-topics.cfm?fips=SCS [Accessed on 28 October 2011].

3. The *Territoriale zee en maritiemekringen-ordonnantie 1939* [Territorial Sea and Maritime Environment Ordinance] of 1939. Andi Hamzah, *Laut, Teritorial dan Perairan Indonesia: Himpunan Ordonansi, Undang-Undang dan Peraturan Lainnya, Akademika Presindo* [*Sea, Territory and Waters of Indonesia: Compilation of Ordinances, Acts, and other Regulations*] (Jakarta, 1984). Indonesia's succession to this claim was confirmed through the Agreement of the Transitional Measures signed in 1949 at the Roundtable Conference involving Indonesia and the Netherlands in The Hague. P. Tangsubkul, *The Southeast Asian archipelagic states: concept, evolution, and current practice* (Honolulu, HI: East-West Environment and Policy Institute, 1984), 30.

4. D. P. Djalal, "Geopolitical concepts and maritime territorial behavior in Indonesian foreign policy," MA Thesis, University of Simon Fraser University, Canada, 1990, 37. Simon Fraser University Institutional Repository at http://ir.lib.sfu.ca/bitstream/1892/6274/1/b14497426.pdf.

5. *Government Declaration concerning the Water Areas of the Republic of Indonesia*, issued by and named after Indonesian Prime Minister Ir. H Djuanda Kartawidjaja. Hamzah, 129-130. An English version of the declaration can be obtained from Djalal, 228.

6. Even though the definition of baselines was made by connecting the outermost points of the outlying islands of Indonesia, enclosing the whole archipelago, the term "archipelagic baseline" was not specifically mentioned in the Djoeanda Declaration.

7. United Nations, *United Nations Convention on the Law of the Sea*, Publication no.E97.V10 (United Nations, New York, 1983). See 1833 UNTS 3, opened for signature 10 December 1982, Montego Bay, Jamaica (entered into force 16 November 1994).

8. Chronological lists of ratifications of, accessions, and successions to the Convention and the related Agreements as of 3 July 2011, http://www.un. org/Depts/los/reference_files/chronological_lists_of_ratifications.htm [Accessed on 29 March 2012].

9. These regulations contain lists of the geographical coordinates of Indonesia's archipelagic baselines. Government Regulation No. 38 of 2002, http://www.setneg. go.id/components/com_perundangan/docviewer.php?id=788&filename=PP_No_38 _th_2002.pdf. Also Government Regulation No. 37 of 2008, http://www.setneg. go.id/components/com_perundangan/docviewer.php?id =2004&filename=PP 37 Tahun 2008.pdf. See Peraturan Pemerintah (PP) [Government Regulation] No 61 of 1998, available at the United Nations Division of Ocean Affairs and the Law of the Sea website at http://www.un.org/Depts/los/LEGISLATIONANDTREATIES /PDFFILES/IDN_1998_Regulation61.pdf.

10. For maritime zone notification and a complete list of the coordinates, see http://www.un.org/Depts/los/LEGISLATIONANDTREATIES/STATEFILES/IDN. htm [Accessed on 24 March 2011].

11. Bakosurtanal, *Map of the Republic of Indonesia* (Cibinong, 2010).

12. Ministry of Marine Affairs and Fisheries' Regulation No. 1 of 2009, http://www.infohukum.kk go.id/files_permen/PER%2001%20MEN%202009.pdf.

13. Ibid.

14. The Fisheries Management Area Map was issued by the Indonesian Navy Hydro-Oceanographic Office (Dishidros) and was officially published by the Ministry of Marine affairs and Fishers in November 2009.

15. Chronological lists of ratifications of, accessions, and successions to the Convention and the related Agreements as of 3 July 2011, http://www.un. org/Depts/los/reference_files/chronological_lists_of_ratifications.htm [Accessed on 29 March 2012].

16. Li Jinming and Li Dexia, "The dotted line on the Chinese map of the South China Sea: A note," *Ocean Development & International Law*, Vol. 34 (2003), 287; See also Hsiung Wang, "The ROC's maritime claims and practices with special reference to the South China Sea," *Ocean Development and International Law*, Vol. 41 (2010), 237-252.

17. Ibid., 290.

18. Ibid., 291-292, 294; Li and Li cite works by Gao Zhiguo, "The South China Sea: From conflict to cooperation," *Ocean Development and International Law*, Vol. 25 (1994): 346; Zhao Lihai, *Haiyang fa wenti yanjiu* [*Studies on the Law of Sea*] (Beijing: Beijing University Press, 1996), 37; Zhao Guocai, "Cong xianxing haiyangfa fenxi nanshaqundao de zhuquan zhengduan" [Analysis of the Sovereign Dispute over the Spratlys under the Present Law of Sea], *Asian Review,* Vol. 9 (1999), 22; Zou Keyuan, "The Chinese traditional maritime boundary line in the South China Sea and its legal consequences for the resolution of the dispute over the Spratly Islands," *International Journal of Marine and Coastal Law*, Vol. 14 (1997), 52; Hasjim Djalal, "Spratly dispute needs democratic settlement," *The Jakarta Post* (2 January 1995), 5; Pan Shiying, *Nanshaqundao·shiyou zhengzhi·guojifa* [Islands of the South China Sea· Petropolitics·International Law] (Hong Kong: Economic Herald Press, 1996), 61.

19. Note from the Permanent Mission of the People's Republic of China to the United Nations to the Secretary-General of the United Nations, 7 May 2009, No. CML/17/2009, http://www.un.org/Depts/los/clcs_new/submissions_files /mysvnm33_09/chn_2009re_mys_vnm_e.pdf.

20. Robert Beckman, "South China Sea: Worsening Dispute or Growing Clarity in Claims?" (Singapore, RSIS Commentary, 16 August 2010). This contention is further supported by the text of a later Chinese protest note of 14 April 2010, issued as a counter-protest to a protest from the Philippines regarding China's nine-dashed line. China's April 2010 note goes a step further, asserting that the disputed South China Sea islands are "fully entitled to territorial sea, EEZ and continental shelf." See Republic of the Philippines Note Verbale No. 000228, 5 April 2011; Peoples Republic of China Note Verbale, CML 8/2011, 14 April 2011, http://www. un.org/Depts/los/clcs_new/submissions_files/vnm37_09/chn_2011_re_phl_e.pdf.

21. Note from the Permanent Mission of Indonesian to the United Nations to the Secretary-General of the United Nations, 8 July 2010, No. 840/POL-703/VII/10, http://www.un.org/Depts/los/clcs_new/submissions_files/mysvnm33_09/idn_2010r e_mys_vnm_e.pdf.

22. Marvin C. Ott, "China's ambition in the South China Sea," *Asia Pacific Bulletin*, No. 17, 29 September 2010.

23. For complete documentation of the agreement, see Choon-ho Park, "Indonesia-Malaysia (Continental Shelf)," in Jonathan I. Charney and Lewis M. Alexander, eds., *International Maritime Boundaries* (The Netherlands: Martinus Nijhoff Publisher, 1993), 1025-1027.

24. Ibid.

25. Oegroseno, 55. Full text of Law No. 18 of 2007, http://legislasi. mahkamahagung.go.id/docs/UU/2007/UU_NO_18_2007.pdf.

26. MoFA. 2010a. "Indonesia sent a diplomatic note conveying protest to Malaysia," http://www.deplu.go.id/Pages/News.aspx?IDP=3878&l=en [Accessed on 20 February 2011]. For Dr. Marty Natalegawa's more detailed explanation, listen to the recorded audio from http://www.deplu.go.id/Pages/Audio.aspx?IDP=39&l=id [Accessed on 20 February 2011].

27. Max Herriman and Martin Tsamenyi, "The 1997 Australia-Indonesia maritime boundary treaty: A secure legal regime for offshore resource development?" *Journal of Ocean Development and International Law*, Vol. 29 (1998), 361-396.

28. Comprising approximately 10,774 nm^2 (37,000 km^2) of maritime space to the south and west of Indonesia's agreed continental shelf boundaries with Malaysia and Vietnam, and around 17,762 nm^2 (61,000 km^2) of maritime space claimed as part of Indonesia's EEZ to the north and west of these seabed boundaries.

29. The "joined up" version of the nine-dashed line was formed by interpolating coordinates of the dashed line segments extracted from a map attached in the Chinese note to the Secretary-General of the United Nations in its response to Malaysia-Vietnam's extended continental shelf submission. http://www.un.org/Depts/los/clcs_new/submissions_files/mysvnm33_09/chn_2009re_mys_vnm_e.pdf.

30. Note from the Permanent Mission of Indonesian to the United Nations to the Secretary-General of the United Nations, 8 July 2010, No. 840/POL-703/VII/10, http://www.un.org/Depts/los/clcs_new/submissions_files/mysvnm33_09/idn_2010r e_mys_vnm_e.pdf.

31. China made this assertion in a note verbale directed to the United Nations Secretary General issued in response to a protest note on the part of the Philippines concerning China's nine-dashed line map. Peoples Republic of China Note Verbale, CML 8/2011, 14 April 2011, http://www.un.org/Depts/los/clcs_new/submissions_files/vnm37_09/chn_2011_re_phl_e.pdf.

32. In accordance with Article 121(3) of UNCLOS: "Rocks which cannot sustain human habitation or economic life of their own shall have no exclusive economic zone or continental shelf." Arguably, many of the above high tide features among the Spratly islands fall into this category. Also, there is a strong trend in maritime delimitation practice to award small islands, especially those far offshore, a reduced effect in the construction of maritime boundary lines.

33. Documentation related to the anniversary can be obtained from the official website of the Chinese Embassy for Indonesia: http://id.china-embassy.org /eng/ztbd/features/ [Accessed on 28 October 2011].

34. Douglas Johnson, "Drawn into the Fray: Indonesia's Natuna Islands meet China's Long Gaze South," *Asian Affairs*, Vol. 24, No. 3 (Fall 1997), 153.

35. Comment by former Indonesian Ambassador Hasjim Djalal during discussions at Law of the Sea Institute Conference on the Limits of Maritime Jurisdiction,

Australian National Centre for Ocean Resources and Security (ANCORS), University of Wollongong, 29 November 2011.

36. John McBeth, "Oil Rich Diet," *Far Eastern Economic Review,* 27 April 1995, 28.

37. Johnson, 155.

38. McBeth, 28; Paul Jacob, "Alatas downplays China's claims in Natuna Islands Map," *Straits Times*, 4 June 1995, 2.

39. Foreign Ministry Spokesperson Qin Gang's Regular Press Conference on 25 June 2009, http://ch.china-embassy.org/ger/fyrth/t569723.htm [Accessed on 28 October 2011].

40. "Eight vessels of Chinese fishermen seized [in Bahasa Indonesia]," *Kompas*, 23 June 2009, http://internasional.kompas.com/read/2009/06/23/22272859 /Delapan.Kapal.Nelayan.China.Ditangkap [Accessed on 28 October 2011].

41. "China protests arrest of fishermen," *The Jakarta Post*, 23 June 2009. According to Indonesia, the number of fishermen was 77 instead of 75. For the purpose of this paper, 75 is used.

42. Qin Gang's Press Conference on 25 June 2009.

43. Asean-China Free Trade Area, "China 'dissatisfied' with Indonesia over detention of fishermen," 2009, http://www.asean-cn.org/Item/726.aspx [Accessed on 28 October 2011].

44. "Indonesia to release 59 Chinese fishermen," *The China Daily*, 8 July 2009.

45. "59 fishermen fly back home from Indonesia," *The China Daily*, 12 July 2009.

46. "Chinese Embassy recorded detained fishermen [in Bahasa Indonesia]," *Kompas*, 25 June 2009.

47. "Indonesia insists to impose punishment to Chinese fishermen," *Antara*, 2009.

48. Qin Gang's Press Conference on 25 June 2009.

49. Foreign Ministry Spokesperson Qin Gang's Press Conference on 26 April 2005, http://id.china-embassy.org/eng/fyrth/t193657.htm [Accessed on 28 October 2011].

50. Keith Loveard, "The Thinker: Caution Over Natuna," *The Jakarta Globe*, 2 July 2009.

51. "South China Sea dispute a potential rift in RI-China ties: Envoy," *The Jakarta Post*, 25 May 2010.

52. Keith Loveard, "The thinker: China's tough talk," *The Jakarta Globe*, 26 August 2009.

53. *Ibid.*

54. As quoted by *Batam Post* from two officials of Indonesia's MMAF: Samuel Sandi and Martin. "Chinese fishermen free to loot Natuna's fish: guarded by patrol vessels, MMAP surrenders [in Bahasa Indonesia]," *Batam Post*, 2010, http://www.batampos.co.id/pro-kepri/pro-kepri/18520-nelayan-china-bebas-jarah-ikan-natuna.html [Accessed on 9 October 2010].

55. Interview with Indonesian military personnel on basis of anonymity. Unfortunately, this news could not be officially confirmed.

56. "Territorial disputes in South China Sea on the increase as China flexes muscles," http://todayjapannews.com/mobile.php?docID=53270 [Accessed on 28 October 2011].

57. "South China Sea dispute a potential rift in RI-China ties: Envoy," *The Jakarta Post*, 25 May 2010.

58. "Navy Chief of Staff suggests Bilateral Meeting between Indonesia and China on fisheries issue (in Bahasa Indonesia)," *Antara*, 2010, http://kepri.antaranews.com /berita/13287/kasal-usul-pertemuan-bilateral-indonesia-china-soal-ikan [Accessed on 28 October 2011].

59. Overall Relations: China and Indonesia, http://id.china-embassy.org /eng/zgyyn/sbgxgk/ [Accessed on 1 May 2011]; Currently, China is Indonesia's second largest trading partner, see "Remarks at China-Indonesia Strategic Business Dialogue," by Wen Jiabao, Premier of the State Council of the People's Republic of China, in Jakarta, 30 April 2011, http://www.bjreview.com.cn/document/txt/2011-06/20/content_369848.htm

60. "60 years Indonesia-China Relations," *The Jakarta Post*, 13 April 2010, http://www.thejakartapost.com/news/2010/04/13/60-years-indonesiachina-relations.html [Accessed on 1 May 2011].

61. Sub-surface features cannot be used to generate maritime claims. Low-tide elevations may be used as base points for making maritime claims but only if they fall wholly or partially within a territorial sea drawn from an above high-tide feature (UNCLOS, Article 13). See Clive Schofield, "Dangerous ground—A geopolitical overview of the South China Sea," in Sam Bateman and Ralph Emmers, eds., *The South China Sea: Towards a Cooperative Management Regime* (London: Routledge, 2009), 7-25.

62. Article 121 of UNCLOS deals with the regime of islands. Article 121(1) of UNCLOS requires that an island be "a naturally formed area of land, surrounded by water, which is above water at high tide."

63. Article 121(3) provides for a sub-category of islands, "rocks," that are incapable of supporting human habitation or an economic life of their own. Such features "shall have no exclusive economic zone or continental shelf."

64. Spratly Island itself has a roughly isosceles triangle shape, the base measuring 750 m with the apex 350 m distant and an area of around 13 hectares. David Hancox and J.R.Victor Prescott, *A Geographical Description of the Spratly Islands and An Account of Hydrographic Surveys Amongst Those Islands*, Maritime Briefing, 1, 6 (Durham: International Boundaries Research Unit, 1995), 8; Schofield, "Dangerous ground," 7-25.

65. Johnson, 155.

66. Simon Sinaga, "No problem with China over Natuna Isles, says Alatas," *Straits Times*, 27 June 1995, 15.

67. Note sent by the Permanent Mission of Malaysia to the United Nations to the Secretary General of the United Nations, http://www.un.org/Depts/los/clcs_new /submissions_files/mysvnm33_09/mys_re_chn_2009re_mys_vnm_e.pdf.

68. Note sent by the Permanent Mission of Vietnam to the United Nations to the Secretary General of the United Nations, http://www.un.org/Depts/los/clcs_new /submissions_files/mysvnm33_09/vnm_chn_2009re_mys_vnm_e.pdf.

69. Like China, Vietnam claims all of the Spratly Islands, while Malaysia claims a number of the southernmost features in the Spratly Islands group.

70. "China Plan Coordinated Sea Patrols," *The Jakarta Post*, 23 May 2011.

71. Nien-Tsu Alfred Hu, "South China Sea: Troubled waters or a sea of opportunity?" *Ocean Development & International Law*, Vol. 41, No. 3 (2010), 211.

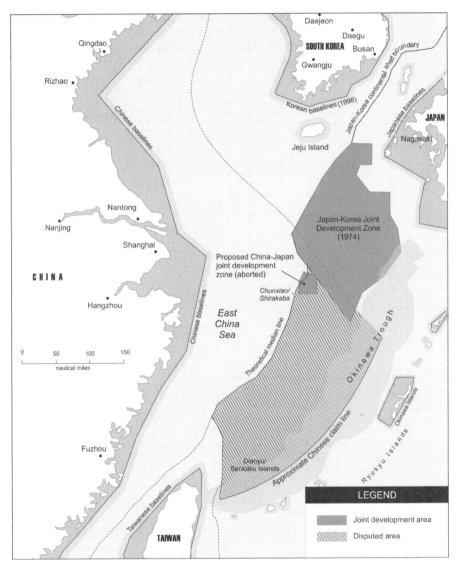

Map 6: Competing Maritime Claims in the East China Sea

6

Sino-Japanese Territorial
and Maritime Disputes

June Teufel Dreyer

China and Japan have several ongoing territorial and maritime disputes in the East China Sea. Both states are parties to the 1982 United Nations Convention on the Law of the Sea (UNCLOS). This convention states that a nation can claim an exclusive economic zone (EEZ) to a distance of 200 nm from coastal baselines, and also a continental shelf to the limits of its natural prolongation of its land territory to the outer edge of its continental margin up to 350 nm or 100 nm seaward of the 2,500 meter depth contour. However, since the East China Sea is only 360 nm across at its widest point, this precludes any easy solution to the dispute.

The three principal territorial and maritime disputes between China and Japan, listed in descending order of importance, are: 1) a group of islands in the East China Sea known to the Chinese as the Diaoyu and to the Japanese as the Senkaku; 2) the delimitation of the Sino-Japanese maritime boundary in the East China Sea and exploitation of the area's oil and gas resources, notably the fields called Chunxiao in Chinese and Shirakaba in Japanese; and 3) Okinotori, a tiny formation that Japan claims is an island capable of generating claims to EEZ and continental shelf rights, but that China, while not contesting Japan's ownership of Okinotori, refuses to recognize as an island capable of extended maritime claims. Control over the Senkaku islands might convey EEZ rights to 20,000 nm^2 (68,686 km^2) and to Okinotori some 116,472 nm^2 (400,000 km^2).

Acting as a mitigating factor on these territorial and maritime disputes is the fact that China is Japan's largest trading partner, and now leads the world in the purchase of Japanese automobiles. Repeated efforts at compromise have failed, a joint "consensus" reached in 2008 has stalled, and both sides have rejected the suggestion that their territorial and maritime disputes be submitted to international arbitration. The Japanese government maintains that the territorial issue has been settled, while China, seemingly a power on the rise relative to Japan, has little incentive to compromise.

Historical Background

The territorial disputes between China and Japan are essentially a continuation of nearly two millennia of intermittently prickly relations between an empire whose ruler believed that he held sway over All Under Heaven and a state that chafed at any inference of its inferiority. In 607, for example, the emperor of the Sui dynasty became incensed at the assumption of equality implicit in the phrase: "The emperor of the land where the sun rises sends a letter to the emperor of the land where the sun sets." A thousand years later, Japanese resentment of the Chinese tribute system, wherein vassal states performed obeisance to the emperor or his representatives and exchanged gifts of local treasures, prompted a Japanese shogun to establish a parallel tribute system whose participants performed similar subordination rituals to the Japanese ruler.

By the mid-19th century, the shrinking distances afforded by advances in technology and the intrusion of Western powers brought China and Japan into more frequent contact in ways that alternately united and divided them, with adversarial ties frequently outweighing ties of amity. After humiliating China with relative ease during the first and second Sino-Japanese wars, Japan established itself as the clearly dominant of the two powers before itself being defeated by the United States in 1945. Japan, though explicitly foreswearing any military role in its post-war constitution, soon established its economic hegemony in ways that irked its larger Asian neighbor. There were complaints that Japan was trying to re-establish the Greater East Asia Co-Prosperity Sphere it had created during the pre-war years, with most of the prosperity in both eras accruing to Japan. A resurgence of nationalistic feeling was evident in China and in Japan as well. To a significant degree, these nationalistic movements reinforced each other.

Territorial disputes, never far below the surface of Sino-Japanese relations, gained increased salience, particularly as both sides began to see themselves in competition for scarce energy resources. The Diaoyu/Senkaku and Chunxiao/Shirakaba disputes are based on the same geomorphology. With regard to the first, the Diaoyu/Senkaku comprises five small islands and three rocky outcroppings with a total land area of just over three square miles (8 km^2). The islands are about 120 nm northeast of Taiwan and 240 nm southwest of Okinawa, at the edge of China's continental shelf. In China's view its shelf ends at the Okinawa trough, an exceptionally deep, roughly north-south oriented, depression in the seabed.

Under Article 57 of UNCLOS, coastal states can claim an EEZ based on a distance extending up to, but not exceeding, 200 nm from their territorial baselines. Article 76, however, allows a coastal state to define the outer limits of its continental shelf up to either a distance of 200 nm or to the natural prolongation of its land territory to the outer edge of the continental margin, up to a maximum extent of either 350 nm or the 2,500 meter depth isobath (contour line) plus 100 nm. Japan, based on article 57, is understood to claim that the median, where China's and Japan's respective 200 nm EEZ claims intersect, should be the border between the nations' EEZs. The PRC cites Article 76, asserting that the maritime boundary should be based on natural prolongation principles and on this basis the delimitation line should be consistent with the Okinawa trough, which is located considerably to the east of the theoretical equidistance line between the Chinese and Japanese coasts. China also claims that its Chunxiao gas field does not cross the median line even were the Japanese method of delimitation to be adopted, because Chunxiao is 2.16 nm (4 km) from Japan's claimed centerline. Japan claims it is due a share of Chunxiao's profits regardless of where China chooses to drill if the extraction draws on resources currently located on the Japanese side of the median line.

China has made a preliminary submission related to extended continental shelf rights in the East China Sea. This sea is, however, roughly divided into two rift complexes, the East China Sea Basin and the Okinawa trough. The Okinawa trough is separated from the East China Sea Basin by the Diaoyudao Uplift Belt, which raises the continental shelf. Hence Japan argues that the presence of the uplift belt refutes China's natural prolongation claim to seabed rights extending beyond the median line between the two states' opposite coastlines—the Senkaku group is located at the middle peak of the uplift. The Okinawa trough is only a few miles away from Japanese territory, so if Beijing can claim the waters up to the Okinawa trough, the PRC would be entitled to exploit virtually the entire East China Sea. A key question that has yet to be determined is whether China's natural prolongation-based continental shelf claims can trump Japan's distance-based EEZ claims.

The Diaoyu/Senkaku Islands

The PRC bases its claim to the Diaoyu/Senkaku islands on three arguments.[1] First, China's initial discovery, use, and ownership. Second, the Japanese government's prior acknowledgement of China's claim to the islands. Third, Japan's cession of the islands to China after World War II. Japan's claims also rest on three bases: that Japan has legal title to the islands, which were *terra nullius*, that is unoccupied, when it took them over; that it has administered the islands peacefully for over a century, holding residual sovereignty even while they were under U.S. administration; and that China previously acquiesced to Japan's sovereignty over the islands, which were and are uninhabited.

Neither country's claim is without problems, not least of which is the difficulty of trying to assign sovereignty to the Chinese empire, which did not recognize the concept until it was forced on the empire by the intrusion of Western powers. By that time, Japan already controlled the islands. So, Japan does not contest that mention of the islands appeared first in Chinese historical records, although it points out that Chinese mariners left no signs of declaring ownership such as markers, plaques, or signs of habitation. China responded that it used the islands for the only purposes they could be used for during this period: as navigational aids and for collection of a particular medicinal herb, *statice arbucula*. In 1893, Empress Dowager Cixi issued a special edict granting the islands to an individual who gathered the herb there to treat one of her illnesses. This, the Chinese side argues, should be sufficient proof that the area was not *terra nullius*.

In early 1894, Japan's interior minister petitioned Okinawa Prefecture to erect national markers on the islands, but was overruled by the country's foreign minister on grounds that this would attract China's attention; such action must wait a more opportune time. That time came quite soon: in January 1895, the Japanese cabinet passed a resolution to erect markers claiming the islands. In the Treaty of Shimonoseki, signed three months later, the Chinese government ceded to Japan Taiwan and all islands appertaining or belonging thereto to China. In China's view, the Diaoyu/Senkaku group was included among these territories; in Japan's, it was not, since by virtue of the January cabinet decree, the islands were already owned by Japan. The Japanese government then leased the islands to a private individual, who used them for agricultural purposes, as did his son after him.

China also rests its claims on a 1931 legal case in which the Tokyo High Court held that the islands historically belonged to Taiwan, thereby acknowledging Taiwan's ownership of the islands. Since Taiwan is, says the Beijing government, part of China, so are the Diaoyu islands. The case may not be legally relevant, however, since no record of the case can be located in the court archives.[2]

As for the ultimately victorious allies' planning arrangements for the disposition of territories after World War II, the Cairo Declaration of 1 December 1943 stated that Japan was to be stripped of all territories "stolen" from China, such as Manchuria, Formosa (an alternate name for Taiwan), and the Pescadores (an alternate name for the Penghu islands), which were to be restored to the Republic of China (ROC).[3] The Diaoyu/Senkaku islands are not mentioned. The Potsdam Declaration of 26 July 1945 was also ambiguous on this point, stating that Japanese sovereignty was to be limited to the four main islands of Honshū, Hokkaido, Kyūshū, and Shikoku and "such minor islands as we determine." The San Francisco Peace Treaty of 8 September 1951 followed Cairo and Potsdam's pattern by not specifically mentioning the Diaoyu/Senkaku group. However, the islands were administered by the United States as part of the Ryūkyūs, including Okinawa, and Washington paid rent to the Japanese national who held a lease on the islands as compensation for using them for bombing practice. Hence, the U.S. implicitly included the Diaoyu/Senkaku group in the minor islands it had determined were under Japanese sovereignty. In May 1969, anticipating an imminent return to Japanese administration, Okinawa prefecture placed a marker on the main Diaoyu/Senkaku Island, signifying that it was to be part of the prefecture.[4] Neither the ROC nor PRC protested at this time.

The dispute over sovereignty emerged only in 1969, when a team of Japanese geologists reported the discovery of an underwater oil field, thought to be one of the ten largest in the world, in the area.[5] The advantage of domestically produced oil was obvious. At the time, Japan imported over 99 percent of the petroleum it used for fuel and power, most of it over long supply lines from the perpetually politically troubled Middle East. While the Tokyo government must have been immediately aware of the potential problems that the discovery involved, it was probably more concerned about the ongoing Sino-Soviet border clashes and therefore the need to increase naval strength on the country's northernmost main island, Hokkaido, to better patrol Soviet maritime activities.[6]

The Beijing government watched U.S.-Japanese negotiations over the return of Okinawa to Japan closely, but said nothing about the Diaoyu/Senkaku implications of reversion until the oil discovery. Its attention was focused on whether "U.S. imperialism" could maintain its nuclear weapons on Okinawa, and to what extent Okinawa would remain "an unsinkable aircraft carrier from which to project American hegemony over Asia."[7] By 1970, however, Chinese media were describing these islands as China's sacred territory.[8]

On 9 April 1971, the U.S. State Department issued a statement that President Richard Nixon and Japanese Prime Minister Sato Eisaku had reached an agreement by which Washington would return Okinawa and the "southwestern islands," which included the Diaoyu/Senkaku group; a minute appended to the agreement specifically delineated an area that included them.[9] As these negotiations were taking place, however, Washington was secretly courting Beijing and did not want to offend it. During Senate hearings prior to the ratification of the treaty, then-Secretary of State William Rogers stated: "We have made it clear that the treaty does not affect the legal status of those islands at all. Whatever the legal status was prior to the treaty is going to be the legal situation after the treaty comes into effect."[10]

As some critics pointed out, Rogers' statement was baffling, given the wording of the U.S.-Japan Treaty of Mutual Cooperation and Security of 1960, article five of which states that:

> Each Party recognizes that an armed attack against either Party in the territories under the administration of Japan would be dangerous to its own peace and safety and declares that it would

act to meet the common danger in accordance with its
constitutional provisions and processes.[11]

Since the islands were unequivocally under the administration of Japan, the U.S.
had in effect pledged itself to help Japan defend them regardless of whether the
islands were legally part of Japan. Subsequent State Department pronouncements
continued to affirm this curious position. On 24 March 2004, deputy spokesperson
Adam Ereli's response to a query was that:

> [the] treaty applies to the Senkaku Islands. Sovereignty of the
> Senkaku Islands is disputed. The U.S. does not take a position on
> the question of the ultimate sovereignty of the Senkaku Diaoyu
> Islands . . . We expect the claimants will resolve this issue through
> peaceful means.[12]

Two days later, in response to further queries on the issue from puzzled reporters,
spokesperson Richard Boucher reiterated Ereli's words, adding "I have stated our
position on this issue. I'll state it again if you want me to, but that's where we
are."[13]

In January 1972, a month before President Nixon's visit to Beijing, and as the
details of the Okinawa reversion were being worked out, *Beijing Review* protested:
"Diaoyu and the other islands have been China's territory since ancient times. There
is no question about this whatsoever . . . It is even more absurd that the United
States wants to include China's territory Diaoyu and other islands it has occupied
into the area of reversion."[14]

Based on the most relevant international law cases, including the island of Palmas,
the Clipperton islands, and the Minquiers and Ecrehos case, the weight of evidence
seems to favor Japan's position on the Diaoyu/Senkaku islands.[15] Courts have
tended to rule that discovery conveys only inchoate title, with more concrete acts of
actual occupation or exercise of authority needed to demonstrate sovereignty over
an island. A state that has inchoate title over a territory may lose sovereignty over it
by prescription if the other state actually occupies or exercises state authority over
the territory in question. The first state must protest the occupation of the second
state, which China did not until after the discovery of oil nearby.

Maritime Delimitation and Chunxiao/Shirakaba

Since no physical territory is involved, and since the oil and gas field was
discovered only in 1995, disputes over Chunxiao/Shirabaka concern only the above-
mentioned controversy over whether equidistance or natural prolongation principles

should be operative in determining the course of the Sino-Japan maritime boundary in the East China. To date, the PRC has observed the median line, at least so far as oil and gas development activities are concerned, although drilling so close to it that the Japanese government has protested that it may be siphoning resources from the Japanese side of the line.[16]

Xinhua's announcement in July 1995 that it had drilled a high-yield well, Chunxiao No. 1, near a theoretical median line, heightened Japanese fears.[17] Tensions were already running high in the area due to aggressive Chinese behavior relevant to Taiwan that had adversely affected Japanese shipping interests and raising the possibility that, should the PRC conquer Taiwan, its maritime claims would impinge still more on Japan's. Two Western companies, Shell and Unocal, initially signed leases with Chinese counterpart organizations for development in the area, but pulled out after the U.S. government warned that its ships might be harassed due to the disputes over sovereignty.

Okinotori

The PRC does not question Japan's sovereignty over Okinotori, "Remote Bird," contending only that it is not an island—*shima* in Japanese—capable of generating EEZ and continental shelf rights, but is only a "rock" within the meaning of Article 121(3) of UNCLOS. Part of the Ogasawara (Bonin) chain and so small that it is not even noted on most maps, it was first discovered by the British ship *Iphigenia* in 1789 and named Douglas Reef. Britain made no claim to the territory, and it disappeared from mention until a Japanese naval vessel investigated the area in 1922 and 1925. Having confirmed that no other nation claimed the reef, Japan asserted ownership, placing it under the jurisdiction of Tokyo municipality and re-naming it Okinotorishima. There were no protests. Plans to build a hydroplane base on the islet were interrupted by World War II.

Administered by the U.S. after World War II, the Ogasawara islands were returned to Japan in 1968. Okinotori attracted no attention until the late 1970s, when nations began to assert claims to 200 nm EEZs. By this time, the depredations of wind and sea had eroded the reef's above-water land area to two outcroppings, each only a few inches above sea level, with the dimensions of king-sized beds and separated by .7 nm.[18] If Japan's contention that Okinotori is an island capable of its own EEZ and continental shelf claims is accepted, Tokyo could claim an EEZ of 116,472 nm^2 (400,000 km^2), which is larger than the total land area of Japan.[19] China has, however, objected. Apart from wanting to preclude the obvious economic advantage that the greatly enlarged EEZ would confer on Japan, the PRC appears to have a strategic motive as well. Midway between Taiwan and Guam, the area would be a logical transit route for American ships based in Guam to protect Taiwan in the event of a PRC attempt to take the island. China wanted to be able to carry out hydrographic mapping that would enable the PLA to better counter the U.S. fleet.

From 1987 on, Japan sought to support its claim that Okinotori is an island by spending more than $600 million to surround the protruding coral outcroppings with 82-foot thick concrete floors and constructing steel breakwaters to stave off further erosion. Slits were made in the concrete casing in order to comply with UNCLOS stipulation that an island be surrounded by water, and the smaller outcropping was covered with a titanium net to shield it from debris thrown up by waves. There are plans to enlarge the size of the reef by breeding calciferous micro-organisms on it. In 1988, Japan's Marine Science and Technology Center built Okinotori's only human-made structure, a marine investigation facility, and regularly repairs it after typhoon damage.[20]

According to UNCLOS, "An island is a naturally formed area of land, surrounded by water, which is above water at high tide. The EEZ and the continental shelf of an island are determined in accordance with the provisions of this convention applicable to other land territory."[21] While this is true of the Okinotori formation, UNCLOS also says that "rocks which cannot sustain human habitation or economic life of their own shall have no EEZ or continental shelf."[22] Since Okinotori cannot sustain either human habitation or economic life of its own, this would seem to rule out island status. However, proponents of the Japanese case argue that neither in UNCLOS nor in international law in general is there a definition of what constitutes a rock. Rocks are not coral reefs; they consist of hard, continental soil. Hence a country can make a claim for an EEZ and continental shelf based on its possession of coral reefs.[23] Furthermore, China has itself asserted sovereignty over tiny islands/islets that are incapable of sustaining human life.[24]

Subsequent Developments

Though the Chunxiao/Shirakaba and Okinotori issues were not yet major factors, differences over the sovereignty of the Diaoyu/Senkaku group loomed in the background of Sino-Japanese normalization talks in the early 1970s. Nixon's shock announcement that Washington had been conducting secret negotiations with Beijing—without informing its close ally, Japan—also gave the Tokyo government incentive to discuss diplomatic recognition with its larger neighbor. Many countries were doing so, and Japan did not want to be the last. Major corporations were eager to enter the Chinese market, and argued that Japan would lose out to Germany, France, and the United States if it did not establish a presence quickly. The Beijing government had made known its interest in acquiring Japanese industrial technology to implement the country's fourth Five Year Plan.

At the same time, however, pro-Taiwan sentiment was strong in the ruling Liberal Democratic Party (LDP), with both the PRC and ROC rejecting the idea of dual recognition. For Beijing to have pressed the issue of the Diaoyu/Senkaku might well have been a deal breaker. Hence the Tokyo government was greatly relieved when envoys reported that Premier Zhou Enlai had agreed to postpone discussion of the issue until an unspecified future date.

In what could have been regarded as a re-enactment of the despised tribute system, Prime Minister Tanaka Kakuei went to Beijing to sign the normalization agreement and received a gift of two pandas. Speaking to the press on his return, Tanaka noted the existence of unspecified problems that would have to be "solved in a realistic manner" between the two sides. The left-of-center daily *Asahi*, which had strongly favored normalization, immediately cautioned that "the country would be well advised to start thinking of the possibility of eventual economic competition" with China.[25]

Japanese fears that they might be in the calm before a storm re-emerged in 1974 when the People's Liberation Army Navy (PLAN) seized the Paracel islands, then held by the government of South Vietnam. There were suspicions that this was the precursor to an invasion of the Diaoyu/Senkaku group. Although no invasion took place, tensions were ratcheted up after the two states extended their maritime claims to 12 nm for the territorial sea and 200 nm, first as fishing zones and subsequently, from 1996, as EEZs. When Japan followed suit, it specified that Chinese and South Korean fishing boats would be allowed to operate within the 200 nm EEZ, though not within the 12 nm territorial zone.[26]

However, in early April 1978, a large number of Chinese ships, variously estimated at from 80 to over 140, appeared within the 12 nm area near the Diaoyu/Senkaku group. Some were armed with machine guns. Most carried large signs claiming the islands as China's sacred territory. Their aggressive behavior caused apprehension not only in Japan but elsewhere in Asia. Still, Beijing's motives were puzzling; it had for several years been pressuring a reluctant Japanese government to sign a treaty of peace and friendship, for which the fishing boats' behavior was scarcely an incentive. Since the proposed treaty contained an anti-Soviet clause thinly disguised as opposition to hegemonism, it was more than its name implies. Moscow had made plain its unequivocal opposition to the pact. Because both the PRC and the USSR were potential markets for Japanese goods and technology, neither the country's government nor its business community wanted to have to choose between them.

If Beijing's motive had been to force Tokyo's hand, the move backfired badly. Japanese nationalism was energized, with even the country's left-wing media and organizations condemning the intrusion and rejecting Beijing's claim that the islands belonged to China. The influential right-wing parliamentary group Seirankai, which had wanted the Diaoyu/Senkaku issue settled before a treaty of peace and friendship was signed, now argued that doing so was an absolute necessity. In the end, the Japanese government accepted highly unconvincing assurances that the incident had been an accident: the boats had inadvertently entered the area in pursuit of a school of fish. Skeptics pointed out that no fishing was taking place, and wondered why the fishermen were equipped with machine guns and anti-Japanese placards. Treaty negotiations resumed nonetheless. In August 1978, after Beijing agreed to a slight rewording indicating that the agreement was not to be interpreted as directed against any third nation, the document was signed.[27] The intrusion had, however, created serious misgivings about China that Beijing made scant effort to soothe. Chinese officials castigated "some Japanese who continue to play up the incident,"[28] and media associated with the government stridently rebutted "persons in Japan" who thought that the PRC had given its tacit consent to Japan's ownership of the islands.[29]

Less incendiary incidents continued to occur thereafter. Japan built a heliport on the largest of the islands; China protested. Each side complained when the other began exploratory drilling activities in the area. Japan regularly protested when Chinese ships intruded into what Tokyo claimed as Japanese waters.

This pattern continued throughout the 1980s, along with intermittent friction over other issues including Chinese discontent with the large trade deficit it was running with Japan, accusations that Japan's textbooks were playing down the country's brutality in World War II, and the visits of its ministers to the Yasukuni Shrine. The shrine, founded in the late 19th century, commemorates the memories of all Japanese soldiers who have fallen in battle—but includes as well some individuals who did not fall in battle, having been executed as war criminals by the victorious allies. Japan had its own list of grievances including Chinese nuclear testing, the PRC's cancellation or postponement of contracts, some of them major, it had signed with Japanese corporations, and what it regarded as Chinese interference in Japan's internal politics. Tensions over disputed territories were an important, but not an overwhelming, part of the fabric of discontent.

By the end of the 1980s, Chinese oil production, which had been expanding for a decade, began to level off. At the same time, the Chinese economy grew quickly, soon absorbing the PRC's entire production and leading Beijing to seek increased exports from abroad. Oil had literally been a lubricant for Sino-Japanese relations. Now the two countries found themselves in competition for exports from third countries. The need for oil and gas also exacerbated tensions over the contested maritime areas. Although trade between the two continued to expand, the trade deficit had shifted in China's favor, and was becoming wider year by year. Japan's difficulties were compounded when its economic bubble burst in 1990, sending the country's once-vibrant economy into a slump from which it has yet to recover. Meanwhile, its larger neighbor's gross domestic product grew by double digits year after year, and its defense budgets by even larger amounts. A further notable development in this period was that in 1996 both the PRC and Japan became parties to UNCLOS and duly claimed 200 nm EEZs.

When a group of right-wing Japanese young people built a makeshift lighthouse on the largest of the Diaoyu/Senkaku islands, patriotic Chinese vowed to destroy it and claim the islands for the PRC. The Beijing government damped down the nationalistic wave within its borders, apparently less because it desired a low-key response than because it feared that anti-government forces might be using anti-Japanese activities as a cover for their real motives.[30] Since Hong Kong was still under British control at that time, activists there were able to charter a boat and set sail. When a combination of poor weather and Japanese coast guard ships convinced the charter boat captain to turn back, several activists jumped overboard, apparently intending to swim to the islands. One drowned, providing the movement with a martyr.[31]

In 2004, seven Chinese activists actually did land on the islands. Since they were from Zhejiang, inside the PRC, some concluded that this time they had received Beijing's support. When the group was apprehended and taken to Okinawa for questioning, the Chinese government accused Japan of violating the nation's sovereignty and ordered that the activists be released, which they were. Again, the Zhejiang activists' actions occurred against a backdrop of other grievances between the two sides.

More worrisome still were demonstrations of Chinese naval strength that seemed calculated to show Japan that the PRC intended to control the entire East China Sea. One such incident was the passage of a submerged Han-class submarine through Japanese territorial waters in November 2004. This transit violated Article 20 of UNCLOS stating that in another country's territorial seas a submarine is required to navigate on the surface and must show its flag. Five days after receiving a formal protest, the Chinese government expressed regret, saying that the submarine had accidentally strayed. While some analysts are inclined to accept this explanation, others argue the delay in issuing a statement indicated that it was intentional, with the PLAN not informing the central government of what it was doing. The latter explanation raises a more worrisome question: whether, to use Mao Zedong's phrase, the Chinese Communist Party still controls the gun.[32]

Recent Efforts at Resolution

Efforts at resolution of competing maritime claims on the delineation of the East China Sea have been ongoing and inconclusive. The two sides held eleven rounds of negotiations between October 2004 and mid-2008. In June 2008, an agreement in principle was reached on working together to develop one of the four gas fields in the East China Sea. A future maritime joint development area would straddle the theoretical equidistance line between the two states, albeit in an uneven fashion since the majority of the proposed zone would be on the Japanese side of the median line. Japanese capital would be injected into the Chinese development company that was working the Chunxiao gas field—an important step for Japan, since it would receive a share of the revenue generated by the field. The details, such as the capital ratio between the two states and the distribution of mining rights, were to be settled in subsequent working-level talks.

While international media portrayed the agreement as a significant breakthrough and there was much talk of turning the disputed area into "a sea of peace and friendship," the reality was quite different. Despite reassurances by leaders of both sides that they had not surrendered their respective nations' sovereign rights over the area, citizens were skeptical. Anger was particularly noticeable on the Chinese side. The country's vice-foreign minister explained that the PRC had not recognized Japan's median line, and that despite some reporting to the contrary,[33] the agreement was for joint development of a proposed joint zone, as well as cooperative development of the gas fields on the Chinese side of the median line. The latter suggests that Japan would operate under Japanese law; the former, that both sides would be governed by Chinese law. Japan's role would be limited to investment only. Infuriated Chinese patriots disagreed strongly.[34] Talks have continued sporadically without resolution.

Nor did the disputed areas turn into a sea of peace and friendship. Two separate incidents in 2010 point to possible difficulties ahead. In April, two Chinese submarines and eight destroyers—a much larger than usual grouping—sailed close to Okinawa and near Okinotori. As Japanese vessels observed its passage, PLAN helicopters twice approached a Japanese destroyer at dangerously low levels, threatening its radio mast. China responded to Japanese protests by saying that the surveillance of Japanese ships betrayed a lack of trust. Major Japanese newspapers opined that these heavy-handed actions indicated Beijing's intention to demonstrate the expansion of its naval strength.[35]

In September 2010, a Chinese fishing boat rammed two Japanese coast guard vessels in separate incidents forty minutes apart. When the ship's captain was taken into custody, China demanded his immediate release. It suspended talks on the cooperative development of the Chunxiao field, hinted that tourism and other exchanges with Japan would be curbed, announced a halt in shipments of rare earths to Japan—they have since resumed on a reduced basis—and subjected imports from Japan to agonizingly slow customs inspection procedures.[36] Beijing also announced that henceforth its ships would patrol the contested maritime areas.[37] The Chinese captain was quickly released.

Conclusions

In the end, legal considerations over the Diaoyu/Senkaku islands, over the Chunxiao/Shirakaba oil and gas fields, and over the Okinotori issue may matter less than great power relationships. As seen, for example, in its return of the Chinese nationals who landed on the Diaoyu/Senkaku islands, the repatriation without trial of the fishing ship captain who rammed two coast guard vessels, and its acquiescence to Beijing's announcement that henceforth Chinese naval vessels would patrol the area around the Diaoyu/Senkaku group, Japan's tendency has been to comply with Beijing's demands.

It is difficult to imagine that, under current circumstances, any Tokyo government, regardless of political party, could do otherwise. While the euphemistically-named Self Defense Force is one of the finest militaries in Asia, it may not be equal to the task of taking on the much larger and increasingly better equipped PLA. For a democracy to augment significantly its defense budget in a time of financial austerity is politically risky domestically as well as provocative to the likely enemy. Although Japan's anti-war constitution does not preclude the right of self-defense, pacifist sentiment remains strong and China's salami tactics—advancing its claims in small, carefully measured increments—would be difficult for any country to respond to. To attack a Chinese naval vessel seeking to patrol contested waters is scarcely imaginable. Moreover, as is clear from Beijing's response to the September 2010 fishing boat incident, the PRC government will skillfully use economic pressure as a lever to induce Japan's compliance.

Assuming that Japan continues its economic and military stagnation and China its economic and military rise, the contested territories could one day come under Chinese control, legal claims notwithstanding. But these assumptions are not foregone conclusions. While the consequences of the earthquake, tsunami, and nuclear disaster of March 2011 were profound, Japan may solve its internal problems and forge ahead again. The PRC faces many difficulties in sustaining its rise: the environment continues to deteriorate, the population dividend—meaning the presence of a large number of young people willing to work for low wages—is ending, and citizen demands for social justice are becoming more strident. But the long-term advantage at present would seem to be on the Chinese side.

Notes

1. The respective claims of the two sides are considered in detail in Jean-Marc Blanchard, "The U.S. Role in the Sino-Japanese Dispute Over the Diaoyu (Senkaku) Islands, 1945-1971," *The China Quarterly*, No. 161 (March 2000), 95-123; William Heflin, "Diayu [*sic*]/Senkaku Islands Dispute: Japan and China, Oceans Apart," *Asian-Pacific Law and Policy Journal*, Vol. 18, No. 1 (2000); Linus Hagström, "Quiet Power: Japan's China Policy in Regard to the Pinnacle Islands," *Pacific Review*, Vol. 18, No. 2 (June 2005), 159-88; Martin Lohmeyer, "The Diaoyu/Senkaku Islands Dispute: Questions of Sovereignty and Suggestions for Resolving the Dispute," Master of Laws thesis, Faculty of Laws, University of Canterbury, 2006; Alexander M. Peterson, "Sino-Japanese Cooperation in the East China Sea: A Lasting Arrangement?" *Cornell International Law Journal*, No. 441 (2009), 441-74.

2. Lohmeyer, 167, 170.

3. The PRC considers itself the successor state to the Republic of China, whose government has ruled only Taiwan and some smaller islands since 1949, and hence the rightful owner of the Diaoyu/Senkaku; the ROC maintains that its sovereignty has never been extinguished.

4. *Kyodo* (Tokyo), 6 May 1969.

5. Philip Shabecoff, "Japanese Oil Find Poses Title Problems," *New York Times*, 28 August 1969, 1. Reference, citing secondary sources, is frequently made to a 1968 report of a United National Committee for the Coordination of Joint Prospecting for Mineral Resources for Asian and the Far East, but the report does not appear in the archives of either the United Nations or the *New York Times*.

6. Takashi Oka, "Japan Planning to Bolster Navy and Patrol Waters Near Kuriles," *New York Times*, 24 September 1969, 5.

7. *Xinhua* (Beijing), 2 June 1969. A survey of Chinese press commentary on Japan in this period shows the nuclear/U.S. base issue on Okinawa to be its primary focus. There were also frequent complaints about violations of fishery agreements and allegations that Japanese capitalism was "plundering" Southeast Asia. The Diaoyu/Senkaku issue was never mentioned.

8. *Xinhua*, 5 December 1970.

9. U.S. Department of State *Bulletin*, Vol. 65, No. 1672 (12 July 1971).

10. Ibid.

11. Text of the treaty can be found at www.mofa.go.jp/region.n-american/US/q&a/ref.1.html [Accessed on 5 January 2010].

12. www.state.gov/r/pa/prs/dpb/2004/30743.htm [Accessed on 7 January 2010].

13. www.state.gov/r/pa/prs/dpb/2004/30837.htm [Accessed on 7 January 2010].

14. "T(D)iaoyu and Other Islands Have Been Chinese Territory Since Ancient Times," *Peking* [after 1979 *Beijing*] *Review*, 7 January 1972, 13-14.

15. www.icj-cij.org/docket/index lists these cases and subsequent determinations thereon.

16. Mark Valencia, "The East China Sea Dispute," *PacNet*, No. 47A, 15 September 2006.

17. *Xinhua*, 2 August 1995.

18. Jon Van Dyke, "Speck in the Ocean Meets Law of the Sea," letter to the editor, *New York Times*, 21 January 1988.

19. Ibid.

20. Norimitsu Onishi, "Japan and China Dispute a Pacific Islet," *New York Times*, 10 July 2005, 4.

21. www.un.org/Depts/los/convention_agreements/texts/unclos/unclos_e.pdf, Article 121.1.

22. Ibid., Article 121.3.

23. These arguments are summarized in Yukio Yoshikawa, "Okinotorishima: Just the Tip of the Iceberg," *Asian Quarterly*, Vol. 9, No. 4 (Fall 2005).

24. Peter Dutton's "Through a Chinese Lens," *Proceedings of the U.S. Naval Institute,* April 2010, 28, has a fascinating picture illustrating this point: three PLA men in heroic postures stand on an outcropping in the South China Sea barely large enough to contain them, vowing to defend it against all comers.

25. *Asahi* (Tokyo), 30 September 1972. Note that the warning appeared on the same day that the normalization agreement, which *Asahi* had long advocated, was signed.

26. *Japan Times*, 15 June 1977, 1.

27. For an analysis of Japanese internal politics at this time, see Daniel Tretiak, "The Sino-Japanese Treaty of 1978: The Senkaku Incident Prelude," *Asian Survey*, Vol. 16, No. 12 (December 1978), 1235-1249.

28. Vice-chair of the National People's Congress Standing Committee Ulanhu, among others, used this phrase to Japanese media. *Mainichi* (Tokyo) 4 May 1978, 2.

29. *Hsin Wan Pao* (Hong Kong), 16 August 1978, 1. Theoretically privately owned and located in what was then a British possession, *Hsin Wan Pao* and other papers like *Wen Wei Pao* not only repeated the official party position but frequently were more strident. They were believed to assert provocative positions on behalf of Beijing while providing it with a plausible deniability if such should be needed.

30. Matt Forney, Sebastian Moffett, and Gary Silverman, "Ghosts of the Past: China Tried to Keep a Lid on Diaoyu Protests," *Far Eastern Economic Review* (Hong Kong), 10 October 1996, 24. For a fuller discussion of the events of this period, see June Teufel Dreyer, "Sino-Japanese Relations: Cooperation and Conflict," *Journal of Contemporary China*, Vol. 10, No. 28 (Spring 2001), 8-26.

31. Edward Gargan, "Man Drowns During a Protest Over Asian Islets," *New York Times*, 27 September 1996, A8.

32. Peter Dutton, *Scouting, Signaling, and Gatekeeping: Chinese Naval Operations in Japanese Waters and the International Law Implications* (U.S. Naval War College, China Maritime Studies No. 2, 2009), analyzes this incident in detail.

33. Some of it in China's own press. The official English-language *China Daily*, for example, used the word "joint" in its 20 June 2008 article on the agreement.

34. Chinese national Ching Cheong wrote a scathing refutation of the vice-minister's claims in the *Straits Times* (Singapore), 20 June 2008.

35. *Yomiuri*, 24 April 2010.

36. *Asahi,* 25 September 2010.

37. *Yomiuri*, 28 September 2010.

Map 7: Kazakhstan's Border with China

7

Kazakhstan's Border Relations with China

Stephen Blank

When the USSR collapsed in 1991, the PRC and Kazakhstan shared a 1,056 mile (1,700 km) border, along which 365 square miles (944 km^2) remained in contention, out of a total Sino-Soviet dispute of about 13,127 square miles (34,000 km^2). In 1994, President Nursultan Nazarbayev attacked national "splittism" and promised Beijing that Kazakhstan would not aid dissident Uyghurs in Xinjiang. In a subsequent 1998 Sino-Kazakh accord, the border was changed by only 72 square miles (187 km^2), with China gaining just over 43 percent of the land still under dispute while Kazakhstan retained just under 57 percent.[1]

The 1996 creation of the Shanghai Five by China, Kazakhstan, Kyrgyzstan, Russia, and Tajikistan may have started the process of delimitating China's borders with the post-Soviet Russian and Central Asian states, but the 2001 creation of the Shanghai Cooperation Organization (SCO), which added Uzbekistan, was integral to China's highly favorable relationship with these states. Indeed, it culminated the first stage of China's successful policy toward Kazakhstan. The 1998 border treaty capped a highly successful—from Beijing's viewpoint—policy toward these post-Soviet states and placed their relations on a strong foundation for the future.

China's border treaty with Kazakhstan, and its subsequent foreign policy toward Central Asia in general, underscores the "intermestic"—the combining of international and domestic policies—nature of Chinese foreign policy toward Central Asia. Meanwhile, the Chinese government's post-treaty foreign policy ties with Central Asian states also illustrates some of the enduring and unresolved—possibly even insoluble—issues in the PRC's relations with Central Asia. In particular, as recently as 2009 Beijing requested that Kazakhstan lease almost 4,000 square miles (one million hectares) of land to Chinese farmers.

Imperial Russian Expansion into Central Asia

During the 19th century, Imperial Russia expanded into Central Asia. After the founding of the city of Vernyi in 1854, the Russians took Tashkent in 1865, the

Uzbek Khanate of Bukhara in 1868, the Uzbek Khanate of Khiva in 1873, and the Uzbek Kokand Khanate in 1876. The Russian administrative system incorporated these areas as the Central Asian border provinces of Semipalatinsk, established in 1854; the governor-generalship of Turkestan, established in 1867; Syr Darya and Semirech'e, both established in 1867; and three others in Uralsk, Turgai, and Akhmolinsk, established in 1868. As a result of the Anglo-Russian Convention of 1907, Russia annexed these lands into its empire. After the October 1917 revolution, they officially became autonomous republics, but largely in name only, within the newly formed Soviet empire—Kazakhstan in 1920, Tajikistan in 1929, and Kyrgyzstan in 1936.

Because of the importance of the Silk Road to China's foreign trade, Beijing had long-standing relations with Central Asia, and considered much of this territory to be part of the Chinese empire, or at least a Chinese tributary. In 1871, during the great Muslim Rebellion (1862-1878) in China, Russian troops moved from modern-day Kazakhstan to occupy the Ili Valley in western Xinjiang, hoping to prevent the spread of revolt into Russian territory. But the Ili Valley was also the necessary invasion route for Russia to project power into Xinjiang, and in 1873 Russia formally incorporated the area into the Russian provincial system as Kuldzha Province. It appeared that Ili might become a permanent part of the Russian empire.

Ili was strategically and politically important to China, however, since the Ili River Valley ran east-west through the mountains linking Chinese with Russian territory. Thus, China deployed large forces under General Zuo Zongtang and, much to Russia's surprise, restored order in Xinjiang. St. Petersburg was not eager to relinquish control over Xinjiang's mountain passes, since they gave Russia the strategic advantage in dealing with China, and provided direct trade routes with Gansu, Shaanxi, and Mongolia. Therefore, the Russian price for withdrawal was that it retain control of the Muzart Pass, the most strategic part of the Ili Valley; acquire trading privileges throughout Xinjiang, Mongolia, and beyond the Great Wall into the heart of China; and receive a five-million-ruble indemnity to defray the occupation costs. The Russians also proposed a separate agreement giving them the right to navigate the Songhua River, in Manchuria, as far inland as Potuna.

China's diplomatic representative, Chonghou, agreed to these terms when he signed the Treaty of Livadia on 2 October 1879. However, when the Tongzhi emperor suddenly died in 1875, a lengthy power struggle had erupted within the Manchu ruling house. Although Chonghou appears to have kept officials in Beijing fully appraised of his 10-month-long negotiations, dynastic matters seem to have completely overshadowed his border negotiations. As soon as China's government understood the treaty terms, therefore, it immediately repudiated the agreement. The resulting diplomatic scandal threatened to end in a war between Russia and China. Russia had thousands of troops stationed near Ili and deployed 23 warships to

Chinese waters, but China had even more soldiers in theater, since Zuo Zongtang had only just put down the Muslim Rebellion in Xinjiang. The Qing put their most famous officers from the Taiping suppression in key positions and hired the former leader of the Ever-Victorious Army, Charles Gordon, to provide military advice. Russia, by contrast, had just fought a costly war with Turkey from 1877-1878. To make matters worse, in 1879 Britain took control of Afghanistan, potentially threatening Russia's position in Central Asia.

Rather than going to war, diplomacy prevailed when Russia agreed to accept a new negotiator, Marquis Zeng Jize, the son of the famous Taiping-era general, Zeng Guofan. Zeng Jize's negotiations in St. Petersburg were acrimonious, but Russia finally agreed to restore most of the disputed territory to China for a nine-million-ruble indemnity. Russia also curtailed its demands for greater trade privileges and dropped the provision concerning navigation rights on the Songhua River. As a result, the 24 February 1881 Treaty of St. Petersburg superseded the Treaty of Livadia. The new treaty halted, temporarily at least, Russia's expansion into China, and established the border between Kazakhstan and China just to the west of Ili Valley.

In 1884, soon after the Treaty of St. Petersburg was ratified, Beijing made Xinjiang a regular province and incorporated it into the Chinese administrative system. While much of Central Asia fell into turmoil following China's 1911 Revolution and Russia's two revolutions in 1917, the borders established in 1881 remained roughly the same when Kazakhstan was formed as the Kazakh Soviet Socialist Republic on 26 August 1920, and when the Republic of Kazakhstan finally gained its independence from the USSR on 25 December 1991.

Central Asian Links with Xinjiang

From China's standpoint, Sino-Soviet relations improved dramatically under Mikhail Gorbachev. Once the USSR collapsed, there were compelling historical, foreign policy, and domestic security issues for demarcating the former Sino-Soviet boundary between Xinjiang and the new Central Asian republics. Xinjiang's ethno-religious makeup, composed largely of Muslim Turkic Uyghurs with kinsmen in what became Tsarist and then Soviet Central Asia, created the potential for rebellion against the distant Han Chinese leadership.[2] As Manchu and Republican power eroded in China, and the Tsars and then Soviets took power in Central Asia, Xinjiang became a political football as Joseph Stalin sought to establish a kind of protectorate there. And even after Stalin, in the 1960s-1970s, during the height of Sino-Soviet enmity, Moscow tried to loosen Beijing's control of this strategic border province.[3]

This historical legacy taught China's current rulers several critical lessons. First, weak central control over provinces, including Xinjiang, coupled with strong external powers' interference, could challenge Beijing's central authority.[4] Second, because Xinjiang is not just a border region, but also has a distinctive ethno-religious character, it requires special handling: as Deng Xiaoping had stated in 1950 when describing China's southwestern frontier, "on a border this long—if the issue of ethnic minorities is not resolved, then the matter of national defense cannot be settled."[5] Third, integrating Xinjiang and astutely handling the "nationality issue" leads analysts like Wu Xinbo to confirm the linkage between domestic and foreign policy when they argue that "China is still a country whose real interests lie mainly within its boundaries, and to a lesser extent, the Asia-Pacific region, where developments may have a direct impact on the country's national interests."[6] Western analysts confirm that a primary, if not the primary, purpose of foreign policy, despite China's new assertiveness vis-à-vis its Asian interlocutors, is to create an environment conducive to domestic stability and growth.[7] Central Asian policy is no exception to this rule.

This fusion of foreign and domestic interests generates what Chinese analysts call an "internationalization of domestic security and domestication of international security."[8] Beijing's Central Asian policy is essentially an outward projection of the PRC's internal security agenda.[9] Chinese analysts tend to believe these threats can be overcome by wise action on China's and other great powers' part.[10] In this context wise action means fostering China's domestic economic growth and restricting Western military and political influence in Central Asia.[11] Such restrictions are necessary because Chinese analysts believe that Muslim minority movements among the Uyghur population in Xinjiang cannot succeed except through foreign assistance, hence any possibility of such assistance must be suppressed.[12]

The origins of China's border treaty with Kazakhstan are linked to a surge in ethnic unrest in Xinjiang during the 1980s.[13] Chinese elites clearly grasp the linkages between Central Asia and Xinjiang. One Chinese school of strategic thought emphasizes the primacy of landward threats to security and asserts that China, to retain its integrity and sovereignty, must retain Xinjiang to ensure that Mongolia and the approaches to Beijing remain in Chinese hands.[14] While it seems to Beijing officials that if Central Asia falls apart then chaos will enter into Xinjiang, conversely if Central Asian countries stabilize and succeed, that could also stimulate deeper drives for self-rule in Xinjiang. Thus, China faces inevitable if not insuperable problems no matter what happens in Central Asia.[15]

Indeed, Chinese scholars make the link between the two areas explicit. For example, Guancheng Xing writes that: "It can therefore be argued that *to a large extent the stability and prosperity of Northwest China is closely bound up with the stability and prosperity of Central Asia.* It is, rightly, because of this consideration that China advocates and promotes active trade and economic cooperation between China and Central Asian states for common economic prosperity."[16] The conjunction of the Soviet collapse, Central Asian independence, U.S. military-political hegemony and with it the primacy of liberalizing global trends, and the rhetoric of Islamic freedom and self-determination visible in increased anti-regime violence in Xinjiang, along with domestic strife among elites and the turmoil concluding in the 1989 Tiananmen massacre, engendered a sizable perceived threat to China's integrity and the stability of communist rule that Beijing recognized and acted to forestall.

Seen from Beijing's perspective, it was essential to prevent Central Asian states from embracing the Uyghurs' cause. If they received foreign backing then they could generate real threats to China's territorial integrity and political stability. Accordingly, China after 1991 began to fashion a Central Asian policy aiming to forge ties with these new Central Asian states that would deter them from intervening in Xinjiang, fix the borders for once and for all by means of a recognized treaty, and irrevocably integrate Xinjiang into a system of central control, thereby forestalling the possibility of internal threats to China's stability and integrity from arising in its borderlands.[17] Since unrest in Xinjiang and Tibet are not far behind Taiwan as potential threats to either China's stability or its integrity, foreign policy must forestall those threats and create auspicious conditions for China's continuing development, the basis of its power abroad.

China's Central Asian Policy Objectives and Strategy

The potential for a crisis in Xinjiang roughly corresponded with the Tiananmen massacre. If the protests and violence in Xinjiang had ever coincided with the domestic unrest that led to the demonstrations in Beijing in 1989, and the elite rivalries that lasted until 1992, then the Communist government could have faced major threats to its continuation in power. Even now, according to the Society for Anglo-Chinese Understanding, 70,000 protests occur annually in China (or about 200 per day).[18]

If China's social unrest ever linked up with ethno-religious rebellions, a highly dangerous situation could easily develop. Therefore, ethno-religious problems had to be detached from Chinese domestic unrest as well as from potential foreign support. Here again foreign policy had to support internal stability and development: "These objectives include assuring domestic order and social well-being; maintaining an adequate defense against threats to the heartland; increasing the level of influence and control over the periphery with an eye to warding off the threats that may eventually menace the political regime; and restoring China to regional preeminence while attaining the respect of its peers as a true great power marked by high levels of economic and technological development."[19]

China's foreign policies toward Central Asia link overall domestic and foreign policy strategy in this so-called peripheral policy.[20] Given the intermestic nature of the problem confronting Beijing, its response utilized all the instruments of national power—economics, diplomacy, and military force—to repress Uyghur unrest. Furthermore, faced with the birth of Central Asian states, Soviet collapse, U.S. hegemony, and domestic turmoil in both Xinjiang and among top cadres, China had to resolve its own leadership issues and simultaneously adopt a new policy line. That policy line framed the political context wherein China could approach the related issues of unrest in Xinjiang, relations with new states, and diplomacy with post-Soviet Russia. In turn, that policy framework allowed for the resolution of outstanding border issues.

By the time of Deng Xiaoping's 1992 "southern tour," Beijing had apparently forged a new strategy.[21] Beijing quickly recognized the new states and opened economic relations with them. This aimed at preventing Taiwan from recognizing the new Central Asian states first and gaining their recognition. But more importantly it was essential for Beijing to get these states to accept Xinjiang as part of China.[22] Simultaneously, recognition opened the way to formalize the processes of interstate trade by which China sought to bind these states economically, and provide incentives for not risking China's anger by supporting Uyghur protests in China. Thus, Kazakh President Nursultan Nazarbayev stated: "In Asia—the key priority is policy toward China. In the context of the processes of economic integration and development of partnership with the region's countries, the effective employment of communication channels connecting Kazakhstan with the region through China is extremely important."[23]

The PRC's tactics blended incentives with coercion. The new states, confronted with a multitude of problems, had no reason to provoke China gratuitously. Trade is the major incentive, plus the fact that China holds foreign businessmen from Central Asia as "collateral," that is hostages for their governments' good behavior on Xinjiang-related issues.[24] Central Asian governments have apparently recognized from the start that local governments perceive China as a uniquely powerful regime that could substantially injure their interests, and therefore make fulsome statements about friendship with it.[25]

Chinese strategy combined foreign and domestic initiatives in 1991-1996 to meet its many and to some degree conjoined domestic-foreign challenges. As the leadership issue clarified and tensions subsided in 1992, Deng Xiaoping's policies for continued domestic growth and security with neighbors began to succeed. His foreign policy strategy comprised building good-neighborly relations and an omnidirectional policy toward developing states to stabilize China's relations with them and build markets for China, including Central Asia. China also moved quickly to negotiate the outstanding border issues with the newly formed Central Asia states and with Russia. The structure of the negotiations combined bilateral talks with each state with joint working groups to maximize expert knowledge.[26]

In Xinjiang, the regime strengthened administrative controls, instituted fairly draconian repression of insurgents, but most of all intensified by an order of magnitude the economic development of the region, believing that ethnic tensions have their origins in economic inequality. The same reasoning was underlying the decade long effort to reorient investment and allocational priorities to China's West, especially in Xinjiang. Those policies grew out of the need to ensure central control over those provinces and that their governance remains a wholly internal one not subject to internationalization and foreign debate.

Arguably a similar reasoning also applies to China's overall policy in Central Asia, which clearly aims to make neighboring states dependent upon China so that they will not dare support their kinsmen across the border.[27] Therefore, economic development through large-scale investment, including major energy projects, entails goals that are broader than overcoming the gap between the richer coastal provinces and the interior and the problem of mass poverty in the interior and Western provinces. China's "go west" program is very much a comprehensive security project. All in all, China's domestic and foreign policies represented a highly sophisticated intermestic policy, combining strong capabilities for repression with those of cooptation of non-Han elites, large-scale Han Chinese colonization of Xinjiang, and equally sophisticated foreign policies toward Central Asia.[28]

China's trade with Kazakhstan is increasing steadily. By 1993, trade with China jumped from $360 million in 1992, the initial year of takeoff, to $434 million. A further growth in economic ties was hailed by the Kazakhstani government. This process, combined with the shift in China's allocational policies, testified to the rise of a "community of interests" among elites in Central Asia and China in upgrading economic ties at the expense of support for Uyghurs in China, that is China's price for continued support and trade.[29] Accordingly, by 1993 President Jiang Zemin was able to tell a military audience that China's relations with its neighbors were the best they had ever been.[30] China's diplomatic initiatives included negotiating a bilateral border treaty with the Kazakhstani government.

Negotiating China's Borders with Central Asia

China's diplomatic initiatives facilitated the reaching of agreements with Russia and the Central Asian states, beginning with the creation of the Shanghai Five in 1996.

This forestalled any possibility that the Central Asian governments or Russia would support the insurgents in Xinjiang either materially or rhetorically and created the basis for linking Central Asian economies to some degree with China's economic development, in which respect Xinjiang would serve as a pivot linking both sides of this equation. Combined with the shift in Chinese investment and spending priorities, the growth of inter-state trade and the intensifying importance of Xinjiang's and Central Asia's energy holdings created strong bonds between those states and China, and between Xinjiang and the rest of China. Thus Beijing could move with confidence, as expressed by Jiang Zemin, to the border talks that had begun before 1991.

China's foreign policy was to a large degree governed by domestic considerations. Where China's internal security is a paramount issue, Beijing seems willing to make concessions on border issues to stabilize its domestic base. Accordingly, in the negotiations with Central Asian states we see a pattern of Chinese compromises. For example, Kazakhstan apparently gained more in percentage terms than China did during their border negotiations. Of course, this perception is tempered by the fact that the PRC's territory is 3.5 times larger than Kazakhstan, so Beijing's relative losses were actually much smaller than what Kazakhstan agreed to forfeit.

China also got what it wanted politically. On the conclusion of a 1994 agreement with Kazakhstan, President Nursultan Nazarbayev stated that Kazakhstan "will never allow factions of 'East Turkestan' to involve themselves in activities here against China that will hurt Sino-Kazakhstani relations." In this and subsequent accords with Kazakhstan, China gained just over a third of the territories in dispute, while Kazakhstan claimed neither to have lost or gained territories. Meanwhile, its policy of non-support for Uyghur activities in China continued. We see a similar pattern in China's border negotiations and subsequent agreements between 1994-2002 with Kyrgyzstan and Tajikistan.[31]

The success of these negotiations with the relevant Central Asian states and Russia has been considerable. It laid the foundations for subsequent developments, most notably the birth and ensuing development of the SCO, which originated as a disarmament and confidence building measure (CBM) in the border zones. It represents an outstanding example of these processes at work in international affairs. But it also came at a price of the Uyghurs as once again Central Asian states announced their unwillingness to raise the issue with China during the summit preparing the 1996 five-power treaty.[32]

Another critical success is that by building a regional structure with Central Asia and Russia, Beijing successfully prevented the internationalization of that issue. Indeed the sense of operating under risk is traceable to U.S power and influence.[33] For example, the state council announced in 1996 that: "As long as China remains to be a socialist country with the Communist Party in power and as long as China does not adopt the American political system, no matter how much the Chinese economy develops, no matter how much democracy in politics, and how much improvement of human rights (the U.S.) will [be] just looking but not seeing and listening but not hearing—[The U.S. is just] using [the] human rights [issue]."[34]

This outlook explains China's fears of Western engagement and cultural penetration in Xinjiang as well as from more classic threats of internal unrest and foreign military intervention. Accordingly, China's presentations of its so-called new security concept, which embraces both definitions of its internal sovereignty and its external policies, all aim to dethrone the regnant U.S. system, including its alliances, and the ideological and intellectual underpinnings of that system in Asia if not globally. A critical aspect of that process is to deny any legitimacy or opportunity for U.S. efforts to interfere in what China calls its internal affairs— Taiwan, Xinjiang, and Tibet—and second, to minimize American presence in Central Asia. Beijing cannot permit any of these issues to become internationalized, or at least is constantly fighting off such attempts. Hence, for example, its 2003 White Paper on Xinjiang reflects its defensiveness about that province.[35]

At the same time, the bilateral border treaty with Kazakhstan was the first example of China embracing its own version of multilateralism in world politics as manifested in the creation of the SCO. China's embrace of groups like ASEAN followed soon thereafter. It is unlikely that this overall turn toward multilateralism was unconnected with the stinging setback on Taiwan it suffered in 1996 when it challenged the U.S. and Taiwan and had to affect a retreat. Beijing's growing interest in multilateral regional security institutions allowed China to defuse domestic challenges and continue its spectacular economic growth in an undisturbed manner.[36] But it also gained several foreign policy advantages for China beyond this one. While this long-term program of support for multilateral regional security could reflect a Chinese adaption to the status quo, it might alternatively be argued that China's approach is actually rather more self-serving and less benign than it appears. Thus, China's "campaign against bilateral alliances" suggests that the "intrinsic worth of the multilateral security approach has yet to be accepted at the highest levels in Beijing and is primarily valued for its possible contribution to the weakening of U.S. ties with its Asian allies."[37]

Similarly, China's policies toward Central Asia, particularly the development of the SCO, exemplifies the process by which China hopes to build a prosperous neighborhood under its auspices:

> Step one for the SCO was to build the group, the first multilateral group China had started on its own. Step two: expand it to discussions of trade, economics and energy. Step three: begin

discussions on more substantive security partnerships. The SCO has gone so far as to conduct its own joint military maneuvers, in China's Xinjiang Autonomous Region. This approach of deepening regional multi-level ties will likely be repeated in other forums, such as ASEAN+3 grouping (ASEAN plus Japan, Korea, and China).[38]

The turn toward supporting regional multilateral security structures is about more than a question of adaptation to international security norms. Clearly it is a way to safeguard Beijing's freedom of action to deal with persistent internal challenges without accounting for nosy international actors and organizations. This safeguards China's domestic sovereignty. At the same time the creation of these structures is an obvious attempt to reduce the U.S. footprint: "China's approach to regional security mechanisms has largely succeeded in allaying near-term fears in the region and in building closer relationships with key partners, including U.S. allies, while also committing China to a deeper stake in regional stability."[39] As one commentator put it, this was at a time when "China showed its claws."[40]

Conclusions

Despite China's undoubted success in meeting its objectives in the 1990s, the subsequent evolution of its capabilities and power means that in some cases we are dealing with unfinished issues, or more precisely success breeds its own challenges. Not only are there clear signs of mounting unease in the U.S. and Southeast Asia about China's rise, but concern in Russia is increasing as well.[41] Some Russian experts charge that Russia is surrendering Russian territory to China and that the border issues with China that were supposedly resolved are in fact unresolved, thereby implying that China's appetite for Russian lands is growing.[42]

Similarly in Central Asia, Beijing's interest in acquiring more land and in altering the borders to meet its new interests has also increased. For example, China approached Kazakhstan in late 2009 with a request to allow Chinese farmers to use one million hectares of Kazakh land to farm soya and rapeseed. Earlier in 2004:

> The Kazakh autonomous region of Ili in Xinjiang obtained permission to rent 7,000 hectares of agricultural land—which had been abandoned since the 1990s—for ten years from the Kazakhstan governor of the border district of Lake Alakol. The lands were rented to about 3,000 Chinese colonists who now grow soya beans and wheat on them. This transaction provoked scathing attacks in the media against the government, apparently

out of concern that the country was being carved up at Beijing's behest. The media recalled that the Russian Far East was also becoming increasingly fragmented through the sale of parcels of agricultural lands and wooded areas to China. Such deals have, however, not been repeated, precisely because Sinophobe social pressures, which are quite palpable on the issue of land possession, have quelled the ambitions of local politicians.[43]

This episode would appear to confirm warnings that despite increased trade and economic relations between China and Central Asia, and rapid economic development in Xinjiang, Beijing's overbearing requests for additional land have in fact aggravated tensions; resentments about the border and about Chinese intentions lie close to the surface.[44] Thus, China's astonishing growth since 1990 has bred new challenges for which the policies successfully implemented in 1991-1996 appear to be inadequate today. Nonetheless it is by no means clear that Chinese leaders fully grasp the degree to which their high-handed behavior has alienated and is estranging past and potentially future partners.

Notes

1. Claes Levinsson and Ingvar Svanberg, "Kazakhstan-China Border Trade Thrives after Demarcation Treaty," *CACI Analyst*, 16 February 2000, http://www.cacianalyst.org/?q=node/367 [Accessed on 7 June 2011].

2. Hassan H. Karrar, *The New Silk Road Diplomacy: China's Central Asian Foreign Policy since the Cold War* (Vancouver: UBC Press, 2009), 19-35.

3. Lowell Tilllet, "The National Minorities Factor in the Sino-Soviet Dispute," *Orbis*, Vol. XXI, No. 2 (1978), 241-260.

4. Karrar, 35.

5. M. Taylor Fravel, *Strong Borders Secure Nation: Cooperation and Conflict in China's Territorial Disputes* (Princeton, NJ: Princeton University Press, 2008), 61.

6. Wu Xinbo, "Four Contradictions Constraining China's Foreign Policy Behavior," Suisheng Zhao, ed., *Chinese Foreign Policy: Pragmatism and Strategic Behavior* (Armonk, NY: M.E. Sharpe, 2004), 58.

7. Stephen Blank, "Xinjiang and Chinese Security," *Global Economic Review*, Vol. XXXII, No. 4 (2003), 121-148; Valerie Niquet, "China and Central Asia," *China Perspectives, Perspectives Chinoises*, No. 67, September-October 2006, 2-10; Huasheng Zhao, "Central Asia in China's Diplomacy," in Eugene Rumer, Dmitri Trenin, and Huasheng Zhao, *Central Asia: Views From Washington, Moscow, and Beijing* (Armonk, N.Y.: M.E. Sharpe, 2007), 137-213; Wu Xinbo, "China," in Muthiah Alagappa, ed., *Asian Security Practice: Material and Ideational Influences* (Stanford: Stanford University Press, 1998), 123, 133-137.

8. Meng Xiangqing, "Domestic Security and International Security Will Become More Interwoven and interdependent in the Future as China Faces Growing Traditional, Nontraditional Security Threats," Beijing, *Shije Zhishi*, 1 June 2005, *Foreign Broadcast Information Service* China *(Henceforth* FBIS CHI) 1 June 2005, quoted in Susan L. Craig, *Chinese Perceptions of Traditional and Nontraditional Security Threats* (Carlisle Barracks, PA: Strategic Studies Institute, US Army War College, 2007), 18.

9. Stephen Blank, "Xinjiang and Chinese Security," *Global Economic Review*, Vol. XXXII, No. 4 (2003), 121-148; Valerie Niquet, "China and Central Asia," *China Perspectives, Perspectives Chinoises*, No. 67 (September-October 2006), 2-10; Zhao, "Central Asia," 137-213.

10. Charles Hawkins and Robert R. Lowe, eds., *The New Great Game: Chinese Views on Central Asia* (Fort Leavenworth, KS: Foreign Military Studies Office, 2006).

11. *Ibid.*

12. Zhao, "Central Asia," 141-144.

13. Lillian Craig Harris, "Xinjiang, Central Asia and the Implications for China's Policy in the Islamic World," *The China Quarterly*, No. 133 (1993), 111-129; Remi Castels, "The Uyghurs in Xinjiang: the Malaise Grows," *China Perspectives*, No. 49 (September-October 2003), 34-48; Nicholas Becquelin, "Xinjiang in the Nineties," *The China Journal*, No. 44 (July 2000), 65-93.

14. Major General Liu Yazhou, "Theory on West Regions," Hong Kong, *Feng Huang Chou Kan*, in Chinese, 5 August 2010, *FBIS CHI*, 20 August 2010.

15. Willem Van Kemenade, *China, Hong Kong, Taiwan Inc: The Dynamics of a New Empire* (New York: Alfred A. Knopf, 1997), 345; Lillian Craig Harris reports the same observation, Harris, 125.

16. Guancheng Xing, "China and Central Asia: Towards a New Relationship," in Yongjin Zhang and Rouben Azizian, eds., *Ethnic Challenges Beyond Borders: Chinese and Russian Perspectives of the Central Asian Conundrum* (New York: St. Martin's Press, 1998), 35.

17. Bates Gill, *Rising Star: China's New Security Diplomacy* (Washington, DC: Brookings Institution Press, 2007).

18. Thomas Mucha, "US-China: Why Obama's Weakness Could Be His Greatest Strength," *The Global Post*, 20 January 2011.

19. Michael D. Swaine and Ashley J. Tellis, *Interpreting China's Grand Strategy: Past, Present, and Future* (Santa Monica: Rand Corporation, 2000), 112.

20. Suisheng Zhao, "The Making of China's Periphery Policy," in Zhao, *Chinese Foreign Policy*, 256-275; Suisheng Zhao "China's Periphery Policy and Its Asian Neighbors," *Security Dialogue*, Vol. XXX, No. 3 (1999), 335-346.

21. Fravel, 128-137.

22. Jean-Pierre Cabestan, "Central Asia-China Relations And their Relative Weight In Chinese Foreign Policy," in Marlene Laruelle, Jean-Francois Huchet, Sebastien Peyrouse, and Bayram Balci, eds., *China and India in Central Asia: A New "Great Game"?* (New York and London: Palgrave Macmillan, 2010), 26-28.

23. Yasmin Melet, "China's political and Economic Relations with Kazakhstan and Kyrgyzstan," *Central Asian Survey*, Vol. XVII, No. 2 (1998), 249.

24. "Kyrgyzstan: China Keeps Nationals and Business' Collateral'," *Radio Free Europe Radio Liberty*, 21 July 2004.

25. Marlene Laruelle and Sebastien Peyrouse, *China As a Neighbor: Central Asian Perspectives and Strategies* (Stockholm: Institute for Security, Development and Policy, 2009), 170.

26. Fravel, 135-136, 158-159.

27. Becquelin, 70; Felix K. Chang, "China's Central Asian Power and Problems," *Orbis*, Vol. XLI, No. 3 (Summer 1997), 401-421.

28. Ross H. Munro, "China's Waxing Spheres of Influence," *Orbis*, Vol. XXXVIII, No. 4 (Fall 1994), 599.

29. Ibid., 601-605.

30. Fravel, 127.

31. Ibid., 160-166.

32. Karrar, 79-82.

33. Joseph Kahn, "China's Leader, Ex-Rival At Side, Solidifies Power," *New York Times*, 25 September 2005, A1, 10.

34. Jing-Dong Yuan, "Studying Chinese Security Policy: Toward an Analytic Framework," *Journal of East Asian Studies*, Vol. XIII, No. 1 (Spring-Summer 1999), 144.

35. Thierry Kellner, *La Chine et la Nouvelle Asie Centrale: De L'Independance des Republiques Centralasiatiques A'L'Apres-11 Septembere* (Brussels, Groupe de Recherché d'Information sur La Paix et la Securite [GRIP], 2002), 6-7, 13; Government of the People's Republic of China, *History and Development of Xinjiang*, 26 May 2003, http://service.china.org.cn/link/wem/Show_Text?info_od=65428&p_qry=xinjiang [Accessed on 7 June 2011].

36. Gill, 68-69.

37. Rosemary Foot, "China in the ASEAN Regional Forum: Organizational Processes and Domestic Modes of Thought," *Asian Survey*, Vol. XXXVIII, No. 5 (May 1998), cited in Gill, 72.

38. Joshua Cooper Ramo, *The Beijing Consensus* (London: Foreign Policy Centre, 2004), 52-53.

39. Gill, 72-73, citing Alastair Iain Johnson and Paul Evans, "China's Engagement With Multilateral Security Institutions," in Alastair Iain Johnston and Robert S. Ross, eds., *Engaging China: the Management of an Emerging Power* (New York: Routledge, 1999), 237.

40. David Shambaugh, "The Year China Showed Its Claws," *Financial Times,* 16 February 2010.

41. "Japan's Chance to Exploit Russian Suspicion of China," *Japan Times*, 24 January 2011.

42. Maria Teploukhova, "Russia and International Organizations in the Asia-Pacific: Agenda for the Russian Far East," *Security Index*, Vol. 91, No. 2 (Spring 2010), 80-81.

43. Laruelle and Peyrouse, 80.

44. Allen Carlson, *Unifying China, Integrating With the World: Securing Chinese Sovereignty in the Reform Era* (Ithaca, NY: Cornell University Press, 2004), 237.

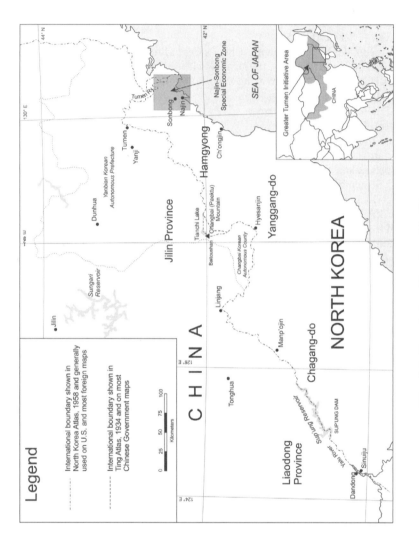

Map 8.1: Korea's Land Border with China

8

Sino-Korean Border Relations

Charles K. Armstrong

China's 880 mile (1,415 km) border with North Korea is not currently under active dispute, and would appear to be among the most straightforward of all the PRC's external boundaries. Administratively, about two-thirds of the Chinese side of the border is in Jilin Province, from the northeastern boundary with Russia, which shares a border of approximately ten-and-a-half miles (17 km) with North Korea, to a point about halfway along the Yalu River. Liaodong Province occupies the remaining southwestern length of the border to the Yellow Sea. On the Korean side are the provinces of P'yongan Pukto, Chagang-do, Yangang-do, and Hamgyong Pukto. For the most part, the rivers are relatively narrow—especially the Tumen—and do not form a major impediment to trans-border population movements.

For much of recorded history until the 18th century, what is now the Korean-Chinese border shifted hands among various contending groups in Northeast Asia. For the past three hundred years, the Tumen and Yalu rivers, flowing northeast and southwest respectively from Changbai Mountain (called Paektu Mountain in Korean) have formed the "natural" geographical boundary between Chinese and Korean states. The PRC and the Democratic People's Republic of Korea (DPRK, North Korea), whose territorial sovereignty meet at this border today, have no current public boundary disputes. Behind the scenes, however, despite a secret agreement that supposedly settled all such problems in 1963, a number of issues regarding control of the waterways, ports, islands, and mountain territories in the border region have emerged since the 1950s and continue to this day.[1]

The most vociferous Sino-Korean boundary dispute of recent years has been between China and the Republic of Korea in Seoul, which—like North Korea—claims sole authority over the entire Korean peninsula, but in fact has no actual jurisdiction over Korea's land boundary with China. The 2004 "Koguryô Dispute" was, strictly speaking, not an argument over a contemporary boundary, but a diplomatic row over an interpretation of history: the South Korean government fiercely disputed the claims of Chinese scholars, supported by the Chinese government, that the ancient kingdom of Koguryô (ca. 37 BC–668 AD) had been a "Chinese" rather than a Korean state. Nevertheless, the Korean challenge to China's interpretation of Koguryô called into question the "naturalness" of the China-

Korean border and might suggest future Korean claims over territory in China's Northeast.[2] At the moment, despite the Koguryô controversy, neither Korean state makes any irredentist claims over Chinese territory. Korean demands for a "return of Manchuria" are confined to a small fringe of South Korean society,[3] and emotions run much higher over territorial disputes with Japan, notably the contention over the Tokdo/Takeshima islets in the sea between South Korea and Japan.[4] If the two Koreas should ever unify, however, border tensions with China could once again come to the fore. It should also be noted that China has yet to delimit its potential maritime boundaries with either of the Koreas, though China and South Korea have established a joint fishing zone in the Yellow Sea.

Historical Construction of the Boundary

The Sino-Korean border region is relatively remote from the historic population centers of both China and Korea, and on the Chinese side was largely settled in the late 19th and early 20th centuries. On the Korean side, the region was long under contention between peninsular kingdoms and states indigenous to the northeast of the continent—"Manchuria"—whether Chinese or non-Chinese. What is more or less the current Sino-Korean boundary was established in 1712, although the exact placement of the border has been contested a number of times since.

Chinese authority extended to the Korean peninsula in the 2nd century B.C.E., when the Han dynasty conquered the kingdom of Chosôn (now called Kochosôn or "Ancient Chosôn," to distinguish it from later Korean kingdoms of that same name) and established military bases on the peninsula. Chinese military bases or "commanderies" remained in the Korean-Manchurian trans-border region for the next 400 years, although their connection to China itself became tenuous after the fall of the Han dynasty in the 2nd century.[5] As Chinese authority weakened, the kingdom of Koguryô rose in power, originating perhaps in the central Yalu region in the 1st century B.C.E. Koguryô came to dominate the vast area between western Manchuria and the southern part of the Korean peninsula by the 4th century.[6] Over the course of the 5th to 7th centuries, Koguryô came into conflict both with continental states to the west, and rival kingdoms on the Korean peninsula to the south. One of these Korean kingdoms, Silla, conquered Koguryô in 668, in alliance with Tang dynasty China. But Silla effectively repulsed Tang's subsequent attempt to conquer the peninsula, and from that time onward no Chinese state would directly control any part of the Korean peninsula.

Tang and Silla did not share a land border, however, as remnants of the former Koguryô elite and other local peoples established the state of Bohai (Parhae in Korean) in the northern part of the Korean peninsula and eastern Manchuria.[7] Silla's northern frontier extended from Pyongyang in the west to the area just north of present-day Wonsan on the east coast; the Yalu-Tumen region was at the center of Parhae territory. In 918, Wang Kôn founded the Koryô kingdom as a self-proclaimed successor to Koguryô, and conquered Silla in 935. Meanwhile Parhae had been destroyed by the Khitan, a nomadic people of Manchuria, in 926. The Khitan consolidated power as the Liao dynasty for approximately one century, before succumbing to another Manchurian tribal people, the Jurchen, who established the Jin dynasty in 1126. Thus, for several centuries after the Silla unification in 668, the trans-Yalu region remained a buffer between states in "China proper" and the Korean peninsula.

This changed after the Mongols created the Yuan dynasty in the late 13th century. Yuan was the first "Chinese" dynasty—although its rulers were of course Mongols—to assert effective control over Manchuria all the way to the Korean (i.e., Koryô) border. From the peninsula side, Koryô had steadily pushed its northern boundary toward the Yalu and Tumen rivers, driving out the Khitan and Jurchen from this territory. Koryô established control over the mouth of the Yalu early in the dynasty, and in 1034 completed a "Great Wall" (*changsông*) from the Yalu estuary in the west to the east coast of the peninsula. Campaigns against the Jurchens in 1107 expanded Koryô territory to the north, almost to the Tumen River, although the Jurchen retook the area in 1109.[8] The Mongols took over Koryô's northern territories in 1258, returning the northwestern area to Korean sovereignty in 1260, but maintaining direct control over the northeast of the peninsula until 1356, shortly before the collapse of the Yuan dynasty.[9] When the Koryô dynasty came to an end in 1392, its administration extended about halfway up the Yalu and across the peninsula to the town of Kyôngsông far up the east coast. The Chosôn dynasty, Koryô's successor, had established control over the mouth of the Tumen by 1398. By 1441, Chosôn had administrative control over the southern banks of the Tumen, establishing the northern boundary of Korea where it would remain until the present day—except for the area of Changbai/Paektu Mountain, which was not fixed until the early 18th century.[10]

Around 1710, China's Kangxi emperor, second ruler of the Qing dynasty established by the Manchus in what is now Northeast China, ordered an investigation to establish the Qing/Chosôn boundary in the Changbai region. Kangxi wanted to take stock of the vast empire he had just consolidated, and was particularly interested in the boundaries of the Manchu ancestral territory in the northeast. By this time, the Yalu and Tumen rivers were considered by both sides to be the dividing line between the Qing empire and Chosôn kingdom. What was at issue, however, was the boundary at the source of the two rivers on Changbai Mountain. In 1712, Kangxi's emissary Mukedeng made the arduous trip up the slopes of Changbai and found what he believed to be the watershed of the Tumen and Yalu rivers. Mukedeng erected a stele marking the border at that point, and this remained the established border until the late 19th century, when the boundary once again became a contested point among the Koreans, Chinese, Russians, and Japanese.[11]

Imperial Unsettlements, 1860-1945

The weakening of the Qing state, the expansion of the Russian empire, and the Japanese advance on the Asian mainland disrupted the China-Korean boundary. The collapse of all three states converging on the continental Korean border—the Qing and Tsarist empires and the kingdom of Chosôn itself—in the second decade of 20th century, all but erased this boundary, which was not fully re-established until the Democratic People's Republic of Korea and the PRC were founded in 1948 and 1949, respectively.

From the mid-19th until the mid-20th century, the Manchurian-Korean borderlands were an area of considerable change, population movement, and political contestation.[12] In 1860, Russia annexed the Pacific coast sections of the Qing empire, pushing the boundary of the Qing south to the Amur and Ussuri rivers and establishing for the first time a border between Russia and Korea, along the final stretch of the Tumen. Russian explorers, merchants, and settlers moved into Manchuria and the Korean border region in increasing numbers over the course of the late 19th century. Koreans, in turn, began to migrate into the Russian Far East, fleeing economic hardship in northern Korea.[13] Koreans also began to migrate clandestinely into Qing territory. Although there had been movement across the boundary for centuries, it was only after 1860, facing famine and rebellion at home and the promise of vast open lands in unsettled Manchuria, that Korean farmers began to migrate into Qing territory in large numbers. Most of the 19th-century Korean migrants settled in the area known as Jiandao (Kando in Korean), along the Tumen.[14]

Facing these demographic pressures from Russia and Korea, as well as the growing interest of Japan, the Qing started to open the Northeast to settlement in the late 1870s. Most of the Chinese migrants into the region were poor farmers from Shandong Province, beset by famine, flood, and social unrest in the 1880s. The region was not fully opened to immigration until 1902, and between 1890 and 1942 some eight million Chinese migrated to Manchuria—comparable to the number of European immigrants moving to the United States in the same period.[15] The collapse of the Qing dynasty in 1911 led to a period of rule in Manchuria by a local military strongman, the "warlord" Zhang Zuolin, from 1916 to 1928. After Zhang's assassination under orders of the Japanese Kwantung Army in 1928, Japan asserted increasingly direct control over Manchuria, ultimately creating a new state called

"Manchukuo" out of the northeastern provinces of the defunct Qing empire in 1932. From 1932 to 1945 the erstwhile Sino-Korean boundary was the porous border between two Japanese-controlled entities; the colony of Korea, and the state of Manchukuo.

Indeed, well before the collapse of the Qing, and even before the official colonization of Korea by Japan in 1910, the Japanese government had taken control of Korea's boundary issues. After Japan defeated Russia in the Russo-Japanese War of 1904-1905, Korea became a Japanese protectorate and ceded control of its foreign affairs to Japan. One of the sources of friction between Korea and China had been a growing contest over the boundary. Chinese settlers arriving in the Tumen region in the 1880s discovered large numbers of Koreans already residing there. Chinese migrants complained to the local government that Koreans illegally occupied Chinese lands; Koreans argued that they were in fact on Korean territory. This led to a reconsideration of the 1712 boundary settlement. A series of negotiations in 1885 and 1887 between Qing and Chosôn officials led to a joint examination of the border on Changbai Mountain. The negotiations were inconclusive, with the Chinese insisting that the Mukedeng stele marked the proper boundary, and the Koreans arguing that the Qing emissary had mistaken another tributary for the Tumen River. Qing and Korean officials both claimed jurisdiction over Jiandao for the next twenty-five years.

When Japan took over the border question from Korea in 1905, the Resident-General initially seemed to pursue Korea's claims in the Kando region, even dispatching Japanese police to the area. However, in 1909 Japan entered a new agreement with China that recognized the Chinese definition of the boundary in exchange for economic concessions in Manchuria. The 1909 agreement established the boundary that still exists to this day.[16]

Liberation, Civil Wars, and New/Old Boundaries, 1945-1952

While the geographical boundary between China and North Korea may be fairly straightforward, the demographic boundary is more ambiguous. Nearly one million people of Korean descent live just across the Tumen River from North Korea in the Yanbian Korean Nationality Autonomous Prefecture (*Yanbian Chaoxianzu Zizhizhou*) of China's Jilin Province. The ethnic Koreans of Yanbian comprise approximately half of the 1.9 million Koreans in China, who constitute the 14th largest of China's fifty-five officially recognized minority nationalities.[17]

Migration in the Japanese colonial period brought one major demographic change to the China-Korean border region: the settlement of some two million immigrants from Korea in territory once claimed by the Qing empire, incorporated into the state of Manchukuo by the Japanese between 1932 and 1945, and "reclaimed" after the end of World War II first by the ROC, then by the PRC. Approximately half of these migrants remained in China in the post-liberation period, most of them residing in the Jiandao region—now being called "Yanbian."[18] By 1945, many of the Koreans had been there for well over a generation and had established their livelihoods there, with nothing to return to on the Korean side of the border. Others feared the uncertainty of circumstances in Korea under the joint Soviet-American occupation. As the Chinese Communist Party (CCP) asserted control of the region, many local Koreans were attracted to the communists' promises of farmland and ethnic cooperation between Koreans and Han Chinese.[19]

Between the end of World War II in August 1945 and the outbreak of the Korean War in June 1950, there was a great deal of relatively unimpeded movement across the Sino-Korean boundary, especially Koreans returning to the peninsula from China. The returning Koreans were mostly farmers, workers, and soldiers; the latter included Korean veterans of the Chinese civil war who would become the core of the Korean People's Army (KPA).[20] The Chinese and Korean communists had a history of close cooperation, going back to the anti-Japanese guerrilla struggles of the early 1930s. Kim Il Sung himself, and many other top leaders in the North Korean military, party, and government, had been members of the CCP before 1945. These CCP-Koreans were experienced guerrilla fighters. Groups of ethnic Korean communists had fought in Manchuria and with Mao's forces in Yanan; among the units that continued operations after the end of World War II was the Yi Hong-gwang Detachment, founded in Manchuria in February 1946, and absorbed into the KPA when the North Korean army was established in February 1948.[21] As many as 100,000 Korean soldiers from North Korea went to Northeast China in 1947-1949 to assist the Chinese communists in their civil war, creating a substantial "Korean Volunteer Army" (*Chosŏn ŭiyonggun*, KVA).[22] KVA members in turn became the leading officers and crack troops of the North Korean Army. U.S. military intelligence estimated in early 1947 that at least 80 percent of the officers in the North Korean security forces at the time were veterans of the Chinese civil war.[23]

The Koreans who remained in Manchuria after liberation in 1945 soon were caught up in the renewed civil war between the Chinese Communist Party and Chiang Kai-shek's Nationalist Party (Kuomintang or KMT). The CCP, with its promises of ethnic inclusion, drew more Korean support than did the KMT's more Han Chinese-centered Chinese nationalism. Local CCP administration was led by a mixed group of Han Chinese and ethnic Koreans. Manchuria would be a critical battleground in the Chinese civil war, and the support of the ethnic Koreans in the region, including many veterans of the anti-Japanese guerrilla struggles of the

1930s, made an important contribution to the Communist victory in Manchuria, and thus in China as a whole.[24]

Kim Il Sung began requesting the return of KVA soldiers to Korea in January 1950—around the time Stalin gave approval for a North Korean invasion—and by June 1950 over half of the entire North Korean army consisted of former KVA, as were more than two-thirds of the KPA cultural cadres.[25] When the Chinese intervened to defend North Korea against the Americans in October 1950, using a "Volunteer Army" of their own, it was partly out of reciprocity for Korean assistance to the Chinese communists.[26]

The DPRK, established in September 1948, and the PRC, established in October 1949, retained the China-Korea boundary as set forth in the 1909 Qing-Japanese agreement. With the outbreak of the Korean War, a conflict known in China as the "Resist-America, Aid-Korea War" (*Kangmei Yuanchao Zhanzheng*) the residents of Yanbian, both Han and ethnic Korean, fully supported the North Korean side and eastern Manchuria became a key staging ground for the training and dispatch of Chinese People's Volunteer (CPV) troops who intervened in Korean in the fall of 1950.[27] On 3 September 1952, the PRC established the Yanbian Korean Nationality Autonomous Region (*Yanbian Chaoxianzu Zizhiqu*), a provincial-level body. Yanbian was administratively downgraded to an "Autonomous Prefecture" (*zizhizhou*) within China's Jilin Province in 1955.

The establishment of Yanbian as a Korean nationality area, negotiated between the Chinese and North Korean governments, clarified the status of Koreans in the region as Chinese citizens. Since that time, North Korea has never claimed political sovereignty over the Koreans in the Yanbian area, and unlike some other minority nationalities in border regions of China (e.g., Tibet, Xinjiang, Inner Mongolia) Chinese-Koreans on the border with North Korea have never demanded independence from China or incorporation into their ancestral "homeland." Since the end of the Korean War there have been several spikes in migration across the border. Many ethnic Koreans fled economic hardship, ethnic discrimination and political unrest in China during the Great Leap Forward in the late 1950s and early 1960s and the Cultural Revolution in the late 1960s, settling in North Korea. Since the North Korean famine of the late 1990s, hundreds of thousands of North Koreans have entered China, some temporarily and others as permanent migrants. All of this population movement remains illegal, however, and the border itself is not challenged on either side.

At the time the autonomous prefecture was established, some 60 percent of its residents were ethnic Koreans, although the proportion of Koreans was much higher in the countryside and most Han Chinese resided in the cities. Like other "autonomous" regions and areas in the PRC, Yanbian maintained a policy of official bilingualism, education in the language and culture of the local minority group, and local self-government, but no significant "autonomy" in a political sense. Over time, Han Chinese immigration into the Yanbian region has shifted the ethnic balance, reducing the ethnic Korean population to about 30 percent, while the degree of Korean assimilation into mainstream Han Chinese culture has accelerated.[28]

Contemporary States and the Border

For most of the period between the end of the Korean War in 1953 and the North Korean famine of the 1990s, the Sino-Korean border was carefully monitored and strictly controlled on both sides, with very little unofficial population movement across the border. Exceptions to this included times of limited illegal migration of ethnic Koreans fleeing China for North Korea during the Anti-Rightist Campaign and Great Leap Forward of the late 1950s and early 1960s, and the Cultural Revolution of the late 1960s and 1970s.[29] The Cultural Revolution period in particular was a trying one for all ethnic minorities in China, Koreans included. This was also a time of great sensitivity on the Sino-Korean border, as PRC-North Korean relations reached a nadir. China's Red Guards criticized North Korean leader Kim Il Sung as a "fat revisionist" and "Korea's Khrushchev." Confrontations between border guards led to skirmishes and even exchanges of gunfire, although it is not known whether there were any casualties. For a period of time during the Cultural Revolution, the border region was put under martial law.[30]

After 1970, Sino-North Korean tensions abated both on the border and in the overall relationship between the two states. At the present time, the Sino-Korean boundary region is rather sparsely populated on both sides, with the exception of the urban centers of Dandong in China and Sinuiju in North Korea, which face each other across the Yalu River near the Yellow Sea. Changbai/Paektu Mountain, a dormant volcano some 8,858 feet (2,700 meters) high with a crater lake (Tianchi or "Heaven Lake") at its peak, is one of the most rugged and spectacular mountains in Northeast Asia. The mountain figures in the creation myths of several Northeast Asian cultures, including the Manchus and Koreans, and is home to many rare flora and fauna. Paektu Mountain is also central to the "myth" of North Korea's founding leader Kim Il Sung and his son and successor Kim Jong Il, who was allegedly born at a secret guerilla camp on the mountain in 1942 during his father's armed struggle against the Japanese.[31] In 1979, the United Nations Educational, Scientific and Cultural Organization (UNESCO) designated a Changbaishan Biosphere Reserve on the Chinese side of the Korean border.[32]

Following the signing of the 1961 Sino-DPRK Treaty of Friendship, Cooperation and Mutual Assistance, the two sides negotiated on the details of the boundary that had been left unresolved since the Korean War. A secret agreement signed in 1963 divided Mount Paektu at the summit, giving three-fifths of Tianchi Lake to North Korea and two-fifths to China. The two countries agreed to joint management and use of the Yalu and Tumen rivers, although China conceded 80 percent of the islands in the two rivers to North Korea. China also conceded 90 percent control over the mouth of the Yalu to the DPRK, in exchange for free navigation rights. The central government of China presumably made such concessions to North Korea in order to offset the influence of the Soviet Union, at a time of intense Sino-Soviet rivalry over the DPRK, despite protests of local Chinese authorities in Jilin and Liaoning provinces.[33] Although territorial control has not changed since the 1963 agreement, the two sides negotiated a new agreement on joint management of border ports in October 2000.[34]

The Russo-Korean border along the Yalu is also an issue of concern for China. The Russia-Qing 1860 Treaty of Beijing deprived China of access to the Sea of Japan; although China has navigation rights to the final stretch of the Tumen, as a result of agreements between the PRC and Russia in the 1990s and early 2000s, Jilin is a landlocked province. Furthermore, the mouth of Tumen is relatively shallow and difficult to navigate. For a time, the UN-sponsored Tumen River Area Development Project (TRADP—now called the Greater Tumen Initiative, or GTI), established in 1994, raised hopes for multilateral cooperation in developing the Tumen River region and incorporating North Korea, Northeast China, Mongolia, and the Russian Far East more fully into the advanced economies of South Korea and Japan.[35] Among other the things, GTI could be linked to North Korea's Najin-Sonbong Special Economic Zone (SEZ), the first free trade zone established in the DPRK, opened in 1991. So far, neither the Tumen River project nor the Najin-Sonbong SEZ has lived up to its early promise. The GTI exists largely on paper, and Najin-Sonbong remains an economic backwater with little outside investment or internal development.

Somewhat more progress has been made at the western end of the border, where the North Korean city of Sinuiju and the Chinese city of Dandong face each other across the mouth of the Yalu. In 2002, North Korea declared Sinuiju and the area around it a Special Administrative Region (SAR), modeled after the Chinese SARs of Hong Kong and Macao, which would be opened to free trade and would have its own laws and administration distinct from the rest of North Korea. The Chinese-Dutch businessman Yang Bin was appointed the first governor of Sinuiju SAR, but was arrested by Chinese authorities for tax evasion before he could take office. The SAR project has languished since that time, but Dandong has rapidly developed and Chinese-North Korean trade thrives across the border.

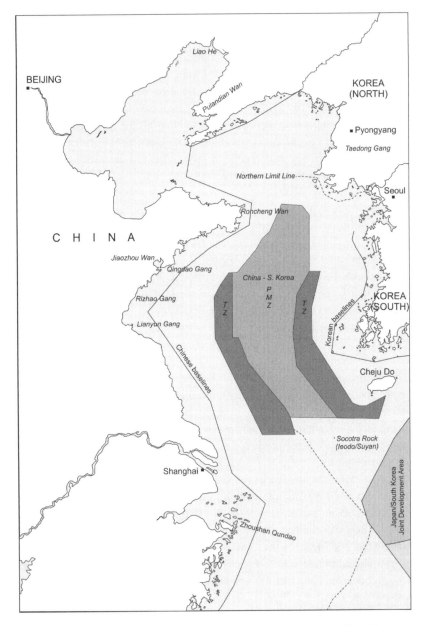

Map 8.2: Maritime Claims and Joint Arrangements in the Yellow Sea

The potential maritime boundary has also been an occasional source of contention between China and North Korea. Overlapping maritime claims have led to disputes over fishing rights. Although neither side has made this a public dispute, fishing and extraction rights in the Yellow Sea have yet to be settled between the two sides.[36] China and South Korea have similar overlapping maritime claims further south in the Yellow Sea. Despite the absence of a maritime boundary agreement for this area, however, in 2001 the two sides moved to manage a key source of friction in their maritime relations by establishing a joint fishing zone in the central part of the Yellow Sea.[37] This agreement provides for a central provisional measures zone (PMZ) and two flanking transitional zones (TZs) (see Map 8.2). After a four year period the TZs were incorporated into the EEZs of the countries nearest to them. These joint arrangements are without prejudice to the delimitation of maritime boundaries between China and Korea. While they have helped to reduce bilateral friction over fishing issues it is notable that enforcement within the joint fishing zone is on a flag-state basis (that is, Chinese fishing vessels may only be apprehended by the Chinese authorities and Korean fishing boats by the Korean authorities). South Korea and China also disagree over ownership of Socotra rock (Ieodo in Korean, and Suyan in Chinese) in the East China Sea.

Illegal migration has also become an issue of bilateral and international concern in the past decade. Whereas migration across the Sino-Korean border during the Cold War period largely consisted of ethnic Koreans crossing into North Korea, since the North Korean famine of the 1990s the population flow has been almost entirely in the other direction, with tens of thousands of North Koreans moving illegally to China. Estimates of the number of such refugees vary widely, as many come across the Tumen River into the Yanbian Korean Autonomous Prefecture and blend in relatively easily with the local Korean-speaking population. Although it is well known that many of these refugees face political repression at home and severe punishment if they return to North Korea, China does not recognize the North Korean migrants as political refugees and has refused to allow the United Nations High Commissioner for Refugees to make a determination of the refugee status of the recently-arrived North Koreans. Instead, the PRC considers such people economic migrants and periodically cracks down on the North Korean refugees, sometimes in cooperation with the North Korean security forces, deporting any uncovered migrants back to North Korea.[38]

Conclusions

Since the founding of the DPRK in 1948 and of the PRC a year later in 1949, boundary and territorial issues have been relatively muted. What disputes arose were generally resolved quietly and behind the scenes. In the Cold War decades, ideological solidarity, close political and economic ties, and Chinese concern with Soviet rivalry over influence in North Korea inhibited conflict over the two countries' mutual border. In the post-Cold War years, China's strategic interests and North Korea's increasing economic dependence on China have also been a restraining factor in boundary disputes.

Conversely, while there has been some cross-border economic cooperation, major projects such as the Sinuiju SAR and the Greater Tumen Initiative have made relatively little progress. For China, probably the biggest issue of the North Korean border is a negative one: how to keep North Korean refugees out. For the DPRK, a country fiercely jealous of its sovereignty and deeply suspicious of the outside world—even of China, its only ally—all national boundaries are "hard" and movement across them is preferably kept to a minimum. China's fear of being flooded by North Korean refugees in the event of instability in the DRPK is an important factor behind its support for the DPRK, and helps explain Beijing's willingness to overlook North Korea's generally provocative behavior toward the outside world.

In fact, China's ability to influence events in North Korea is severely limited. Should ongoing economic hardship and the current leadership transition lead to unexpected changes in North Korea, perhaps even a change in the regime itself, China's cross-border relations—whether through a deeper Chinese penetration into Korea, or by new and more open disputes over the boundary, or in some other ways not yet foreseen—may also be transformed. Should Korea once more become a unified state, this change could be even more profound, with a renewed Korean nationalist interest in renegotiating fishing and water rights with the PRC. Unresolved overlapping claims to maritime jurisdiction, and thus valuable marine resources, in the Yellow Sea are a potential source of friction between China and Korea, although China and South Korea have moved to moderate such tensions through the establishment of a joint fishing zone in 2001. Ultimately the Sino-Korean border established by Kangxi in 1712, by the Japanese in 1909, and by means of the as-yet secret Sino-DPRK treaty in 1963, might be viewed very differently by the leaders of a newly reunified Korea.

Notes

1. Daniel Gomà Pinilla, "Border Disputes between China and North Korea," *China Perspectives* [Online], 52, March-April 2004, http://chinaperspectives.revues.org/806 [Accessed on 31 October 2011].
2. Peter Hays Gries, "The Koguryo Controversy, National Identity, and Sino-Korean Relations Today," *EAST ASIA* Vol. 22, No. 4 (Winter 2005), 3-17.

3. Andre Schmid, *Korea between Empires, 1895–1919* (New York: Columbia University Press, 2002), 273-275; Andrew Schmid, "Rediscovering Manchuria: Sin Ch'aeho and the Politics of Territorial History in Korea," *Journal of Asian Studies,* Vol. 56, No. 1 (February 1997), 26-46.

4. For a general historical overview of the Tokdo/Takeshima controversy, see Mark Selden, "Small Islets, Enduring Conflict: Dokdo, Korea-Japan Colonial Legacy and the United States," *Asia-Pacific Journal,* Vol. 9, Issue 17, No. 2 (25 April 2011).

5. Although the commanderies were originally established by Han Chinese governments, Korean historians tend to see them as part of Korean history, somewhat like Roman Londinium in British history. See Hyung Il Pai, *Constructing "Korean" Origins: A Critical Review of Archaeology, Historiography, and Racial Myth in Korean State-Formation Theories* (Cambridge: Harvard University Asia Center, 2000).

6. For a wide-ranging historical overview of the relations among Chinese, Korean, and Manchurian states in pre-modern times, see Gari Ledyard, "Yin and Yang in the China-Korea-Manchuria Triangle, " in Morris Rossabi, ed. *China Among Equals: The Middle Kingdom and Its neighbors, 10th – 14th Centuries* (Berkeley: University of California Press, 1983), 313-353.

7. Ibid., 322.

8. Gari Ledyard, "Cartography in Korea," in J.B. Harley and David Woodward, eds., *The History of Cartography, Volume Two, Book Two: Cartography in the Traditional East and Southeast Asian Societies* (Chicago: University of Chicago Press, 1994), 290.

9. Ledyard, "Yin and Yang," 325.

10. Ledyard, "Cartography in Korea."

11. Schmid, *Korea Between Empires,* 206-207.

12. George A. Lensen masterfully covers the late 19th century diplomatic competition over the region in *Balance of Intrigue: International Rivalry in Korea and Manchuria, 1884–1899* (Tallahassee: University of Florida Press, 1982).

13. Alyssa Park, "A Borderland Beyond: Korean Migrants and the Creation of a Modern Boundary Between Korea and Russia, 1860-1937," Ph.D. Dissertation, Columbia University, 2009.

14. Henry G. Schwartz, *The Minorities of Northern China: A Survey* (Bellingham: Western Washington University Press, 1982), 207.

15. Prasenjit Duara, *Sovereignty and Authenticity: Manchukuo and the East Asian Modern* (Lanham, MD: Rowman & Littlefield, 2003), 44; Adam McKeown, "Global Migration, 1846-1940," *Journal of World History,* Vol. 15, No. 2 (June 2004).

16. Schmid, *Korea Between Empires,* 215.

17. Lee Kwang-kyu, *Overseas Koreans* (Seoul: Jimoondang, 2000), 45-48.

18. Sun Chunri, "The Formation of Korean Areas in Yanbian, Jilin Province," *Minzu Yanjiu,* (January 1980), 86-87.

19. Chae-Jin Lee, *China's Korean Minority: The Politics of Ethnic Education* (Boulder: Westview Press, 1986), 53-55.

20. Bruce Cumings, *The Origins of the Korean War, Volume Two: The Roaring of the Cataract, 1947-1950* (Princeton: Princeton University Press, 1990), 446.

21. *Ri Hong-gwang chidae* [The Yi Hong-gwang Detachment] (Shenyang: Liaoning minzu chubanshe, 1986), 16; Yi Hong-gwang was the name of a Korean guerrilla killed in Manchuria in 1935.

22. United States Department of State, *Foreign Relations of the United States 1949*, Vol. 7 (Washington, DC: United States Government Printing Office, 1976), Part 2, 974.

23. National Archive and Record Administration, United States Army, Record Group 319, *Intelligence Summaries—North Korea* (ISNK), No. 31 (15 – 28 February 1947), 4.

24. Steven Levine, *Anvil of Victory: The Communist Revolution in Manchuria* (New York: Columbia University Press, 1987).

25. Nie Rongzhen, *Inside the Red Star: The Memoirs of Marshal Nie Rongzhen* (Beijing: New World Press, 1988), 642-664; Cumings, 446; U.S. National Archive and Record Administration, Record Group 242, "Record Seized by US Military Forces in Korea," shipping advice 2009, item 9/120. KPA Cultural Cadre Bureau, *Munhwa kanbu sŏngwŏn t'onggyep'yo* [Statistical Table of Cultural Cadre Members]. 15 December 1949 ("top secret").

26. Cumings, 363, 357-364.

27. See for example Hong Xuezhi, *Kang-Mei Yuan-Chao zhanzheng huiyi* [Recollections of the Resist-America Aid-Korea War] (Beijing: Jiefangjun wenyi chubanshe, 1991).

28. Andrei Lankov, "The Gentle Decline of the 'Third Korea'," *Asia Times*, 16 August 2007.

29. Lee, *China's Korean Minority*, 79-91.

30. Ibid., 90.

31. The "secret guerilla camp" was established in North Korean media as Kim Jong Il's birthplace in the early 1980s, when the younger Kim emerged as his father's successor for political leadership. Historical records outside of North Korea suggest Kim Jong Il was born near Khabarovsk in Russia, where his father had joined a brigade of the Soviet Army during World War II. Charles Armstrong, "Centering the Periphery: Manchurian Exile(s) and the North Korean State," *Korean Studies*, Vol. 19 (1995), 1-16.

32. On the Changbaishan (Changbai Mountain) Biosphere Reserve, see http://www.unesco.org/mabdb/br/brdir/directory/biores.asp?mode=gen&code=CPR +01 [Accessed on 31 October 2011].

33. Chae-Jin Lee, *China and Korea: Dynamic Relations* (Stanford: Hoover Institution, 1996), 99-100.

34. Goam Pinilla.

35. Andre Marton, Terry McGee, and Donald G. Paterson, "Northeast Asian Economic Cooperation and the Tumen River Area Development Project," *Pacific Affairs*, Vol. 68, No. 1 (Spring 1995), 8-33.

36. Goam Pinilla.

37. The agreement entered into force on 30 June 2001. See S.P. Kim, "The UN Convention on the Law of the Sea and New Fisheries Agreements in North East Asia," *Marine Policy*, Vol. 27 (2003), 97-109.

38. Yoonok Chang, Stephan Haggard and Marcus Noland, "Migration Experiences of North Korean Refugees: Survey Evidence from China," Peterson Institute for International Economics, Working Paper 08-4, March 2008.

Map 9: Kyrgyzstan's Border with China

9

Kyrgyzstan: China's Regional Playground?

Erica Marat

During 1999, China and Kyrgyzstan settled their dispute along their 533 mile (858 km) border, with Bishkek ceding almost 480 square miles (1,240 km²) of land to Beijing.[1] Domestic opposition over border delimitation between the PRC and the Kyrgyz Republic was one of the defining issues for Kyrgyzstan President Askar Akayev, who ruled from 1990 until 2005. In 2001, rumors surfaced claiming that Akayev had reaped personal financial gains from the deal.[2] On 17 March 2002, Akayev ordered police to quell protests in Aksy, a village in southern Kyrgyzstan. These protests were organized by supporters of MP Azimbek Beknazarov, who had been arrested for opposing the president's 1999 agreement. Six demonstrators were shot dead during clashes with the police.[3]

The incident provoked an uproar in Kyrgyzstan and energized the opposition movement. It also forced Akayev to distance his regime from opposition forces. Akayev's popularity at home plummeted in the years following the Aksy shooting. Squeezed out of the country's political system, parliamentary candidates mobilized crowds to challenge Akayev's regime in 2005. Choosing not to shoot at civilian demonstrators this time around, the president fled the country. Although China's role in Akayev's political demise was indirect, the 2002 incident was the first major signal of China's growing political and economic role in Kyrgyzstan and across Central Asia in general.

Since Kyrgyzstan resolved its border disputes with China, the country's economic relations with Beijing have grown quickly, pulling the country away from its traditional ties to Moscow. Even though Beijing has never directly challenged other regional players' influence in Kyrgyzstan, Russia and the United States have been wary of China's potential political leverage in Kyrgyzstan. Russia, in particular, has tried to limit China's influence in Kyrgyzstan through regional organizations such as the Collective Security Treaty Organization and the Russia-Belarus-Kazakhstan Customs Union. U.S. experts, in the meantime, have advised Washington to demand that China develop its economic relations within the framework of international institutions, rather than rely on backroom deals with Kyrgyzstan's political elites.[4]

Historical Background of Sino-Kyrgyz Relations

Kyrgyzstan belongs to several multinational organizations that have impacted its relations with China. The Collective Security Treaty Organization (CSTO) was founded in 1992 by Russia, Belarus, Armenia, Kazakhstan, Kyrgyzstan, Tajikistan, and Uzbekistan. This organization is primarily driven by its members' common Soviet history, which could allow for further expansion of its functions beyond military cooperation. As such, the CSTO has sought to strengthen the ideological similarities among its members by promoting the Kremlin's projects as part of the organization's platform. In 1996, the Shanghai Five was created, which included China, Kazakhstan, Kyrgyzstan, Russia, and Tajikistan.

In 1999, China and Kyrgyzstan were some of the first Shanghai Five members to settle their disputed borders. Bilateral negotiations resulted in a 1996 treaty, ratified by Kyrgyzstan's parliament, which agreed to delimit their mutual 533 mile (858 km) border. In 1999, a secret amendment to this earlier treaty was signed in which Bishkek ceded to Beijing 480 square miles (1,240 km^2) of its territory. The process of demarcating the new border was constantly disrupted by protesters in Kyrgyzstan claiming that the parliament never ratified this amendment.[5] President Askar Akayev's government eventually collapsed, in part due to this unrest. After the new government finally quelled the protests, border demarcation continued and was reportedly completed on 14 July 2009, with China ceding "part of the Khan Tengri Peak located in the mountains of Tien Shan while Kyrgyzstan ceded Uzengi-Kush, a mountainous area located south of the Issyk Kul region."[6]

Meanwhile, during 2001 the Shanghai Five was changed to the Shanghai Cooperation Organization (SCO) with the addition of Uzbekistan.[7] In August 2007, the SCO held its largest annual summit to date in Bishkek, attended by official representatives of 12 countries. Participants included the presidents of the SCO's six member states: Chinese President Hu Jintao, Kazakh President Nursultan Nazarbayev, Kyrgyz President Kurmanbek Bakiyev, Russian President Vladimir Putin, Tajik President Emomali Rahmon, and Uzbek President Islam Karimov. They were joined by high-ranking officials from the SCO's observer members: Afghanistan's President Hamid Karzai, Indian Minister of Oil and Gas Murli Deora, and Pakistan's Foreign Minister Khurshid Kasuri. In addition, Iranian President Mahmoud Ahmadinejad, Mongolian President Nambaryn Enkhbayar, and Turkmen President Gurbanguly Berdimukhamedov attended as distinguished guests. UN Under-Secretary-General Lynn Pascoe attended as well.

All of the participants expressed their satisfaction with the SCO's development and hoped that the organization would continue to further consolidate in the "Shanghai spirit." The SCO members often appeal to the Shanghai spirit, a concept meant to represent a shared identity within the organization. However, the concept's meaning is unclear, and every member can interpret it differently. From the organization's early days, the concept has caused confusion, and it remains a rather abstract notion in SCO activities. Some analysts have focused on political similarities, interpreting the phrase as China's attempt to promote authoritarian norms of governance.[8] Other interpretations are social and cultural. The Shanghai spirit becomes particularly ambiguous when SCO leaders insist that the organization unites the world's four major religions—Christianity, Confucianism, Hinduism, and Islam. The SCO has also supported cultural cooperation ahead of the Beijing 2008 Summer Olympics and the upcoming 2014 Winter Olympics in Sochi, Russia. Furthermore, Kazakhstan is planning to organize a conference on cultural exchanges among the SCO members, while China already hosts a Silk Road Program that promotes inter-confessional cooperation with neighboring states.

Energy cooperation and security issues were the 2007 summit's main focus. Nazarbayev invited the SCO observer states and distinguished guests to participate in the organization's energy collaboration. Raising another regional issue, Karzai called on the SCO member states to prioritize the fight against the drug economy. Putin was satisfied with the summit's productivity and promised to invest $2 billion into Kyrgyzstan's hydropower sector. Ironically, Hu's speech was not translated from Chinese because the Kyrgyz side had forgotten to provide an interpreter. Although Russian and Chinese are the SCO's official languages, the majority of the organization's members and guests are more familiar with Russian. Therefore, Hu's speech remained inaccessible to most of the summit's participants.

The summit adopted a "Bishkek Declaration" focusing on four main themes. First, member states agreed on the "strengthening of strategic stability, non-proliferation weapons of mass destruction" and preventing the use of weapons against "objects in the cosmic space." Second, the declaration emphasized the importance of the struggle against the "three evils" of terrorism, separatism, and extremism. Third, the SCO agreed to coordinate the activities of a special Contact Group dealing with the narcotics industry in Afghanistan. Lastly, the SCO member states agreed that energy cooperation should be the basis for "sustainable economic growth and security." The Bishkek Declaration postulates that a "reliable and mutually-beneficial partnership in various fields of the energy sector will be conducive to the provision of security and stability on the SCO territory, as well as in the global perspective." The declaration specifies that energy dialogues will include producer, transit, and consumer countries.[9]

The summit also endorsed a "Long-term Treaty of Good-neighborliness, Friendship, and Cooperation." However, the new treaty largely duplicates the existing treaties on "Eternal Friendship" adopted by the Central Asian states in the early 1990s. Central Asian leaders have often referred to the Eternal Friendship treaties at official meetings; however, they proved ineffective when Uzbekistan decided to mine its borders with Kyrgyzstan and Tajikistan.

In terms of mutual security, the SCO has become a major international player in the Central Asian region and beyond.[10] Since 2002 the SCO has sought to conduct annual collective anti-terrorism military exercises, with Russia and China providing most personnel and armaments. Collective military exercises, such as "Peace Mission," represent a central part of the SCO functioning, provide a sense of institutional evolution, help consolidate the organization's agenda, and foster military development among the organizations' member states. The SCO's annual anti-terrorist exercises are also designed to train a joint force to deal with security threats arising on the territories of its member states. Collective military activities have particularly grown since 2003, involving greater numbers of troops and more sophisticated technologies. SCO exercises have used practice scenarios such as a mass uprising similar to the one in Andijan, Uzbekistan, in May 2005, and violent regime change such as that which occurred in Kyrgyzstan during 2005.

Annual military drills have been the hallmark of the SCO; nearly the entire budget of the organization is spent on staging joint military exercises and organizing annual security summits. However, military drills still remain more window dressing than substantive. Large-scale collective military maneuvers and the technology involved do not appear to align with the organizational goals of fighting transnational threats such as organized crime and ethnic separatism, which require smaller-scale military and policing operations. Indeed, the previous experience of multilateral exercises demonstrates that the SCO member states prefer to utilize their conventional military equipment and personnel, rather than developing new skills in police activities or intelligence exchange.

Since 2007, SCO members have also explored opportunities for energy cooperation, as well as expressed interest in consolidating their efforts in Afghanistan. Cooperation in the energy sector includes the construction of new pipelines linking Turkmenistan, Kazakhstan, Russia, and China. The organization's two major members—China and Russia—have seen their interests converge in some key issues. Arguably, both countries share a common concern with secessionist movements on their territories. Moscow's experience with secessionist Caucasian rebels and Beijing's strained relations with Taiwan and counter-secessionist campaigns in Xinjiang Uyghur Autonomous Region and Tibet Autonomous Region form a common interest between the two countries. Both partners also seek to increase loyalty among the Central Asian states.

China, although the key driving force behind the SCO, is the sole member that was never part of the Soviet Union. The shared Soviet background, along with widespread knowledge of the Russian language, greatly simplifies communication between Russia and the Central Asian members. China remains an unknown and unpredictable partner for the post-Soviet states. To a large degree, however, it is through the medium of the SCO that China exerts influence over Kyrgyzstan.

Sino-Kyrgyz Economic Cooperation

The 1999 border agreement between China and Kyrgyzstan paved the way for increased economic cooperation. Bilateral economic cooperation picked up noticeably starting in 2003-2004 and had almost tripled by the late 2000s, reaching $1.6 billion and making up 94 percent of Kyrgyzstan's cross-border commerce.[11] According to other estimates, cross-border commerce reached $10 billion in 2009. Kyrgyzstan's two largest bazaars—Dordoi in the country's north and Kara-Suu in the south—were largely stocked with Chinese wares; 75 percent and 85 percent of the goods traded, respectively.[12]

Since the mid-1990s Beijing has provided soft loans to Kyrgyzstan. That is, the Chinese government allocates low-interest credits to the Kyrgyz government on the condition that Chinese employees lead most of the related construction projects. For example, in 1994 China invested $7.4 million into a paper manufacturing plant in which the majority of workers were Chinese. But despite an additional $14.7 million investment in 1998 by the Chinese side, the factory still declared bankruptcy.[13] China also invested $70 million to build a cement plant in southern Kyrgyzstan. The plant is expected to generate up to 2,500 tons of cement a day and export its products to neighboring countries.[14]

Thanks to its membership in the World Trade Organization since 1998, Kyrgyzstan has become an important transit zone for Chinese goods going to neighboring countries. Kyrgyzstan is the only Central Asian state in the WTO. Despite Bishkek's new status as an important player in Sino-Central Asian relations, however, Sino-Kyrgyz economic ties grew mostly in the trade sector, while direct investment and financial cooperation remain insignificant.

To a large extent, this can be explained by Kyrgyzstan's unpredictable political situation. In early 2010 President Kurmanbek Bakiyev's son Maksim visited Beijing to strengthen economic relations with China. At a meeting with Chen Jian, the Chinese Assistant Minister of Commerce, Maksim Bakiyev expressed strong interest in building links with China in finance, energy, mineral resources, and agriculture. According to the younger Bakiyev, "The progress of China, especially in the financial crisis sphere, excites admiration."[15] However, his plans were interrupted when his father's regime collapsed in April 2010.[16]

China's economic expansion has generated fears in Kyrgyzstan about the potential demographic impact on the country. It is estimated that as many as 100,000 Chinese entrepreneurs are currently working in Kyrgyzstan, mostly in local bazaars.[17] The

Kyrgyz government does not know the exact number of Chinese migrants, which explains the wide range of estimates. Instances of brutal treatment of Chinese laborers at the hands of Kyrgyzstan's law-enforcement agencies have been reported in the past few years.[18] Chinese merchants and labor migrants live in segregated areas in Bishkek, rarely mixing with local residents. The largest Chinese market on the outskirts of Bishkek is known to be a "city within a city," with its own residential facilities, food industry, hospital, and mosque, since most of the inhabitants are Muslim.

The Central Asian Railroad and Energy Projects

Another major development is a planned railway link with China. In the late 1990s, the Chinese government opened official talks with Kyrgyzstan and Uzbekistan on the construction of a railroad that would connect all three countries. The idea was born almost simultaneously with the Shanghai Five when the organization was formed in 1996. The railroad project has been repeatedly discussed at SCO meetings. Although a timetable for the railroad's construction is still unclear, the project is likely to proceed in the foreseeable future.

In 2009, Beijing and Bishkek agreed that China's National Machinery Import & Export Corporation would be responsible for constructing the railroad, with the Chinese side providing equipment and labor.[19] The estimated construction cost is over $2 billion, and it will take roughly 12 years to become profitable.[20] If fully constructed, the 166 mile (268 km) railroad would considerably shorten the current 560 mile (900 km) connection between China and the rest of Central Asia and provide better access to the sea for the landlocked Central Asian countries. Potentially, Iran and Turkey might also join the project. The railroad would help connect East Asia with Europe, since it would take about one week to transport cargo from the Chinese Pacific coast to the European market instead of current time of several weeks to even a few months. Lacking its own efficient railroad system, Kyrgyzstan would greatly benefit from this project. The railroad would connect Naryn oblast with Osh oblast and possibly Issyk Kul as well.[21] In addition, Kyrgyzstan would profit from cargo transit levies.

Initially, planners considered two main options, a southern and northern route. The first option would link China and Uzbekistan through southern parts of Kyrgyzstan, while the northern option entails crossing Kyrgyzstan's heartland. Tashkent lobbied for the northern route, but Bishkek regarded the southern route as more attractive, since it might provide much needed over-land infrastructure within the country.[22] After continuous negotiations, all parties agreed to build the southern route. In 2008, Beijing projected construction to be finished by the end of 2010.[23] Yet, several unresolved issues have kept the project at the planning stage. For example, the terms of the contract between China and the Central Asian countries remain ambiguous. Beijing is clearly interested in receiving access to Kyrgyzstan's minerals in exchange for railroad construction. Since both the Chinese and Kyrgyz governments lack transparency, details of this rail-for-minerals agreement are hidden from the public.

Although the Russian government has not voiced any direct criticism of the railroad, Moscow has repeatedly said that the China-Central Asia railroad is unlikely to become a serious rival to the Trans-Siberian line.[24] Already, railroad links have been expanding between Central Asian countries and Russian cities. Another obstacle is getting all three countries to agree on a standard track width. The Chinese insist on building a narrow track to meet European, rather than Russian, standards. Uzbekistan has already begun adapting its rails to meet international standards, and it is now up to Kyrgyzstan to comply with Beijing's request. Unlike Bishkek, which fully relies on Chinese investment, Tashkent agreed to pay for its own segment of the railroad.

Despite these difficulties, negotiations among China, Kyrgyzstan, and Uzbekistan were ongoing. As the railroad's prospects became clearer two years ago, Chinese investors stepped up activity in cities that will be linked by the railroad. New hotels and shops are already being built to serve future passengers.[25] The new government led by Prime Minister Almazbek Atambayev renewed talks with China's Communications Construction Company and by mid-2010, Beijing and Bishkek agreed to sign the "China-Kyrgyzstan-Uzbekistan" railroad construction agreement.

Similarly complex negotiations have been undertaken to utilize the region's hydropower. Beijing has already shown interest in importing electricity from Kyrgyzstan. In early 2010 Kyrgyzstan's national power company, Natsionalnaia electricheskaia set, and China's Tebian Electric signed a $342 million deal to build the Datka-Kemin 500 kv power transmission lines. This would potentially enable Kyrgyzstan to develop an internal power transmission system and break its dependence on the Central Asia power grid.[26]

Other projects on the table include China's possible investment in the construction of the Kara-Keche coal factory in the country's south and helping to renovate the Bishkek thermal power plant.[27] Both sites are crucial components of the country's energy system. However, their economic viability is less clear and is contingent upon other energy projects in the country. The Bishkek plant also needs to have its Soviet-era infrastructure modernized, but such a project is unlikely to generate revenue due to low electricity and hot water tariffs in Kyrgyzstan and the wider region. Therefore, any energy investment from China will probably generate greater political payoffs than economic profits.

Convergence of Economic Rather Than Political Interests

Chinese officials have expressed interest in continuing to deepen economic ties with Kyrgyzstan by providing economic assistance and training Kyrgyz specialists: "We are interested in developing cooperation with Kyrgyzstan. Our nations benefit from cooperation, it provides security and stability in the region. This [cooperation] also meets the goals and challenges of the Shanghai Cooperation Organization," Chen Jian said in early 2010.[28] Chinese Vice-Premier Zhang Dejiang also acknowledged Kyrgyzstan's support of China's core interests, particularly, "Taiwan and Tibet-related issues, and fighting 'East Turkistan' forces." Zhang promised that China "would always support Kyrgyzstan's efforts for realizing its development and safeguarding national independence, state sovereignty and security."[29]

The Bakiyev regime was able to secure large financial deals thanks to its political ties, rather than on access to the open market. The $2 billion loan from Russia promised in February 2009 and the deal with China were the results of political cooperation. President Bakiyev has further stated that some Kyrgyz companies might be included in the Shanghai Stock Exchange, and both Kyrgyzstan and China have agreed to facilitate opening banks in each other's country.

Russian and Chinese partners are willing to navigate in Kyrgyzstan's corrupt political system without applying any pressure to increase the transparency of either the political or economic conditions. The Kyrgyz government, in turn, has centralized its control over financial institutions, building a system where any major international business deal is brokered through the regime. In this environment, both parties rely on mutually agreeable political decisions, while a competitive market is regarded as a hurdle. Over time, however, differences between China and Russia have become more evident. The most visible of all is their treatment of the West.[30] Russia has been counteracting the presence of foreign powers, particularly the United States, on the territory of Central Asia. In contrast, China generally agrees that the Central Asian states have the right to build their own regional organizations.

On a number of occasions Russia has tried to use the SCO as a platform to voice disagreement with the U.S. presence in Central Asia. The most notorious case was at the Astana summit in 2006, when Russia requested that Kyrgyzstan evict the U.S. military base from its territory. Moscow has also used soft power to press this issue—the Russian mass media regularly condemns Western negative perceptions of the SCO's cooperation with the CSTO, especially after Russia and China conducted the bilateral Peace Mission 2005 exercises in China. Unlike Moscow, however, Beijing was not eager to issue open statements against the United States or the West in general. In fact, the SCO's charter states that the organization is not "directed against other states and international organizations."[31]

In the run-up to the 2007 summit, for example, the Kyrgyz government experienced increasing pressure from Russia to close the U.S. military base at Manas airport. One day prior to the summit, U.S. Secretary of Defense Robert Gates and Assistant Secretary of State for Central and Southern Asia Richard Boucher both visited Bishkek to discuss U.S.-Kyrgyz relations with then-president Kurmanbek Bakiyev, Parliament Speaker Marat Sultanov, and Defense Minister Ismail Isakov. The U.S. officials emphasized the importance of Kyrgyzstan's cooperation with the United States within the international anti-terrorism framework and stressed that the issue of the U.S. military base in Bishkek should not be raised at the SCO summit. Soon after the U.S. delegation departed, Russian Foreign Minister Sergei Lavrov arrived to make Moscow's case to the SCO members.

Yet, Beijing's attempts to oust the U.S. airbase from Kyrgyzstan might be more subtle than Russia's. While Beijing avoided expressing anti-U.S. sentiments publicly, evidence suggests that China may have sought to reduce the American presence through more informal avenues. According to a U.S. State Department cable released by Wikileaks, the Chinese government allegedly offered the Bakiyev regime $3 billion to shut down the U.S. airbase. U.S. Ambassador Tatiana C. Gfoeller confronted Zhang Yannian, China's Ambassador to Kyrgyzstan, about the secret deal. "Visibly flustered, Zhang temporarily lost the ability to speak Russian and began spluttering in Chinese to the silent aide diligently taking notes right behind him," according to the cable.[32] This suggests that both China and Russia pursued similar policy goals in Kyrgyzstan yet used different means to achieve them.

Another important difference between China and Russia is the SCO's relations with Western actors and their differing view of the Central Asian states' autonomy in conducting domestic and international politics. While Russia seeks to be the dominating actor in the region and to reduce the presence of Western countries, China agrees that the Central Asian states have the right to form their own regional organizations. Chinese experts have asserted that, contrary to speculations, the SCO is by no means an anti-American or anti-Western alliance. According to Pan Guang, Head of the SCO Studies Center in Shanghai, China affirms the right of Central Asian states to organize and deal with other states, including Westerns states, while Russia alone opposes such outreach.[33]

Finally, unlike Beijing, Moscow rarely supports economic cooperation within the SCO that doesn't involve Russia's participation. Instead, in 2006 then-Russian President Vladimir Putin suggested establishing an energy club within the SCO framework.[34] This proposal suggests that Russia's interest in establishing a price-coordination mechanism amid uncertainties in the development of gas and oil commercial relations is present in all of the SCO's energy ties. Putin's suggestion was a rather reactive move following the growing energy cooperation between Kazakhstan and China, as well as increased coordination between Turkmenistan and Uzbekistan.

The Russia-Belarus-Kazakhstan Customs Union

In 2009, Bakiyev promised to join a new Russia-led Customs Union (CU), saying that Bishkek could quickly settle the over 10,000 contradictions between the WTO regulations and those of the union. Bakiyev made this pledge at a time when Moscow disapproved of his leadership. Interest in joining the CU continued under the new regime in Kyrgyzstan. In April 2011, Prime Minister Almazbek Atambayev announced that Kyrgyzstan will join the Russia-Belarus-Kazakhstan Customs Union starting from 2012.[35]

As a WTO member for over a decade, Kyrgyzstan has much lower import and export tariffs compared to what the Customs Union has to offer. The WTO helped Kyrgyzstan to diversify its imports, significantly decreasing its dependence on Russia and Kazakhstan. These two moves promoted a local class of small and medium entrepreneurs who import goods from China, Turkey, and India and then sell to traders from neighboring states. According to estimates by the Kyrgyz research institute "Proekt budushchego," the number of traders in Kyrgyzstan benefiting from re-exports has reached 800,000, out of a population of 5.5 million. Russia and Kazakhstan are the primary markets for roughly 90 percent of those traders.[36]

By joining the Customs Union, Kyrgyzstan will, in effect, play by Russia's rules and regulations. Russia's average customs tariff amounts to roughly 10 percent, whereas Kyrgyzstan's is half that amount due to its WTO membership.[37] Russia keeps its import tariffs high and export tariffs low to shield local manufacturers from external competition. For Kyrgyzstan this will mean higher prices for most goods imported from Russia and Kazakhstan. Customs Union membership will also increase prices for commodities imported from Europe and the Middle East, including cars and consumer electronics.

Bakiyev and Atambayev's decision was political rather than economic. Kyrgyzstan is the only Central Asian and CU country with WTO membership. By joining the Customs Union, Kyrgyzstan voluntarily submitted to Russia's stronger political control. Atambayev's announcement came shortly after his deputy, Omurbek Babanov, returned from Moscow. Both Atambayev and Babanov hope to secure the posts of president and prime minister, respectively, during presidential elections in late 2011. Moscow's support would be a huge boost for them.

Growing Security Partnership

Hundreds of military personnel from China and Kyrgyzstan annually participate in exercises designed to protect the border from infiltration by terrorists and extremists.[38] Both countries conduct annual bilateral drills and under the China-led SCO framework. Thanks to such regular drills, the SCO quickly earned a reputation in Kyrgyzstan as a regional structure guaranteeing security. Despite the regularity of such activities, however, the SCO's practical value at times of crisis has been limited.

Almost a decade after being formed, the SCO still struggles to find its own niche as a security actor in Central Asia and Russia. Among other issues, the SCO's paralysis is caused by the continuing competition between its two largest members, China and Russia, and cultural differences because China does not share the common Soviet past that links the other members.[39] The SCO has experienced troubles in formulating its identity and finding common criteria for its existing and prospective member states. The organization's numerous agreements in the security and cultural sectors have not been implemented efficiently. The SCO is based more on bilateral ties between member states than multilateralism.

It is important to note that in June 2010, Moscow turned a deaf ear to the pleas of Kyrgyzstan's provisional government to deploy CSTO troops to help quell the ethnic violence in southern Kyrgyzstan. However, Russia has been actively involved in the region since the violence. Moscow specifically sought to influence Kyrgyzstan's parliamentary elections by supporting favorable candidates.[40] Overall, Kyrgyzstan's crisis provided an opportunity for the United States and Russia to collaborate along the lines of the Obama Administration's "reset" policies. Officials from both Moscow and Washington have emphasized that they have been coordinating their activities in the aftermath of the crisis.

Russia had previously been seeking to gain greater leverage by using the SCO's military arm. The Kremlin had even suggested staging joint military exercises between the SCO and CSTO. However, Chinese experts often note that since the SCO is not a military alliance, it will not cooperate with the CSTO, which declares itself a military alliance. The June 2010 ethnic violence in southern Kyrgyzstan once again demonstrated that the SCO, along with other regional security organizations, is unable to meet the most critical challenges the Central Asian region faces today. To date, the SCO's annual security summits and military drills have failed to prepare its members states to deal with inter-ethnic strife in Kyrgyzstan or the spread of insurgent groups in the Ferghana Valley.

It is important to note that following the Tashkent summit in June 2004, the SCO expanded its activities and established a Regional Anti-Terrorism Structure (RATS) to deal with transnational drug trafficking and insurgencies. Since 2003 the SCO has staged joint military exercises in Russia, Kazakhstan, China, and Uzbekistan. After Uzbekistan evicted the U.S. Karshi-Khanabad airbase from its territory in July 2005 and became a more active player in the organization, the SCO informally emerged as a regional political, security, and economic bloc to counter U.S. interests in the region. Similar to the CSTO, the SCO's mutual pact precludes Western intervention into the Central Asian states, Russia, and China in cases of instability.

However, the SCO chose not to describe the June 2010 events in Kyrgyzstan as instances of terrorism, separatism, or extremism—the main "three evils" the organization has pledged to combat. Unable to stop the spread of violence on its own, Kyrgyzstan's government found it could not turn to the SCO for assistance.[41] Over 450 people reportedly died in the June violence and 110,000 residents fled to neighboring Uzbekistan.[42] During these events the SCO was exposed as a toothless regional security mechanism unwilling to react to crises swiftly. The organization's lack of response once again confirmed that the cooperation advanced under its aegis is primarily political and economic, not military. In particular, SCO members continue to draw support from each other's political recognition, as nearly all of its member states have at one time or another been criticized for embracing features of authoritarianism.[43]

Conclusions

The 1999 Sino-Kyrgyz border agreement, although controversial, appears to have settled all outstanding border claims. Subsequently, the border was successfully demarcated on the ground. By the early 2000s, China and Kyrgyzstan had agreed to negotiate all future border disputes through the SCO. China's growing political and economic influence has fueled concerns, however, that Beijing may attempt to annex additional land from Kyrgyzstan. Allegations that Akayev personally benefited from the 1999 border deal have not been officially confirmed or denied through any investigation by Bishkek. Rumors have spread that Bakiyev initially intended to give up Kyrgyzstan's eastern territories to China as well.

Soon after settling border issues with Kyrgyzstan in 2002, China initiated bilateral border control drills with Bishkek. China's growing presence in Kyrgyzstan over the past decade has stirred hope that it would lead to greater regional security, as well as fears of increased Chinese political influence. Despite settling all border disputes with China, and in spite of its decision to join the WTO, and thereby become an important transit hub for Chinese goods, fears in Kyrgyzstan persist about its eastern neighbor's rapid political expansion. The 2002 incident in Aksy, in which police fatally shot six civilians, marked the beginning of Akayev's decline.

Although China's involvement in the incident was indirect, its actions proved that Beijing was ready to cooperate with the Kyrgyz regime behind closed doors, preferring to put his personal political gain ahead of Kyrgyzstan's national interests. Reports that Beijing allegedly tried to bribe Bakiyev to oust the U.S. base is another example.

As with Russia, China has demonstrated the ability to navigate Kyrgyzstan's corrupt political system without applying sufficient pressure to increase the transparency of either the political or economic conditions in that country. However, China's economic presence has not yet translated into direct political influence. Russia's economic ties with Kyrgyzstan might be fading compared with those of China, but historical and cultural links still pull Kyrgyzstan toward Moscow rather than Beijing. As China's economic presence has increased in Kyrgyzstan, Russia has tried harder to lure that country back into its own orbit. In 2011, for example, Russia and Kyrgyzstan agreed to expand the Moscow-led Customs Union, which could potentially weaken Bishkek's commercial relations with Beijing. More importantly, however, despite China and Russia's rivalry over influence in Kyrgyzstan, neither the SCO nor CSTO was able to meet Kyrgyzstan's security needs during the ethnic conflict in June 2010. Both organizations confirmed their purely declaratory character by failing to answer pleas for help by a weaker member state.

Notes

1. Turat Akimov, "Echo Aksy," *Obshchestvennyi reiting*, 12 December 2002; the amount of land ceded was listed as 1,270 km^2 according to http://www.angelfire. com/rnb/bashiri/Kyrgyzstan/Kyrgyz.html [Accessed on 27 October 2011]. Other sources round it down to 1,200 km^2, see investigation by Russian human rights group Memorial, http://www2.memo.ru/uploads/files/42.pdf; others say Kyrgyzstan gave up roughly 1,000 km^2, see *Eurasia Insight*, http://www.eurasianet.org/ departments/rights/articles/eav031703a.shtml [Accessed on 27 October 2011].

2. Turat Akimov, "Asksy Events in Kyrgyzstan: Anatomy of Political Conflict," *Obshchestvennyi reiting*, 12 March 2002.

3. David Gullette, "Akayev's Legacy in Kyrgyzstan Proving Difficult to Overcome," *Eurasia Insight*, 9 May 2005.

4. "Strengthening Fragile Partnerships: An Agenda for the Future of U.S.-Central Asia Relations," *The Project 2049 Institute*, February 2011, http://www.project2049 .net/documents/strengthening_fragile_relationships_central_asia_feigenbaum.pdf.

5. Alisher Khamidov, "Dispute over China-Kyrgyz Border Demarcation Pits President Vs. Parliament," Eurasianet.org, http://www.eurasianet.org /departments/insight/articles/eav062801.shtml [Accessed on 27 October 2011].

6. "Kyrgyzstan and China Complete Border Demarcation," *International Boundaries Research Unit* (IBRU), 17 July 2009.

7. The SCO also includes three observers—India, Mongolia, and Pakistan—and three special guests—Afghanistan, Iran, and Turkmenistan.

8. Thomas Ambrosio, "Catching the 'Shanghai Spirit': How the Shanghai Cooperation Organization Promotes Authoritarian Norms in Central Asia," *Europe-Asia Studies*, Vol. 60, No. 8 (October 2008).

9. http://www.pircenter.org/kosdata/page_doc/p1540_2.pdf.

10. "SCO Summit Is Held in Tashkent Hu Jintao Attends and Delivers an Important Speech to the Summit," *Ministry of Foreign Affairs of the People's Republic of China,* 11 July 2010, http://www.fmprc.gov.cn/eng/wjdt/wshd /t708530.htm [Accessed on 27 October 2011].

11. Umed Erkinov, "Kyrgyzstan: Is China a Hidden Power in Bishkek?" *Eurasia Insight,* 17 March 2009.

12. Chris Rickleton, "Kyrgyzstan: China's Economic Influence Fostering Resentment," *Eurasia Insight,* 28 April 2011.

13. Nargis Kassenova, "China as an Emerging Donor in Tajikistan and Kyrgyzstan," IFRI/Russian NIS *Center*, January 2009.

14. Ibid.

15. "Maksim Bakiyev: Kyrgyzstan is Interested in China's Help and Experience Sharing in Creating a Successful Economic Development Model," www.24.kg, 12 January 2010.

16. Kurmanbek Bakiyev was ousted as a result of protests in central Bishkek on 7 April 2010.

17. Erkinov, "Kyrgyzstan: Is China a Hidden Power in Bishkek?" *Eurasia Insight,* 17 March 2009.

18. "The Great Silk Road Today: Chinese Influence in Kyrgyzstan Today," www.ferghana.ru, 6 May 2008.

19. "China National Machinery Im & Ex Corporation Will Construct China-Kyrgyzstan-Uzbekistan Railroad," Ministry of Natural Resources of the Kyrgyz Republic, 22 September 2009, http://www.geo.gov.kg/index.php/ru/news/geology-news/488-news [Accessed on 27 October 2011].

20. "China Is Ready to Build a Railroad through Kyrgyzstan," www.for.kg, 31 May 2009.

21. "Transport connections: Market Overview," http://www.centralasia-biz.com/cabiz/kirgizstan/transport/abt_transport_obzor_kg.htm [Accessed on 20 November 2011]; "A demonstration against the construction of new China-Kyrgyzstan-Uzbekistan railroad was held in Naryn," www.akipress.kg, 19 September 2011.

22. Ibid.

23. Yuliya Mazykina, "Kyrgyzstan-Uzbekistan. A Railroad of Disappointments," www.24.kg, 9 August 2011.

24. "International Transport Corridors," Eurasian Development Bank, http://transtec.transtec-neva.ru/files/File/eurozec.pdf.

25. Damir Usenbayev, "Iron Step," www.ca-oasis.info, April 2008.

26. Elena Avdeyeva, "Wishes and Opportunities: Kyrgyzstan Is Improving Its Doctrine of Multi-vector Cooperation," *Belyi parus*, 18 January 2010.

27. Ibid.

28. "Maksim Bakiyev: We Are Interested in Deepening Cooperation between Governments of Kyrgyzstan and China," www.akipress.kg, 13 January 2010.

29. "Chinese Vice Premier Pledges to Advance Cooperation with Kyrgyzstan," www.xinhuanet.com, 12 January 2010.

30. For in-depth analysis see Alexander Cooley, "Russia and the Recent Evolution of the SCO: Issues and Challenges for U.S. Policy," in Timothy Colton, Timothy Frye, and Robert Legvold, *The Policy World Meets Academia: Designing U.S. Policy toward Russia* (American Academy of Arts and Sciences, 2010).

31. http://www.sectsco.org/EN/show.asp?id=69 [Accessed on 30 April 2011].

32. Edward Wong, "China Quietly Extends Footprints into Central Asia," *New York Times*, 2 January 2011.

33. Erica Marat, "The SCO and Foreign Powers in Central Asia: Sino-Russian Differences," *Central Asia–Caucasus Analyst*, 28 May 2010.

34. Stephen Blank, "The Shanghai Cooperation Organization as 'Energy Club', Portents for the Future," *Central Asia–Caucasus Analyst*, 4 October 2006.

35. "Kyrgyzstan Will Keep Its WTO Membership and Join the Customs Union," *Kazakhstan Today*, 26 August 2011.

36. "The Customs Union: Kyrgyzstan in Front of a Difficult Choice," *International Centre for Trade and Sustainable Development*, May 2010, http://ictsd.org/i/news/ bridgesrussian/76721/ [Accessed on 27 October 2011].

37. Ibid.; "Kyrgyzstan faces a tough choice," http://ictsd.org/i/news/bridgesrussian /76721/, May 2010 [Accessed on 9 January 2012].

38. "China and Kyrgyzstan Launch Anti-Terrorism Exercises," *China Daily*, 11 October 2002.

39. David Wall, "The Shanghai Cooperation Organization: Uneasy Amity," *Open Democracy*, 15 June 2006.

40. Erica Marat, "Moscow Seeks Influence in the Kyrgyz Elections," *The Jamestown Foundation*, 5 October 2010.

41. "SCO Expresses 'Grave Concern' over Kyrgyzstan Violence," *Xinhuanet*, 21 June 2010; "Statement of Shanghai Cooperation Organization in Connection with Events in Southern Kyrgyzstan," 20 June 2010, http://www.sectsco.org/EN/show .asp?id=219 [Accessed on 30 April 2011].

42. "Report of the Independent Commission of Inquiry into the Events in Southern Kyrgyzstan in June 2010," *Kyrgyzstan Inquiry Commission,* http://www.k-ic.org/images/stories/kic_report_english_final.pdf.

43. All SCO members belong to the "not free" category according to the Freedom House's ratings.

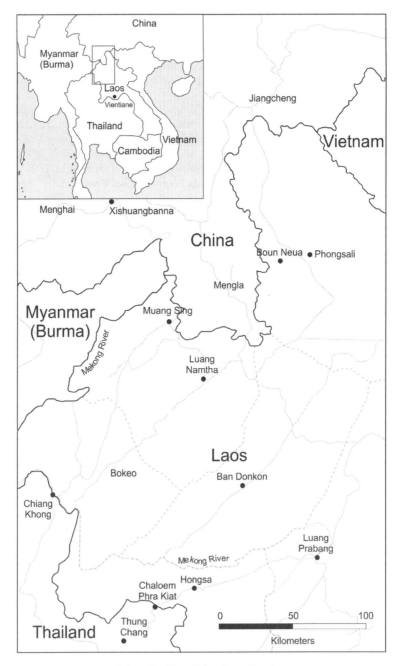

Map 10: The China-Laos Border

10

The China-Laos Boundary:
Lan Xang Meets the Middle Kingdom

Ian Townsend-Gault

Of all the boundaries examined in this book, the undisputed border between China and Laos (formerly the Kingdom of Lan Xang) might at first appear to be one of the least important, at only 264 miles (425 km).[1] Perhaps because it is land-locked, many writers treat Laos as less interesting and vital than its neighbors.[2] The country and its people have always attracted much less attention than Vietnam and even Cambodia. The French liked to distinguish between the different parts of what they called L'Union d'Indochine by claiming that the Vietnamese plant the rice, the Cambodians watch it grow, and the Lao listen to it grow. Certainly the Lao gave their colonial masters much less trouble than the Vietnamese.[3] Southeast Asia's only land-locked (or "land-linked") state, Laos is strategically well placed to constitute one or more east-west land bridges—potentially linking northern Myanmar and Thailand to ports on the South China Sea—and allowing for the development of north-south trade routes from China's Yunnan Province. Former Deputy Prime Minister Khampoui Keoboulapha has even stated: "We want to become the link between Vietnam, China, Thailand, Burma and Cambodia."[4]

During the 19th and 20th centuries, Laos was never able to avoid degrees of domination by its powerful neighbors to the east, north, and west, a process that continues to some degree to this day. In particular, Vietnamese influence is very clear in the eastern parts of the country, and there are many signs of Chinese encroachment from the north. Meanwhile, the Thais took the western provinces constituting Issan from pre-colonial Laos, and indeed tried to annex Lao territory to the west of the Mekong in Champasak Province at the outbreak of World War II; France subsequently forced them to withdraw to the previously agreed borders when it attempted to resume colonial rule in 1946.

During the first decade of the 21st century, more intense exploration has shown that the country's natural resource and energy generation potential is much greater than had been previously thought. Yet Laos remains the poorest country in mainland Southeast Asia. Given this fact it is hardly surprising that its government has entered into cooperative arrangements with China, the economic and military hegemon to its immediate north. In light of the cross-border linkages with China and other neighboring states, the extent to which Laos can retain full sovereign control over its territory along the Sino-Lao border remains to be seen. This shift toward China, which is comparatively recent, also suggests a move away from a very close—and asymmetric—relationship with Hanoi, which has tended to regard itself as the patron of Vientiane. To better understand this dynamic, this chapter will begin with a description of the geography of Laos and basic facts about its people. Since the spatial limits of the country were fixed during the colonial period, important decisions taken then, which still have ramifications today, will be summarized next. Finally, several current outstanding border problems with China will be considered.

Laos: Geography and History

The total area of the Lao People's Democratic Republic is 91,429 square miles (236,800 km^2), divided into 89,112 square miles (230,800 km^2) of land and about 2,317 square miles (6,000 km^2) of water. The country has 3,158 miles (5,083 km) of land boundaries with Burma (146 miles/235 km), Cambodia (336 miles/541 km), China (263 miles/423 km), Thailand (1,090 miles/1,754 km), and Vietnam (1,324 miles/2,130 km).[5]

It is estimated that the population of Laos was about 6.5 million (July 2011), with up to 60 percent of the population ethnic Lao, and the rest divided among the many ethnic minorities, most of whom live in the more remote mountain areas—such as those in the vicinity of the Lao-China border.[6] Relations between the majority and some of the minorities have not been easy: many of the latter have little commitment to the Lao People's Democratic Republic either ethnically or politically. In fact, the pre-colonial history of the country was marked by the waxing and waning empires of the emerging dominant ethnic groups, which included the Siamese in Ayutthaya, the Khmers in Angkor then Phnom Penh, the Cham in what is now southern Vietnam, the Viets, and different clans, dynasties, and warlords in what is now China.

The modern states that have emerged in this region tend to present their histories in "Westphalian state" terms, but this European model of the state did not take root in Southeast Asia until the late 19th century. The role of colonial powers was key to this process. Before their arrival, the applicable geopolitical model was the mandala, the area over which a ruler actually held sway, dominating it in terms of ritual or religion, as well as the exercise of economic and military power.[7] This essentially fluid concept does not incorporate a defined territory and thus formal—and by implication permanent—borders, which international lawyers hold to be one of the four essential elements of statehood.[8] To illustrate, the furthest extent of the Khmer empire (Kampuchea Krom) included modern Bangkok, Vientiane, and Ho Chi Minh City.

In Laos, the mandala established in 1353 by King Fa Ngum was known as Lan Xang Hom Khaothe, the Kingdom of a million elephants and the white parasol, which was the manifestation of kingship.[9] At its greatest extent, Lan Xang included northern Cambodia, and northeast Thailand. This entity managed to survive until the early 18th century when, after Siamese intervention, it was divided into two kingdoms, Luang Phabang to the north and Champasak to the south. Lan Xang and its successors seem to have acknowledged the overlordship of China through the payment of occasional tribute, but unlike the case with Vietnam (the northern part of which had been a Chinese colony for a millennium until the 12th century), China did not interfere directly in the political affairs of the small kingdom(s) to the south. It seems fair to state, however, that northern Laos was part of a Chinese economic "sphere of influence."

Matters were very different between the Lao and Siam. Continual strife with Siam led the King of Luang Phabang to request French protection, which was eventually to lead to colonial status for it and Champasak, as part of French Indochina, and overall control by governors appointed by Paris. The French united what they called "Upper" and "Lower" Laos into a single administrative unit, while preserving the local royalty, and it was these entities that were to achieve independence in 1954, albeit dominated by the northern kingdom, as modern Laos.

Throughout the pre-colonial period, and to some extent during it, Laos faced predatory threats to its territory, and even its very existence, from Vietnam to some extent, but mostly from Siam. The cultural and linguistic ties between these two are very much greater than with Vietnam, Cambodia, and certainly China. Nowhere in the literature has it been suggested that China represented the same degree of territorial threat to Laos as it did to Vietnam, with which its cultural and indeed historical ties were much stronger. To a great degree the modern border between China and Laos was determined during the late 19th century, in the Sino-French Treaty of 1895.

The Sino-French Border Agreement of 1895

As with other European colonizers in Asia, the French were keen to establish clear boundaries between their possessions and the territories of their neighbors. The Sino-French Treaty of 1895 determined the borders between China and France's colonial possessions in Southeast Asia.[10] Under the terms of this treaty, China renounced all claims to sovereignty south of the border stipulated in the agreement, which included China's border with Laos.

French exploration of Laos began in the mid-19th century. In 1850, Father Emile Bouillevaux became the first known European to visit the ruins at Angkor, an account of which he published. But the first major European explorer into Laos was Henri Mouhout, who visited Angkor ten years later, and whose accounts were by far the most detailed. Mouhout was to make his way up the Mekong, dying in Louang Phabang of fever in 1861.[11] A subsequent expedition led by Doudant de Lagreé, sponsored by the French authorities, traced the course of the river from the South China Sea to the Chinese interior. They hoped, of course, to find it navigable all the way, but the rapids south of Pakxe proved too much of a barrier.[12] Other explorers, such as Garnier, stimulated French interest in forming viable colonies, which had hitherto been regarded as less than successful ventures, by publishing somewhat optimistic accounts of undiscovered mineral and other riches.[13]

This was the period during which France established L'Union d'Indochine, or French Indochina as it will henceforth be referred to. Although various altruistic motives were advanced for expanding French presence in Asia—including bringing Christianity, the "civilizing mission," and the like—the powerful catalysts of national pride and economic opportunity combined perfectly here as they were to do elsewhere and for other colonizing powers. Having said this, the Catholic lobby in the France of the day was a formidable voice in domestic politics, and one not to be ignored. The same might be said of the French army and navy. France believed firmly in the concept of "Indochina." It believed it was creating a new French-led polity, with Vietnam, divided as it was, at its core.[14]

To this end, the movement of colonial subjects was encouraged. Trained and trusted Vietnamese would be sent to Laos and Cambodia as administrators, while laborers were recruited from and transferred throughout the region. Although there had always been some migration across borders, these movements were now more directed. The Vietnamese minority in Cambodia would become the first target of Khmer Rouge ethnic cleansing policies after 1975, while that in Laos seems to have been less contentious so far as local populations were concerned. This may be because the country was already something of a multi-ethnic melting pot.

By the time they came to negotiate the 1895 treaty, France and China had already had a number of diplomatic exchanges.[15] The need for a border treaty was supported by the Siamese King Mongkong and his son Chulalongkorn. Conscious that Siam was the only part of South and Southeast Asia to escape colonial status, these monarchs determined that the best way of avoiding that fate was to bring their country up to date as swiftly as possible. Chulalongkorn (reigned 1868-1910) in particular modernized the Siamese legal and governmental systems by introducing the Torrens system of land-holding and registration.

But it is one thing to agree on the need for a border, and quite another to undertake the work of delimitation and demarcation itself. The Mekong furnished the easiest way of establishing a border, and the easy terrain of Champasak facilitated the work there also. But the more remote mountainous and jungle areas were formidably different, and work here tended to lag. The treaty's main purpose was to extend the already agreed border between Tonkin—which is what France called the northern part of what is now Vietnam—and China, signed in 1887, "from the red River (west) to the Mekong." Thus, the border between Laos and China was very much the creation of the colonial master of the former.

The delimitation and demarcation of the Sino-Lao boundary was largely based on water-courses and watersheds, where possible. Commissioned agents or authorities of the parties were charged with fixing the border on the ground, in accordance with the treaty and the maps signed by the Delimitation Commission:

> Leaving the sources of the Nam-wou, the frontier follows the watershed between the Nam-wou basin and the basin of the Nam-la, leaving to China, to the west, Ban-noi, I-pang, I-wou, and the six tea mountains and, to Annam, to the east, Mong-wou and Wou-te and the confederation of the Hua-panh-ha-tang-hoc. The frontier goes in a north-south direction southeast as far as the sources of the Nan-nuo-ho, then it moves, along the watershed, in a west-north-westerly direction, the valleys of the Nan-ouo-ho and its tributaries to the left of Nam-la, as far as the confluence of the Mekong and the Nam-la, to the northwest of Muong-poung.[16]

The border extended east from the trijunction of Laos, China, and Burma in the Mekong River to the trijunction of the boundaries among Laos, China, and Vietnam. To the north of the line was the Chinese province of Yunnan, while to the south were the three most northerly provinces of Laos, including Luang Namtha to the west (bordering Burma), and Oudomxay and Phongsaly to the east, bordering Vietnam.

The authorities agreed that the border between Laos and China was "sharper" than with other neighbors—with the possible exception of the area of the Sinicized ethnic minority the Tai Lu (or Lue), of Sipsong Panna. Following an attempted revolt in 1914, its leader Ong Kham fled for refuge into China, where he remained until his death there in 1923.[17] The Lu rebellion lasted for two years, and was suppressed only after three French military expeditions.[18] Perhaps because of this revolt, the promised demarcation of the border on the ground did not happen, nor were the exact locations of the east and west trijunctions established. This would only be accomplished more than 100 years later.

From the Colonial Period to the Present Day

French administration in Laos was continued under Japanese control during World War II, as it was in neighboring Vietnam and Cambodia. As the Japanese retreated, the provisions of the agreement of the Allied Powers at Potsdam came into effect. Nationalist China occupied the former French colonies as far south as the 16th parallel, while British forces occupied the territories to the south of the 16th parallel.

After World War II, France decided to reclaim its Asian empire just as Britain, the Netherlands, and the United States sought to regain their possessions lost to Japan. Ho Chi Minh had in the meantime declared the independence of Vietnam in August 1945, and neither he nor his supporters were willing to submit to the colonists whom they had seen subjugated by Japan, another Asian power.[19] In Laos, the Lao Issara ("Free Laos") had attempted to seize power, but France was intent on reasserting control—French officials and army personnel had been in situ throughout the war, and indeed had harried the Japanese from behind the lines in its final month—and France's allies did nothing to prevent it. The end result was the conflict known as the First Indochina War.[20]

Like Cambodia, Laos did not play a significant role in this conflict. The royal family appeared to their people to be in control, and there was no popular leader of the charismatic stature of Ho Chi Minh, plus revolutionary army, to challenge it. In Laos, French authority was re-established after the king affirmed his loyalty to France in May 1946, and a *modus vivendi* to this effect was signed in August. Seven years later, France granted Laos independence under a treaty of 1953, under which Laos would remain within the French Union. The war in Vietnam, however, lasted until the Geneva Conference of 1954, which was actually in progress when news came of the defeat of the French forces at Dien Bien Phu at the hands of the Vietminh under General Vo Nguyen Giap. Paris had had enough, and now signaled its intention to withdraw from Indochina. King Norodom Sihanouk also decided that it was time for Cambodia to become fully independent, while Laos retained membership in the French Union until 1958.

During the Vietnam War, Laos suffered greatly from repeated bombings and the planting of mines. The Pathet Lao gradually grew in strength, assisted by Hanoi, not to mention incessant royalist in-fighting.[21] The country started to suffer from the conflict in Vietnam, since part of the "Ho Chi Minh Trail," the means by which the North supplied its guerrillas, the Vietcong, in the South, ran through Laos, and was a target for U.S. bombing. The war resulted in massive incursions of Vietnamese into Lao territory, and a great many decided to stay; Lao authorities were powerless to prevent this, if indeed they wished to. This explains the very high percentage of

Vietnamese—exact numbers are not available—living to this day in Huaphan Province, which is bordered by three Vietnamese provinces. There are also significant numbers of Vietnamese in Champa and Savanakhet.

The Vietnamese and their supporters were keen to export revolution to Laos and Cambodia, and found ready clients in the Pathet Lao[22] and Khmer Rouge respectively. North Vietnam unified the country as the Socialist Republic of Vietnam in 1976, which helped precipitate the coming to power of communist regimes in Laos and Cambodia. Laos did not experience horrors on the scale of the Pol Pot regime, but the Pathet Lao government did institute a carbon copy of the rigid version of Marxism chosen by Hanoi, with which it maintained very close ties. Most royalist officials and thousands of soldiers were sent to "re-education" camps, mainly in the remote and relatively inaccessible northeast of the country, but there were no killing fields, nor institutions resembling the infamous Tuol Sleng.

This situation lasted until 1986, when the Communist party of Vietnam found itself obliged to abandon its Marxist orthodoxy and institute radical reforms under the policy of *doi moi*, or restructuring (modeled on the Soviet policy of *perestroika*). By this time, it was becoming clear that the Soviet Union was no longer in a position to assist its Asian client states, and one of the purposes of *doi moi* was to introduce a mixed economy based on the model in China already adopted under Deng Xiaoping. Laos followed suit, and the disintegration of the Soviet Union forced Laos to re-evaluate its relations with their heretofore despised capitalist neighbors. Lao PDR was admitted to the Association of Southeast Asian Nations (ASEAN) in 1997, something that had seemed inconceivable a few short years before.[23]

Moving to Complete the Sino-Lao Border

The gradual warming of relations between Laos and China during the 1990s was facilitated by the ease with which a process was instituted to demarcate the border with marker posts between the two countries as exactly as possible. A Treaty and Supplementary Protocol, signed in 1991, established a Border Commission, which completed its work the following year. A further agreement in 1994, which came into force the following year, between Laos and Myanmar established the western border trijunction, and the trijunction among Laos, China, and Vietnam to the east was fixed by treaty in 2006.

The current Sino-Laos border issues are largely identical to those between other regional states, including facilitating trade, control of illegal activities such as smuggling people, narcotics, and other goods, and security. These dominate the bilateral and usually annual meetings of the Border Commissions of the Greater

Mekong Sub-region states, as they have for decades. Hard facts are not easy to come by, but the central governments have encouraged cooperation at the provincial level.

Building new roads has been a high priority. As long ago as 1962, the governments of Laos and the PRC agreed at the request of the former that the latter would build a series of roads south from Yunnan Province to Muang Sing, Nam Tha, and Ban Houay, all three river ports on the Mekong. Another road would be constructed to Phongsaly. The plan was for these roads to be connected to the Lao highway system, but the coalition government of the day collapsed, and this did not come to pass. Significantly, however, Chinese workers, who may have numbered 15,000 at one time, remained in northern Laos. They were to remain there during the war, and left only when relations were broken off after Vietnam invaded Cambodia in 1978, driving out the Chinese-backed Khmer Rouge.[24]

There are two possible legacies of this engagement with China. First, Beijing has long seen the strategic importance of Laos as a road/rail land-bridge, though the Lao-Viet alliance has been something of a stumbling block to furthering engagement. But patient diplomacy, and the fact that, economically speaking, China is better placed to assist Laos than its neighbor to the east, has started to yield concrete dividends. During the late 1990s, Laos-watchers became aware that a pro-China faction was emerging in the governing party. This led to initiatives designed to increase China's profile, the most significant of which was rescuing Laos from the worst consequences of the 1997 Asian financial crash.

Subsequent signs of a warming relationship between Laos and the PRC included meeting the costs of construction of the largest auditorium in the center of Vientiane, a highly visible symbol of a least a degree of political realignment toward China, although this is not to say that ties with Vietnam are no longer close. China also financed the construction of a major sports stadium for the ASEAN games. A controversial plan to build a major housing complex—allegedly mostly for Chinese nationals—near the revered That Luang monument in Vientiane was, however, abandoned due to fears that China's leverage was becoming too marked.

But Chinese influence continues nonetheless and, in 2011, it was announced the Soochow University would open the first foreign campus in Laos, in Vientiane. It has even been reported that in areas near Chinese manufacturing plants only Chinese security guards are hired to protect the factories. A group of consultants, armed with official passes and all the necessary documentation to enter the factory, and accompanied by the district government official, were refused access to the area and ordered off the premises.

According to the BBC, a large Chinese-owned casino was built right across the Sino-Laotian border in the town of Boten, and all local street signs were changed to Chinese characters.[25] There is evidence that the casino at least was totally out of Lao control at one point.[26] Subsequent anecdotal evidence suggests that Chinese border guards were preventing their nationals from crossing into Laos to visit it, fearing that it was a front for money laundering and the smuggling of narcotics. Other reports suggest that pressure from China has since forced the casino to close. But the Chinese presence in the town remains strong. This raises the obvious question as to who really controls the area, and even the extent to which it can be said to still be under the actual sovereignty of Laos.

In a recent incident, two Chinese cargo ships were attacked on the Mekong in October 2011, apparently by renegade Thai soldiers. Thirteen Chinese sailors were murdered when the vessels were boarded. This has resulted in joint patrols on the river undertaken by China, Laos, Myanmar and Thailand, which began in December 2011.[27]

Another important development are indicators that China might extend its high-speed railway line into Laos. It would appear that this undertaking is being carried out with little or no regard to environmental or social impact. Villagers are simply informed of what is going to happen; they are not consulted. In addition to China's highly negative environmental record, many Chinese initiatives have been criticized on the grounds that local laborers and other workers and suppliers benefit very little from the Chinese-built projects, and this in a country with perennially high unemployment.

Conclusions

The history of Southeast Asia shows that both Lan Xang and colonial and independent Laos have often been regarded as less important than their neighbors. However, this attitude is changing with the present generation, especially in the major cities. The previous isolation of Laos, which was imposed by its government and by geography, is gradually disappearing. As Grant Evans has put it: "Not so long ago to be in the mountains of Laos . . . was to feel cut off from the world in ways increasingly unimaginable. Now Hmong walk into post offices . . . and easily call their refugee relatives in Australia, France, or the U.S."[28]

Still, vast asymmetries in the relations between China and Laos remain, and have been exacerbated recently by the latter's under-development, and its desire to find any means possible to pull itself out of its relatively impoverished state. As in similar cases elsewhere, this leaves Laos extremely vulnerable to outside political and economic pressure. In the case of Laos, the situation is not helped by the weak state of the country's government and administration. Matters are gradually improving, however, as the emerging private sector offers educated Lao vastly better opportunities than does working for the state.

Even though the Lao-Chinese border is officially delimited and demarcated, the fluid situation in northern Laos along parts of its border with China are of increasing concern to Lao nationalists. Historically, Laos faced territorial depredations from its neighbors to the west and east, and occasionally from south. There are thus valid concerns that the fourth direction of the compass to the north might now be added.

Notes

1. "Laos" was coined by the French colonizers to mean "the place where the Lao peoples live," despite the fact that a sizeable percentage of the population are not ethnic Lao. Laos is officially the Lao People's Democratic Republic, or Lao PDR (as per UN documents). "Laos" will be used here for convenience sake, but it should be noted that many people follow the lead of the people of that country and do not pronounce the "s." Where variations in English language spelling occur, especially in official documents (e.g., Tongking versus Tonkin), the original has been retained. See, *The Geographer*, "China-Laos Boundary," International Boundary Study, No. 34, (Office of the Geographer, Bureau of Intelligence and research, United States Department of State), 24 June 1964.

2. Many guidebooks refer to it as "tiny" Laos, but according to the CIA World Factbook, Laos is 83rd out of 249 countries and territories world-wide, https://www.cia.gov/library/publications/the-world-factbook/rankorder/2147 rank.html?countryName=Laos&countryCode=la&regionCode=eas&rank=83#la [Accessed on 27 October 2011].

3. Nor were they entirely quiescent, see Geoffrey C. Gunn, *Rebellion in Laos: Peasant and Politics in a Colonial Backwater* (Boulder: Westview Press, 1990).

4. Randi Jerndal and Jonathan Rigg, "From Buffer State to Crossroads State: Spaces of Human Activity and Integration in the Lao PDR," in Grant Evans, ed., *Laos–Culture and Society* (Chang Mai, Thailand: Silkworm Books, 1999), 35-60: 50.

5. *CIA World Factbook*, 2011. See https://www.cia.gov/library/publications/the-world-factbook/geos/la.html [Accessed on 10 January 2012].

6. Ibid.

7. Martin Stuart-Fox, *Historical Dictionary of Laos* (Metuchen, NJ: Scarecrow Press, 1992).

8. The others being fixed population, a government, and capacity to enter into relationships with other states (Montevideo Convention on the Rights and Duties of States, 1933, Article 1).

9. During the Second Indochina War, it was not uncommon for westerners to refer dismissively to the "Land of a million Irrelevants."

10. *Complementary Convention to the Convention delimiting the Frontier between Tongking and China of June 26, 1887*, Beijing, 20 June 1895. English translation at http://www.chinaforeignrelations.net/treaties/4 [Accessed on 27 October 2011].

11. Mouhout's grave lies just outside the town, on the banks of the Nam Kham River.

12. This problem was solved by the construction of a small railway to by-pass the rapids. The rusting remains of some of the rolling stock can still be seen.

13. Milton Osborne, *The Mekong: Turbulent Past, Uncertain Future* (New York: Atlantic Monthly Press, 2000).

14. Christopher E. Goscha, *Vietnam or Indochina ? Contesting Concepts of Space in Vietnamese Nationalism, 1887-1954* (Copenhagen: Nordic Institute of Asia Studies, 1995).

15. Treaties concluded before this dealt with matters such as customs duties, approved border crossings for trade, and the installation of consular and other officials in border areas.

16. *Complementary Convention*, Beijing, 20 June 1895.

17. The Lu were a constant problem for France. Early in the 20th century their leader, Ong Kham, encouraged his and other ethnic peoples not to perform corvée labor, a form of forced labor whereby villages were required to provide a given number of able bodied workers for a period of years to work for the colonialists.

18. "The Lu Revolt," in Stuart-Fox, 83.

19. France also played no role in securing the Japanese withdrawal, so there was to be no triumphant return along the lines of General Douglas MacArthur wading ashore in the Philippines.

20. The Second Indochina War is otherwise known in the west as the "Vietnam War," and to the Vietnamese, the "American War."

21. One prominent member of the royal family decided to further his aims by actually joining the Pathet Lao.

22. The name translates literally as "Laotian state."

23. Such a union, which would have included Yunnan, was called for by the Laotian scholar and intellectual Katay Don Sasorith in 1948. Grant Evans, "What Is Lao Culture and Society?" in Evans, 21.

24. "Chinese Roads," in Stuart-Fox, 22.

25. "Fears over growing Chinese industry in Laos," BBC News, 4 June 2011, http://news.bbc.co.uk/2/hi/programmes/from_our_own_correspondent/9498760.stm [Accessed on 27 October 2011].

26. The casino in Boten, situated along the Chinese border, greeted the outgoing head of the Swiss Development Agency Martin Sommer with a belligerent Russian thug backed by rooftop snipers when he visited in 2010, according to people familiar with the situation." Beaumont Smith, "Local losers in Lao casino capitalism," *Asia Times Online*, 2 August 2011, http://www.atimes.com/atimes /Southeast_Asia/MH02Ae01.html [Accessed on 10 January 2012].

27. "Mekong patrols start from Chinese port," *International Herald Tribune*, 12 December 2011, 4.

28. Evans, 30.

154

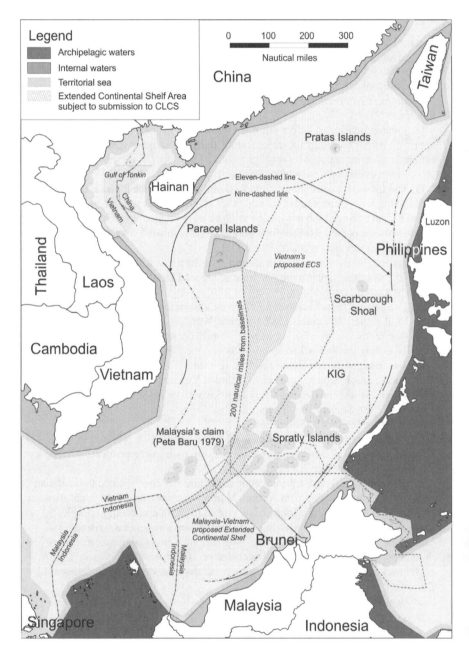

Map 11.1: Competing Maritime Claims in the South China Sea

11
Malaysia and China: Economic Growth Overshadows Sovereignty Dispute

Vivian Louis Forbes

The PRC and Malaysia are not land neighbors, since the distance between China's international border and Malaysia along longitude 100° E. is nearly 2,082 miles (3,350 km), but they share a potentially lengthy maritime boundary in the southern sector of the South China Sea. A dispute over these maritime borders concerns Kuala Lumpur particularly because of Beijing's apparent claim to all the South China Sea, as shown on Chinese maps that depict the nine-dashed line, an area that is approximately 648,000 nm^2 (2,225,420 km^2) in size.

China and Malaysia have yet to delimit their maritime boundaries and resolve their territorial dispute in the South China Sea. In particular, they must first determine sovereignty over the Spratly islands, which include numerous small features encompassing 3 square miles (7.8 km^2) of land scattered over 69,883 nm^2 (240,000 km^2) of water. Determining sovereignty over these highly disputed islands, islets, reefs, and sand cays is the first step in resolving this complex border problem.

Despite their maritime and territorial disputes in the South China Sea, recent political and economic relations between China and Malaysia have been warming. The PRC's impressive economic growth has been linked to Beijing's strengthening international profile, in league with the PLA's expanded military might. Malaysia has also experienced stable economic growth, notwithstanding external negative factors such as the financial crash in 1997 and the global financial crisis of 2008. By April 2010, Malaysia's foreign trade with China reached $74.2 billion, reflecting an annual growth rate of 22.34 percent since 2000, thus making Malaysia China's largest Asian trading partner.[1]

Historical Background, Geography, and ASEAN Links with China

Malaysia comprises two major parcels of land mass, plus numerous small islands, whose collective surface area is approximately 127,414 square miles (330,000 km^2). The Malay peninsula, which borders Thailand, is the first of these areas, while the second includes the northwestern one-third of the island of Borneo, comprising Sabah and Sarawak, which borders Indonesia's Kalimantan to the south even while semi-encompassing Brunei.

Soon after World War II, the Malaysian "emergency" broke out, and from 1948-1960 the government conducted a counter-insurgency operation against the Malayan Races Liberation Army, which was the military force of the Malayan Communist Party. From the mid-1960s, and for about a decade, the PRC continued to place ideology over state-to-state relations by supporting Communist insurgents in non-communist countries and implicitly granting ethnic Chinese in the Southeast Asian region citizen status when they travelled to China. During most of the Cold War period (1947-1990), China's relations with the original group of five ASEAN (Association of Southeast Asian Nations) members—namely, Indonesia, Malaysia, the Philippines, Singapore, and Thailand—were generally hostile.

In their 1967 *Bangkok Declaration*, members of ASEAN committed themselves to raising the standard of living of their people, as well as securing peace, freedom, and prosperity. Malaysia established diplomatic ties with China on 31 May 1974. Relations warmed after China's introduction of its "open and reform" policies of the early-1980s.[2] In July 1991, at the invitation of Malaysia, China's Foreign Minister, Qian Qichen, representing China as a Consultative partner of ASEAN, attended the 24th ASEAN Ministerial Meeting (AMM) in Kuala Lumpur. This visit led to a further deepening of Sino-Malaysia relations.

Since 1991, the members of ASEAN and China have resolved many of their differences through multilateral negotiations: 1) signing of the Treaty of Amity and Cooperation; 2) proposing and then forming an ASEAN-China Free Trade Agreement; and 3) maintaining its "peaceful development" foreign policy in the region. During the China-ASEAN Commemorative Summit held at Nanning, China, in October 2006, ASEAN and Chinese leaders pledged to enhance the strategic partnership between the two political entities.

Major achievements since the early-1990s in Sino-ASEAN relations have contributed to the strengthening of the bilateral relationship.[3] Indeed, significantly improved relations have been witnessed through multilateral dialogues that were designed to promote cooperation, economic development, and regional peace. The future of this partnership is dependent on whether ASEAN and China are willing to continue to uphold this high level of cooperation. The close partnership could be de-stabilized if either party failed their commitments and obligations to their agreements, or fail to expand socio-cultural cooperation.[4]

China's relationship with ASEAN and its peaceful rise are integral to Beijing's economic reform and development.[5] China's growth has catalyzed sustainable development in ASEAN economies, and has therefore enhanced the economic integration between Southeast Asia and China.[6] However, studies of China's trade and investment ties with ASEAN reveals that Chinese influence in the region has actually been fairly minimal.[7] The complex and multifaceted historical relationships that exist were predominantly molded by both geopolitical dynamics and internal political forces in individual countries within ASEAN.

Ideological barriers have largely been removed, thereby highlighting the importance of economic links and the emergence of multilateralism as a mode of diplomatic interaction: "China-ASEAN relations are back to normalcy and improvements are now at their historical best."[8] The promising China-Malaysia relations should be viewed in the context of how Malaysia overcame the "China-threat" theory as well as their expanding bilateral economic partnership since the mid-1970s.[9] These, in turn, were a result of improving Sino-Malaysia diplomatic relations between 1957-1973.

Rationale for Diplomatic Relations, 1957-1973

After Malaysia gained independence from Great Britain in 1957, foreign relations between China and Malaysia were strained due to a clash of ideologies. The nation, Malaya, as it was then known, was adversely affected between 1948 and 1960 by communist insurrection within Peninsular Malay and on Borneo Island, particularly in present-day Sabah and Sarawak.[10] Under the administration of the first prime minister, Tunku Abdul Raham (1957-1970), China was perceived as an ideological and security threat. Additionally, China's support for the Malayan Communist Party (Parti Komunis Malaya), its refusal to recognize Malaysia's state formation in 1965, and the upheaval in China during the Cultural Revolution (1966-1976) were all major hurdles to the normalization of diplomatic relations.

In May 1974, the government of Malaysia's Prime Minister Tun Abdul Razak Hussein (1970-1976) established formal diplomatic ties with the PRC. Malaysia established an Embassy in Beijing and four Consulate Offices in Shanghai, Guangzhou, Kunming, and Hong Kong (Special Autonomous Region). Malaysia also maintains a Malaysian Friendship and Trade Centre (MFTC) in Taiwan. In return, China has an Embassy in Kuala Lumpur and a Consulate-General located in Kuching, Sarawak.

A period of detente, diplomatic normalization, and peaceful coexistence followed the opening of Sino-Malaysian relations. For example, the conduct of diplomatic relations were embodied in the communiqué signed in Beijing between Razak and Premier Zhou Enlai. Bilateral relations were based on the principles of respect for one another's sovereignty and non-interference in one another's internal affairs. Further exchanges of visits soon included Premier Deng Xiaoping to Malaysia in 1978, followed soon afterward by Prime Minister Tun Hussein Onn to China. In

May 1999, Chinese Foreign Minister Tang Jiaxuan and the Malaysian Foreign Minister signed a Joint Statement Concerning Future Cooperation Framework.

Since the two countries established diplomatic ties, bilateral links have witnessed great progress. Having established a strategically cooperative relationship, mutual political trust has been continuously deepened and economic and trade cooperation has yielded remarkable results, bringing substantial benefits to the two peoples. Both countries have carried out pragmatic cooperation in a wide range of fields, including trade, investment, tourism, agriculture, education, science, and technology. There have also been frequent exchanges of high-level visits and rapid growth of people-to-people contacts. Both sides have recognized that it is particularly important for the two countries to step up bilateral economic cooperation amid the current global economic recession. The two governments share common views and cooperate closely on many regional and international issues, which has served to safeguard their legitimate interests.

When Premier Wen Jiabao and Malaysian Prime Minister Abdullah Badawi met in Beijing on 28 May 2004, they pledged to work together more closely as they commemorated the 30th anniversary of diplomatic relations between the two countries. The Chinese Premier described the relationship as the best it has ever been with great political trust, expanding common interests, closer economic ties, and increased consultation and coordination in the international arena.

Premier Wen made a five-point proposal to further expand and deepen bilateral relations. He noted that China and Malaysia should maintain high-level visits and discuss their views on major issues so that bilateral ties could develop in a steady and healthy manner. They should expand mutually beneficial relations across the board and work within the framework of China's strategic partnership ASEAN. He noted in particular that they should promote cooperation in key areas such as agricultural, high technology, exploration of resources, infrastructure construction, and tourism to increase trade volume. Furthermore, the two countries should consolidate their traditional friendship by promoting exchanges between peoples from all walks of life, especially youth. Indeed, no fewer than 27 agreements, memoranda of understanding, or treaties have been signed by the two governments. He suggested that China and Malaysia should enhance their cooperation in dealing with international and regional issues, and push for the widening of the ASEAN process through the "10 plus 3" process, which means the cooperation between the 10-member ASEAN and China, Japan, and Korea.

A visit by President Hu Jintao to Malaysia on 11 November 2009 underscored the rising importance of bilateral trade ties between China and Malaysia. The parties signed five new memoranda of understanding (MOUs), which included increased collaboration between the two countries' financial regulatory agencies and educational institutions. In terms of capital markets, China and Malaysia complement each other very closely. Malaysia has already been considered as China's trading partner for equities investments through the Qualified Domestic Institutional Investor (QDII) agency. Malaysia is only the second ASEAN country to be recognized as an authorized market, and there is confidence that the interest will further flow into Malaysia's capital market investment sectors.

China's economic growth is not a threat, but is actually quite beneficial to Malaysia, because the former is a big producer of goods and the latter is a consumer. This was the main theme discussed by former Prime Minister Tun Dr. Mahathir Mohamad when he delivered a keynote address at a forum called *A Strong China—Implications and Challenges,* which was organized by the National Chamber of Commerce and Industry of Malaysia in Kuala Lumpur, Malaysia, on 26 April 2010. He further suggested that Malaysia should not unduly fear China's strength, but should see it as an important engine of the world economy, which is an asset. He commented that many Malaysians were investing in China because they had certain expertise that China would like to have, and so China was seeking to import these skills to cater to a large population. He also acknowledged that the substantial Malaysian-Chinese population in the country that shares the same language and culture with China provides an important link to communicate smoothly and efficiently.[11]

Mahathir was convinced that China would become one of the most powerful economies in the future. It had found a way to develop into a strong economy without giving up the single party authoritarian system from the past. He observed that China retains a political system that ensures stability, combined with a modified form of Western market system. He concluded that Malaysia should maintain its generally good relationship with China.[12]

The rapid economic development experienced in both Malaysia and the PRC was, in part, brought about by the mutual trade agreements for commodities and manufactured goods. Under the administrations of two former prime ministers, Mahathir Mohamad (1981-2003) and Abdullah Badawi (2003-2009), economic cooperation with China was a top priority, notwithstanding some lingering political and strategic ambivalence. This cooperation has been enhanced and continues uninterrupted under the present leaderships. However, recent disputes over the South China Sea threaten to undermine this history of improved bilateral relations.

The South China Sea Disputes

Past and present Chinese governments have maintained their claims to sovereignty over the Spratly islands in the South China Sea, something which, from Beijing's perspective at least, is indisputable and is based on historical data.[13] However, because of the Confucian tradition—which holds that territory was expressed in spheres of influence rather than definitive linear boundaries—it is difficult to prove many of China's territorial claims in the South China Sea.

The first formal claim of sovereignty over the South China Sea was made in 1876 when the Paracel islands were claimed as Chinese territory. In 1883, a German survey team was expelled by China from the Spratlys, but by the late-1930s, Japan established its military presence in the South China Sea, and utilized the island of Itu Aba as a submarine base for the purpose of intercepting maritime commerce in the South China Sea.

In 1947, the ROC produced a map featuring a series of eleven dashes forming an elongated U-shaped boundary that encompassed most of the territory in this semi-enclosed sea (see Map 11.2). Various versions of the U-shaped map have been published subsequently, including the PRC nine-dashed map, but each fails to state specifically the extent of the land claims. Special attention is given to the historic creation of this U-shaped boundary line in an article by two scholars from Xiamen University, Fujian, who cite numerous official documents and other scholarly articles from China.[14] Li Jinming and Li Dexia conclude in their article:

> Nevertheless, the dotted line shown on the Chinese map is also China's maritime boundary in the South China Sea because of two characteristics of the dotted line. First, the location of the dotted line followed the international principles regarding maritime boundaries then in existence. . . Second, the dotted line was the manner of designating a claimed national boundary line. Thus, "the nine-dotted line" had a dual nature.[15]

It would appear, therefore, that the nine-dashed lines portrayed on the PRC map has a dual purpose. Not only does it define China's sovereignty over the South China Sea islands, but it also plays a role as China's claimed ocean boundary in the South China Sea. However, a careful study on the topic has suggested that China never claimed the entire water area of the South China Sea, but only the islands and their adjacent seas within the lines.[16]

In the past, China has demonstrated flexibility on matters concerning technical and scientific cooperation, but this merely underscores that in general Beijing refuses to discuss sovereignty claims on a multilateral basis. The reluctance on the part of the Chinese government to participate in multilateral discussions relating to sovereignty over the South China Sea, coupled with its extensive territorial claims and expanding military strength, has raised grave concerns in the region. The influence of China's historical legacy and the impact it will have on any future settlement must also be considered.

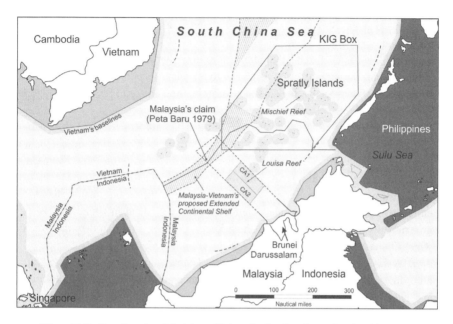

Map 11.2: Overlapping Maritime Claims in the Southern South China Sea

There may be significant differences among ASEAN members on how best to manage potential conflicts with other claimants. However, it is likely that the Chinese will not compromise on the sovereignty issue—whether because of conviction or political realities on the Chinese mainland. The stance adopted by Beijing has been to continue dialogue and negotiations with various disputants, so long as they do not appear to be "trading away" what many Chinese argue is their territory—the islands of the South China Sea, namely the Paracels (Xisha), Scarborough Shoal (Huangyan Dao), and the Spratlys (Nansha). Of these three, the Spratly islands are of the greatest importance to Malaysia.

The Spratly Islands

One of the most contentious areas in the South China Sea are the Spratly islands. The Spratlys' east-west extent is about 480 nm (874 km) and about as much in its north-south alignment. For ease of reference it can be considered as being located within the latitudes of 4° to 12° north and longitudes 110° to 118° east. Among the features a reported three dozen or so rise above sea level, and only seven of these have a land surface area exceeding a fifth of a square mile (0.5 km²).

In 1958, the PRC issued a declaration defining its territorial waters as encompassing the Spratlys. In 1959, the islands were made part of the country's bureaucratic structure, at the administrative level of banshichu. In 1988, the banshichu were switched to the administration of the newly founded province of Hainan. China strongly asserted its claims to the islands again on 25 February 1992, in Article 2 of the national legislation reinforcing its Territorial Sea and Contiguous Zone limits.

In July 2010, the Communist Party-controlled *Global Times* stated that "China will never waive its right to protect its core interest with military means." China currently occupies ten of the marine features, including Cuarteron Reef, Fiery Cross Reef, Gaven Reef, Hughes Reef, Johnson Reef, Mischief Reef, and Subi Reef. The ROC also claims all the Spratly islands, but only occupies one major island, the largest of the Spratly group, named Itu Aba (Taiping Island in Chinese). The two governments agree that the South China Sea is China's, although they disagree on which China.

Malaysia does not simply have to deal with China, since Vietnam likewise claims all of the Spratly islands. In 1973, they were made part of the Phuoc Tuy Province, and later of the Khanh Hoa Province. Currently, Vietnam occupies 21 islands or reefs, including Alison Reef, Amboyan Reef, Barque Canada Reef, Central London Reef, Cornwallis South Reef, Da Gri-san, Da Hi Gen, East London Reef, Great Discovery Reef, Ladd Reef, Landsdowne Reef, Namyit Island, Pearson Reef, Petley Reef, Sand Cay, Sin Cowe Island, South Reef, South West Cay, Spratly Island, Tennent Reef, and West London Reef.

The Philippines too claims most of the Spratlys, terming them the Kalayaan Island Group (KIG). These are administered by Palawan Province. The Philippines, however, only occupies eight islands, including Kota or Loaita Island, Lawak or Nansham Island, Likas or West York Island, Panata or Lamkian Cay, Pag-asa or Thitu Island, Parola or North East Cay, Patag or Flat Island, and Rizal or Commodore Reef.

As discussed above, Brunei claims a rectangular-shaped area of the sea, which includes Louisa Reef, and Brunei and Malaysia have recently clarified their competing claims to this area. Meanwhile, Malaysia occupies three marine features it considers to be on its continental shelf, including Ardasier Reef (Terumbu Ubi), Mariveles Reef (Terumbu Mantanani), and Swallow Reef (Terumbu Layang). But Malaysia claims eleven features in total, many of them currently under the control of other countries involved in this dispute.

The difficulty of precisely identifying the numerous marine features—atolls, islands, islets, sand cays and sandbanks, reefs, and rocks—comprising the Spratly archipelago is complicated by the coexistence of different systems for naming these marine features. Chinese (two versions), English, Filipino, French, and Vietnamese names have been superimposed on each other, without any clear correspondence between them.

China's willingness to voice its claim to sovereignty over all of the Spratlys has been increasing in recent years. During the Cold War, China and Vietnam had military skirmishes over the Paracels in 1974 and the Spratlys in 1976.[17]As China's concerns about the Soviet Union have decreased, it has arguably become even more focused on Southeast Asian disputes. All this greatly complicates Chinese claims to the islands in its territorial dispute with such countries as Brunei, Malaysia, the Philippines, and Vietnam.

An important factor in Malaysia's defense modernization strategies since the late-1980s has been its ability to defend itself in case of a military dispute over the overlapping claims to some of the features of the Spratlys. Since the 1990s, the Malaysian Armed Forces have taken delivery of ships, submarines, and MIG-29 fighter jets, at least in part in the context of a potential South China Sea conflict. A definitive delimitation of the maritime boundary, or rather, maritime boundaries, assuming this were to ever happen, would undoubtedly ease political and military tensions.

In its diplomacy, China has demonstrated a conciliatory attitude toward Malaysia. After the PRC signed the *Treaty of Amity* and the *Declaration of the Code of Conduct in the South China Sea* in 2002, tensions eased between China and Malaysia over their competing claims to some of the marine features within this group. Many of Malaysia's natural gas and oil fields located offshore of Sarawak also fall under the Chinese claim, as well as within the Philippine hydrocarbon reserves. To date, China has not specifically objected to their development by Malaysia. However, recent Malaysian efforts to assert its claim to an extended continental shelf have been met with stiff opposition.

Malaysia's Continental Shelf Claim

Malaysia claims a portion of the southeastern section of South China Sea, together with eleven marine features in the Spratly islands, on the basis that they are within its legal continental shelf. Malaysia currently occupies Swallow Reef or Pulau Layang-Layang, which has a .023 square mile (.060 km^2 or six hectares) island at the eastern fringe of the reef. It also claims two marine features currently occupied by Vietnam, namely Barque Canada Reef and Amboyna Cay; Amboyna Cay is also claimed by the Philippines. Malaysia also claims Commodore Reef, which is occupied by the Philippines, and Royal Charlotte Reef, which is not currently occupied by any nation. All the features claimed by Malaysia are also claimed by Vietnam and China, as well as by Taiwan.

The five features currently occupied by Malaysia are also claimed by the Philippines and one is generally thought to be claimed by Brunei. All of these features are encompassed within the unilateral claim that Malaysia issued in 1979 and whose boundary was delineated on a map that was published in that year.[18] As noted above, Malaysia's basis for claiming sovereignty over as well as occupying certain islands in the Spratly group is that these are part of its continental shelf. However, control of the continental shelf is not a basis for a claim to title over islands, but only a basis for a claim to the resources of the shelf. Malaysia's position therefore appears to be at odds with the longstanding legal principle that claims to maritime space arise from sovereignty over territory rather than the other way around.

On 6 May 2009, Malaysia and Vietnam made a joint submission to the UN Commission on the Limits of the Continental Shelf in accordance with Article 76, paragraph 8, of the 1982 United Nations Convention on the Law of the Sea (UNCLOS), relating to extended continental shelf areas located beyond 200 nm from their baselines along their mainland coasts into the southern sector of the South China Sea. The joint submission was made without prejudice to the question of delimitation of the continental shelf between the states with opposite or adjacent coasts. Similarly, the joint submission is without prejudice to the position of the states that are parties to a land or maritime dispute in consonance with paragraph 5 (b) of Annex I to the Commission's rules of procedure.

A day later, China lodged a protest against this submission. On 7 May 2009, the government of China submitted a *Note Verbal* and a copy of a map as an attachment to the Commission on the Limits of the Continental Shelf as a legal counterpoint to the joint submission by Malaysia and Vietnam relating to the claims by these countries to an extended continental shelf in accordance with Article 76 of UNCLOS. The *Note* stated that:

> China has indisputable sovereignty over the islands in the South China Sea and the adjacent waters, and enjoys sovereign rights and jurisdiction over the relevant waters as well as the seabed and subsoil thereof . . . a position consistently held by the Chinese Government, and is widely known by the international community.[19]

The protests lodged by the PRC, as indeed by some of Malaysia's other neighbors as well as Malaysia's own counter-protests, appear to be mere formalities, as any final approval by the UN will only be possible when the sovereignty disputes are resolved.[20] For this reason, Malaysia's continental shelf claims will probably not be resolved for some time to come.

Conclusions

Aggressive moves by China against Japan over an island dispute in the East China Sea during early November 2010 caused concern in Malaysia. These events prompted Malaysia's Defence Chief to state on 10 November 2010 that his nation's confidence in a traditional friend, China, is based on a trading relationship dating back thousands of years, with particular reference to sea-borne trade.[21] The PRC and Malaysia acknowledge that they are good neighbors, and that the peoples of these countries share a long history of friendly exchanges. During recent years, political trust has been deepened and economic and trade cooperation has yielded remarkable results, bringing substantial benefits to both nations. Malaysia's adoption of the "One China Policy," even while pursuing close economic relations with Taiwan, reflects commercial expediency in the face of political realities.

The PRC and Malaysia have adopted a constructive approach to resolve outstanding problems, including overlapping claims and the determination of land and maritime boundaries. Every diplomatic effort is being made to ensure that bilateral relations do not become adversely affected by these territorial problems. In the past, the Malaysian government has even agreed to refer territorial disputes with Indonesia and Singapore to the International Court of Justice. This indicates the extent to which Malaysia is prepared to go in achieving amicable solutions to bilateral problems.

Notwithstanding these outstanding Sino-Malaysian territorial disputes over the Spratlys, past and present Malaysia government administrations have demonstrated great reluctance to the joint development of the Spratly islands. Instead, Malaysia is actively exploiting these resources on its own, even while trying to enhance its claim over the area through military presence and commercial development. Most importantly, Malaysia's 2009 decision to submit with Vietnam a joint continental claim to the UN Commission on the Limits of the Continental Shelf will almost certainly interfere with China's apparent claim to the entire South China Sea, as per its nine-dashed line map.

Notes

1. "Malaysian Businesses Set to Take Advantage of Using RMB as Trade Settlement," 9 June 2011, http://www.bernama.com/bernama/v5/newsindex.php?id=592681 [Accessed on 27 October 2011].

2. George T. Yu, "Political Change and Reform in China," in K.C. Hou and K. K. Yeoh, eds., *Malaysia and Southeast Asia and the Emerging China: Political, Economic and Cultural Perspectives* (Kuala Lumpur: Institute of China Studies, 2005), 91.

3. Kim Yong Gan, "China-ASEAN Relations: a key to the Region's Stability and Prosperity," in Lai Hongyi and Lim Tin Seng, eds., *Harmony and Development ASEAN-China Relations* (Singapore: World Scientific Publishing Co. Pte., 2007), 3-5.

4. Ibid., 11-14.

5. Lai Hongyi, "China's Evolving Relations with Southeast Asia: Domestic and Strategic Factors," in Ibid., 17-35.

6. Lu Jianren, "China's Economic Growth and Its Impact of the ASEAN Economies," in Ibid., 107-116.

7. Sheng Lijun, "China's Peaceful Rise and Its Political and Security Implications for South East Asia," in Ibid., 36-48.

8. Wu Xiao An, "China Meets Southeast Asia: A Long-Term Historical Review," in Khai Leong Ho, ed., *Connecting and Distancing, Southeast Asia and China* (Singapore: Institute of Southeast Asian studies, 2009), 22.

9. Stephen Leong, "Malaysia-China Relations: Looking Beyond Fears and Inadequacies," in Lai and Lim, 145-148.

10. V.L. Porritt, *British Colonial Rule in Sarawak 1946-63* (Oxford: Oxford University Press, 1997), 423; P. Lee and K.H. Lee, "Malaysia-China Relations: A Review," in Hou and Yeoh, 1-27: 2-5.

11. "China not a threat, says Dr Mahathir," *Brunei Times*, 27 April 2010, http://www.bt.com.bn/news-asia/2010/04/27/china-not-threat-says-dr-mahathir [Accessed on 1 February 2011].

12. Ibid.

13. J. Rowan, "The U.S.-Japan Security Alliance, ASEAN and the South China Sea Dispute," *Asian Survey*, Vol. XLV, No. 3 (2005), 414-436.

14. Han Zhenhua, ed., *Woguo nanhai Zhudao Shiliao Huibian* [The Compilation of Historic Materials on the South China Sea Islands] (Beijing: The Oriental Publishing House, 1988); Gao Zhiguo, "The South China Sea: From Conflict to Cooperation," *Ocean Development and International Law*, Vol. 25 (1994), 346; Zou Keyuan, "The Chinese Traditional Maritime Boundary Line in the South China Sea and its Legal Consequences for the Resolution of the Dispute over the Spratly Islands," *International Journal of Marine and Coastal Law*, Vol. 14 (1997), 52.

15. Li Jinming and Li Dexia, "The Dotted Line on the Chinese Map of the South China Sea: A Note," *Ocean Development and International Law*, Vol. 34 (2003), 294.

16. Gao, 346.

17. Leo Suryadinata, *China and the ASEAN States: The Ethnic Chinese Dimension* (Singapore: Singapore University Press, 1985), 43.

18. The *Peta Menunjukkan Sempadan Perairan dan Pelantar Benua Malaysia* or "Map Showing the Territorial Waters and Continental Shelf Boundaries of Malaysia," published by the Malaysian Directorate of National Mapping in two sheets. This map is often referred to as the *Peta Baru* or New Map.

19. CML/17/2009, Communications received with regard to the joint submission made by Malaysia and Viet Nam to the Commission on the Limits of the Continental Shelf in 2008, 7 May 2009, chn_2009re_mys_vnm_e.pdf.

20. For details of Malaysia and Vietnam's joint submission to the United Nations Commission on the Limits of the Continental Shelf, as well as the protests and counter protests connected to it see: http://www.un.org/Depts/los/clcs_new /submissions_files/submission_mysvnm_33_2009.htm [Accessed on 20 December 2011].

21. Anne Gearan, "Malaysia defense chief says China no bully," *Daily Caller,* 9 November 2010.

Map 12: Mongolia's Border with China

12
Sino-Mongol Border:
From Conflict to Precarious Resolution

Morris Rossabi

Mongolia's position between two great empires has shaped its modern boundaries and its border disputes. Before the 17th century, the boundaries between Mongolia, China, and Russia had not been well defined. The Mongol nomadic lifestyle precluded a careful delineation of frontiers, and China's tribute system of foreign relations, which treated foreigners as vassals and so could not conceive of diplomatic parity, prevented it from negotiating on border issues with alleged subjects of the emperor. A treaty would presume equality with the Mongol peoples and confederations, an untenable proposition for most Chinese dynasties.

For this reason, border delimitation and demarcation between China and Mongolia required outside intervention, in particular from Imperial Russia and, later, the Soviet Union. As a result of Stalin's 1945 negotiations with Chiang Kai-shek, during January 1946 China recognized Outer Mongolia's independence. This meant that 603,909 square miles (1,564,116 km^2)—greater than the state of Alaska—of what had formerly been internationally recognized as Chinese territory were dominated by Moscow until the end of the USSR in 1991.

Following the PRC's creation in 1949, Mao Zedong expected Mongolia to return to China, as per Soviet promises during the 1930s. When this did not happen, Sino-Soviet tensions increased, particularly along their lengthy borders. During August 1962, Beijing sought to resolve its territorial disputes with Mongolia through diplomacy. On 25 December 1962, China and the Mongolian People's Republic (MPR) signed an agreement officially beginning the process of delineating the Sino-Mongolian border. Later, in 1988, a second treaty settled the 2,886 mile (4,645 km) border.

Mongolia under the Qing Dynasty

Sino-Mongolian border disputes stem from three-centuries' old events. The struggle between the peoples of the steppe and the Chinese agricultural lands stretches back to the Han dynasty (206 B.C.E.-C.E. 220) and the Xiongnu confederation in

Mongolia, but the expansion of the Tsarist and Qing (1644-1911) empires in the 17th and 18th centuries made conducting proper border delineation more urgent. The Mongols who had earlier been free to roam around from southern Siberia to what is now Inner Mongolia began to be hemmed in and restricted by powerful neighboring countries, mainly Russia and China.

The arrival of the Russians in Northeast Asia undermined the previous system of Chinese foreign relations, which relied more on informal structures—such as the tribute system—rather than signed diplomatic agreements. Starting in the middle of the 17th century, clashes erupted between Qing forces and Russian settlers and prospectors along the borders of Manchuria.[1] At the same time, Galdan, a leader of the Zunghar or Western Mongols, rose to prominence and sought to unify the Mongols and to challenge China's economic and political domination. Qing fears that the Zunghars and the Russians would form an alliance against China prompted negotiations with the Tsarist state.[2] In the ensuing Treaty of Nerchinsk of 1689, China permitted Russia to dispatch merchants to trade in Beijing, to send students to learn Chinese and Manchu, and to establish a Russian Orthodox ecclesiastical mission and, in turn, received concessions from the Tsarist Court on delineation of the border.[3] Most of this delimitation centered on Manchuria. In general, "the Russians were forced to withdraw from their advance positions."[4] Later still, in 1727, the Treaty of Bura and the Treaty of Kyakhta provided an even more detailed delineation of the border.

An important consequence of the Sino-Russian treaties was that Galdan was isolated and vulnerable, creating a great opportunity for the Qing. With no place to escape, Galdan fought a losing battle with the Qing forces in 1696 and was defeated. The following year, he appears to have committed suicide. Even earlier, the Qing, in 1636, had overwhelmed the last important Khan of Inner Mongolia and had brought that sizable land within its domains. The Manchu Court established the Lifanyuan (Office of Colonial Affairs) to govern these lands. Territorial divisions were irrelevant because China was the only government. The only substantial boundary was between Inner Mongolia and Outer Mongolia, which was due partly to the different times the Qing brought them under its control and partly due to the Gobi Desert separating the two.

The Qing ruled Mongolia for more than two centuries in what many Mongols believe to have been a brutal and oppressive manner. Chinese merchants allegedly exploited both herders and the nobility, placing them in debt and pauperizing the country. The Qing authorities meted out harsh punishments for even minor infractions. The Mongols complained that the Chinese and the Manchus had a stranglehold on the economy. The Buddhist monasteries were virtually the only institutions that profited from Qing governance. Seeking to ingratiate itself with the Bogdo Gegen, the Mongol equivalent to the Dalai Lama, and to monks, the Manchu

Court provided the monasteries with laborers and special subsidies in hopes that Buddhist injunctions against killing and support of pacifism would translate into a less bellicose Mongol population. Except for one outbreak in the middle of the 18th century, peace prevailed, and in Mongolia the Qing did not face the insurrections it encountered in Xinjiang. To be sure, most Mongols resented and were hostile to foreign rule, but they were unable to extricate themselves from foreign control, even as the Qing dynasty declined in the 19th century.

Russia sought to capitalize on the Qing court's weakness. Nikolai Muraviev-Amursky, the Governor General of Siberia in the 1850s, ignored the Sino-Russian treaties of 1689 and 1727 and occupied territories along China's northeastern border, compelling the Qing to sign a new treaty, which ceded these lands. However, Tsarist officials did not at this time encroach on Mongolia. Russian scientists and adventurers studied and wrote about Mongolia's natural environment and physical geography, but Russian merchants rarely ventured into the countryside and could not challenge itinerant Chinese peddlers who traveled to the steppes and thus monopolized trade with the herders. Without a large contingent of Russian settlers in Mongolia, the Tsarist government could not lay claim to the land of the nomads. The boundaries were not altered, and the 1689 and 1727 treaties remained in force.

A Chaotic Post-Qing Mongolia

The Qing dynasty's collapse in 1911 offered Mongols an opportunity to liberate themselves, a possibility that they, in part, subverted by aligning too closely with Russia. Mongol princes quickly declared independence, and the Bogdo Gegen became the head of state. Some Mongols, who were finally allowed to express their antipathy toward their opponents, looted Chinese businesses and attacked Chinese merchants. After the initial violence, the Mongol elite sought to preserve its independence. However, factional disputes among the Mongol princes both in Outer Mongolia and Inner Mongolia prevented unity and undermined efforts at independence.

The disunited Mongol leaders turned to the Russians for protection and aid. Beginning in the 1890s, the Russians began building the Trans-Siberian Railroad immediately to the north of the Russian-Mongol border, which gave them enormous leverage over Mongolia. However, the Tsarist government did not favor a union of all Mongols nor did it wish to antagonize Japan, which sought greater influence in Inner Mongolia through twenty-one demands it presented to the Chinese government in 1915. Although the new government in China was relatively weak, Russia did not approve of total independence for the Mongols. Thus, in 1915, it joined together in a tripartite treaty with China and Mongolia, which proclaimed Mongolia autonomous but under Chinese suzerainty and also delineated the border between Outer Mongolia and Inner Mongolia. This ambiguous treaty created considerable uncertainty and led to turbulence.

The Russian revolutions of 1917 and the increasingly ineffective Chinese central government generated even greater chaos in Mongolia, which realigned itself with China once again in 1919. Other foreigners, including adventurers who did not represent any specific State, capitalized on the disarray among the Mongol leaders. A Chinese commander named Xu Shuzheng, the Manchurian warlord Zhang Zuolin, and the Japanese-backed White Russian Grigori Semenov all sought to dominate this central area of Northeast Asia. The culmination was the short-lived military occupation during 1920-1921 of Urga—the present-day Mongolian capital of Ulaanbaatar—by the fanatical, violent, and reportedly mad anti-communist Baron Roman Ungern-Sternberg.[5]

Several of these foreigners conceived of a Pan-Mongol state composed of Outer Mongolia—what is now the country of Mongolia—Inner Mongolia, the Buryat Mongol lands, Tuva, and the territories inhabited by the Mongols in Manchuria. Under these turbulent conditions, questions of boundaries were not addressed. In the end, however, the formation of the Soviet Union, and its victory over various "White" factions during the Russian civil war, allowed the Bolshevik government to exert indirect control over Mongolia.

Socialist Mongolia and Relations with China

The involvement of the USSR shaped many of Mongolia's territorial issues. During early 1921, Mongol nationalists turned for assistance to the Bolsheviks in deposing Ungern-Sternberg. In July 1921, a combined Mongol-Bolshevik force expelled him from Urga and eventually executed him.[6] Mongol nationalists proclaimed independence, yet depended on the USSR for political and military support, in particular against China.

The USSR sent advisers to aid the Mongols. Communist International (Comintern) agents all too often dictated events, however, leading to executions in the early 1920s of top Mongol officials considered anti-Soviet or overly ardent nationalists. The Chinese naturally objected to the projected establishment of an independent Mongolia and pressured the USSR to accept their claim that Mongolia was part of China. After considerable negotiation, the warlord-supported government in Beijing finally elicited a major concession from the USSR in a treaty signed on 31 May 1924. The USSR acknowledged Chinese sovereignty over Mongolia, but was not compelled to withdraw its troops. The Soviets were, to say the least, disingenuous. They knew that, within a short time, Mongol leaders would proclaim the country to be an independent MPR—consisting of 602,909 square miles or 1,564,116 km^2—on 26 November 1924. Moreover, if offered an opportunity, the Soviets would eagerly renounce the treaty. In 1927, when Chiang Kai-shek overwhelmed the warlord government and simultaneously severed an alliance with both the Chinese Communists and the USSR, the Soviets would and did break this agreement.[7]

However, the Soviets capitalized upon their dominant position in Mongolia to enlarge their own influence. In 1921, they encouraged the independence of and gave formal diplomatic recognition to the Tannu Tuva People's Republic, a region that had long been considered to be part of Mongolia because it adhered to Tibetan Buddhism and had the same language and economy. Tannu Tuva does not share a common border with China. Five years elapsed before the MPR signed a treaty recognizing Tannu Tuva's independence. Yet Tuvans and Mongols appear to have harbored a desire to unify through the creation of a Pan-Mongol state. In 1929, the USSR attempted to quash those efforts by having the Tuvan prime minister deposed for seeking to establish such a new state. Continued Mongol nationalist aspirations prompted Joseph Stalin, in 1944, to incorporate the so-called independent Tannu Tuva as the Tuvan Autonomous Oblast within the USSR. This meant the USSR annexed 65,830 square miles (170,500 km^2) of formerly Mongol and, arguably, formerly Chinese territory, to the Soviet Union.

At the same time, Stalin pressured Chiang Kai-shek as part of the post-war settlement to agree to a new boundary that increased Mongol territory to its south and east at China's expense; he thus compensated Mongolia and deflected criticism from Mongol nationalists for the loss of Tannu Tuva. Like Chiang, Mao Zedong was upset by the loss of Chinese territory but had scant leverage to prevent Stalin from doing so. In 1962, the USSR further consolidated its position by establishing Tannu Tuva as an Autonomous Republic, and even after the USSR's collapse in 1992, the Tuvan Republic remained within the Russian Federation.

The principal issue concerning the border during the 1920s and early 1930s was that the Chinese government persisted in its view that Mongolia was part of China, as per the terms of the 1924 Sino-Soviet treaty. Indeed even after the establishment of the MPR, numerous Chinese lived in Mongolia. As one specialist on modern Mongolia has noted, "the Mongols depended on Chinese merchants for tea, Chinese peasants for farming, Chinese artisans for the building of monasteries and making of Buddhist artifacts, Chinese money-lenders for capital, and Chinese labor for hard work other than livestock herding."[8]

However, the late 1920s and early 1930s witnessed a forced exodus of Chinese from the MPR.[9] The Chinese government was in no position to protest the treatment of its citizens or to reassert its right to rule. Chiang Kai-shek still faced the opposition of prominent warlords and the Chinese Communists, along with Japanese encroachment, declines in world prices for agricultural goods, and corruption, and ultimately the Japanese attack in 1937. His government objected to a 1936 mutual security agreement between the USSR and the MPR, complaining that Mongolia, as part of China, had no right to sign such a document.[10] The onset of the Sino-Japanese War and World War II overshadowed the status of Mongolia and its boundary with China.

Toward the end of World War II, the Mongols added to the confusion. Their authoritarian leader Khorloogiin Choibalsan (1895-1952) had his own territorial ambitions.[11] Aware of the civil war between Chiang Kai-shek and the Chinese Communists, he continued to hope that he could detach Inner Mongolia from China. That desire came to a grinding halt in 1947 when the Communists occupied and established the Inner Mongolian Autonomous Region. However, Choibalsan persisted in his grand ambitions for expansion. The revolt of the Kazakh leader Osman Batyr (1899-1951) starting in 1944 offered an opportunity to influence or perhaps to expand in the neighboring land of Xinjiang. Stalin at first supported Choibalsan's aspirations by assisting Osman in order to weaken Chiang Kai-shek.[12] Thus Choibalsan provided Osman with Soviet weapons and planned to lay claim to part of the Kazakh regions in Xinjiang. Because Kazakhs constituted 5 percent of Mongolia's population, Choibalsan believed that he had a strong case.[13] Osman also received considerable support from local Kazakhs who resented Chinese exploitation, and he appeared to be on the verge of victory.

However, at the end of 1945, Stalin withdrew his support because of a rapprochement with China. After considerable pressure, Chiang Kai-shek agreed to accept a vote by the Mongol population on the future status of Mongolia. On 20 October 1945, almost 100 percent of the Mongol electorate reputedly opted for independence. In January 1946, the Nationalists agreed that Mongolia was independent in exchange for Stalin's promise not to help the Chinese Communists. The very next year, Chiang renounced his pledge because of Stalin's support for the CCP and Mongol support for Osman. But Stalin, with legal justification, ignored Chiang's renunciation and broke with Osman, compelling Choibalsan to follow suit. Although Mongolia did not become a part of the USSR, like Tannu Tuva, its territory was dominated by Moscow until the end of the USSR in 1991. In 1951, the Chinese Communists captured and executed Osman, finally ending Choibalsan's dream of a base in Xinjiang.

The PRC's Relations with Mongolia

The Chinese Communist victory in 1949 did not necessarily bode well for Sino-Mongol relations. In his renowned interviews with the journalist Edgar Snow, Mao

Zedong had said that Mongolia would inevitably return to Chinese jurisdiction after the Communist victory in China.[14] Such views greatly concerned Mongolia, which feared that it would suffer the same fate as Inner Mongolia and that Chinese colonists would swamp the native population.[15] Once again, the Mongols turned to the USSR for support.

Mongol concerns subsided somewhat when Mao signed the February 1950 Treaty of Friendship, Alliance, and Mutual Assistance with the USSR, which tacitly accepted Mongolia as an independent country by not mentioning it in the treaty. Shortly thereafter, the MPR and China signed agreements, in which the Chinese pledged economic aid and dispatched Chinese laborers to Mongolia to build sizable construction projects.[16] Chinese and Mongol workers built the Trans-Mongol Railroad, which was completed on 7 December 1955 and linked the Chinese town of Jining to the Mongol border town of Erlian (Mongol Erenhot) and then to Ulaanbaatar, after which it connected to the Trans-Siberian Railroad.[17]

As a result of these projects, Mongolia's trade with China increased dramatically throughout the 1950s. But Mongolian leaders remained suspicious of Chinese intentions, fearing that China still planned to annex Mongolia. China had already gained control not only over Inner Mongolia but also over Tibet, with which Mongolia had traditionally maintained strong links. Although the Soviet-inspired collectivization and the 1930s purges in Mongolia had generated hostility toward the Russians, the Mongols did not fear a massive arrival of Russians into Mongolia. China, with its huge population, was perceived as a far greater threat to Mongol independence.

Despite this latent fear, the MPR benefited from Chinese economic aid until the onset of the Sino-Soviet split in 1960. However, deepening ideological, territorial, and economic conflicts between China and the USSR eventually compelled the MPR to choose sides. Yumjaagiin Tsedenbal (1916-1991), who had ascended to power after Choibalsan's death in 1952, was married to a Russian woman and had been educated in the USSR. He supported an alliance with the USSR and overcame opponents who proposed a balanced approach toward China and the USSR.[18] Early in 1962, the Soviet leadership bolstered Tsedenbal's decision by inviting Mongolia to become the first non-European member of the Council for Mutual Economic Assistance (COMECON), the major organization for economic planning and cooperation in Eastern Europe. Mongolia's entrance into the COMECON ensured significant Soviet and Eastern European economic and technical assistance.[19]

In December 1962, the Chinese countered by agreeing to a treaty that delimited the border in Mongolia's favor.[20] China was motivated to cede territory because of threats other than those posed by the USSR. It was engaged in territorial disputes with India, which shortly erupted into a border war, and 60,000 Kazakhs and

Uyghurs had recently fled from Xinjiang to the USSR, an indication of instability along China's northwestern frontier. Mongolia had attempted for five years to negotiate an agreement, but China had stalled. In August 1962, China, encountering domestic disturbances and external conflicts, called for a meeting to resolve a dispute over 16,808 square miles (43,533 km^2). In the ensuing treaty, signed on 25 December 1962, China compromised, turning over substantial grazing areas, the Beita and Bogeda mountain regions, Qinghe, and Hongshanzui. Settlement of this territorial dispute permitted China to cope with the violence and disruptions in Xinjiang. The negotiations also appeared to confirm the view that "China has not been highly prone to using force in its territorial disputes."[21]

Hoping to ingratiate themselves to the Mongols, the Chinese officials had made major concessions on boundary delimitation in negotiations with Tsedenbal in Beijing, but to no avail. A month later Tsedenbal condemned the Chinese for defaming the USSR and for undermining the unity of the Communist bloc through disparagement of the Soviet policy of peaceful coexistence with the capitalist world.[22] In July 1964, Mao further strained his relations with Tsedenbal and the Mongol leadership in an interview he had with Japanese journalists.[23] He accused the USSR of manipulating the Mongol government and hinted that Mongolia was a part of China that had been detached by the Soviets. His intemperate remarks reignited fears of Chinese territorial designs on Mongolia and bolstered Tsedenbal in his tilt toward the USSR.

Capitalizing on Tsedenbal's decision, the Soviet leadership almost immediately provided the support the Mongols required. In April 1965, they pledged to offer over six hundred million rubles of aid, and shortly thereafter, negotiated a trade agreement favorable to the Mongols.[24] During January 1966, the USSR and Mongolia signed a Treaty of Friendship, Cooperation, and Mutual Assistance, which entailed a Soviet guarantee of its neighbors' territorial integrity. Troops from the USSR arrived, and as the Sino-Soviet conflict intensified, tens of thousands of Soviet soldiers were stationed in Mongolia.[25]

The Chinese responded by sending troops to their side of the border. The onset of the Chinese Cultural Revolution, especially as it affected Inner Mongolia, generated even greater animosity between China and the MPR. In Inner Mongolia, violence erupted between the Red Guards, mostly wandering bands of Chinese youths, and the Mongols, and eventually between the Chinese army and the Mongols.[26] Many Mongols and Chinese lost their lives in the ensuing battles, and the press in Mongolia began to publish severe critiques of China's "oppressive" policies in Inner Mongolia. It also accused China of seeking to annex Mongolia.

During 1972-1980, Sino-Mongol relations continued to be hostile. The Mongols feared that as the Chinese population increased, China would need *lebensraum*, jeopardizing all neighboring lands including Mongolia. They accused China of threatening Mongolia by conducting over 150 military exercises adjacent to the border, of trespassing on Mongol territory, of rustling or killing livestock, and of undertaking reconnaissance flights over Mongolia. They repeatedly referred to China's "chauvinism" and "hegemonism."[27] In turn, the Chinese were concerned by the large number of Soviet troops in Mongolia. With more than 100,000 soldiers in Mongolia, the USSR was perceived as a threat to China's security.[28] The Chinese also accused the Mongols of violating Chinese territory in Inner Mongolia, requiring Chinese forces to expel them.[29]

Warming Sino-Mongol Relations

Beginning in the early 1980s, China and the USSR began to move toward a rapprochement, which naturally influenced Mongolia's relations with China. Trade, tourism, and cultural relations between Mongolia's two neighbors were restored at a rapid pace.[30] The Mongols did not at first follow their Soviet patrons. Tsedenbal, for example, complained that Chinese officials continued to issue maps claiming Mongolia and Lake Baikal as part of China. His government also accused the Chinese who still resided in Mongolia of gambling, smuggling, and other criminal activities.[31] Mongolian leaders repeatedly insisted that China sought to interfere in Mongolia's internal affairs and stated that "China may not and does not have the right to demand the withdrawal of Soviet military units from Mongolia."[32]

Tsedenbal had become a stumbling block in attempts to improve relations. The USSR leaders, who from 1982 on supported change, found Tsedenbal to be a throwback to a pre-reform era and played a role in his ouster in August 1984. Jambyn Batmönkh (1926-1997), who was more willing to compromise than his predecessor, became the new Secretary of the Mongolian People's Revolutionary Party (MPRP) when Tsedenbal went to the USSR and reputedly resigned because of "poor health."[33]

Sino-Mongol relations rapidly improved. In October 1984, the foreign ministers of Mongolia and China held private talks during the United Nations General Assembly convocation in New York, the first such meetings since the 1960s. Even more telling was a speech by Hu Yaobang, the Secretary of the Chinese Communist Party. Visiting Inner Mongolia in the fall of 1984, he spoke about its future and of China's links with Mongolia. He proclaimed that peaceful resolution of border disputes was essential for the region's economic developments. Erlian, a town on the Mongol side of the border, could, he noted, become a vital commercial entrepot.[34]

The most dramatic development though was Mikhail Gorbachev's speech in Vladivostok on 29 July 1986. The reform-minded leader of the USSR proposed the withdrawal of a Soviet division from Mongolia. This concession caught all the participants by surprise. The Chinese Vice Minister of Foreign Affairs responded that such an "outcome is expected to have great impact on the future of Sino-Soviet negotiations for the improvement of their relations."[35] Although the Chinese were delighted, they soon signaled that this concession was too limited.[36] For the Mongols, Gorbachev's speech and his pledge posed serious questions about their vulnerability to Chinese attack. Batmönkh traveled to Moscow to seek reassurance that the USSR would continue to act as Mongolia's ultimate protector, but he was apparently not satisfied with Gorbachev's response.[37]

After his interview with Gorbachev, Batmönkh and his government began to improve relations with China, partly because their faith in Soviet guarantees of their security was shaken. The pace of Sino-Mongol interchanges quickened. At the same time, Mongol officials, who were less certain about the protections offered by the Soviet umbrella, sought to broaden their links with the outside world as insurance against possible Chinese attempts at expansionism. In any event, trade volume between China and Mongolia increased throughout the late 1980s,[38] and political and diplomatic interchanges continued apace.[39]

One of the first concerns in Mongolia's warming relationship with China was problems relating to the Sino-Mongol frontiers. In spring of 1987, government negotiators reached preliminary agreements and, perhaps as important, devised mechanisms to resolve disputes along the 2,886-miles (4,645 km) long border. After a series of meetings between representatives of both parties, they signed a new treaty governing the border, which tended to favor Mongolia.[40] By 1989, the Chinese Communist Party and the MPRP had restored ties, and a new agreement permitted Mongolia to open a consulate in Höhhot in Inner Mongolia and eliminated visa requirements for Chinese and Mongol citizens crossing their respective borders.[41]

While the Mongols fostered better relations with China, they simultaneously sought to widen their contacts with the outside world. Their greatest success occurred on 27 January 1987, with the establishment of diplomatic relations with the United States.[42] Recognition by the United States was invaluable, because it signaled acceptance in the Western capitalist world. With growing concerns about the USSR's flagging commitment to Mongolia and with the fear that the only alternative was China, Mongolia sought to join the Western and Asian community of states to avert total dependence on the Soviet bloc or on China. Mongolia's break with its socialist past facilitated contacts with the outside world. Demonstrations starting late in 1989 compelled the MPRP government to resign in March 1990 and to consent to the first multi-party elections in Mongol history.[43]

Mongolia's New Policies and China

Having decided to seek Western and Japanese aid and technical assistance, Mongolia committed itself to so-called westernizing reform. The International Monetary Fund, the Asian Development Bank, and other international financial agencies would proffer aid, in the form of grants and loans, on condition that Mongolia adopt a market economy, which included liberalization of prices, privatization of state assets, austerity, minimalist government, and abandonment of protectionism.[44] In 1993, the World Bank estimated that Mongolia would require at least $150-200 million of aid per year for the indefinite future. Almost two decades later, its prediction seems prescient.

One of the unanticipated effects of the reform policies has been the numerous avenues offered to the Chinese to influence the Mongol economy. For example, privatization in Mongolia has been viewed as riddled with favoritism and corruption. In a poll conducted in October 1998, 14.1 percent of the Mongols surveyed believed that Mongol agents for foreign states, principally China, were the great beneficiaries of the privatization process.[45] China could now own property in Mongolia. Liberalization meant higher prices for most goods, impoverishing many Mongols while providing opportunities for the sale of cheap Chinese products.

Meanwhile, pressure from the international financial agencies, as well as from Mongol proponents of the market economy, led to the removal in May 1997 of tariffs on almost all imported commodities. Nascent Mongol industries were unprotected, and inexpensive Chinese goods flooded the market and undermined local products and manufacturing. Native enterprises could scarcely secure loans from the hastily developed banking system, which was plagued by favoritism and extraordinarily high rates of interest. Without accessible loans, Mongol processing industries could not compete with the Chinese in purchasing Mongol raw materials.[46]

The official Mongol government's line over the past two decades has been that China has abandoned efforts to expand into Mongolia.[47] There is some truth in this view. With no menacing Soviet troops in Mongolia, China need not fear for the security of its borderlands, and it has scarcely shown interest in adopting a belligerent stance about border delimitation. Instead it appears to have decided that economic influence and possible economic dominance are both better strategies in Mongolia than rule over still another so-called national minority area.

The Mongol population, however, seems less sanguine than its leaders. As early as 1993, the Economist Intelligence Unit found that "many ordinary people express the traditional fear that the growing presence of Chinese, mainly small businessmen, in Mongolia could be a prelude to a Chinese takeover."[48] By late 1997, "rumors that companies have been bought by Chinese individuals or companies have aroused some popular criticism."[49]

Despite these concerns, the various Mongol governments since 1990 have persisted in a policy of maintaining good relations and seeking even closer contacts with China. The visit of Chinese Premier Li Peng to Ulaanbaatar in April 1994 was perhaps the most important of these exchanges. Li signed a Treaty of Friendship and Cooperation on 29 April.[50] The new treaty recognized the independence, sovereignty, and territorial integrity of Mongolia and committed the two countries to non-aggression, non-interference in internal affairs, and peaceful coexistence. Neither would allow its lands to be used by the troops of another country for an attack against the other. Four and a half years later, Mongol President Natsagiin Bagabandi met with China's President Jiang Zemin.[51] The two sides pledged to cooperate about the most important border issues at this stage—halting serious violations along the frontiers, including illegal entry, smuggling, money laundering, and narcotics.[52] These border issues, rather than potential Chinese expansion, have been the Mongols' central concerns in the 21st century, and collaboration, not conflict, has been emphasized.

Such cooperation has culminated in a professed reconciliation of Mongol-Chinese security relations. The *Mongol Defense White Paper*, an official work issued by the Ministry of Defense in 1998, asserted that neither Russia nor China "is striving to exert dominant influence in Mongolia."[53] It also documented increasing collaboration in military affairs between China and Mongolia and China's acceptance of Mongolia's neutrality and nuclear-free status. Joint military conferences, roundtables, military exchanges, and Chinese grants for military equipment and for Chinese language training for the Mongol military have reduced Mongol concerns about security.[54]

China's Economic Dominance and Border Issues

A dramatic increase in Sino-Mongol trade has accompanied peace along the border. By 2009, total turnover amounted to 48 percent of Mongolia's foreign trade, with China receiving 73.9 percent of Mongolia's exports and supplying 25.2 percent of its imports.[55] However, this trade has been inequitable in the sense that China receives raw materials from Mongolia and then reaps substantial additional value that accrues from processing or refining cashmere, copper, and other products it imports. As early as 2000, one source expressed concern, noting that "for the first three months of this year . . . China has sucked up all 100 percent of the copper concentrate, the main export item of Mongolia. This is in addition to the total value of raw cashmere and skins, [and] on top of the 14 percent of the combed cashmere. China's share of the total Mongol exports was 83.5 percent." These figures do not include the illegal (or "suitcase") trade conducted at various points along the border. In addition, "100 percent of the rice, 99.6 percent of all vegetables, [and] over 80 percent of fruits came from China in 1999."[56] Since then, China has invested in and obtained aluminum, coal, fluorspar, and zinc, among other minerals.[57] As of 2010, it provided 60 percent of foreign investment in Mongolia, with Canada, the closest competitor, supplying 6.6 percent of such investment. In short, China has become a dominant force in the Mongol economy.

China also has a vital role in regional economic development projects. Since the early 1990s, the United Nations Development Programme has been touting the development of Northeast Asia as an integrated unit, with individual countries providing complementary assets. China and North Korea could supply cheap and abundant labor, Mongolia and Siberia natural and mineral resources, and Japan and South Korea capital and technical expertise.[58] So far, this project has not led anywhere. An even more elaborate project entails development of the Tumen River zone. Customs among the participating countries would be removed or at least reduced, and a special economic zone would be created among the same six countries. Mongolia would benefit because of direct access to the sea, more sustained development of its natural resources, and a larger market for its products. Cooperation has so far proved elusive, as each country has focused on its own needs and supports different versions of the project.[59]

Serious problems have persisted, however, in the relations between the densely populated Han Chinese-dominated lands in the south and the sparsely populated but sizeable Mongol lands in the north. For example, Chinese smuggling has become rampant. In April 1999, Mongol authorities stopped 100 trucks with 200 tons of raw cashmere heading to China. Customs officials have also arrested smugglers of cement and clay, cedar nuts, and gold.[60] Mongol authorities have repeatedly accused Chinese nationals of smuggling illegal substances, and border officials have captured Chinese smuggling cars, alcohol, and narcotics.[61] They have detained Chinese trying to bring large sums of money into Mongolia.[62] However, most smugglers have not been captured. The Sino-Mongol border is too long to be adequately policed, and, in addition, corrupt customs officials have facilitated such illegal activities.[63]

The Mongol authorities have been concerned about Chinese trespassers. Livestock rustling and illegal fishing in Mongol waters have posed continual problems.[64] Chinese enterprises have encouraged illegal cutting in Mongol forests by paying desperate and unemployed Mongols to provide timber for them. Chinese have also been accused of trading in wildlife.[65] The Mongol deer population, valued by the Chinese for their antlers, has declined precipitously because of poaching.[66] Poachers, many from China or representing Chinese agents or companies, threaten the survival of wild sheep, camels, donkeys, red fox, wolves, and snow leopards.[67] China continues to build better roads to Xinjiang and Mongolia principally to foster economic development, but better transport also facilitates smuggling of everything from narcotics to weapons to endangered species.[68] China professes to be concerned about smuggling, and in a recent visit to Mongolia, Wen Jiabao, the Premier of China's State Council, and his Mongol counterparts discussed more vigorous policing of the border.[69]

Human trafficking was perhaps of greatest concern.[70] Most of these cases involved the transport of women to China, Russia, South Korea, Malaysia, Japan, Israel, Turkey, Switzerland, and Hungary.[71] Such trafficking seems to be accelerating, although it is possible that greater attention and more reports about the practice, rather than a dramatic increase, may have contributed to more media awareness. Spectacular cases such as the railroad police halting the kidnapping of an under-sixteen year old girl to China have aroused the public.[72] Surveys about trafficking have also been disturbing. An Asia Foundation study reported that some street children in Ulaanbaatar were kidnapped and sent to Erlian and Beijing to work in the sex trade. It also concluded that friends or relatives sold some children into prostitution. Some adults were misled by false advertisements promising jobs in China, Russia, Japan, South Korea, or other countries, but then were virtually enslaved into prostitution.[73]

No wonder then that many Mongols are hostile to China. A survey by the most reputable polling organization in Mongolia found that 44.3 percent of those surveyed believed that Russia was Mongolia's best present and future partner and only 2.3 percent considered China to be the best partner.[74] A U.S. Peace Corps volunteer who lived for several years in Mongolia captured the mood of many Mongols when he wrote:

> China, in one sense, is already invading the country. There are the towels at the market, the fruits in the shops; the cheap electronic equipment in the stores . . . the number of Chinese restaurants in the capital . . . Mongolians . . . complain that Chinese attain land through local contacts, Chinese companies take jobs away from Mongolian companies, Chinese workers take jobs away from Mongolian workers, and Chinese men take Mongolian women away from Mongolian men.[75]

To be sure, this view is exaggerated, but it does, nonetheless, reflect the attitudes of numerous Mongols.

Recognizing the perils of over-dependence on China, the Mongol government has attempted to cultivate relations with other countries. As early as 1989, Mongolia had joined the Group of 77, the organization for the so-called underdeveloped countries, and had established relations with the European Economic Community (now European Union). Mongol authorities have been aggressive in initiating closer contacts with numerous countries, a striking contrast to the pre-1990 period when they dealt almost exclusively with the Soviet bloc. They have also sought assistance from the Japan International Cooperation Association, the United States Agency for International Development, and the Konrad Adenauer Foundation, and have joined the Asia Pacific Economic Organization and the World Trade Organization, among other international organizations.[76]

Another recent development is closer Mongol relations with Russia, which has recovered from its virtual collapse in the early 1990s. Wary of China's increasing influence in Central Asia and Mongolia, Russia has begun to affirm its interest in its southern neighbor.[77] Russian Prime Minister Vladimir Putin visited Mongolia in May 2009 and pledged Russian assistance in energy, railways, airlines, and agriculture.[78] About three months later, President Dmitry Medvedev arrived in Mongolia and reaffirmed Russian solidarity with Mongolia and promised an expansion of trade, training for veterinarians, help on environmental issues and space technology, scholarships for study in Russia, and joint development of Mongol uranium resources.[79] In 2010, Russia agreed to provide additional military equipment, and the Mongol government, in turn, approved of joint military exercises.[80] These agreements with Russia offer Mongolia another outlet, but China is and, for the foreseeable future, appears that it will remain Mongolia's foremost trading partner and investor.

China has its own concerns about relations with Mongolia. It has complained about the Dalai Lama's visits to Mongolia. Some Mongols who still believe in Tibetan Buddhism have invited him, which is a repeated irritation for the Chinese government. The Chinese are not favorably disposed toward any show of support for the Dalai Lama and regard Tibet as an internal issue, with which they will brook no interference from the Mongols or other outsiders.[81] They have been even more concerned about a Mongolia-Inner Mongolia link. Until the late 1990s, Mongols often demonstrated in Ulaanbaatar in support of fellow Mongols in Inner Mongolia.[82] However, the Mongol government has tried to avoid alienating the Chinese government. For example, in December 1998, President Bagabandi visited Inner Mongolia and stated that he was "impressed with China's efforts to protect the culture and education of the Mongol minority."[83] The joint U.S.-Mongolia military exercises, which began in 2006 and are known as "Khan Quest," have been even more irritating for the Chinese, who have responded with "Sharpening, 2008," a military exercise of their own just across the border in Inner Mongolia.[84]

Conclusions

Without armed conflict, China has become a dominant force in Mongolia. Abiding by the Marxist dictum that economics often dictates political relations, China has already attained a powerful position in Mongolia. Chinese enterprises have flooded the market with cheap consumer goods and have thus undermined Mongol native industries. Mongolia has had little choice but to trade its natural and mineral resources for Chinese finished or processed products. Lack of regulation on foreign capital has enabled the Chinese to purchase quite a number of Mongol enterprises. With such considerable economic leverage, China does not need to occupy Mongolia physically to exert enormous influence. In the foreseeable future, therefore, any Chinese attempt to annex Mongolia outright is unlikely. However, China's increasing assertiveness in 2010 in dealings with Japan and its Southeast Asian neighbors about disputed islands and territorial waters may presage greater difficulties on Sino-Mongol border issues.[85]

   The definitive delineation of the border between China and Mongolia has become largely irrelevant, especially as the two economies become more and more integrated. Communist China has frequently acquiesced to Mongol territorial claims along the border, perhaps looking to a rapidly approaching future where it can dictate the terms of their relationship. In theory, Beijing has also sought to cooperate with Mongolia on rustling, illegal fishing and lumbering, narcotics, weapons, minerals smuggling, and human trafficking, although some corrupt Chinese and Mongol border officials have clearly profited from such criminal activities.

   If Mongolia hopes to avert Chinese domination and to guarantee its border and its territorial integrity, however, it needs to retain its economic independence. Duties on foreign goods and regulation of foreign, specifically Chinese, capital would be required. Tariffs on some products would offer native industries a breathing space to restore themselves and to elicit state funds and indigenous bank credit. Mongol enterprises cannot, on their own, compete with state-supported Chinese enterprises. With strong native industries, however, Mongolia could develop a more equitable relationship with China—a relationship that would not be colonialist and that would permit Mongolia to avoid a status as a Chinese economic satellite. It could then better protect its territorial integrity and current border with the PRC.

Notes

1. The latest work on these events is Peter Perdue, *China Marches West: The Qing Conquest of Central Eurasia* (Cambridge: Harvard University Press, 2005).
2. Translations of the Chinese sources detailing the complicated tripartite relationship among the Zunghars, Russia, and China may be found in Fu Lo-shu, *A Documentary Chronicle of Sino-Western relations (1644-1820)* (Tucson: University of Arizona Press, 1966).
3. On these missions, see Eric Widmer, *The Russian Ecclesiastical Mission in Peking During the Eighteenth Century* (Cambridge: Harvard University Press, 1976).
4. Mark Mancall, *Russia and China: Their Diplomatic Relations to 1728* (Cambridge: Harvard University Press, 1971), 158; the book also offers translations of the treaties on pages 280 to 310.
5. On Ungern-Sternberg, see the popularly-written biography by James Palmer, *The Bloody White Baron* (New York: Basic Books, 2009).
6. Hillel Salomon, "The Anfu Clique and China's Abrogation of Outer Mongolian Autonomy," *Mongolia Society Bulletin*, Vol. 10, No. 1 (Spring 1971), 74-75.
7. For a concise view of these events, see Charles Bawden, *The Modern History of Mongolia* (New York: Frederick Praeger, 1968).
8. Robert Rupen, *The Mongolian People's Republic* (Palo Alto: Hoover Institution Press, 1966), 19.
9. Ibid., 36; Owen Lattimore, *Nomads and Commissars: Mongolia Revisited* (New York: Oxford University Press, 1962), 98; For a Mongol interpretation of the "nefarious" activities of Chinese traders, see William Brown and Urgunge Onon, trans., *History of the Mongolian People's Republic* (Cambridge: Harvard University Press, 1976), 221, 248.
10. Gerard Friters, *Outer Mongolia and Its International Position* (London: George Allen & Unwin, 1951), 203-204.
11. For Choibalsan, see Mary Rossabi and Morris Rossabi, trans. and introduction, *From Herder to Statesman: The Autobiography of Jamsrangiin Sambuu* (Lanham: Rowman and Littlefield, 2010), 12-14, 16-18.
12. Sergey Radchenko, "Choibalsan's Great Mongolia Dream," *Inner Asia*, Vol. 11, No. 2 (2009), 236.
13. Alexander Diener, *One Homeland or Two? The Nationalization and Transnationalization of Mongolia's Kazakhs* (Stanford: Stanford University Press, 2009), 68-73; See also Peter Finke, *Nomaden im Transformationsprozess: Kasachen in der post-sozialistischen Mongolei* (Münster: Lit Verlag, 2004).
14. Edgar Snow, *Red Star over China* (New York: Random House, 1938), 88-89, fn. 1.
15. Urdadyn Bulag, "The Cult of Ulanhu: History, Memory, and the Making of National Heroes," *Central Asian Survey*, Vol. 17, No. 1 (March 1998), 11-33.
16. Barry Bartow, "The Policy of the Mongolian People's Republic Toward China, 1952-1973," Ph.D. Dissertation, West Virginia University, 1974, 51.

17. Elizabeth Green, "China and Mongolia: Recurring Trends and Prospects for Change," *Asian Survey*, Vol. 26, No. 12 (December 1986), 1346-1348; Sun-ho Kim, *Die Entwicklung der politischen Beziehungen zwischen der Mongolischen Volksrepublik und der Volksrepublik China (1952-89)* (Hamburg: Mitteilungen des Instituts für Asienkunde, 1992), 46-47.

18. One, somewhat sensationalized, account of this struggle within Mongolia was written by D. Dashpurev and S. K. Soni, *Reign of Terror in Mongolia, 1920-1990* (New Delhi: South Asian Publishers, 1992), 59-63; Another primary source by influential leaders who were subsequently purged but not killed is by Mary Rossabi and Morris Rossabi, *Socialist Devotees and Dissenters: Interviews with Three Twentieth-Century Mongolian Leaders* (Osaka: National Museum of Ethnology, 2010).

19. Kim, 46-47; Green, 1349.

20. Foreign Broadcast Information Service (hereafter, FBIS) (China), 4 June 1990, 14-15; on the negotiation of this treaty, see Rossabi and Rossabi, *Herdman and Statesman*, 135.

21. M. Taylor Fravel, *Strong Borders, Secure Nation: Cooperation and Conflict in China's Territorial Disputes* (Princeton: Princeton University Press, 2008), 300.

22. Udo Barkmann, *Die Beziehungen zwischen der Mongolei und der VR China (1952-1996)* (Hamburg: Mitteilungen des Instituts für Asienkunde, 2001), 62-63.

23. *New York Times*, 8 September 1964, 3.

24. Green, 1351.

25. Kim, 51.

26. For the turbulence in Inner Mongolia, see William Jankowiak, "The Last Hurrah? Political Protest in Inner Mongolia," *Australian Journal of Chinese Affairs* 19-20 (1988), 269-288; David Sneath, "The Impact of the Cultural Revolution in China on the Mongolians of Inner Mongolia," *Modern Asian Studies*, Vol. 28, No. 2 (1994), 409-430.

27. Alan Sanders, "Mongolia 1975: 'One Crew in Battle, One Brigade in Labour' with the USSR," *Asian Survey*, Vol. 16 (January 1976), 66-67; William Heaton, "Mongolia: Troubled Satellite," *Asian Survey*, Vol. 13, No. 2 (February 1973), 251.

28. Heaton, 249, offers an estimate of half a million troops, a vastly inflated figure.

29. William Heaton, "Mongolia 1978: Continuing the Transition," *Asian Survey*, Vol. 19, No. 1 (January 1979), 62.

30. *FBIS* (China), 11 August 1983, A1; 9 September 1983, C1; 11 October 1983, C1; 15 November 1983, C1; 7 May 1984, C2; 12 October 1984, C1.

31. *FBIS* (China), 31 May 1983, D1; 1 June 1983, D1; 3 June 1983, D1; 8 June 1983, D1.

32. William Heaton, "Mongolia in 1983: Mixed Signals," *Asian Survey*, Vol. 24 (1984), 128.

33. On Batmönkh, see Alan Sanders, "Restructuring and Openness," in Shirin Akiner, ed., *Mongolia Today* (London: Kegan Paul, 1991), 59-62.

34. *FBIS* (China), 30 October 1984, D3-D4.

35. *FBIS* (China), 7 August 1986, D1.

36. Green, 1363; This author fell into the trap of attempting to foretell the future and wrote: "It is highly improbable that the Soviet Union would remove all of its forces or otherwise weaken Mongolia's security, given the importance of Mongolia to Soviet defenses in East Asia." Within five years, all of the Soviet troops had been withdrawn.

37. *FBIS* (China), 13 August 1986, C3.

38. *FBIS* (China), 16 March 1987, D2; Kenneth Jarrett, "Mongolia in 1987: Out from the Cold?" *Asian Survey*, Vol. 28 (1988), 80.

39. *FBIS* (China), 13 March 1987, D1; 8 June 1987, D5.

40. *FBIS* (China), 29 November 1988, 14-15.

41. *FBIS* (China), 13 September 1988, 13; 24 March 1989, 4.

42. Jarrett, 78-80; Ministry of External Relations, *Foreign Policy Blue Book* (Ulaanbaatar, 2000), 96.

43. For the events that led to these political changes, see Morris Rossabi, *Modern Mongolia: From Khans to Commissars to Capitalists* (Berkeley: University of California Press, 2005), 1-29.

44. *FBIS* (China), 29 July 1991, 8-9; Elizabeth Milne, John Edward Leimone, F. Rozwadowski, and Padej Sukachevin, *The Mongolian People's Republic: Toward a Market Economy* (Washington, DC: International Monetary Fund, 1991), 30-32; Alan Sanders, "Foreign Relations and Foreign Policy," in Ole Bruun and Ole Odgaard, eds., *Mongolia in Transition: Old Patterns, New Challenges* (Richmond: Curzon Press, 1996), 241-242.

45. Sant Maral Foundation, "Public Perception of Privatization in Mongolia," Ulaanbaatar, April, 1999.

46. Frederick Nixson, "The Economic Development Experience of Mongolia," in K. T. Liou, ed., *Handbook of Economic Development* (New York: Marcel Dekker, 1998), 675-695; Keith Griffin, ed., *Poverty and the Transition to a Market Economy in Mongolia* (New York: St. Martin's Press, 1995), 1-14; Georges Korsun and Peter Murrell, " Politics and Economics of Mongolia's Privatization Program," *Asian Survey*, Vol. 35, No. 5 (May 1995), 472-486.

47. R. Tuya, Minister of External Affairs, Lecture, Asia Society, New York City, 19 April 2000.

48. Economist Intelligence Unit, *China and Mongolia: Country Report* (3rd quarter, 1993), 38.

49. Economist Intelligence Unit, *China and Mongolia: Country Report* (4th quarter, 1997), 41.

50. Economist Intelligence Unit, *China and Mongolia: Country Report* (3rd quarter, 1994), 41; Ministry of Defense of the Government of Mongolia, *Mongolia Defense White Paper 1997/1998* (Ulaanbaatar, 1998), 93, 95.

51. *UB Post*, 15 December 1998; *Mongol Messenger*, 16 December 1998.

52. *Email Daily News* (Ulaanbaatar), 18 November 1997, 18 June 1999.

53. *Mongol Defense White Paper*, 52.

54. Economist Intelligence Unit, *China and Mongolia Country Report* (1st quarter, 1997), 51, and (1st quarter, 1998), 42.

55. National Statistical Office of Mongolia, *Mongolian Statistical Yearbook, 2009* (Ulaanbaatar, 2010), 260-272.

56. "Is China Becoming 'Dangerously' Important in Mongolia's Foreign Trade?" *Mongolia This Week*, 26 May-1 June 2000, 1.

57. *World Mongol News*, 23 June 2006; *Mongol Messenger*, 14 June 2006.

58. Andrei Adminin and Elena Devaeva, "Economic Cooperation of Russia's Far East and Northeast Asia," *Far Eastern Affairs*, Vol. 1 (1999), 29-38.

59. Andrew Marton, Terry McGee, and Donald Patterson, "Northeast Asian Economic Cooperation and the Tumen River Area Development Project," *Pacific Affairs*, Vol. 68, No. 1 (Spring 1995), 8-33; Ickoo Kim, "Tumen River Area Development Program and the Prospects for Northeast Asian Economic Cooperation," *Asian Perspective*, Vol. 19, No. 2 (Fall-Winter 1995), 75-102.

60. *UBPost,* 4 November 2004, 9 December 2004, and 6 December 2007.

61. *Mongol Messenger*, 10 May 1997 and 26 September 2007.

62. *Mongol Messenger*, 28 March 1997; *Email Daily News*, 30 January 1998 and 5 April 1999.

63. *Montsame News Agency*, 30 June 1999; *Email Daily News*, 22 April 1999.

64. *Mongol Messenger*, 26 November 1997; Economist Intelligence Unit, *China and Mongolia: Country Report* (1st quarter, 1994), 39; *UBPost*, 3 January 2008.

65. World Bank, *Wildlife Trade in Mongolia* (Ulaanbaatar, 2005).

66. *Email Daily News*, 13 May 1998 and 4 March 1999.

67. See a popular account in John Noble Wilford, "In Mongolia, An 'Extinction Crisis' Looms," *New York Times*, 6 December 2005, F1, F3.

68. *Mongol Messenger*, 26 July 2006; *World Mongol News*, 1 January 2007.

69. *Mongol Messenger*, 4 June 2010.

70. *Mongol Messenger*, 13 April 2005, 12 October 2005, and 19 November 2008; *UBPost*, 24 April 2009.

71. *UBPost*, 24 February 2008; Jessica Farmer, *Trafficking in Persons and Prostitution at Mine Sites in Mongolia* (Ulaanbaatar: Asia Foundation, 2008) for a full report.

72. *UBPost*, 27 September 2006.

73. Asia Foundation, *Human Trafficking in Mongolia* (Ulaanbaatar, 2006); On Chinese involvement, see Sheldon Zhang, *Chinese Human Smuggling Organization: Families, Social Networks, and Cultural Imperative* (Stanford: Stanford University Press, 2008).

74. Sant Maral Foundation, *Politbarometer* (Ulaanbaatar), May 2008.

75. Matthew Davis, *When Things Get Dark: A Mongolian Winter's Tale* (New York: St. Martin's Press, 2010), 156.

76. *FBIS* (China), 13 June 1991.

77. Sergei Blazov, "Russia Presses for Stronger Ties with Mongolia," *Eurasianet* 30 May 2007, http://www.eurasianet.org/departments/insight/eav053007a.shtml [Accessed on 3 June 2007].

78. *Mongol Messenger*, 20 May 2009.

79. *Mongol Messenger*, 2 September 2009; For more on uranium, see Andrew Kramer, "Rosatom, A Russian Power Company, to Mine Uranium in Mongolia," *New York Times,* 26 August 2009, B2.

80. *Mongol Messenger*, 12 February 2010.

81. They repeatedly refer to him as a "splittist," not as a religious figure. *World Mongol News*, 22 August 2006.

82. *Email Daily News*, 3 December 1996; *Montsame News Agency*, 4 June 1999.

83. Economist Intelligence Unit, *China and Mongolia Country Report* (1st quarter, 1999), 47.

84. Uradyn Bulag, "Mongolia in 2008: From Mongolia to Mine-golia," *Asian Survey* 49:1 (January-February, 2009), 133-134.

85. Christian Caryl, "China Gets Tough," *New York Review of Books*, Vol. 57, No. 19 (9 December 2010), 32-37.

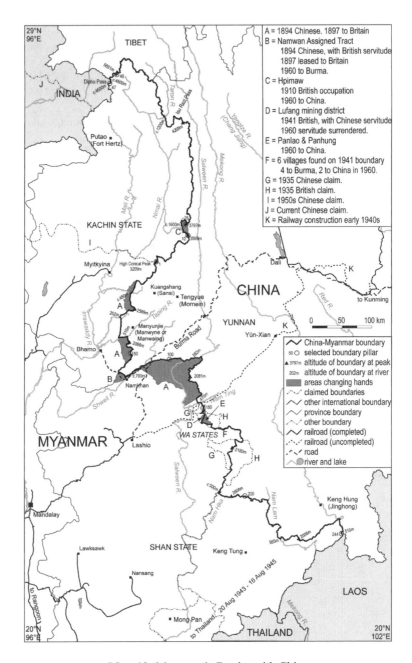

Map 13: Myanmar's Border with China

13

The Sino-Myanmar Border

Brendan Whyte

China's 1,367 mile (2,200 km) boundary with the Republic of the Union of Myanmar (before 1989 called Burma) falls geographically and historically into two sections.[1] The two sections meet at a 10,528 foot (3,209 meter) mountain peak situated at 98° 9' 18" east and 25° 32' 46" north, and called, in all the various boundary treaties, the "high conical peak" (尖高山, pronounced jiāngāoshān in Mandarin), but also known as Mulang, or Manang, Pum (木浪凸, pronounced mùlàngtū in Mandarin).

The 900 mile (1,450 km) boundary section south of this peak was the first to be delimited in 1894. This section runs from the "high conical peak" in a series of generally southward then eastward steps, cutting across the grain of the country until it meets the Mekong River, which it follows downstream for 18.3 miles (29.5 km) to the trijunction with Laos. The northern section, by contrast, runs through much higher altitudes, in a region of much more difficult terrain and lower population density. This boundary follows the Irrawaddy watershed (although it leaves most of one tributary, the Taron River, to China), at altitudes of 10,000-20,000 feet (3,000 to 6,000 meters), which provides an obvious natural, physical, historical, and cultural divide, even though no official agreement was reached on this section until the 1960s.

The Sino-Burmese boundary treaty delineating their mutual border was signed on 1 October 1960, and was ratified a year afterwards. As a result of this treaty, China gained approximately 44 square miles (114 km²) of territory from Burma. While most of the Sino-Myanmar border remains unchanged to this day, the exact location of the China-Myanmar-India trijunction remains in dispute. In addition, domestic rebellion in the Han Chinese-dominated Kokang region of Myanmar has led to recent border tensions between the PRC and Myanmar.

Early 19th Century History of the Sino-Burmese Border

The modern history of the boundary begins with the British conquest of Upper Burma in late 1885 and that kingdom's proclamation as British territory on 1 January 1886. Later that year Britain and China signed a convention regarding their new relations with respect to Burma and Tibet. Three of the convention's five articles dealt with Burma: Britain agreed that Burma would continue to send to China "the customary decennial Missions." In turn, China acknowledged British rule in Burma and agreed Britain was "free to do whatever she deems fit and proper." The Sino-Burmese boundary was to be "marked by a Delimitation Commission, and the conditions of frontier trade to be settled by a Frontier Trade Convention, both countries agreeing to protect and encourage trade between China and Burmah [*sic*]."[2]

Although the "customary missions" were soon forgotten, the delimitation of much of the boundary was drawn up eight years later in 1894.[3] Beginning at "the high conical peak" and running southward, a complicated topography had led to the existence of a patchwork of small hill-tribe polities, whose allegiance was inconstant, paying tribute to the lowland powers in Yunnan or Burma, but often both, and sometimes neither, as circumstances and personalities changed over time. The greater population density and resource potential of this section, its relatively low altitude, the general lack of any obvious natural boundaries, and the British desire to develop trade with China, were all factors in the British push for delimitation of a boundary here.

The boundary was defined southwards in three consecutive sections. The first ran from the peak to the Taiping River. The second section ran from the Taiping to the Shweli River, via the Namwan River, but left to China a triangular promontory including the land between the Namwan and Nammak rivers, which contained three of eight massive stone gates built by the Chinese in the 15th and 16th centuries to command the passes up the Taiping and Shweli valleys.[4] As this salient contained "the most direct of the roads between Bhamo and Namkhan," the road was to remain open for "travellers, commerce and administrative purposes," and Britain had the right to improve the road, as well as, within certain restrictions, to move troops along it. The third section of boundary ran from the Shweli to the Salween, and on to the Mekong. This third section was the least well-defined, as it ran through little-known country, and was shaped by both physical features and the boundaries of hill-tribe polities that were rather optimistically described as "locally well-known."[5] Britain renounced rights to the Shan state of Keng-Hung, but insisted that China not cede it to any other nation—meaning the French, who were in the process of defining their Indochinese boundaries with China—without British agreement.

North of the "high conical peak" Britain hoped for a scientific frontier using the watershed of the Irrawaddy, but as the headwaters of this river were still unknown, the Chinese suspected British of having designs upon parts of Tibet and Sichuan. As a result, this section was "reserved for a future undertaking between the High Contracting Parties when the features and condition of the country are more accurately known." A boundary commission was to demarcate the boundary within three years, and was given some power to vary the alignment if necessary.[6]

Other clauses of the 1894 agreement regularized cross-border relations, including such issues as:

> • No fortifications or camps were to be situated within ten miles of the boundary.
> • Trade was to be allowed across the boundary for six years, duty-free, except for salt imported to Burma and rice imported to China.
> • Salt exports from Burma to China were prohibited, as were the export from China to Burma of cash, rice, and grains.
> • Trade was initially only to be conducted via Manwyne (Manwaing, now Manyunjie) and Sansi (Kuanshang).
> • Weaponry and munitions were prohibited as trade items, as were opium and "spirituous liquor."
> • Chinese trade vessels were permitted on the Irrawaddy River.
> • Consuls were to be exchanged, and passports issued to those wishing to cross the border.
> • Fugitives were to be extradited as required.
> • The telegraph systems in each country were to be connected across the border "as soon as the necessary arrangements can be made."

A separate agreement on a telegraph line was made within a fortnight. This new treaty aimed for a connection before 31 May 1895, between the British station at Bhamo and the Chinese one at Tengyue (Momein), with an intermediate station at Manwyne.[7] This agreement was slightly revised, with an updated fee schedule, in 1905.[8]

The Foreign "Scramble for Concessions" in China

In 1895, a year after the initial boundary convention, China, under pressure from France, ceded part of Keng-Hung to the latter, as part of the delimitation of the Sino-Indochina boundary. This derogation of an explicit clause in the 1894 convention also allowed Britain the opportunity to revise the 1894 agreement in a new convention of 1897.[9] Several sections of the Sino-Burmese boundary were adjusted in Britain's favor, and a map showed the changes made. In particular, the salient south of the Namwan River was recognized "as belonging to China" but "[i]n the whole of this area China shall not exercise any jurisdiction or authority whatsoever. The administration and control will be entirely conducted by the British Government, who will hold it on a perpetual lease from China, paying a rent for it, the amount of which shall be fixed hereafter." The rent for the "Namwan Assigned Tract," or "Meng-Mao triangular area" as it came to be known, was subsequently settled at Rs.1,000 per year.[10]

Again, a boundary commission was to demarcate the boundary within three years, and, as an acknowledgement of the lack of accurate knowledge of terrain and its tribal distributions, empowered to modify the line on the basis of mutual concession "if a strict adherence to the line described would intersect districts, tribal territories, or villages." Another addition was a clause requiring the Chinese to "consider whether the conditions of trade justify the construction of railways in Yunnan" and if so, "to connect them with the Burmese lines."[11]

This was an attempt by the British to divert Yunnanese trade away from French Indochina, where a railway line from Hanoi up the Red River to Kunming was begun in 1904 and opened by 1910. The boundary commission was duly formed, and operated over three cold seasons between 1897 and 1900. It demarcated the boundary south from the "high conical peak" and west from the Mekong, but it was unable to come to any agreement on the alignment of the frontier between the Nam Ting and Nam Kha rivers in the remote and dangerous Wa states.[12] This impasse was due to ambiguities in the 1897 delimitation, coupled with the presence of mineral and gemological wealth. Further negotiations were necessarily suspended during the Boxer Uprising (1899-1901), which paralyzed China, but were not revived for over 30 years.

Subsequently, the British signed two agreements with Tibet in 1914, which created the McMahon line boundary between India (including Burma) and Tibet.[13] Britain now considered the Burma-Tibet boundary to run east, from a trijunction with Assam just north of the Diphu (or Talok) L'Ka Pass, along the Irrawaddy watershed to the Isu Razi Pass, but leaving the upper reaches of the Taron River to Tibet.[14] To connect this Burma-Tibet boundary with the demarcated Burma-China boundary beginning at the "high conical peak," the most obvious line was along the Irrawaddy watershed, and toward establishing this de facto limit, Britain had, in 1910, occupied several Chinese-claimed villages at Hpimaw (Pianma or Pienma) on the Irrawaddy side of the crest.[15]

Final Changes to the Sino-Burmese Border

Another 20 years were to pass before further boundary definition was attempted. The catalyst was the attack, in 1934, by Wa tribesmen and Chinese bandits, on a British prospecting party in the vicinity of the undemarcated Wa sector. British troops were sent in, and China took the matter to the League of Nations.[16] In early 1935, an agreement was reached under the League's auspices for a commission of two representatives from each side, led by a neutral chairman—Colonel Frédéric Iselin of Switzerland—appointed by the President of the Council of the League.[17] The Commission worked from December 1935 to April 1937, presenting its report in the latter year.[18] Only in 1941 did China accept its findings.[19] The final boundary followed, in the main, the line decided by the majority of the commissioners. As part of the agreement, the British granted Chinese interests the right to form up to 49 percent of the capital in any British mining concerns operating in a roughly 3 by 6 mile (5 by 10 km) area "on the eastern slopes of the Lufang ridge," on the Burmese side of the boundary.[20]

Assisting the two sides to reach an agreement quickly was the increasing Japanese military threat. In order for Britain to supply Chinese Nationalist forces in Sichuan Province, they opened the famous Burma Road up the Shweli Valley in January 1939. Preparations also began, beginning in 1941, for a never-completed railway to join Lashio with Kunming, as presaged by the 1897 convention.[21]

During World War II, Thai forces, allied to Japan, invaded Burma's Shan states. On 1 August 1943, Japan declared Burma "independent," but on 20 August gave Thailand the Shan states of Mong Pan and Keng Tung, creating a short-lived theoretical Sino-Thai boundary between the Sino-Indochinese and Sino-Burmese lines.[22] Burma, and Thailand's two Shan states, returned to British control at the time of Japan's surrender in August 1945.[23]

The Modern Sino-Burmese Border

Burma became independent on 4 January 1948.[24] Shortly afterwards, the Chinese Kuomintang (KMT) government refused to accept the annual rent for the Namwan Assigned Tract; the Communists who succeeded the KMT in October 1949 followed suit. In December that year, Burma recognized the Mao Zedong regime, the first Asian country, and the first non-communist one, to do so. This was making a virtue of necessity, given Burma's neutralist international position, its adjacency to China along a still only half-demarcated boundary, and its own internal strife, including two underground communist groups supported by China seeking the government's overthrow.

In 1950, General Li Mi, the last KMT governor of Yunnan, and several thousand KMT soldiers, retreated uninvited into Burma. For Rangoon, this presented the nightmare scenario of a potential cross-border PLA offensive. In line with its neutralist policies, Burma placed the matter before the UN in March 1953.[25] A U.S.-led evacuation of 6,000 KMT troops, combined with Burmese military offensives against the rest, reduced the problem, but many remained or returned, and merged into the general instability of Burma's hill-tribe regions. China's restraint in the matter was due to its own internal exhaustion, and the danger of overt aggression pushing Burma into the western camp. Nevertheless, the PRC sent troops into Burma in 1952, where they remained for five years, but the Burmese government remained silent on the issue until the situation was revealed by the Rangoon newspaper *The Nation* in 1956.[26]

The Chinese were not unwilling to negotiate a complete boundary settlement with Burma "at an appropriate time,"[27] but refused to be bound by any of the previous Sino-British agreements. Latent claims to all of northern Burma,[28] ongoing support for Burma's communist insurgent groups, and the potential fifth column of Burma's ethnic Han Chinese community, all gave China the whip hand. Yet ultimately Beijing was content with a few relatively minor rectifications to the de facto line, probably as a result of several much larger foreign policy issues, and so achieved a political victory by demonstrating its munificence and soothing international fears of the hard-line ideology it had spouted in the early 1950s. According to one expert ". . . the Chinese position had only little room left for maneuvering in the diplomatic and foreign policy field at that time (insurrection in Tibet, skirmishes and escalating tension on the Sino-Indian border, beginnings of the Sino-Soviet ideological schism, necessity to maintain a moderate 'peace-loving' image in the aftermath of the Bandung conference)."[29]

After several years of political hardball, Beijing signed a boundary agreement with Burma on 28 January 1960.[30] This set up a committee to discuss the boundary questions, erect boundary pillars, and draft a full boundary treaty. Specifically, it was agreed that from the "high conical peak" northward to the—still-undetermined—trijunction with India, the boundary would follow "the traditional customary line," that is, the watershed between the Irrawaddy and Salween, but leaving the Taron to China. While the McMahon line was followed here, it was used not because it was the McMahon line, but because it happened to be a sensible boundary. However, this treaty and the subsequent Sino-Burmese agreements avoided specific reference to the McMahon line, or even references to the previous Sino-British treaties, which the Chinese claimed were "unequal."

Burma agreed to return to China the villages of Hpimaw, Gawlum, and Kangfang, but the areal extent of this agreement was still to be finalized. South of the "high conical peak," the Namwan Assigned Tract would be gifted to Burma, in exchange for "the areas under the jurisdiction of the Pan[g]hung and Pan[g]lao tribes" west of the 1941 line. The new boundary treaty would replace all previous treaties, and describe the alignment of the entire boundary from India to Laos. Finally, China "in line with its policy of being consistently opposed to foreign prerogatives and respecting the sovereignty of other countries" renounced its right to participate in mining enterprises at Lufang.[31]

The Sino-Burmese Boundary Treaty was signed on 1 October 1960.[32] It confirmed the already-demarcated sections of the boundary, the agreed changes to the 1941 line, and the "traditional customary line"—that is, the McMahon line—elsewhere, and defined for the first time in a single document the two sections of the boundary, north and south of the "high conical peak" respectively. China received 59 square miles (153 km^2) at Hpimaw and 73 square miles (189 km^2) in the Panglao and Panghung areas, in exchange for giving up all claims to the 85 square miles (220 km^2) of the Namwan Assigned Tract. Minor adjustments at the Taron and Shweli rivers also gave about 3 square miles (8 km^2) to Burma. The resurvey of the 1941 line found six villages straddling it. Two of the villages—Yawng Hok and Lungnai—were given to China, and the other four—Umhpa, Pan Kung, Pan Nawng, and Pan Wai—to Burma. Overall, China gained 44 square miles (114 km^2) from Burma.

The boundary was depicted on 1:250,000 scale maps from each country, and on 1:50,000 scale maps for the Hpimaw "returned area," the Namwan tract, the Shweli river rectification, the Panglao and Panghung concessions, and the six reunited villages. The treaty also stated that a boundary protocol would be drafted to define and map in exact detail, the locations of all boundary pillars, once these had been erected.

An Exchange of Notes signed on the same day as the treaty specified that residents of areas changing hands were to be considered citizens of the country to which the lands were given, but they had a year to declare any desire to remain citizens of their original country, and two years in which to move back into that country, taking all their possessions and receiving monetary compensation for their lands.[33] Approximately 2,400 families in the areas transferred by this treaty to China—1,400 in the Kachin State and 1,000 in the Wa State—opted to remain Burmese citizens and were resettled in Burma before 4 June 1961.[34] In addition, no new cultivation of trans-frontier lands would be allowed, and all existing trans-frontier cultivation was to be abandoned within three years.

The Boundary Protocol was signed a year later.[35] It included maps of the entire boundary at 1:50,000 scale, and areas on the Shweli and Nam Lam river areas at 1:5,000. A total of 402 boundary markers were erected, from the trijunction with Laos up to, but not including, the Diphu L'Ka Pass, the "provisional western extremity pending its final determination," that is the trijunction with India. Although the Sino-Burmese alignment simply followed what India already considered the Indo-Burmese boundary, as defined in 1837, did not intrude into Indian-claimed territory per se, and was expressly left undemarcated, India nevertheless protested the delimitation of the Sino-Burmese boundary west of what India considered the trijunction: "5 miles [8 km] north of the Diphu L'Ka Pass, and not at the Diphu L'Ka Pass itself. The coordinates of the trijunction are approximately longitude 97° 23' east and latitude 28° 13' north."[36] From the "high conical peak" to Laos, the boundary is officially described as 896.54 miles (1,442.84 km) long, and from the "high conical peak" to Diphu L'Ka Pass, 461.61 miles (742.89 km), for a total length of 1,358.16 miles (2,185.75 km).

Since the signing of the 1960-1961 boundary treaty and protocol, the only modification to the boundary has been to tie it to the termini of the China-Lao and Myanmar-Lao boundaries. A treaty to this effect was signed by China, Myanmar, and Laos on 8 April 1994 and came into force on 11 October 1995. Two new markers were placed on opposite banks of the Mekong to demarcate the trijunction at the confluence of the Mekong and Nam La rivers.[37]

Conclusions

While the boundary's "provisional western extremity" still awaits the settlement of the Sino-Indian boundary, the Sino-Burmese boundary as defined in 1960-1961 has proved relatively stable and apparently uncontested throughout the last 50 years.[38] However, this situation could change, since in recent years a predominantly Han Chinese militia in the Kokang region of the Shan State, called the Kokang Myanmar National Democratic Alliance Army (MNDAA), has attempted on several occasions to secede from Myanmar. This breakaway region runs right along the Sino-Burmese border.

The domestic rebellion in Kokang has simmered under the surface for many years, with as many as 50,000 ethnic Han Chinese having fled across the border to China over the past ten years. Tensions increased after an August 2009 attack by Myanmar central government forces against the MNDAA, reportedly "to liquidate the largest remaining rebel forces ahead of next year's 'election'," which violated a 20-year-old ceasefire. There are valid concerns that the Chinese government might even intervene in the conflict. Even though the Myanmar foreign minister has reportedly "apologized" for the instability on the border, the Chinese foreign minister warned the Myanmar government they must "'properly handle domestic problems and maintain stability in the China-Myanmar border region'."[39]

The Chinese government continues to provide Myanmar with humanitarian assistance, but it has perhaps linked this aid to offers to mediate the conflict in Kokang. More ominously, China is also reinforcing the Sino-Myanmar border with troops to stop refugees; during February 2010, it was reported that the "China's People's Liberation Army (PLA) deployed an unknown number of soldiers in border towns close to the Wa States where armed conflict is anticipated."[40] A protracted conflict could severely disrupt bilateral trade along the border, thereby undermining the economic development of China's landlocked southwest provinces, trigger an outpouring of refugees into China, interfere with construction of the pipeline from Kunming to the Burmese port of Kyaukphyu, which passes close to Wa controlled areas, and perhaps even lead to major increases in narcotics production in northern Myanmar, which could fuel drug addiction in the PRC. For all of these reasons, the August 2009 "Kokang Incident has laid bare the fault lines in Sino-Burmese relations."[41]

Notes

1. The Geographer, *Burma—China Boundary*, International Boundary Study No. 42 (Washington, DC: Office of the Geographer, Bureau of Intelligence and Research, Department of State), 2; J.R.Victor Prescott, *Map of Mainland Asia by Treaty* (Melbourne: University of Melbourne Press, 1975), 347; J.R.Victor Prescott, Harold J. Collier, and Dorothy F. Prescott, *Frontiers of Asia and Southeast Asia* (Melbourne: University of Melbourne Press, 1977), 50.

2. *Convention between China and Great Britain Relative to Burmah and Thibet*, signed at Peking [Beijing], 24 July 1886. Ratifications exchanged at London, 25 August 1887. Text given in Clive Parry, ed., *Consolidated Treaty Series* (Dobbs Ferry, NY: Oceana Publications, 1969-86), Vol. 168, 135-137.

3. *Convention between China and Great Britain giving effect to Article III of the convention of 24 July 1886 relative to Burmah and Thibet*, signed at London, 1 March 1894. Ratifications exchanged at London, 23 August 1894. The text without the map is given in Parry, Vol. 180, 15-24. The map is reproduced only in the original publication in the *British and Foreign State Papers*, 1894, Vol. XCVI, 89-101 (C. 7547; Treaty Series No. 19, 1894).

4. Hugh Tinker, "Burma's Northeast Borderland Problems," *Pacific Affairs*, Vol. 29, no. 4 (1956), 330, 335.

5. *Convention between China and Great Britain,* 1 March 1894, Parry, Vol. 180, 15-24.

6. Ibid.

7. *Convention between Great Britain and China, Respecting the Junction of the Chinese and Burmese Telegraph Lines*, signed at Tien-tsin [Tianjin], 6 September 1894. Text given in Parry, Vol. 179, 321-24.

8. *Telegraph Convention between China and Great Britain*, signed at Peking, 23 May 1905. Text given in Parry, Vol. 198, 315-318.

9. *Agreement between China and Great Britain Modifying the Convention of 1 March 1894 relative to Burmah and Thibet*, signed at Peking, 4 February 1897. Ratifications exchanged at Peking, 5 June 1897. The text without the map is given in Parry, Vol. 184, 197-202. The map is reproduced only in the original publication in the *British and Foreign State Papers*, 1898, Vol. CV, 129-38 (C. 8564; Treaty Series No. 7, 1897).

10. Richard J. Kozicki, "The Sino-Burmese Frontier Problem," *Far Eastern Survey*, Vol. 26, No. 3 (March 1957), 33.

11. *Agreement between China and Great Britain,* 4 February 1897. Parry, Vol. 184, 197-202.

12. A description of the 9 February 1900 incident, in which the heads of two British officers on the Commission were taken by Wa tribesmen, is given in Sao Saimong Mangrai, *The Shan States and the British Annexation*, Data Paper 57, Southeast Asia Program (Ithaca: Department of Asian Studies, Cornell University, 1965), 291-297.

13. *Exchange of Notes between Great Britain and Tibet regarding the India-Tibet Frontier*, signed at Delhi, 24 March 1914, and *Convention between China, Great Britain and Tibet*, signed at Simla, 3 July 1914. The texts without the maps are given in Parry, Vol. 219, 339-340, and Vol. 220, 144-147. The maps were apparently published for the first time in *Atlas of the Northern Frontier of India* (New Delhi: Ministry of External Affairs, 1960) maps 22 & 24. Also see Alastair Lamb, *The McMahon Line: a study in the relations between India, China and Tibet, 1904 to 1914*, 2 vols. (London: Routledge & Kegan Paul, 1966); and Karunakar Gupta, "The McMahon Line 1941-45: The British Legacy," *China Quarterly*, No. 47 (July-September 1971), 521-545.

14. For why Diphu L'Ka Pass itself is not the trijunction, see Lamb, 544 fn. 22; for why the Taron was excluded from Burma, see Lamb, 543-545.

15. For the 1910-11 "Pianma Incident" and the Chinese reaction to this incident, see Thomas E. McGrath, "A Warlord Frontier: The Yunnan-Burma Border Dispute, 1910-1937," *Proceedings*, Ohio Academy of History, 2003, 9-14, www.ohio academyofhistory.org/2003McGrath.pdf, and www2.uakron.edu/OAH/Proceedings/2003/McGrath.pdf.

16. Tinker, 338; Harold C. Hinton, *China's Relations with Burma and Vietnam: a brief survey* (New York: Institute of Pacific Relations, 1958), 35.

17. *Exchange of Notes between His Majesty's Government in the United Kingdom and the Government of India and the Chinese Government Regarding Establishment of a Commission to Determine the Southern Section of the Boundary between Burma and Yunnan*, signed at Nanking [Nanjing], 9 April 1935. The text of this agreement is given as treaty no. 3766 in *League of Nations Treaty Series* (LNTS), Vol. 163, 177-183.

18. The work of the commission is described in the first-hand accounts of W.A. Prestre, "Au Pays des Coupeurs de Têtes: Rites étranges d'un pays inconnu," *L'Illustration*, no. 4950, 15 January 1938, 78-81; W. Stark Toller, "The Burma-Yunnan Boundary Commission 1935-37," *Eastern World*, May 1949, 4-6 and June 1949, 4-6; and J.B.P. Angwin R.E., "The Sino-Burmese Boundary," which is a 7 page report including in the *Papers on the Burma Frontiers*, a bound typescript collection of documents and reports produced by the Burmese embassy in London in the 1950s, part of the papers of G.H. Luce, former professor at the University of Rangoon, now held in the National Library of Australia. An overview of the commission's work, and its broader context is also given by Martin R. Norins, "Tribal Boundaries of the Burma-Yünnan Frontier," *Pacific Affairs*, Vol. 12, No. 1 (March 1939), 67-79.

19. *Exchange of Notes on the demarcation of the Southern Section of the Yunnan-Burma Boundary and the joint exploitation of the Lufang mines*, signed at Chungking [Chongqing], 17 June 1941. Text and two maps given as treaty no. 64 in *United Nations Treaty Series* (UNTS), Vol. 10, 1947, 227-42.

20. Ibid.

21. A contemporary account of British attempts to access trade with Yunnan Province, and the subsequent development of the Burma Road, is given by John LeRoy Christian, *Modern Burma: A Survey of Its Political and Economic Development* (New York: International Secretariat, Institute of Pacific Relations, 1942), 223-247.

22. For the Thai text of the treaty see Charnvit Kasetsiri, "The First Phibun Government and its Involvement in World War II," *Journal of the Siam Society*, Vol. 62, Part 2 (July 1974), 87-88.

23. The text of Thailand's proclaimed annulment of the 1943 treaty on 16 August 1945 appears in Kasetsiri, 75-76. The text of the final peace treaty between Great Britain and Thailand is presented as treaty no. 1375 in *UNTS*, Vol. 99, 132-146.

24. An overview of Sino-Burmese relations from independence until the Burmese military coup of September 1988 is presented by Chi-shad Liang, "Burma's Relations with the People's Republic of China: from delicate friendship to genuine co-operation," in Peter Carey, ed., *Burma: The Challenge of Change in a Divided Society* (Basingstoke & Oxford: Macmillan Press & St. Anthony's College, 1997), 71-93.

25. For the Burmese side of the issue, see *Kuomintang Aggression against Burma* (Rangoon: Ministry of Information, 1953).

26. *The Nation* (Rangoon), 31 July, 7, 14, 23, and 25 August, and 16 September 1956.

27. "Communique on Talks between Chinese and Burmese Premiers (December 12, 1954)," in *A Victory for the Five Principles of Peaceful Coexistence: Important Documents on the Settlement of the Sino-Burmese Boundary Question Through Friendly Negotiations and on the Development of Friendly Relations between China and Burma* (Peking: Foreign Languages Press, 1960), 5.

28. Ralph Pettman, *China in Burma's Foreign Policy* (Canberra: Australian National University Press, 1973), 19.

29. Michael Strupp, *Chinas Grenzen mit Birma und mit der Sowjetunion: volkerrechtliche Theorie und Praxis der Volksrepublik China* (Hamburg: Mitteilungen des Instituts für Asienkunde, 2nd edition, 1987), 532. The propaganda potential of the agreement is, however, largely dismissed by Luke T. Lee, *China and International Agreements: A Study of Compliance* (Leyden & Durham, NC: A.W. Sijthoff & Rule of Law Press, 1969), 35. However, for an example of Chinese propaganda regarding the agreement see *A Victory for the Five Principles*.

30. *Sino-Burmese Agreement on Boundary Question*, signed in Peking, 28 January 1960. Text given as document 64 in G.V. Ambekar and V.D. Divekar, eds., *Documents on China's Relations with South and Southeast Asia, 1949-1962* (Bombay: Allied Publishers, 1964), 188-191.

31. Ibid.

32. *Boundary Treaty (with* [25] *attached maps)*, signed at Peking, 1 October 1960; came into force 4 January 1961. Text and maps given as treaty no. 14847 in *UNTS,* Vol. 1010, 1947, 114-123 (Burmese), 124-134 (Chinese), 135-143 (English), 151-159 (French translation). For a discussion of Burma's position on the treaty, see Nu, U, *Speech by Hon'ble Prime Minister Asking for the Approval of the Parliament to the Ratification of the Boundary Treaty between the Union of Burma and the People's Republic of China, 5th December 1960* ([Rangoon]: Sarpay Beikman Press, [1960]). A contemporary western analysis is given by Daphne E. Whittam, "The Sino-Burmese Boundary Treaty," *Pacific Affairs,* Vol. 34, No. 2 (Summer 1961), 174-183.

33. *Exchange of Notes constituting an Agreement between the Union of Burma and the People's Republic of China annexed to the Boundary Treaty of 1 October 1960,* signed at Peking, 1 October 1960. The text appears as part of treaty no. 14847 in *UNTS,* Vol. 1010, 1984, Chinese note 144-145, English translation 146-147, Burmese reply 148-149, English translation 150, French translation of both notes 160-161.

34. Whittam, 183.

35. *Protocol to the Boundary Treaty of 1 October 1960 (with* [191] *maps)*. Signed at Peking, 13 October 1961; came into force 22 February 1962. Text as part of treaty no. 14847 in *UNTS,* Vol. 1010, 1984, 162-396 (Burmese) and Vol. 1011, 4-210 (Chinese), 211-347 (English) & 348-490 (French translation). Vol. 1012 contains 87 Burmese-English maps; Vol. 1013 contains 104 Chinese-English maps.

36. See documents 52 to 54 in Ambekar and Divekar, 166-170.

37. The treaty, which was written in Chinese, Burmese, Lao, and English, does not yet appear to have been published in full, but there is a version of just the Chinese text available online at www.law-lib.com/law/law_view.asp?id=77504 [Accessed on 27 October 2011].

38. Strupp, 1987, 531 suggests a "'latent' instability" exemplified by a 1986 "Sino-Burmese Draft Protocol on the first Joint Inspection (and Re-Demarcation)." However, this conclusion appears invalid 25 years on. In contrast, an earlier conclusion by Alastair Lamb in *Asian Frontiers: Studies in a Continuing Problem* (Melbourne: F.W. Cheshire for the Australian Institute of International Affairs, 1968), 157, seems to have become increasingly valid over time: "[The Chinese] were prepared to abandon extensive territorial claims which neither the Manchus nor the Kuomintang had been willing to give up. It seems likely that the departure of the British has altered profoundly the strategic nature, in Chinese eyes, of the Sino-Burmese border. . . . Burma has becomes a kind of Chinese 'protectorate' in the sense that it has adopted a 'neutral' foreign policy—that is to say, a policy of exclusion from its soil of potential or actual anti-Chinese influences. . . . So long as Burma remains 'neutral', it seems likely that the Sino-Burmese border will remain stable."

39. http://southeastasia.foreignpolicyblogs.com/2009/08/31/update-sino-burmese-border-crisis/ [Accessed on 27 October 2011].

40. http://www.peopleforum.cn/viewthread.php?tid=47468[Accessed on 27 October 2011].

41. http://www.jamestown.org/single/?no_cache=1&tx_ttnews%5Btt_news%5D=35468 [Accessed on 27 October 2011].

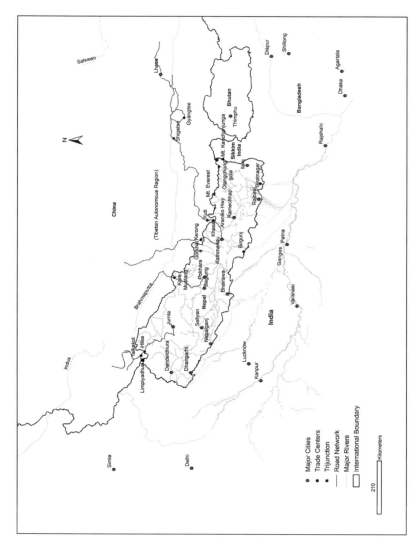

Map 14: Nepal's Border with China

14

China-Nepal Border: Potential Hot Spot?

Chitra K. Tiwari

China's first recorded official relations with Nepal, a country located southwest of Tibet, occurred near the middle of the 7th century. Although boundary delimitation between the two countries began almost 1,300 years later, during 1961, the two trijunctions—where the Nepalese, Chinese, and Indian territories meet—have yet to be negotiated on both the western and eastern ends of Nepal. The as yet unfinished boundary line between China and Nepal extends for 881.6 miles (1,414.8 km), touching seven counties in Tibet from Drenthang Township of Dinggue County in Shigatse Prefecture to Purang County of Nagri Prefecture.

On the Nepali side, the boundary extends from the Olangchunggola township in the east to Tinkar village and Kalapani-Limpiyadhuri in the west. The elevation of the borderline begins from almost 10,000 feet (3,000 meters) and reaches to 29,029 feet (8,848 meters) at the peak of Mount Everest (Tibetan name—Chomolungma; Nepalese name—Sagarmatha). The border area is almost a no-man's land, with only 10 villages on the Nepali side and 18 villages on the Chinese side of the border. There are 34 major passes between the two countries but only four—Hilsa, Rasuwagarhi, Kodari, and Olangchunggola—are operational. Two all-weather roads connect central Nepal with Tibet through Rasuwagarhi and Kodari.

While the Sino-Nepal Boundary Treaty was signed fifty years ago in Beijing during October 1961, China's and India's ongoing boundary dispute means that India has consistently refused to discuss the location of their mutual trijunctions, which has left this strategic border unfinished. Meanwhile, there have been a few bilateral disputes between the PRC and Nepal, including over the exact ownership of Mount Everest, and Nepal's relaxation of its border that made it easier for the supporters of the Dalai Lama to enter Nepal as refugees.

Sino-Nepal Historical Relations

The first contact between Nepal and China appears to have occurred in the mid-7th century. Chinese and Tibetan records assert, and the Nepalese chronicles concur, that Tibetan King Srong-tsen Gampo visited Nepal in about 640 and that he married a Nepali princess named Bhrikuti Devi. King Gampo had also married a Chinese princess earlier. The Nepali princess, Bhrikuti, is said to have introduced Buddhism into Tibet and then to China.[1]

A Chinese pilgrim, Xuanzhuang visited Nepal in 637 and the first official Chinese mission to Nepal arrived in Kathmandu via Tibet in 644. In 647, a Nepali envoy visited China with presents for the emperor. In 651, shortly after the death of Tibetan King Srong-tsen Gampo, Nepali King Narendra Deva sent another mission to China by way of Tibet. As hostilities between the Chinese and Tibetans began to grow a decade after King Gampo's death, Tibet closed its territory for any trans-Himalayan movement of people. As a result, references to China's relations with Nepal disappeared from Chinese documents for another 700 years.

The contacts between China and Nepal were opened once again during the Ming dynasty (1368-1644). In the period 1384-1427, five Chinese missions and seven Nepali missions were exchanged between the two countries. But with the emergence of the Malla dynasty in 1427 in Kathmandu Valley (also called Nepal Valley), all diplomatic contacts with China were abruptly terminated. Relations were reestablished with the Manchu dynasty when it established a Chinese presence in Tibet in the early 18th century with two Ambans (resident representatives) in Lhasa. Kathmandu sent a mission to the Ambans in 1732.

Nepal-Tibet Wars

By the beginning of 17th century, taking advantage of the internal chaos in Tibet marked by conflicts between competing Buddhist sects as well as regional conflicts between Lhasa and Shigatse, Ram Shah (1606-1633), the King of Gorkha, a small principality located west of Kathmandu Valley, invaded Tibet, and seized strategic Kerong Pass located northwest of Kathmandu Valley and reached an agreement with Tibet defining the boundary line between Gorkha and Tibet. Pratap Malla (1626-1674), the King of Kathmandu, also invaded Tibet from the northeast and brought Kuti, a second major trading route, under his control.

These invasions led to a treaty that established joint authority with Tibet over the border trading towns of Kerong and Kuti; the Nepalese merchant community of Kathmandu Valley was allowed to establish 32 trading houses in Lhasa along with a Kathmandu government's representative; Tibet agreed not to impose any charges or customs duties on Nepalese merchants and promised to make a token payment in gold and silver annually to Kathmandu. It was also decided that Kathmandu would mint coins for Tibet, while Tibet further acknowledged that all trade with India would be channeled through Kathmandu. The joint authority over the border trading town of Kerong and Kuti, however, came to an end before the death of the Fifth

Dalai Lama in 1683 when Tibet regained the territories seized by the kings of Gorkha and Kathmandu.

The mid-18th century was marked by political upheavals in Nepal as Prithvi Narayan Shah, the King of Gorkha, embarked on conquering the 46 little principalities scattered all over present day Nepal and the three Kingdoms inside Kathmandu Valley. With the capture of the three Malla kingdoms of Kathmandu Valley in 1769, the general outlines of modern-day Nepal had been carved out.

Relations with Tibet worsened with the rise of the Shah dynasty in Nepal. There were three major issues contributing to the worsening of relations: First, the Nepalese King wanted to develop Kathmandu as the trading hub between India and Tibet, thereby blocking other routes. This proposal was not acceptable to Tibet, and as a result Tibet in 1770 closed the trade routes and suspended all commercial activities between the two countries. Second, there was a dispute over the Nepal-minted coins circulating in Tibet. Tibetans complained that the value of the coins minted was debased thanks to an improper ratio of silver to other metals being used and demanded compensation. The Nepali side refused, arguing that the debased coins were minted by their enemies, the Mallas, and hence Nepal could not take the responsibility for Tibetan losses. Third, Nepal complained that the salt the Tibetans were supplying was adulterated with dust.

These disputes led to the Nepalese invasion of Tibet in July 1788. Nepalese forces captured Kuti and Kerong areas and imposed a treaty in June 1789 that was largely in favor of Nepal. Under the terms of the treaty Tibet agreed to pay an annual tribute of 9,600 taels of Chinese silver to Nepal; to accept and use newly minted Nepalese coins; to maintain a Nepali envoy in Lhasa; and to conduct trade with India only through Nepal while closing the alternative trade routes through Sikkim and Bhutan. In return, Nepal promised not to invade Tibet again.

The Tibetans, however, failed to honor the terms of the treaty signed by its representative on grounds that the tribute amount was far beyond the capacity of Tibetan economy to deliver. In August 1791, the Nepalese invaded Tibet, capturing the border trading towns of Kuti and Kerong. The Nepalese advanced all the way to Shigatse, home of Panchen Lama, and captured it too. After taking Shigatse, the Nepalese force commander, Damodar Pande, demanded that Tibet pay 550 pounds (250 kilograms) of gold as penalty for the violation of the treaty, as well as 19,200 taels of Chinese silver due to Nepal as tribute for the years 1790 and 1791. When Tibet rejected the demand, Nepalese forces plundered Tashilhunpo monastery. The value of the stolen property—gold, silver, and jewels donated by devotees from centuries—has never been estimated.

China Enters the Nepal-Tibet War

The plundering of the Tashilhunpo monastery and the possibility of a Nepalese advance into Lhasa brought the imperial Chinese army to the defense of Tibet. In October 1791, a combined Tibetan-Chinese army drove Nepali troops out of Tibet and in June 1792 they launched a military campaign against Nepal. Nepalese forces defended their territory fiercely but were overwhelmed by the Chinese.

The Chinese intervention in favor of Tibet led to the signing of the Sino-Nepalese Treaty in September 1792 that stated Nepal and Tibet should maintain fraternal relations and seek Chinese arbitration in case of any disputes. Nepal was to return all articles plundered at Tashilhunpo monastery and was never again to raise claims based on the 1789 treaty. A Chinese officer would demarcate the boundary between Nepal and Tibet in Kuti and Kerong areas. China promised to come to Nepal's assistance in the event of an attack by a foreign power. Finally, Nepal was to send a mission to China every five years with a gift to the emperor. This treaty clearly established the political supremacy of China in Nepal.

China, however, ignored the treaty obligation of assisting Nepal in the event of foreign aggression when Nepal sought Chinese help during the Anglo-Nepalese War of 1814-1816. The imperial representative in Lhasa wrote to the Nepalese King, "When you fight with the British, this happens outside our borders. The soldiers of the Emperor cannot go there."[2] By refusing Nepal's requests for military as well as financial assistance, China, by default, surrendered its dominant position in Nepal to the growing British influence in India.

Taking advantage of China's internal conflicts, the Taiping Rebellion (1850-1864) in particular, Nepal decided to settle the old scores and invaded Tibet in 1854. China intervened again and the war was quickly terminated, resulting in a treaty concluded in Kathmandu in March 1856. The treaty reinforced the special status of China requiring Nepal to continue sending tribute missions every five years, Nepal agreeing to assist Tibet in the event of foreign aggression, and Tibet agreeing to pay annual tribute to Nepal.

Nepal, however, refused to assist Tibet when British India sent an armed expedition in 1904 to open a direct trading route between India and Tibet. In fact, Nepal helped the British expedition by supplying necessary porters and mules. Nepal's trade with Tibet, mostly the bartering of agricultural produce, however, went into decline with the opening of alternative routes. Taking advantage of internal political troubles in China as well as increased British activism across the Himalayas, Nepal stopped paying tribute to China beginning in 1908. By 1910, however, China had become apprehensive of British activity in Tibet and reasserted its claim to sovereign rights in Tibet and feudatory missions from Nepal. Nepal broke relations with China when the Tibetans, taking advantage of China's 1911 revolution, drove the Chinese out of Lhasa.

Sino-Nepal Relations with Communist China

Post-World War II political developments in China and India led to a drastic change in relations between Beijing and Kathmandu. While the British withdrew from India in 1947, the Nationalists were defeated by the Communists in 1949. Nepal, too, experienced a limited revolution under India's careful supervision in 1950. While China claimed sovereignty over Tibet and sent the PLA to Lhasa in 1950, India signed a Peace and Friendship Treaty with Nepal in the same year, establishing New Delhi's dominance over Nepal's foreign and defense policies. In 1954, New Delhi and Beijing signed a treaty that recognized China's sovereignty in Tibet.

The Sino-Indian Treaty of 1954 had an immediate impact on Kathmandu's relations with Beijing. Nepalese and Chinese representative began extensive talks in New Delhi and later in Kathmandu leading to the establishment of diplomatic relations between the two countries in 1955. In September 1956, both countries signed a treaty under which Nepal recognized China's sovereignty over Tibet and agreed to surrender all privileges and rights granted by the old treaty of 1856. In February 1957, Chinese Premier Zhou Enlai visited Kathmandu, giving high level attention to relations with Nepal.

A series of agreements and a treaty followed the establishment of diplomatic relations between China and Nepal.[3] An agreement to delimit the boundary line was signed in March 1960, which was followed a month later by signing a Treaty of Peace and Friendship in Kathmandu. The Sino-Nepal Boundary Treaty was signed in Beijing in October 1961. But the trijunctions, where the Nepalese, Chinese, and Indian territories meet, on both the western and eastern ends of the borderline, have not yet been fixed due to the ongoing Sino-Indian dispute: India was formally invited to discuss the demarcation of the boundary, but declined to attend.[4]

The treaty instituted a Sino-Nepal Joint Commission to study and decide on issues related to the alignment, location, and maintenance of the seventy-nine border demarcation markers. It was also agreed to create a 12.4 mile (20 km) demilitarized zone on both sides of the border to avoid movement of the armed personnel. The commission's findings were incorporated through a protocol to the original treaty.

The speed with which Beijing moved to establish good relations with Nepal in the late 1950s and early 1960s was prompted by political crisis in Tibet, Beijing's worsening relations with India, and the Cold War between Western democracies and communism. In March 1959, the PLA suppressed a Tibetan rebellion, also known as Lhasa Uprising. The Dalai Lama and his supporters fled the country toward India and thousands of Tibetan refugees began to cross into Nepal through the freezing Himalayan passes. The Khampa rebels, armed and trained by U.S. Central Intelligence Agency (CIA) in guerrilla warfare, began to operate their hit-and-run activities against the Chinese military fortifications from across the Nepalese border.[5]

China Claims Mount Everest

While delineating the boundary, the maps produced by both sides showed inconsistencies in 35 places on the Sino-Nepal borderline. These disputes were solved quickly and amicably, mostly in favor of Nepal. Indeed, Nepal actually received more lands than its maps had shown. Mount Everest, however, became a bone of contention between the Chinese and the Nepalese governments. The news was leaked in the aftermath of Nepalese Prime Minister B.P. Koirala's visit to Beijing in March 1960 where the Chinese leadership, including Mao Zedong, reportedly laid claim on Mount Everest, the highest mountain on earth. Koirala refused to entertain the Chinese claim. In Nepal, the response to this news was the display of massive anti-Chinese demonstrations to protest Beijing's claim to the world's highest mountain that had long remained a symbol of Nepalese pride.

In the discussions on boundary issues, the Chinese side questioned that if the mountain belonged to Nepal then it must have a name in the Nepali language—Everest is the English name and Chomolungma is the Tibetan name—since these names are clearly written on the maps published by respective countries, but that there is no word for it in the Nepali language. The Nepali side gave the Nepali name as Sagarmatha, which was coined by a famous Nepali historian Baburam Achayra in 1938, and explained that Nepal was yet to publish its map with name and script.

When the maps were presented during the border delineation it was found that the Chinese map showed the mountain within Chinese territory while the Nepali map showed the mountain on the boundary line. It was also found that the mountaineering expedition teams received permission from Nepal while climbing from the southern side and from Tibet while climbing from the northern side. The visit of Chinese Premier Zhou Enlai to Kathmandu in April 1960 settled the dispute when he made it clear that Beijing had not claimed the whole of Everest as reported in the press but was prepared to accept the demarcation of boundary line along the peak. Consequently, the Chinese side agreed to follow the Nepalese delineation, which shows the mountain on the boundary line, with the northern slope belonging to China and the southern slope belonging to Nepal.

China Violates the Demilitarized Zone

In late June 1960, the PLA violated the demilitarized zone and fired on an unarmed Nepali police team near Kore Pass in the Mustang section of Nepal-Tibet border, killing one and capturing seventeen others. The incident provoked massive anti-Chinese demonstration in Kathmandu. The Chinese foreign ministry stated that the Chinese troops had mistaken the Nepali policemen for Tibetan rebels and claimed that the incident occurred inside Chinese territory about one-kilometer to the north of Kore Pass.

In sharp contrast to Beijing's explanation, the Nepali side claimed that the incident occurred inside Nepali territory 300 meters south of the Kore Pass. The Chinese government eventually admitted that a mistake had been made by low ranking personnel and agreed to pay 50,000 Nepali Rupees to the family of the dead policeman. It is interesting to note, however, that when the boundary demarcation took place later on both sites were placed well inside Nepali territory.

China Supports Nepal's Absolute Monarchy

China and Nepal's relations were strengthened after King Mahendra staged a coup in December 1960 in Nepal against the elected government headed by Prime Minister B.P. Koirala. India expressed its unhappiness with the king's action, describing it as "a setback to democracy." In response King Mahendra moved to play the "China card" at a time when Beijing's relations with New Delhi were tense, as they were on the verge of fighting a border war, and signed an all-weather road, named the Kodari Highway, construction agreement with China to connect Nepal with Tibet in October 1961. While the Kodari Highway had minimal economic or commercial value, it was a symbol of independence from India for Nepal and of strategic military importance to China.

In the period 1961-1962, Nepal's king faced political and guerrilla opposition from the ousted Prime Minister Koirala's party, based in India with New Delhi's tacit support. During this difficult period, King Mahendra received unequivocal support from Beijing when Chinese Foreign Minister Chen Yi declared that: "In case any foreign army makes a foolhardy attempt to attack Nepal . . . China will side with the Nepalese people."[6] India's relations with the king's government continued to worsen. Meanwhile, the Chinese won the heart of King Mahendra when Mao Zedong told him during his visit to Beijing in 1962 about the "possibility of a big country like China injuring the feelings of small neighbor such as Nepal out of sheer ignorance and arrogance," but assured the King that "China would be more than careful to respect Nepal's national sentiments."[7]

During the 1962 India-China border war, Nepal declared its neutrality but continued to support China's application for membership in the United Nations. The regime in Nepal took India's emergence since the 1970s as the dominant power in South Asian region as a threat to the survival of monarchy in Nepal. Nevertheless, Nepal did not abandon its policy of equidistance between China and India but wanted to be close to China to counter India's dominance in the region. However, by this time, China had implicitly recognized India's predominance in the South Asian region, and hence was unwilling to compete with New Delhi in Nepal. In 1978, when Deng Xiaoping visited Nepal, he reportedly advised the Nepali king to maintain good relations with India and said that China could help Nepal only to the extent of pledging support in safeguarding its national independence and preventing foreign interference.

Nepal, however, negotiated a deal in 1988 for the purchase of Chinese weapons, including anti-aircraft guns, a move that angered India, leading to the imposition of a blockade in 1989. Policy-makers in New Delhi argued that China-Nepal arms deal violated the 1965 Indo-Nepal arms agreement that obliges Nepal to secure all defense supplies from India. The Nepali monarchy lost its mandate in 1990 when the country was rocked by pro-democracy protestors, who thronged the streets of Kathmandu and other major towns with the known support of India.

Tibetan Problem as an Irritant in Sino-Nepal Relations

In the mid-1970s, Nepal mobilized its military forces to disarm the Tibetan Khampa guerrillas, numbering around 1,500-men, camped in different passes along the Himalayas inside the Nepali territory, from where they carried out hit-and-run activities against the Chinese army. The presence and activities of these guerrillas in Nepal had been an irritant not only to Kathmandu's relations with Beijing but also to the general Nepali population living along the Himalayan region. These Khampa guerrillas were trained in Colorado and their military hardware and other supplies were provided by the CIA in the aftermath of 1959 Lhasa Uprising. These guerrillas, however, were abandoned by the CIA after U.S. President Richard Nixon's 1972 visit to Beijing. Taking advantage of the changed international situation, which gave Nepal an opportunity to please China, Nepal's royal army moved to disarm them. Wang Di, the leader of the Khampas, was shot dead when he refused to surrender.

China's entry into Tibet in 1950, and the internal turmoil in Tibet since then, has been a sensitive issue in Nepal's relations with China. Nepal had to bear the burden of thousands of refugees in the 1950s and early 1960s and the process of refugees entering Nepal continues unabated. Coinciding with the refugee problem, the Sino-

Nepalese border also faces political problems created by Tibetan nationalists in the name of the Free Tibet Movement.

The flow of Tibetan refugees into Nepal began in the early 1950s, but the first major influx crossed the border into Nepal in 1959, following the Lhasa Uprising. While no one knows the exact number of Tibetan refugees in Nepal, they are estimated to be around 50,000; approximately 20,000 of them are living in 12 different settlements across Nepal, and another 30,000 are estimated to be in Kathmandu. These refugees were taken care of by the relief programs of the International Committee of the Red Cross (ICRC). In order to manage the refugee's plight, the Tibetan Government in Exile in Dharmashala in India established the Tibetan Welfare Office in Kathmandu to coordinate between the refugees, international aid organizations, and the Nepalese government.

In 1966, China and Nepal signed an Agreement on Trade, Intercourse, and Related Questions between the Tibet Autonomous Region (TAR) of China and Nepal allowing the citizens living in the border regions and "religious pilgrims" to cross the Tibet-Nepal border without a passport or visa. They needed only to register at the border. The agreement was renewed in 1976 for another ten years. As the flexibility of this agreement led to the influx of more anti-Chinese Tibetan refugees into Nepal, China and Nepal signed a new treaty that significantly restricted Tibetans entering or traveling through Nepal. Nepal introduced a strict border policy under Chinese government pressure and refused to accept or recognize Tibetans entering Nepal as refugees. Nepal has not signed the 1951 UN Refugee Convention and considers all asylum seekers—with the exception of the pre-1989 Tibetan population and certain Bhutanese—to be illegal immigrants and arrests them as they enter Nepal.

Nonetheless, the flow of Tibetan refugees into Nepal continues unabated; an estimated 3,000 Tibetans entered Nepal as refugees in 2007, but the number precipitously declined in 2008 to about 500 due to strict border controls imposed by Nepali authorities. An informal "gentlemen's agreement" between the government of Nepal and the United Nations High Commissioner for Refugees (UNHCR) now protects Tibetans passing through Nepal to India. Since 1990, the agreement has provided that any Tibetans who are apprehended by the police within Nepal's borders should be detained and turned over to the Nepalese Department of Immigration, who in turn will contact UNHCR. All apprehended Tibetans generally wait at the Tibetan Refugee Reception Center in Kathmandu until they are authorized to travel on to Tibetan refugee centers in India.

The Chinese government, however, considers these Tibetans as separatists and puts pressure on the Nepal government for their prompt handover to Chinese border authorities. Chinese sensitivities increased as the refugee issue became a matter of political propaganda launched by the activists of Free Tibet Movement, an anti-Chinese outfit established in 1987 and based in London with chapters in the U.S., other Western countries, and India.

The PRC's traditionally good relations with Nepal changed abruptly in 2008 with the collapse of monarchy and the establishment of the Nepalese Republic. Chinese were concerned that the uncertain political climate and instability brought about by the fall of monarchy in Nepal had the potential to increase anti-Chinese activities. The Chinese concerns turned out to be correct when Kathmandu became a center of anti-Chinese demonstrations by activists of the Free Tibet Movement, who gathered in Nepal from all over the world, during the Beijing Olympics in the summer of 2008. China closed the Nepal-Tibet border for tourist traffic, and halted the bus services between Kathmandu and Lhasa for more than a year.

The Tibetan issue has become a matter of sustained irritation for Nepal's government as it is under constant pressure from both the Western countries and China. The representatives of Western governments want Nepal to provide safe passage to refugees heading to Dharmashala in India and to other countries in the West. Chinese authorities, on the other hand, want the Tibetan refugees to be handed over to them or locked up behind bars. The Tibetan problem is unlikely to find a solution in the near future as China is unlikely to give in to any pressures coming from Western powers and India. Beijing's defense policies in Tibet, as in imperial China, places importance on controlling the country's minority-dominated periphery for the purpose of protecting the core Han Chinese majority heartland.[8]

Sino-Nepal Relations in Post-Monarchy Nepal

China was concerned about the political chaos in Nepal, due to armed uprising launched by Nepal Communist Party, which is openly Maoist. Beijing had no relations with the Maoist rebels, but as they carried Mao's name it became a matter of embarrassment to the Chinese government. The government-controlled Chinese press used to describe the Maoist rebels in Nepal as anti-government guerrillas and carefully avoided mentioning the word "Maoists" in their news articles. Although Chinese authorities never liked the use of their former leader's name by the Nepalese Maoists when they were fighting the monarchy, Beijing had no choice but to accept them as a political force for years to come as they emerged as the largest party in the Nepalese constituent assembly and led a coalition government in the summer of 2008. Beijing now appears comfortable in dealing with the Nepalese Maoists, mainly due to their ideological affinity with the Chinese Communist Party and their anti-Indian pronouncements, especially their expressed interest to neutralize New Delhi's influence.

Since the country was declared a republic in 2008, there have been visible signs of reorientation in China's foreign policy toward Nepal. China had earlier followed quiet diplomacy of maintaining good relations with the monarchy. However, in the political vacuum created by the ouster of the monarchy, Nepal saw the emergence of several political parties each vying for a larger share of political power. Since the 1990s, Nepal has been embroiled with acute ethnic, religious, and linguistic contradictions and economic disparities leading to a Maoist communist insurgency. Even though the Maoist insurgency officially ended in 2006, the economic and ethnic dimensions of the conflict are as strong as ever. The objectives of the various ethnic groups involved in this conflict vary from local autonomy to outright separation.

With the exception of the Maoist party, all other political parties in Nepal have pro-Indian proclivities. Criminals, too, have taken refuge inside the political parties and all sorts of social miscreants have taken the opportunity to fish in the troubled waters. As Tibetans, who were otherwise quiet in the past, began organizing protest demonstrations in Kathmandu, Beijing began to show its concern over the possibility of the Tibet-Nepal border being misused. By sending high-level Chinese political, economic, and military delegations to Nepal since the end of the monarchy in 2008, Beijing has sought to establish good relations with the emerging leaders of all political parties. In these visits, Nepal has been repeatedly assured by the Chinese of the continuation of economic, technological, and military aid.

In 2009, Beijing increased its annual grant assistance to Nepal by 50 percent— from $15 million to $22 million. In March 2011, the chief of the PLA, General Chen Bingde, visited Kathmandu and pledged 130 million Yuan ($19.80 million) worth of support to the Nepali army to build a hospital for military personnel. In return for this aid, the Chinese asked the Nepal government not to deviate from a "One China" policy, not to allow Nepalese land to be used for anti-China activities, to block the Tibetans at the border and take strong action against them, and to grant special facilities for Chinese investments in strategic sectors such as development of hydropower and tourism industries. In early 2011, China's Export Import Bank provided a soft loan of $97.2 million (equivalent to seven billion Nepali Rupees, or Rs) at 1.75 percent interest for a period of 20 years to develop a major hydropower plant (60mw) in Trishuli River.[9]

Ever since an economic aid agreement between China and Nepal was concluded in 1956, Nepal has benefited from Chinese economic and technical assistance in developing its industrial infrastructure, even though the balance of trade has been heavily and steadily in favor of China. The latest figures show that Nepal suffered a trade deficit worth $431 million (Rs 31 billion) in 2009-2010 with China. It was only $299 million (Rs 21.5 billion) a year earlier. Beijing has also initiated an exchange of scholars program and has invited Nepalese scholars to attend Chinese universities and think tanks to study. These engagements suggest that China is trying to draw Nepal into becoming a strategic partner.

Conclusions

While China lives peacefully with Nepal without any territorial disputes along their boundary, this frontier, however, is likely to continue to be a hotspot for cross-border activities by anti-Chinese Tibetans. Since the headquarters of these anti-Chinese Tibetans is located in Dharmashala in India, China suspects New Delhi's role in fomenting troubles across the border by taking advantage of the Indo-Nepalese open border. Consequently, China's pressures on Kathmandu for a special status on a par with New Delhi will continue to be Beijing's main diplomacy in Nepal in the near future.

Even more importantly, Nepal's border with China cannot be resolved without India's cooperation. Both the eastern and western trijunctions—where the Nepalese, Chinese, and Indian territories touch—remain unresolved. Until delegates from the three countries meet and reach an agreement on the location of these trijunctions, then Nepal's border with the PRC will remain undemarcated. Thus, final resolution of the Sino-Nepali border dispute is contingent on the ultimate resolution of the Sino-Indian dispute.

Notes

1. There are many sources on the history of Nepal-Tibet-China relations. For an excellent executive summary of Nepal's relations with China and Tibet that provides reference to Chinese, Tibetan, and Nepali sources, see Leo E. Rose, *Nepal: A Strategy for Survival* (Berkeley: University of California Press, 1971).

2. Quoted in Ibid., 86.

3. Avtar Singh Bhasin, *Documents on Nepal's Relations with India and China, 1949-1966* (New Delhi: Academic Books, 1970).

4. Buddhi Narayan Shrestha, "Nepal-China Border Demarcation: A Token of Friendship," http://www.bordernepal.worldpress.com [Accessed on 19 January 2007]; Vidhya Vir Singh Kansakar, "Nepal-India Open Border: Prospects, Problems and Challenges," a paper presented at the Nepalese Institute of Foreign Affairs, no date.

5. For details of Tibetan crisis, see Warren W. Smith, Jr., *China's Tibet? Autonomy or Assimilation* (Lanham, MD: Rowman and Littlefield, 2008); John W. Roberts II, and Elizabeth A. Roberts, *Freeing Tibet: 50 Years of Struggle, Resilience and Hope* (New York: AMACOM, 2009); Kenneth Conboy and James Morrison, *The CIA's Secret War in Tibet* (Lawrence: University Press of Kansas, 2002).

6. Rose, 248.

7. Rishikesh Shaha, *Nepali Politics: Retrospect and Prospect* (New Delhi: Oxford University Press, 1978), 126.

8. D.S. Rajan, "Settling Tibet Issue—Problems and Prospects," *South Asia Analysis Group*, Paper No. 4365, 4 March 2011.

9. *The Republica*, 1 January 2011, 18 August 2011.

218

Map 15: Pakistan's Border with China

15

The Sino-Pakistan Border: Stability in an Unstable Region

Christopher Tang

Scholarly discourse concerning Sino-Pakistani relations is dominated by the notion of a "special relationship" or "entente cordiale."[1] Largely still applicable today, this description derives support from a close examination of border relations shared by Pakistan and the PRC. Since settling their 325 mile (523 km) border through secret negotiations in 1963, the two allies have avoided any major boundary disputes and remain in regular dialogue about the myriad implications of their mutual frontier.

The Sino-Pakistani relationship has proven "remarkably durable" during the past fifty years, based as it is on a "realistic power calculation," emerging from their mutual enmity toward India.[2] While this strategic algebra remains valid today, friendly Sino-Pakistani relations have survived not simply because of the 1962 Sino-Indian border war. Instead, the relationship has evolved to accommodate changing circumstances, both regional and global.

In fact, Islamabad and Beijing have sporadically redefined and reasserted the meaning and intentions underlying their strategic friendship. From Beijing's careful negotiation of providing Pakistan nuclear assistance while easing its position on the Kashmir issue, to a heightened focus on terrorism in recent years, Pakistan and the PRC have adapted their relations to evolving regional and geopolitical contexts and, in so doing, have ensured continued cooperation across the Karakoram Highway. With Sino-Pakistani interaction now overtly assisting the PRC's efforts to secure a presence in the Indian Ocean via the deep-water port at Gwadar, it remains clear that the stable Sino-Pakistani border allows bilateral relations to flourish and affords security in an often insecure region of the world.

Cold War Conveniences, 1962-1971

Though Sino-Pakistani relations have developed to accommodate a host of shared concerns, the friendship begins and ends with India. Emerging from a sense of urgency initiated by the 1962 Sino-Indian border conflict, the Sino-Pakistani border settlement of March 1963 formally commenced the friendship between Beijing and

Islamabad in earnest. Previously, relations had been minimal and limited by Sino-American hostility. A member of two pro-American alliance systems in the Southeast Asian Treaty Organization (SEATO) and the Central Treaty Organization (CENTO), Pakistan worried about the PRC. Although a cordial exchange between Zhou Enlai and Mohammad Ali Bogra at the Bandung Conference in 1955 worked to minimize mutual suspicion, settling the undefined border was not yet diplomatically feasible. Not until the late 1950s would diplomatic exchanges begin, after Karachi grew fearful of improving Indo-American ties, and approached Beijing about settling the border.

If the Chinese were initially hesitant to define formally the boundary given Pakistan's pro-American leanings, they were also unsure as to what actually constituted a realistic delineation for the borderline. Since the creation of Pakistan in 1947 and the formation of the PRC in 1949, neither side had published their mutual border on a map. Karachi did, however, gain access to Chinese maps dating from the late 1950s, which seemed to lay claim to the Hunza region that Pakistan felt was its own.[3] When formal border discussions began, therefore, talks continued for several months between May and December 1962 before the two sides agreed on where the line should be drawn.[4] In March 1963, foreign ministers Chen Yi and Zulfikar Ali Bhutto signed the Sino-Pakistan boundary agreement in Beijing.

The agreement is generally considered to be a compromise on Beijing's part. In the estimation of Pakistani China-hand Agha Shahi, Chinese negotiators agreed to the boundaries Pakistan proposed, since they admitted they were not sure where the line should, in fact, be drawn.[5] While, to be sure, Beijing was unclear on this issue, it is perhaps more likely that the Chinese were willing to compromise in negotiations for the sake of, first, expediting a resolution after the Sino-Indian conflict and, second, settling definitively the frontier of restive Xinjiang Province.

China maintained control over much of the territory in question, but the final arrangement closely resembled the actual line of control Karachi had proposed.[6] In fact, Pakistan retained authority over all territory it had heretofore administered, and the Chinese retreated in their claims to the Hunza. Additionally, China transferred to Pakistan 750 square miles (1,942 km^2) in the Oprang Valley. Three-fourths of K2 stayed with Pakistan, which also held six of seven disputed Karakoram passes. In the wake of the agreement, Sino-Pakistani relations commenced in earnest and a *de facto* alliance was born.

As was to be expected, Nehru's India was outraged at the border settlement. Aside from its concern for the apparent emergence of an anti-India alliance between Pakistan and the PRC, New Delhi was incensed at what it perceived to be a Sino-Pakistani agreement over Indian land. Since the settlement between Beijing and Karachi dealt with territory in the disputed Kashmir region, India felt the rug had been pulled out from under its feet. Worse, the initial Sino-Pakistani communiqué signaling a provisional border agreement was released on the eve of Indo-Pakistani talks on Kashmir at Tashkent.[7] While the unresolved Sino-Indian boundary dispute is tied to a number of discrete territorial grievances, the Sino-Pakistani settlement remains an annoyance for New Delhi.

By settling their shared boundary, Pakistan and the PRC effectively neutralized the only major potential issue that could have spoiled the formation of a meaningful relationship. For the duration of the Cold War period, Sino-Pakistani relations would remain intact and prove a valuable tool at the disposal of both parties. Throughout the 1960s, with Ayub Khan increasingly wary of a United States that seemed interested in providing weapons to India, Pakistan was eager to use the border settlement as a springboard to better relations. In August 1963, an aviation agreement was concluded that commenced regular Pakistan International Airlines (PIA) flights from Dacca to Shanghai and Guangzhou. The following February, Beijing upped the ante by continuing its support for worldwide national liberation movements and officially began backing Pakistan in the struggle for Kashmir.

Although the 1965 Indo-Pakistani war dealt a crushing blow to Pakistan, the Chinese supported their battered ally, offering rhetorical condemnation of India throughout the hostilities, and stepping up aid to Pakistan in the wake of its defeat. While Chinese foreign relations were largely derailed throughout the Cultural Revolution, Sino-Pakistani ties survived remarkably well, and proved a critical prerequisite for the Sino-American backchannel communication that facilitated Nixon's historic February 1972 visit to the PRC. Even though Sino-Pakistani relations had blossomed after settling the shared border in 1963, Pakistan's devastating dismemberment in 1971 compelled Beijing and Islamabad to redefine the relationship's meaning.

Karakoram Diplomacy, 1971-2000

After the 1971 Indo-Pakistani war, Sino-Pakistani relations transitioned from an emphasis on navigating Cold War geopolitical alignments toward bilateral interaction conducted through a more covert kind of diplomacy. This adaptation was both influenced and facilitated by the introduction of the Karakoram Highway (KKH) in the late 1970s. The highest international road in the world, KKH construction began in 1959, reached completion in 1978, and was opened to civilian and third-country access in 1982.

In the early to mid-1970s, before the KKH was opened, Sino-Pakistani ties were sustained largely through Chinese aid and development programs in addition to vast sales of conventional weapons.[8] Though the 1970s saw continued cooperation and partnership between Pakistan and the PRC, only after the KKH became operational did the alliance regain strategic value in regional affairs. While Beijing and Islamabad had been regularly concluding barter trade agreements since 1964, the KKH, as expected, improved cross-border trade.[9] Among other things, these exchanges included Pakistani leather, nylon, cloth, cotton, dry fruit and herbs, for Chinese silk, textiles, technical hardware, and farming equipment.[10]

Although cross-border trade was one major product of the highway, the KKH also rejuvenated Sino-Pakistani interaction more broadly by literally and figuratively paving the way for covert Chinese nuclear assistance to Pakistan. Throughout the 1980s and 1990s, this Chinese nuclear support would fundamentally come to define and sustain the relationship. Though the salient facts of the story remain a closely guarded secret, it is widely believed that the Chinese provided Pakistan with the information, technical assistance, and some of the materials necessary to construct their nuclear bomb.[11] After Pakistan's demoralizing results in the 1971 war with India, Zulfikar Ali Bhutto set out to acquire a nuclear deterrent. Bhutto's urgency naturally intensified after India's successful test of its nuclear device in 1974. As Swaran Singh indicates, it is believed that somewhere among Bhutto's three visits to Beijing in February 1972, September 1974, and April 1976, he was able to secure Chinese support for the nascent Pakistani nuclear program.[12] In one estimation, PRC nuclear assistance likely began after India's successful May 1974 test.[13] Whenever it was that these agreements were actually first initiated, most historians agree that by mid-1976 Chinese backing was consolidated.[14] Over the ensuing two decades, PRC nuclear support continued.

During the early 1980s, the Chinese reportedly transferred to Pakistan a blueprint for a nuclear device from China's October 1966 test, along with highly enriched uranium, tritium, and essential components required for a nuclear weapons production complex.[15] Additionally, Chinese scientists travelled to Pakistan to oversee production. It is believed that midway through the 1990s Beijing sold Islamabad ring magnets crucial for gas centrifuges that produce weapons-grade enriched uranium. Further, the Chinese offered Pakistan heavy water necessary for plutonium production reactors, an industrial furnace to melt plutonium and uranium, and high-tech diagnostic equipment.[16] Above all, the PRC has helped the Pakistani nuclear program achieve self-sustainability by directly assisting construction of the Khushab nuclear reactor, which continues to produce weapons-grade plutonium.

While it is unclear when exactly the Pakistan nuclear device came into existence, in May 1998 the country conducted its first successful test in response to the Indian detonation a few weeks prior. From across the KKH, Chinese nuclear assistance and a turn toward secretive diplomacy had breathed new life into post-Mao Sino-Pakistani relations. Indeed the cross-border KKH may even have directly facilitated the nuclear exchange. In May 1983, Pakistan's Foreign Minister Yakub Khan was present at the Chinese nuclear test at Lop Nor in Xinjiang.[17] Further, in May 1990 there was suspicion in both India and the West that the PRC permitted Pakistan to test covertly its own nuclear device on Chinese soil at Lop Nor, thereby keeping secret Pakistan's nuclear capacity.[18] While the notion of a Pakistani nuclear test on Chinese soil remains mere speculation, it exists as a possibility precisely because of the strategic Karakoram backdoor.

Beijing was also instrumental in providing Islamabad with the delivery systems for its nuclear devices. Throughout the late 1980s and into the mid-1990s, the Chinese sold M-11 Short Range Ballistic Missiles (SRBM) to Pakistan.[19] With a range of over 186 miles (300 km), these missiles provided Pakistan with the ability to hit a wide range of Indian targets along their border. Additionally, Beijing agreed to help train the Pakistani military how to operate these missiles, supplied Pakistan with the missile technology itself, and even helped construct a factory to produce the devices. While some observers claim Beijing was acting defiantly to irritate the United States after its 1992 sale of F-16 fighters to Taiwan, it is more likely that the Chinese sought to strengthen Pakistan's nuclear capacity as a means to limit India's rise and prevent its challenge to China's dominance in Asia.[20] Whatever Beijing's definitive motive, covert Chinese nuclear assistance was facilitated by their secure shared border, and the Karakoram Highway that bridged its mountainous path. Even as late as 2001, American intelligence reports claimed to have spotted Chinese trucks travelling across the KKH carrying missile components into Pakistan.[21]

Improving Sino-Indian Relations

Perhaps the most intriguing aspect of the emergence of this Karakoram diplomacy and Chinese nuclear assistance is that it occurred alongside the PRC's dual effort to improve relations with India, while adopting a more neutral stance on Indo-Pakistani tensions. By the late 1970s Beijing was interested in seeking better ties with India as a means to isolate the Soviet Union.[22] In so doing, however, the Chinese astutely endeavored to protect the Sino-Pakistani friendship by insisting on "delinking" that relationship from any rapprochement with New Delhi.[23] Naturally, this policy required careful Chinese maneuvering. Before Foreign Minister Huang Hua's highly anticipated June 1981 visit to India, the first such contact since Zhou Enlai's 1960 effort, Premier Zhao Ziyang traveled to Pakistan to reassure the Zia regime that any improvement in Sino-Indian relations would not disrupt China's military ties to Pakistan. At the same time, Zhao told Zia that it was important for China to improve its relationships throughout South Asia, and the PRC thus had to begin pursuing a more impartial stance on South Asian regional affairs.

Despite this concession, New Delhi did not consent to China's delinkage of Sino-Indian and Sino-Pakistani relations until 1987, months before Rajiv Gandhi's celebrated December 1988 trip to the PRC. After Premier Li Peng's visit to India in December 1991, delinkage was henceforth entrenched in Sino-Indian contacts. Perturbed as New Delhi was at continued military ties between Beijing and Islamabad, the covert nature of Sino-Pakistani Karakoram diplomacy allowed India to proceed with Sino-Indian rapprochement without having to appear as befriending the enemy's benefactor. By going underground, relations between Pakistan and the PRC allowed China, India, and Pakistan to all step beyond the loggerheads imposed by Cold War alliance systems, and move closer toward improved regional security and facilitated bilateral contact.

In addition to making possible China's delinkage of improved Sino-Indian ties amid continued military assistance to Pakistan, Karakoram diplomacy allowed Beijing to reappraise its policy on Kashmir, and shift to impartiality on the issue. Since early 1964, the Chinese had backed the Pakistani call for a plebiscite in Kashmir, situating the issue within its larger support for national liberation struggles throughout Asia, Africa, and Latin America. Chinese support on the issue effectively intensified its friendship with Pakistan and accentuated the relationship as primarily an anti-Indian endeavor. With the conclusion of the Mao era and the "reform and opening" ushered in under Deng Xiaoping in the late 1970s, however, Beijing was ready to abandon revolutionary struggle and focus on achieving regional stability and security. After 1971, as the essence of Sino-Pakistani relations gradually shifted from overt Cold War relations to covert backdoor diplomacy manifested largely in military assistance, the Chinese were loath to withdraw their support of Kashmir too abruptly.

As such, throughout the 1980s, Beijing set out gently but consistently to alter its discourse on the topic. This policy shift began with Deng Xiaoping's June 1980 statement that the Kashmir issue should be "solved peacefully" between India and Pakistan, since it was a "bilateral dispute."[24] Thereafter, Kashmir made fewer and fewer appearances in Chinese discourse, yet was occasionally mentioned alongside reference to "the relevant United Nations resolutions"—a tacit yet subtle nod of support to Pakistan in that it suggested the dual validity of UN protocol and the Simla Agreement calling for bilateral negotiations. When the Kashmir crisis of 1989-1990 broke out, however, Beijing was compelled to make a statement. During the next several months, the PRC fluctuated between discarding, and then returning to, veiled statements of support for Pakistan by way of referencing the UN.[25] Ultimately, by May 1990, Beijing had settled on backing "peaceful negotiations" between India and Pakistan. At the same time that Karakoram diplomacy was bringing Chinese nuclear assistance and missiles to Pakistan, therefore, the Chinese were able to disentangle themselves from Kashmir, and emerge publicly as a neutral and responsible member of the international community.

The duality of Sino-Pakistani relations throughout this period was visible again during the 1998 Indo-Pakistani nuclear crisis. In many ways the product of Chinese Karakoram diplomacy with Pakistan, the respective May 1998 nuclear tests by India and Pakistan greatly concerned Beijing. Though its nuclear assistance to Islamabad had been driven by a concern for the regional balance of power and a latent desire to frustrate and limit India's rise, the PRC leadership feared a nuclear arms race raging on its southwestern frontier, and the subsequent problems posed for improving Sino-Indian ties.[26] Publicly, therefore, Beijing expressed "deep regret" after the 1998 tests and only mildly professed sympathy with the Pakistani test—a position designed more as a response to New Delhi's assertion of the China threat as the motivation behind its own test.[27]

While Sino-Indian diplomacy was icy in the months following May 1998, the path toward rapprochement was eventually resumed and the PRC continued pursuing its policy of neutrality on the subcontinent. Most observers in India and the West understood very well that the PRC had supported and nurtured the Pakistani bomb, but the shift toward covert Sino-Pakistani relations beginning in the mid-to-late 1970s allowed Beijing to temper the Indian challenge to Chinese regional supremacy, even while working to secure stability on its southwestern frontier.

If the 1998 nuclear crisis exposed a slight lingering of China's public leanings toward Pakistan, the Kargil conflict of the following year confirmed PRC impartiality in South Asia as far as outward appearances were concerned. After Kashmiri mujahideen backed by Pakistani troops moved across the Line of Control and took position in the mountains of Indian-controlled Kargil, India responded with airstrikes and artillery fire over the next two months. With both states now nuclear powers, the situation threatened to spiral out of control. This worried Beijing, which supported stability in South Asia. Focused as it was on facilitating a "peaceful and stable environment on its periphery" to continue its economic rise unimpeded, as Fazal-ur-Rahman writes, China's response to Kargil was "neutral but not detached" and representative of the larger "discernible adjustments" in its South Asia policy since the 1980s.[28] For Islamabad, the Chinese response "fell short of [its] expectations," conditioned as it was by historical Chinese support for Pakistan in times of crisis spanning the previous three and half decades.[29]

At the turn of the 21st century, therefore, while Chinese missiles continued secretly crossing the Karakoram, on the international stage Beijing was proclaiming itself neutral on South Asia. Although the PRC carefully protected Sino-Pakistani relations throughout the 1980s and 1990s by shifting toward covert Karakoram diplomacy, the new century saw a new transnational challenge in the form of Islamic fundamentalism. The emergence of the Taliban regime in Afghanistan, social unrest among Uyghur Muslims in Xinjiang, and America's "War on Terror" after 2001, caused the security of the shared Sino-Pakistani border to be reappraised and the Beijing-Islamabad friendship was forced to confront new challenges, thereby reinventing its meaning amid a new and uncertain context.

The Transnational Challenge of Terrorism

The unstable Chinese West has been of great concern to PRC leaders since securing power in 1949, but the issue of Beijing's rocky relationship with Xinjiang's Uyghur Muslim population did not heavily influence Sino-Pakistani relations until very recently. Though Islamabad pays little attention to the fate of Uyghur Muslims, despite their common thread of Islam, it has been exceedingly careful to avoid ruffling Beijing's hypersensitive feathers on the issue. However, amid the rise of Islamic fundamentalism and the emergence of sustained Uyghur unrest in Xinjiang, both of which date back to the mid-1990s, Beijing has recently taken the initiative to bring up the issue with Pakistan. In so doing, it has stressed its premium on a Sino-Pakistani border impervious to the osmosis of militant influences, both direct and indirect. Given the myriad problems posed for America's "War on Terror" by Pakistan's seemingly porous border with Afghanistan, Chinese leaders are determined to ensure that Islamabad understands that any Pakistani culpability in the militarization of Xinjiang's Uyghurs will not be tolerated. Beijing's concerns have become greatly intensified since 9/11 and the subsequent war against the Taliban in Afghanistan, even though Chinese security concerns regarding Islamic fundamentalism in fact date back to the Soviet war in Afghanistan.

Although sporadic acts of violent Uyghur nationalism in China throughout the 1990s can be traced to a variety of causes, one impetus driving these militant elements is the legacy of the Soviet-Afghan War on Uyghur political consciousness. Though it is critical not to generalize across the Uyghur population, select groups of Uyghur men were recruited to fight alongside Afghan mujahideen (many of whom would later become members of the Taliban) against the invading Soviets. Portions of this Uyghur force were even trained and armed by a Chinese government eager to play its part in repelling Soviet encroachment on their western periphery.[30]

Beijing was keen to disavow these Uyghurs soldiers after the war, even though many made their way back to China via the Karakoram Highway.[31] Along the way, some of these Uyghurs were exposed to Pakistani madrassas, which, in conjunction with their experience fighting alongside Afghan mujahideen, worked to militarize them for their domestic struggle against Beijing.[32] The formation of these "cross-border linkages" form a critical portion of the story by which a segment of Xinjiang's Uyghur population became radicalized, and helps to explain Beijing's deepening concern throughout the 1990s and into the 2000s.[33] Indeed, even before 9/11 and the American call to defeat "terror" worldwide, Beijing was increasingly worried about the tenuous situation in Xinjiang, and endeavored to use Sino-Pakistani relations in its efforts to suppress Uyghur unrest.

As militarized Uyghurs funneled back into Xinjiang and Beijing faced its first encounter with sustained violent revolt in the region, throughout the 1990s it increasingly took measures to secure the Sino-Pakistani border.[34] Following a failed 1992 Islamist rebellion near Kashgar, the PRC closed the Karakoram at the border for several months. In 1996, Beijing launched its "Strike Hard" campaign designed to intercept "major common criminals," "ethnic splittists," and "illegal religious forces."[35] After the Taliban seized power in Afghanistan with Islamabad's support in September 1996, the Chinese grew fearful of the ramifications for Sino-Pakistani ties. In August 1997, Chinese leaders announced they would be installing a fence along the border with Pakistan designed to guard against terrorists and Islamic fundamentalism.[36] When, in January 1999, PRC authorities arrested 16 allegedly militant Uyghurs that had received military training on Pakistani soil, Beijing issued a complaint to Islamabad. For the Chinese government, engagement with Pakistani authorities has become an essential component of its program to control the Uyghur population in Xinjiang.[37]

This sentiment hardened after the events of 9/11 and the commencement of the American war in Afghanistan. The Taliban and affiliates of al-Qaeda recruited over 1,000 Uyghurs from madrassas in Pakistan to fight alongside them against U.S. forces.[38] It is a continual fear on the part of Chinese authorities that these embattled Uyghurs will elude Beijing's eye and either make their way back into Xinjiang unnoticed, or influence Uyghur separatist movements from across international borders. In recent years, Beijing has reportedly pressured Pakistan to repatriate Chinese Uyghur radicals apprehended within Pakistani borders, a request that Islamabad seems to have largely obliged.[39]

Shortly after 9/11, the Chinese were quick to gain American endorsement for officially labeling one prominent Uyghur group, the East Turkestan Independence Movement, a terrorist organization. This discursive maneuver added credibility to Beijing's goal of controlling militant Uyghur activists both inside and outside the PRC's borders. In November 2003, President Hu Jintao and General Pervez Musharraf signed the China-Pakistan Joint Declaration, agreeing to bilateral cooperation in opposing "separatism, extremism, and terrorism."[40] Asif Ali Zardari's July 2010 trip to the PRC was set against the third installment of Sino-Pakistani joint counterterrorism exercises in Ningxia Province.[41]

Though the Uyghur issue and Xinjiang's stability in general are at the crux of Beijing's current concern for border security with Pakistan, Chinese authorities are also worried about the impact of violence in Pakistan on Sino-Pakistani relations more broadly. In recent years Beijing has grown fearful for the safety of Chinese citizens in Pakistan on private or state business. In May 2004, three Chinese engineers were killed in Gwadar, likely the result of a local Balochistani separatist group's discontent with Islamabad.[42] During Pakistan's 2007 crisis at Lal Masjid (Red Mosque), 10 Chinese workers were kidnapped. Several days later, three other Chinese workers were executed in Peshawar, prompting Beijing to demand that Islamabad do more to protect Chinese nationals working in Pakistan.[43] More recently, several Chinese engineers were kidnapped in the troubled Swat region.[44]

Pakistan's internal struggles are probably not enough to derail Sino-Pakistani relations, but they remain a nagging hindrance and a concern for Beijing. It is perhaps for this reason that in 2005 the Shanghai Cooperation Organization (SCO) agreed to admit Pakistan as an observer state. Serving primarily as a means to improve China's relations in Central Asia, the SCO also functions as a regional anti-terrorism security forum.[45] Aside from striving to counter U.S. influence in the region, the group is dedicated to seeking regional stability and countering cross-border radicalism.[46] Pakistan's admission as an observer thus bespeaks its importance confronting militancy in the area, and eliminating violence as an impediment to trade and economic interaction.

Even though China and Pakistan have been both careful and fortunate to avoid any major boundary disputes along their shared frontier, the threats raised by Islamic fundamentalism, and terrorism more generally, represent relatively new challenges to a secure and stable Sino-Pakistani border. Despite a variety of difficulties encountered in responding to these challenges, Beijing and Islamabad continue to adapt their relationship to an increasingly transnational context.

Beyond the Karakoram

If terrorism and security concerns have posed a difficult challenge to Sino-Pakistani relations at the border, China's current effort to create a strategic corridor connecting the Karakoram Highway, through Pakistan, to the Indian Ocean has injected the relationship with a renewed sense of purpose. Geographically limited in its access to the Indian Ocean and, by association, the Middle East and Africa, over the past decade the PRC has made a strategic push to secure permanent access to these regions via Pakistan's southern coast. At the heart of Beijing's plan is the emerging Pakistani port city of Gwadar on the Arabian Sea, situated in Balochistan Province roughly 47 miles (75 km) east of the Iranian border. Gwadar offers a deep-sea port, warehouse storage, and industrial facilities. Only recently completed, from the very start of planning on Gwadar the Chinese have been actively involved. Built largely by the China Harbor Engineering Company Group, construction commenced in 2002 and the port became operational in late 2008. The Chinese government is believed to have contributed over 80 percent of the funding for the project, estimated at around $200 million.[47] Additionally, much of the technical assistance has come from the PRC, with over 450 Chinese workers participating.

Widely perceived to be part of China's so-called String of Pearls naval strategy, a Chinese presence at Gwadar offers Beijing advantages of "both a military/political and economic nature."[48] From a political and military standpoint, the Gwadar port grants the PRC the ability to monitor foreign activities in the Indian Ocean— particularly those of the United States and India. From this vantage point, the Chinese could also eventually challenge U.S. naval power in the region, while circumventing entirely the Indian subcontinent—an advantage that would be particularly useful should an enemy seek to block Chinese ships at the Malacca Strait.[49]

Economically, Gwadar has the potential to facilitate Chinese crude oil imports from the Persian Gulf and Africa.[50] Gwadar is particularly well located, since it is a mere 180 nm from the Straits of Hormuz, through which over 40 percent of all globally traded oil passes. In conjunction with the emerging Chinese maritime presence at ports in Bangladesh, Sri Lanka, and Myanmar, Gwadar significantly upgrades Chinese access to previously distant regions. Although it is only over the past decade that Gwadar has emerged as a major strategic port supporting China's rise, Beijing's plans there are intricately connected with the Karakoram Highway.

In the PRC's vision, the port at Gwadar is most valuable as a means to connect western China with the Indian Ocean. In addition to establishing a maritime presence at Gwadar, therefore, the Chinese long-term plan calls for two land-based connections between Gwadar port and Xinjiang Province. The first is a pipeline, capable of carrying crude imports unloaded at Gwadar across Pakistan to Xinjiang. Beijing has recently completed two similar pipeline projects across Central Asia, one to transport oil from the Caspian Sea across Kazakhstan, and the other carrying natural gas from Turkmenistan.

The second connection is a network of improved roads to ease transport of import-export goods between Gwadar and the Karakoram. Between 2002 and 2004, a two-lane highway was constructed linking Gwadar with Karachi. Beijing is ultimately interested, however, in connecting Gwadar with Kashgar, some 2,175 miles (3,500 km) away. Anticipating this, Beijing and Islamabad are currently at work widening the KKH to accommodate the increased traffic they expect in the near future.[51]

Reports indicate that in addition to building roads, bridges, and tunnels, they may also be at work on a high-speed rail system in the region.[52] Chinese oil tankers currently require 16 to 25 days to reach the Persian Gulf.[53] If all goes according to China's Gwadar-Karakoram linkage plan, the time necessary for transporting cargo between Gwadar and eastern China would be just 48 hours. In support of the construction of these transportation links, possibly as many as 10,000 Chinese troops have recently been spotted in Gilgit, a Pakistani-controlled region of disputed Kashmir.[54] This has triggered concern in both New Delhi and Washington.

While Sino-Pakistani transportation links between Gwadar and the KKH remain somewhat unclear, China's strategic corridor through Pakistan to the Indian Ocean represents a turn away from the covert Karakoram diplomacy defining the 1980s and 1990s, and a step toward overt strategizing between an increasingly strong China and one of its more valuable regional allies. While this overt foreign policy by no means indicates an increasingly aggressive or hostile China as some commentators have suggested, it is nevertheless unabashedly self-confident.[55] Even while the PRC maintains concern for the way its actions are perceived by the international community, its recent foreign policy is imbued with a sense of assertiveness, which was clearly visible in Sino-Pakistani ties over the past decade.

Conclusions

The stable Sino-Pakistani border has, in many ways, enabled these neighbors' bilateral relations to stand the test of time since their commencement in 1962; Pakistan could well be considered China's closest bordering ally. To be sure, Beijing and Islamabad have faced a number of challenges concerning their shared border, including protests by New Delhi that it encroaches upon Indian-claimed territory in the disputed Kashmir region. However, to date the Sino-Pakistani boundary has existed largely without dispute since its settlement in 1963.

By negotiating their borders early on, Pakistan and the PRC were able to proceed with their mutual alignment against India, and develop a strategic friendship that helped both countries to navigate the uneasy conditions of Cold War geopolitics. After the early 1970s saw the dismemberment of Pakistan and the Sino-American rapprochement, Sino-Pakistani relations were reinvented, inspired by the emergence of the Karakoram Highway, as a covert axis of military assistance. Secret Chinese nuclear support and missile sales to Pakistan in the 1980s and 1990s allowed the PRC stealthily to continue its effort to limit India's rise, while publicly emerging as a responsible member of the international community by pursuing improved Sino-Indian relations and adopting neutrality on Kashmir.

The challenge of transnational terrorism and Islamic fundamentalism has posed a threat to Sino-Pakistani border diplomacy since the mid-1990s. At the same time, the past decade has seen the relationship redefined yet again, with a contemporary focus on Gwadar and China's strategic corridor through Pakistan to the Indian Ocean. Beijing's pipeline plans and anticipated linkage with the Karakoram denote a more assertive and confident Chinese foreign policy, which has shifted Sino-Pakistani strategy and diplomacy from covert to overt. Over the past half century, Beijing and Islamabad have occasionally been compelled to reinvent the meaning of their ties in the face of a number of diverse challenges. Nevertheless, free of any major boundary disputes since 1963, the Sino-Pakistani border remains a beacon of stability in an otherwise unstable region.

Notes

1. Anwar Hussain Syed, *China & Pakistan: Diplomacy of an Entente Cordiale* (Amherst, MA: University of Massachusetts Press, 1974); Yaacov Vertzberger, *The Enduring Entente: Sino-Pakistani Relations, 1960-1980* (Washington, DC: Praeger, 1983); Yaacov Vertzberger, *China's Southwestern Strategy: Encirclement and Counterencirclement* (New York: Praeger, 1985); John W. Garver, *Protracted Contest: Sino-Indian Rivalry in the Twentieth Century* (Seattle: University of Washington Press, 2001); L. Bhola, *Pakistan-China Relations: Search for Politico-Strategic Relations* (Jaipur: R.B.S.A. Publishers, 1986); Jagdish Jain and Rajendra Kumar Jain, *China, Pakistan, Bangladesh* (New Delhi: Radiant Publishers, 1974).

2. Garver, 187-188.

3. Syed, 82.

4. Zhonggong zhongyang wenxian yanjiushi bian [Chinese Communist Party Central Documents Research Office, ed.], *Zhou Enlai nianpu, 1949-1976* [A Chronicle of Zhou Enlai's Life: 1949-1976] (Beijing: Zhongyang wenxian chubanshe, 1997), Vol. 2: 535.

5. Dennis Kux, *The United States and Pakistan, 1947-2000: Disenchanted Allies* (Washington, DC: Woodrow Wilson Center Press, 2001), 136-137.

6. M. Taylor Fravel, *Strong Borders, Secure Nation: Cooperation and Conflict in China's Territorial Disputes* (Princeton: Princeton University Press, 2008), 116.

7. "Kashmir Talks Hasten," *Christian Science Monitor*, 28 December 1962, 4; "Pakistan and Indian Prepare for Talks," *Christian Science Monitor*, 5 January 1963, 10.

8. Vertzberger, *China's Southwestern Strategy*, 87-104.

9. Hermann Kreutzmann, "The Karakoram Highway: The Impact of Road Construction on Mountain Societies," *Modern Asian Studies*, Vol. 25, No. 4 (October 1991), 725; Sean R. Roberts, "A 'Land of Borderlands': Implications of Xinjiang's Trans-border Interactions," in S. Frederick Starr, ed., *Xinjiang: China's Muslim Borderland* (Armonk, NY: M.E. Sharpe, 2004), 220-225.

10. Vertzberger, *China's Southwestern Strategy*, 88.

11. Matthew Kroenig, *Exporting the Bomb: Technology Transfer and the Spread of Nuclear Weapons* (Ithaca, NY: Cornell University Press, 2010); George Perkovich, *India's Nuclear Bomb: the Impact on Global Proliferation* (Berkeley: University of California Press, 1999); Swaran Singh, *China-South Asia: Issues, Equations, Policies* (New Delhi: Lancer's Books, 2003).

12. Singh, 192.

13. Garver, 325.

14. Ibid., 327; Singh, 192; Vertzberger, *China's Southwestern Strategy*, 102.

15. T.V. Paul, "Chinese-Pakistani Nuclear/Missile Ties and Balance of Power Politics," *Nonproliferation Review*, Vol. 10, No. 2 (2003), 24; Kroenig, 112.

16. Paul, 24.

17. Singh, 195.

18. "China Raises Nuclear Stakes on the Subcontinent," *New York Times*, 27 August 1996, A6; Thomas C. Reed, "The Chinese Nuclear Tests, 1964-1996," *Physics Today*, September 2008, http://www.cfr.org/china/physics-today-chinese-nuclear-tests-1964-1996/p17360 [Accessed on 16 November 2011].

19. Garver, 237.

20. For U.S. missile sales to Taiwan, see J. Mohan Malik, "South Asia in China's Foreign Relations," *Pacifica Review*, Vol. 13, No. 1 (February 2001), 82. For limiting India's challenge to Chinese hegemony in Asia, see Paul, 24. Garver argues that although Chinese missile assistance *became* linked with U.S. fighter sales to Taiwan, "among the important motives" was "a desire to strengthen Pakistan against India." Garver, 237.

21. "China ships components for missile to Pak: report," *The Times of India*, 7 August 2001, 12.

22. Garver, 216.

23. Ibid., 218.

24. Ibid., 228.

25. For Beijing's changing views on Kashmir in 1989-1990, see Ibid., 229-231.

26. Malik, 84; See also Michael Dillon, *Xinjiang–China's Muslim Far Northwest* (New York: Routledge Curzon, 2004), 154.

27. "China Voices 'Regret,' but Still Faults India," *New York Times*, 29 May 1998, A10; Garver, 336-337.

28. Fazal-ur-Rahman, "Pakistan-China Relations: The Shadow of Kargil and 9/11," in Shiping Tang, Mingjiang Li, and Amitav Acharya, eds., *Living with China: Regional States and China through Crises and Turning Points* (New York: Palgrave Macmillan, 2009), 153.

29. Ibid., 154.

30. John K. Cooley, *Unholy Wars: Afghanistan, America, and International Terrorism* (London: Pluto Press, 2000), 51-63.

31. Ziad Haider, "Sino-Pakistan Relations and Xinjiang's Uyghurs: Politics, Trade, and Islam along the Karakoram Highway," *Asian Survey*, Vol. 45, No. 4 (July-August 2005), 529-530.

32. Roberts, 227-230; See also Dillon, 139-140.

33. Haider, 530.

34. For a summary of unrest and revolt in Xinjiang throughout the 1990s, see Ibid., 527 and Justin Jon Rudelson, *Oasis Identities: Uyghur Nationalism Along China's Silk Road* (New York: Columbia University Press, 1997), 131.

35. Quoted in Haider, 527. For a detailed discussion of the "Strike Hard" campaign and its initial application in 1996 and 1997, see Dillon, 84-109.

36. "China is fencing its border with Pakistan, says daily," *The Times of India*, 11 August 1997, 18; "China's fence against 'Islamic fundamentalism'," *The Times of India*, 12 August 1997, 18; Haider, 532.

37. Malik, 85.

38. Haider, 530; Ziad Haider, "Clearing Clouds Over the Karakoram Pass," *Yale Global Online*, 29 March 2004, http://yaleglobal.yale.edu/content/clearing-clouds-over-karakoram-pass [Accessed on 27 October 2011].

39. Haider, "Sino-Pakistan Relations and Xinjiang's Uyghurs," 535-536; Roberts, 232.

40. Haider, "Sino-Pakistan Relations and Xinjiang's Uyghurs," 537.

41. Andrew Small, "Intensifying China-Pakistan Ties," Interview with Andrew Small, *Council on Foreign Relations*, 7 July 2010, http://www.cfr.org/china/intensifying-china-pakistan-ties/p22603 [Accessed on 27 October 2011].

42. Ziad Haider, "Oil Fuels Beijing's New Power Game," *Yale Global Online*, 11 March 2005, http://yaleglobal.yale.edu/content/oil-fuels-beijings-new-power-game [Accessed on 27 October 2011]; "City of Fishermen in Pakistan Becomes Strategic Port," *New York Times*, 28 September 2004, W1.

43. Small interview; Willem van Kemenade, "China and Pakistan: New Friends Can't Compare," *Yale Global Online*, 12 March 2008, http://yaleglobal.yale.edu/content/china-and-pakistan-new-friends-can%E2%80%99t-compare [Accessed on 27 October 2011].

44. Small interview; Lisa Curtis, "Swat militants free Chinese engineer," *Dawn*, 15 February 2009.

45. Rizwan Zeb, "Pakistan and the Shanghai Cooperation Organization," *China and Eurasia Forum Quarterly*, Vol. 4, No. 4 (2006), 51.

46. David Kerr, with Laura C. Swinton, "China, Xinjiang, and the Transnational Security of Central Asia," *Critical Asian Studies*, Vol. 40, No. 1 (2008), 113.

47. Haider, "Oil Fuels Beijing's New Power Game"; Rina Saeed Khan, "Gwadar: Pakistan's new Great Game," *The Guardian*, 8 April 2011, http://www.guardian.co.uk/commentisfree/2011/apr/08/gwadar-pakistan-great-game [Accessed on 27 October 2011].

48. Jeffrey Henderson, "China and global development: Towards a Global-Asian Era?" *Contemporary Politics*, Vol. 14, No. 4 (December 2008), 388.

49. James R. Holmes and Toshi Yoshihara, "China's Naval Ambitions in the Indian Ocean," *Journal of Strategic Studies*, vol. 31, No. 3 (June 2008), 379.

50. Haider, "Oil Fuels Beijing's New Power Game."

51. Khan.

52. Anna Mahjar-Barducci, "New War Ahead: China-Pakistan vs. U.S.A.," *Hudson New York*, 2 March 2011, http://www.hudson-ny.org/1918/china-pakistan-usa-war [Accessed on 27 October 2011]; J.E. Dyer, "China, Gilgit-Baltistan (Memorize it Now), and the Balance of Power in Asia," *Hot Air*, 5 March 2011, http://hotair.com/archives/2011/03/05/china-gilgit-baltistan-memorize-it-now-and-the-balance-of-power-in-asia/ [Accessed on 27 October 2011]; Selig G. Harrison, "China's Discreet Hold on Pakistan's Northern Borderlands," *New York Times*, 28 August 2010.

53. Ibid.

54. Dyer.

55. Robert Kaplan, "The Geography of Chinese Power," *Foreign Affairs*, Vol. 89, No. 3 (May/June 2010), 22; see also Mahjar-Barducci.

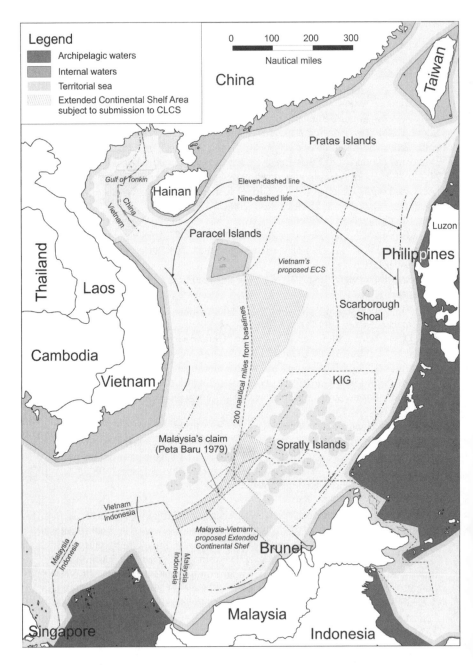

Map 16.1: Competing Maritime Claims in the South China Sea

16
Philippine-China Border Relations: Cautious Engagement Amid Tensions

Lowell Bautista and Clive Schofield

Conflicting claims to sovereignty over islands, related overlapping maritime claims, and undelimited maritime boundaries are an enduring source of tension between the Philippines and China. In particular, an influential and often corrosive factor in their bilateral relations is their competing claims in the South China Sea. China asserts territorial sovereignty over numerous islands in the southern South China Sea, generally referred to as the Spratly (Nansha) islands, on historic grounds. Meanwhile, the Philippines claims sovereignty over many of the same islands, which it refers to as the Kalayaan Island Group (KIG), on the basis of discovery and effective occupation (see Map 16.1).

Both countries are parties to the United Nations Convention on the Law of the Sea (UNCLOS)[1] and both refer to international law to support and bolster their respective claims. The Philippines and China also contest sovereignty over Scarborough Shoal, located in the northeast of the South China Sea, with a potential exclusive economic zone (EEZ) of approximately 54,000 nm^2 (185,500 km^2). Moreover, the Philippines has yet to delimit its overlapping maritime claims to the northwest with the Republic of China (ROC) administered Pratas islands and to the north with respect to the island of Taiwan.

As contentious as these maritime disputes appear, they need to be set in context. The Philippine-China relationship is one of the most important bilateral ties that the Philippines has forged. The Philippines is keenly aware and recognizes, in common with other nations around the world, the increasing economic, political, and military capabilities of China. However, Philippine relations with China, whilst increasingly strong, especially in economic terms, can in political and diplomatic terms be characterized largely as cautious, at best, and even hostile, at times.

Overview of Philippine-China Relations

The Philippines and China formally established diplomatic relations on 9 June 1975.[2] However, cultural and trade relations between the two countries can be

235

traced as far back as the 10th century. In modern times, economic and trade relations remain the key drivers that reinforce the ties between the Philippines and China. In 2009, China was the Philippines' third largest trading partner, its third largest donor partner, and fourth largest source of foreign tourists. Since the 1990s, Philippine bilateral trade with China has registered double-digit growth. From 1997 to 2007, Philippine trade with China grew by over 30 percent annually.[3] The Philippines has consistently enjoyed a positive trade balance with China. In 2007, bilateral trade was $30.6 billion, representing an impressive 75 percent growth from 2005 figures of $17.6 billion.[4]

In April 2005, Chinese President Hu Jintao and Philippine President Gloria Macapagal-Arroyo referred to bilateral relations between the Philippines and China as enjoying a "golden age of partnership."[5] Despite the hyperbole, it is nevertheless true that Philippine-China bilateral relations have expanded substantially, and show every sign of continuing to do so. Further, since 1975 the two countries have signed close to 100 bilateral agreements covering a wide range of areas including defense, trade, transnational crime prevention, infrastructure, agriculture, science and technology transfer, and cultural exchanges.[6] It is undeniable that China is strategically important in Philippine foreign and security policy for historical, cultural, geographic, economic, and political reasons.[7]

Overlapping Maritime Claims and Maritime Boundaries

Despite this broadly positive trend in Philippine-China diplomatic and economic relations overall, the two countries' incompatible territorial and maritime claims provide a notable source of friction, and, at times, serious diplomatic conflict, between them. As mentioned above, both the Philippines and China are parties to UNCLOS.[8] The PRC claims a territorial sea of 12 nm,[9] a contiguous zone out to 24 nm,[10] and an EEZ extending to 200 nm,[11] all measured from its territorial sea baselines.

China's baselines include an extensive system of straight baselines that encompasses much of its mainland coastline and around the Paracel islands. Accordingly, the PRC treats waters landward of its territorial sea baselines as its internal waters.[12] The PRC's straight baseline claims have aroused international criticism, in large part because of their application along coastlines arguably not deeply indented or fringed by islands, as required under Article 7 of UNCLOS, the use of long baseline segments, and the apparent use of inappropriate baseline points.[13]

Further, the PRC submitted preliminary information indicating the outer limits of the continental shelf beyond 200 nm with respect to the East China Sea on 11 May 2009 but reserved the right to make further submission for "other sea areas," presumably meaning the South China Sea.[14] It is also worth noting that Taiwan, since it is not a member of the UN and so has been unable to become a party to UNCLOS, has likewise defined straight baselines around its shores[15] and claimed maritime zones, including a 12 nm territorial sea, a 200 nm EEZ, and continental shelf rights.[16]

The Philippines has also enacted domestic legislation related to maritime claims that is largely consistent with UNCLOS. Moreover, in 2009 the Philippine Congress passed Republic Act No. 9522, a new law amending its old baselines law and defining archipelagic baselines for the Philippines.[17] These claimed baselines are consistent with the relevant provisions of UNCLOS. That said, the Philippines claims a territorial sea that is unique in international law. The breadth of the Philippine territorial sea is variable, defined by coordinates set forth in the Philippine Treaty Limits. In Philippine law, all the waters beyond the outermost islands of the archipelago, but within the Philippine Treaty Limits, comprise the territorial sea of the Philippines.[18] The Philippines also claims a 200 nm EEZ,[19] and a continental shelf up to the limits of exploitability.[20] Further, the Philippines submitted a partial submission on the limits of its continental shelf beyond 200 nm with respect to the Benham Rise region located to the east of Luzon Island on 8 April 2009. The Philippines specifically reserved its rights to make submissions with respect to other areas, suggesting a further potential extended continental shelf submission relating to parts of the South China Sea.

The maritime claims of the Philippines and China overlap with one another and are complicated by the fact that the two states contest territorial sovereignty over multiple islands in the southern South China Sea and over Scarborough Shoal, located in the northeastern part of the South China Sea. Overall, four parts or sections to the overall China-Philippine maritime boundary delimitation can be distinguished. First, a potential maritime boundary exists due north of the Philippines between the Philippine archipelago and Taiwan. Second, to the northwest of the Philippines a potential maritime boundary exists involving the Pratas islands, which are administered by Taiwan. Third, and further to the south, China and the Philippines potentially have a maritime boundary to delimit in the vicinity of Scarborough Shoal. Finally, the various states may have maritime boundaries to define with respect to the disputed Spratly islands in the southern South China Sea.

The Philippines and Taiwan share overlapping EEZ claims to the north of the Philippines and south of Taiwan, having both proclaimed EEZs that potentially extend 200 nm from their respective baselines. If a theoretical equidistance line is constructed, it would proceed from a trijunction between the claims of China (specifically the Taiwanese island of Lan Yu which is it's easternmost island),

Japan (the Sakishima islands group), and the Philippines (particularly Amianan Island located due north of the major Philippine island of Luzon) and proceeds through the Bashi Channel into the South China Sea (see Map 16.2).[21] In this context it is notable that, due to the presence of Japan's Sakishima islands and the northerly islands of the Philippines to the east of Taiwanese territories, the application of equidistance means that Taiwanese maritime entitlements to the east would be curtailed well before the 200 nm limit is reached.[22] It is also notable that from the Bashi Channel proceeding to the south and west, the line of equidistance between the nearest features on the Taiwanese and Philippine sides lies within the Philippine Treaty Limits—something that would be likely to complicate any future negotiations, even if the complications inherent in negotiating a maritime boundary with Taiwan rather than the PRC were somehow to be overcome.

Proceeding further to the south and west, a theoretical line equidistant between China and the Philippines relies on base points located on the Pratas islands (Dongsha islands in Chinese) on one side and the western coast of the major Philippine island of Luzon on the other. The Pratas islands are located between the Chinese mainland coast and the Philippines and are currently occupied and administered by Taiwan, but also, unsurprisingly, claimed by the PRC. The Pratas islands comprise three islands made up of coral atolls and reef flats in the northeastern side of the South China Sea, 459 nm (850 km) southwest of Taipei and 184 nm (340 km) southeast of Hong Kong. The main island, Pratas, is above sea level and is 1.74 miles (2.8 km) long and 0.54 miles (0.865 km) wide. Given the small size and thus restricted coastal front of the Pratas islands in comparison to Luzon, if maritime boundary delimitation negotiations were ever initiated, the Philippines would in all likelihood argue that Pratas islands be accorded a reduced effect. It is also important to note that the equidistance line between these features and the Philippines cuts deep into the Philippine Treaty Limits.

The primary obstacle in the delimitation of the equidistance line between the PRC and the Philippines, however, is the presence of Scarborough Shoal, the ownership of which is contested. Scarborough Shoal, which the Philippines refers to as Bajo de Masinloc and China calls Huangyan Dao, is located in the northeastern South China Sea between the Macclesfield Bank—a submerged feature claimed by the PRC— and the Philippine island of Luzon. It is claimed by the Philippines, China, and Taiwan. The shoal is triangular in shape, and comprised of a chain of reef and island features with heights ranging from half a meter to three meters, which are mostly below water at high tide.[23] The shoal has an area of around 44 nm^2 (150 km^2) and is considered valuable for the fisheries resources associated with it. It is 189 nm (350 km) to the northeast of the Spratly islands and 119 nm (220 km) away from the nearest landmass, Palauig, Zambales, in the Philippine island of Luzon.

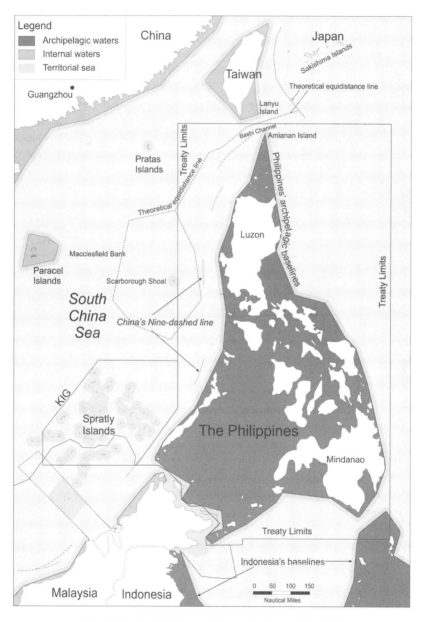

Map 16.2: The Philippine Treaty Limits and the KIG

The Scarborough Shoal lies outside the Treaty Limits. Aside from the issue of sovereignty, the main problem is whether the features can be classified as islands capable of generating EEZ and continental shelf claims or as "rocks" incapable of advancing such extended maritime claims consistent with Article 121 of UNCLOS. The general rule is that islands are to be treated in the same manner as other land territory.[24] However, Article 121(3) of UNCLOS provides that "rocks which cannot sustain human habitation or economic life of their own shall have no exclusive economic zone or continental shelf." Despite its small size, remote location, and lack of habitation, it is highly likely that, whichever state ultimately obtains sovereignty over the feature, they will claim that Scarborough Shoal is capable of generating an EEZ and continental shelf rights and will seek to use it as a base point for maritime boundary delimitation.

In contrast, whichever of the two claimants does not obtain sovereignty over the feature is liable to argue that it should be treated as a mere "rock." If it were to be accorded full weight in the generation of maritime claims, the maritime spaces associated with Scarborough Shoal have been estimated at approximately 54,000 nm^2 (185,500 km^2).[25] That said, even if regarded as being capable of generating extended maritime claims, it would seem highly unlikely that Scarborough Shoal would be accorded full weight as a base point for the construction of a maritime boundary, regardless of ownership. In either case, Scarborough Shoal would present an extremely limited coastal front as compared to the coasts of either mainland China or the Philippine major island of Luzon, and on this basis its influence on any boundary line would likely be significantly reduced or eliminated altogether.

The Philippine claim to the Scarborough Shoal is based on the principles of discovery, proximity, and effective occupation. Since the 1950s, the Philippines has used the shoal as an impact range for defense purposes and conducted oceanographic surveys of the area with the U.S. Navy, then based in the U.S. Naval Base in Subic Bay, Zambales, and in 1965 the Philippines built a lighthouse on Scarborough Shoal. However, since the days of Spain's colonization, Filipino fishermen were already using the area as a fishing ground and as place of shelter during bad weather. The 2009 Philippine Archipelagic Baselines Law reiterated Philippine sovereignty and jurisdiction over the shoal and provided that baselines over the shoal should be determined using the regime of islands provision of UNCLOS (Article 121). It should be noted, however, that this claim on the part of the Philippines was protested by China.

China and Taiwan, on the other hand, base their claims over Scarborough Shoal on historical evidence dating as far back as the Yuan dynasty, with records as early as 1279 mentioning the area as being used by Chinese fishermen. It was reportedly also used as a surveying point in a 1279 survey of the South China Sea for Kublai

Khan. China regards the shoal as part of Macclesfield Bank or Zhongsha islands, and administered under Hainan Province.

The foregoing issues are arguably relatively minor disputes when compared to that over the South China Sea. The six neighbors that have overlapping and conflicting claims to sovereignty over the numerous small islands that dot the South China Sea are, in clockwise order from the north, China, Taiwan, the Philippines, Malaysia, Brunei, and Vietnam; Beijing also argues that Indonesia should delimit a maritime boundary with China. All of these countries base their claims on principles of international law, both customary and conventional. These principles are mainly discovery and effective occupation.[26]

The Basis of the Chinese Claim over the South China Sea

The PRC claims territorial sovereignty over the islands of the South China Sea, notably the Paracel and Spratly islands. The PRC primarily anchors its claim on the principle of discovery based on historical records that date as far back as 200 B.C.E.[27] China also relies on an 1887 treaty between France and China delimiting the territories of China and Vietnam, which was at that time a French protectorate.[28] China has maintained troops on at least seven of the Spratly islands since 1988, including: Da Chu Thap (Fiery Cross Reef); Da Chau Vien (Cuarteron Reef); Da Gac Ma (Johnson Reef); Da Hu-go (Hughes Reef); Da Gaven (Gaven Reef); Da Su-bi (Subi Reef); and Mischief Reef. The PRC has erected structures on some of them, including a naval airfield on Fiery Cross Reef.

Taiwan's claim to the South China Sea is based on the principles of discovery and occupation.[29] In 1946, Taiwan was the first claimant to establish its presence in the Spratlys following the Japanese withdrawal after World War II. It has physically occupied and exercised sovereignty over Itu Aba (Taiping Island), the largest island in the Spratlys, since 1956.

The PRC claims "indisputable sovereignty over the South China Sea islands and adjacent waters" and this claim is often associated with a controversial map depicting nine dashes. This is often referred to as the nine-dashed map, or, if the dashes are joined up, the "U-shaped line" that encloses the main island features of the South China Sea.[30] However, Beijing has never defined the precise locations of the dashes or provided their exact coordinates, or, indeed, depicted them as a continuous "joined up" line. It likewise remains unclear whether the dashed lines pertain merely to the enclosed island features, over the entirety of the waters they enclose, or to both. Therefore, it is uncertain whether the nine-dashed line represents a unilateral maritime boundary claim, a delineation of China's ownership over the islands, or a depiction of its historic right of title over the South China Sea.[31]

On 7 May 2009, the PRC attached a map showing the nine-dashed line to two notes submitted to the UN Commission on the Limits of the Continental Shelf (CLCS). This is the first time China has officially publicized its nine-dashed line map and represents arguably an important, recent articulation of China's official position on its maritime claims in the South China Sea. China used these notes and attached maps to challenge the joint submission made by Malaysia and Vietnam on 6 May 2009, and that of Vietnam alone made on the following day, over their extended continental shelves in the South China Sea. Malaysia and Vietnam lodged diplomatic counter-protests in response to China's protest in May 2009. On 4 August 2009, the Philippines also filed a diplomatic protest over the submissions made by Vietnam and Malaysia. Further, on 5 April 2011, the Philippines filed a diplomatic protest in response to China's 7 May 2009 diplomatic protest.

The Basis of the Philippine Claim Over the South China Sea

The Philippines bases its claim to the South China Sea on the principle of discovery and effective occupation.[32] The Philippines asserts that the Spratly islands were *terra nullius* when Tomas Cloma, a Filipino lawyer and businessman, discovered them in 1947. On 11 June 1978, President Ferdinand Marcos issued Presidential Decree 1596, which placed the cluster of islands enclosed by defined coordinates starting from the Philippine Treaty Limits, "including the sea-bed, sub-soil, continental margin and air space" as "subject to the sovereignty of the Philippines." The law stated that "these areas do not legally belong to any state or nation but, by reason of history, indispensable need, and effective occupation and control established in accordance with the international law, such areas must now [be] deemed to belong and [be] subject to the sovereignty of the Philippines." The area was constituted as a municipality of the province of Palawan and collectively referred to as the KIG. The Philippines occupies eight islands, including: Pag-asa (Thitu Island); Rizal Reef (Commodore Reef); Patag (Flat Island); Dagahoy Dugao/Kota (Loaita Island); Panata (Lankiam Cay); Lawak (Nanshan Island); Likas (West York Island); and Parola (North East Cay).[33] Presidential Decree 1599, also enacted on 11 June 1978, which proclaimed a 200 nm EEZ for the Philippines, includes the KIG.

Of relevance here are the Philippine Treaty Limits, which have been a major impediment in the delimitation of the Philippines' maritime boundaries.[34] Negotiations over overlapping maritime zones with its neighbors have been stalled over this particular issue. The national territory of the Philippines has been defined in its constitution, in treaties, and in numerous domestic legislations. The Philippine national territory consists of, first, all the islands and waters embraced within the Philippine archipelago, and, second, all other territories belonging to the Philippines by historic right or legal title, over which the Philippines has sovereignty or jurisdiction, which includes the KIG.[35] The provision on the national territory embodied in the Philippine Constitutions contradicts rules embodied in UNCLOS, which the Philippines signed and ratified.

The declaration submitted by the Philippines on its ratification of UNCLOS likewise seriously cast doubts on its willingness to implement UNCLOS and caused confusion regarding how the Philippines really defines its maritime claims and boundaries. This ambiguity springs from the Philippine interpretation of the archipelago concept and its claim that the limits of its national territory, and consequently of its territorial sea, are the boundaries laid down in its Treaty Limits. The Philippines argues that it has consistently treated these "international treaty limits" as defining the Philippine archipelago, consisting of the unity of sea, land, and air-space. However, as noted above, in 2009, the Philippines revised its baselines through Republic Act No. 9522.[36] This law reiterated the sovereignty of the Philippines over KIG and asserted that baselines over the features shall be determined consistent with the "regime of islands" under UNCLOS.[37]

The extensive historic claims to territorial waters of the Philippines have been the subject of much academic debate and serious criticisms.[38] They are raised here mainly to highlight a basic point: the Philippine claim to the KIG and the delimitation of its potential maritime boundaries with China faces challenges related to ambiguities in the definition of Philippine land and sea boundaries. Analogous challenges exist for the Philippines with respect to China's own historically-based claims in the South China Sea. It must be emphasized, however, that other than those involving disputed sovereignty, such as to islands within the KIG and Scarborough Shoal, the other overlapping maritime boundaries between the Philippines and China could be potentially negotiated and even resolved without difficulty, should the political will to do so exist.

Recent Developments

On 14 March 2005, representatives from national oil companies of the PRC, the Philippines, and Vietnam entered into the Tripartite Agreement for Joint Marine Seismic Undertaking in the Agreement Area in the South China Sea (JMSU Tripartite Agreement) in Manila, Philippines.[39] In this document, the three parties affirmed that the signing of the JMSU Tripartite Agreement does not undermine the basic positions held by their respective governments on the South China Sea issue.[40] The tri-nation agreement covers 41,606 nm^2 (142,886 km^2) and was set to remain in effect for three years. Philippine President Gloria Macapagal-Arroyo, who witnessed what she termed a "historic signing" of the agreement, said the accord was "a breakthrough in implementing the provisions of the 2002 [Declaration on the] Code of Conduct in the South China Sea among ASEAN and China."[41]

On 28 April 2005, China and the Philippines issued a joint statement as Chinese President Hu Jintao concluded a two-day state visit to the Philippines that welcomed the signing of the JMSU Tripartite Agreement as a historic step toward the transformation of the South China Sea into a sea of friendship and cooperation. In addition, the two countries agreed to continue efforts to safeguard peace and stability in the South China Sea and reaffirmed their commitments to the China-ASEAN strategic partnership for peace and prosperity, the China-ASEAN Free Trade Area, and the process of East Asian cooperation.[42]

The JMSU Tripartite Agreement lapsed in June 2008 and was not extended by the parties. Since its termination, no other substantive cooperative undertakings among the disputants have been launched. However, this apparent setback does not remove the rationale for scientific studies to appraise the resources in these disputed areas upon which potential future unilateral or joint development activities of an economic nature would be based.

On 3 March 2011, the Philippines filed a diplomatic protest against Chinese incursion into Reed Bank, where oil exploration activities were in progress. The Reed Bank is located about 80 nm (148 km) from the Philippine island of Palawan and therefore within what the Philippines regards as its 200 nm EEZ. The Philippines maintains that Reed Bank is not a disputed area and is independent of its KIG claim. Parts of the Reed Bank are, however, within the area encompassed by China's nine-dashed line map. The Philippines complained that Chinese patrol boats inappropriately harassed a Philippine oil exploration vessel undertaking hydrographic surveys in the Reed Bank. In response, two warplanes were deployed by the Philippine military, but the vessels in question had already left when the aircraft arrived. The Philippines announced that its own oil exploration activity would resume at the Reed Bank, and deployed an unarmed Philippine Coast Guard patrol ship to accompany the oil exploration vessel.[43] In 2012, the Philippines declared that it will proceed with oil and gas exploration in the vicinity of Reed Bank, amid protests from China. Whilst reports and accusations of incursions and aggressive posturing from both parties continue, tension in the area remains high. This issue appears likely to remain an ongoing source of friction between the Philippines and China.

On 5 April 2011, the Philippines submitted to the CLCS a diplomatic protest against China's nine-dashed line territorial claim including most of the South China Sea. As noted above, Vietnam and Malaysia had previously filed their own protests on 7 May 2009, a day after China deposited a map showing its nine-dashed line claim to the United Nations. Indonesia, despite not having a formal claim over any of the disputed islands in the South China Sea, filed a similar protest in 2010.[44]

The Philippine protest, through a *note verbale* sent through the country's permanent mission to the UN, asserted the following three points: first, the KIG constitutes an integral part of the Philippines over which it has sovereignty and jurisdiction; secondly, the Philippines exercises sovereignty and jurisdiction over the waters around or adjacent to each relevant geological feature in the KIG under the international law principle "the land dominates the sea," as provided for under UNCLOS; and thirdly, the PRC's claim to "relevant waters, seabed and subsoil" related to the KIG has no basis under UNCLOS as that jurisdiction belongs to the Philippines.[45]

On 14 April 2011, China submitted a *note verbale* to the United Nations in reply to the Philippine protest, reiterating its "indisputable sovereignty over the islands in the South China Sea." The harshly worded Chinese protest note went on to assert that the Philippines, since the 1970s, "started to invade and occupy some islands and reefs of China's Nansha islands and made relevant territorial claims, to which China objects strongly." The Chinese note also mentioned that the Philippine "occupation of some islands and reefs of China's Nansha islands as well as other related acts constitutes infringement upon China's territorial sovereignty."[46]

The PRC's diplomatic protest refuted Philippine sovereignty over the KIG and argued that the Philippines cannot invoke such "illegal" occupation to support its territorial claims under the legal doctrine *ex injuria jus non oritur*, or "a right cannot rise from a wrong." In addition, China claimed that under the relevant UNCLOS provisions, "as well as the Law of the People's Republic of China on Territorial Sea and Contiguous Zone (1992) and the Law on the Exclusive Economic Zone and the Continental Shelf of the PRC (1998), China's Nansha Islands is (sic) fully entitled to Territorial Sea, EEZ, and Continental Shelf."[47] The latter statement is a potentially significant one in that it suggests that China asserts maritime claims from the South China Sea islands rather than some type of historic waters claim on the basis of its nine-dashed line map.

The exchange of diplomatic protests between the PRC and the Philippines came at an inopportune time. Bilateral relations between the two countries were tense after three Filipinos convicted of drug-related offenses in China were executed on 30 March 2011, despite concerted efforts by the Philippine government seeking leniency in their sentence. The Philippines, however, clarified that its territorial protest was independent of and unrelated to any other event.

Conclusions

The resolution of the border disputes between the Philippines, on the one hand, and the PRC and Taiwan, on the other hand, will not be easy. The issue of the South China Sea is particularly complex, first, because of the number of parties directly and indirectly involved; second, because of its geopolitical and strategic importance; and, third, because of its real or perceived economic resource potential. Outstanding ambiguities, uncertainties, and longstanding, yet problematic historic claims on the part of both China and Taiwan versus the Philippines will undoubtedly hamper dispute resolution.

To achieve an equitable agreement, the Philippines must settle once and for all its confusion over its Treaty Limits in order to move the agenda forward in any maritime delimitation negotiations with neighboring states. It would be similarly helpful if the PRC were finally to clarify its position regarding the infamous nine-dashed line. Without resolving these uncertainties, a firm basis for negotiations is lacking, and suspicions will linger, with the potential to poison otherwise generally cordial bilateral relations. Further, the absence of jurisdictional clarity will not only prevent access to, and the effective management of, potentially valuable and vulnerable living and non-living marine resources within areas of overlapping maritime claims, but also continue to serve as a source of friction and potential confrontation between the Philippines and China.

In general, it should be expected that the relationship between the Philippines and the PRC will continue to be robust, especially in the economic sphere. However, a certain degree of caution and mutual suspicion will continue to plague their relationship until such time as they are able to resolve all of their territorial and maritime jurisdictional differences. From a Philippine perspective, the protection and defense of its sovereignty, territorial integrity, and the natural resources lying therein cannot be compromised. However, the Philippines has to be aware of geopolitical realities and must, therefore, continue to engage China constructively within existing regional and international frameworks so as to ensure long-term peace and stability in the region.

Notes

1. *United Nations Convention on the Law of the Sea*, 1833 UNTS 3, opened for signature 10 December 1982, Montego Bay, Jamaica (entered into force 16 November 1994) (hereinafter "UNCLOS" or "the Convention").

2. Joint Communiqué of the Government of the Philippines and the Government of the People's Republic of China. Signed in Beijing on 9 June 1975.

3. Archimedes C. Gomez, "China-Philippines Economic and Trade Cooperation," http://www.ecdc.net.cn [Accessed on 28 June 2011]; Xu Lingui, "China to Become 2nd Largest Trade Partner of Philippines as Recovery Takes Hold," 30 December 2009, http://news.xinhuanet.com [Accessed on 28 June 2011]. The contraction in trade between China and the Philippines in 2008-2009 was due to the global financial crisis. In the first half of 2010, bilateral trade between the Philippines and China increased by 52.6 percent to $13.1 billion over the same period in 2009. Public Information Service Unit, "Philippines-China Trade Continues to Increase," 1 September 2010, http://www.dfa.gov.ph [Accessed on 28 June 2011].

4. Philippine Embassy in the People's Republic of China, Bilateral Economic Relations, http://www.philembassychina.org [Accessed on 27 April 2011].

5. Philippine Embassy in the People's Republic of China, Overview of Philippines-China Relations, http://www.philembassychina.org [Accessed on 27 April 2011].

6. Ibid.

7. Rommel Banlaoi, "The China Challenge in Philippine Foreign and Security Policy," 12 January 2011, http://declassifiedrommelbanlaoi.blogspot.com /2011/01/china-challenge-in-philippine-foreign.html [Accessed on 27 April 2011].

8. The Philippines ratified UNCLOS on 8 May 1984 while China ratified UNCLOS on 7 June 1996.

9. Article 3, Law on the Territorial Sea and the Contiguous Zone of 25 February 1992.

10. Article 4, Law on the Territorial Sea and the Contiguous Zone of 25 February 1992.

11. Article 2, Exclusive Economic Zone and Continental Shelf Act, 26 June 1998.

12. Article 2, "Law on the Territorial Sea and the Contiguous Zone of 25 February 1992." See also Declaration of the Government of the People's Republic of China on the baselines of the territorial sea, 15 May 1996.

13. United States Department of State, "Straight Baseline Claim: China," *Limits in the Seas*, No. 117 (Washington, DC: Office of Ocean Affairs, Bureau of Oceans and International Environmental and Scientific Affairs, U.S. Department of State, 9 July 1996), http://www.state.gov/g/oes/ocns/opa/convention/c16065.htm [Accessed on 31 October 2011].

14. Preliminary Information Indicative of the Outer Limits of the Continental Shelf Beyond 200 Nautical Miles of the People's Republic of China [translation], 11 May 2009, para.10, http://www.un.org/depts/los/clcs_new/submissions_files /preliminary/chn2009preliminaryinformation_english.pdf.

15. This system of straight baselines is extensive and applies not only to Taiwan's main islands but also to Pratas Island and the Macclesfield Bank. A comprehensive and critical analysis of this claim is provided by the U.S. Department of State. U.S. Department of State, "Taiwan's Maritime Claims," *Limits in the Seas No. 127,* Washington, DC, 15 November 2005.

16. For a detailed treatment of Taiwan's maritime claims see, see Kuan-Hsiung Wang, "The ROC's Maritime Claims and Practices with Special Reference to the

South China Sea," *Ocean Development and International Law*, No. 41 (2010), 237-252.

17. Republic Act No. 9522, An Act to Amend Certain Provisions of Republic Act No. 3046, as amended by Republic Act No. 5446, to define the Archipelagic Baseline of the Philippines and for other Purposes, 10 March 2009.

18. Lowell Bautista, "The Legal Status of the Philippine Treaty Limits in International Law," *Aegean Review of the Law of the Sea and Maritime Law*, No. 1 (2010), 111-139.

19. Presidential Decree No. 1599, 11 June 1978.

20. Presidential Proclamation No. 370, 20 March 1968.

21. J.R. Victor Prescott and Clive Schofield, *The Maritime Political Boundaries of the World* (Leiden/Boston, Martinus Nijhoff, 2005), 434.

22. Ibid., 435.

23. The British Admiralty sailing directions, for example, indicate that Scarborough Reef is "steep-to on all sides and consists of a narrow belt of coral enclosing a lagoon of clear blue water" and that South Rock, at 3 meters high, is the "tallest rock" located at the southeast extremity of the reef. United Kingdom Hydrographic Office, *China Sea Pilot*, Vol. 2, 9th ed., Admiralty Sailing Directions, (UKHO, Taunton, 2010), 74.

24. UNCLOS, Article 121(1).

25. Prescott and Schofield, 434.

26. For details of these submissions, as well as the reactions and counter-reactions associated with them, see http://www.un.org/Depts/los/clcs_new/submissions_files/submission_mysvnm_33_2009.htm [Accessed on 11 January 2012].

27. Jianming Shen, "China's Sovereignty over the South China Sea Islands: A Historical Perspective," *Chinese Journal of International Law*, No. 1 (2002), 94.

28. Hungdah Chiu and Choon-Ho Park, "Legal Status of the Paracel and Spratly Islands," *Ocean Development and International Law*, No. 1 (1975), at 11 citing the Convention Respecting the Delimitation of the Frontier Between China and Tonkin (Vietnam), signed on 26 June 1887. The 1887 treaty created a boundary line ("west of 105 degrees 43 minutes east of Paris") which ceded to China all territory east of this line. China posits that since the Spratlys lie east of this line, it belongs to China. On this point, also see Brian K. Murphy, "Dangerous Ground: The Spratly Islands and International Law," *Ocean and Coastal Law Journal*, No. 1 (1995), 187, 191.

29. China incorporates the claim of Taiwan into its own because China does not recognize Taiwan as an independent state separate from the PRC. See Michael Bennett, "The People's Republic of China and the Use of International Law in the Spratly Islands Dispute," *Stanford Journal of International Law*, No. 28 (1992), 425, 448. For a separate discussion of Taiwan's maritime claims with respect to the South China Sea, see Wang.

30. Li Jinming and Li Dexia, "The Dotted Line on the Chinese Map of the South China Sea: A Note," *Ocean Development & International Law*, No. 34 (2003), 287–295. The map was originally issued by the Republic of China (Taiwan) and included eleven rather than nine dashes. See Kuan-Hsiung Wang, 247-249. It should also be noted that official PRC depictions show a series of discontinuous dashes rather than

a continuous "joined-up" line, although the ROC has issued postal stamps in 1996 showing just such a line.

31. Li and Li, 291.

32. For a more thorough discussion of the Philippine claim, see Haydee Yorac, "The Philippine Claim to the Spratly Islands Group," *Philippine Law Journal*, No. 58 (1983), 172.

33. Map of the South China Sea, U.S. State Department Geographer, 2010.

34. Victor Prescott and Clive Schofield, "Undelimited Maritime Boundaries of the Asian Rim in the Pacific Ocean," *Maritime Briefing*, Vol. 3, No. 1 (2001), 3.

35. Lowell Bautista, "The Historical Context and Legal Basis of the Philippine Treaty Limits," *Asian Pacific Law and Policy Journal*, No. 10 (2008), 1-31.

36. Republic Act No. 9522, An Act to Amend Certain Provisions of Republic Act No. 3046, as amended by Republic Act No. 5446, to define the Archipelagic Baseline of the Philippines and for other Purposes, 10 March 2009.

37. Section 2, Republic Act 9522.

38. Joseph W. Dellapenna, "The Philippines Territorial Waters Claim in International Law," *Journal of Law and Economic Development*, No. 45 (1970-1971).

39. CNOOC/ PETROVIETNAM/ PNOC Joint Statement on the Signing of a Tripartite Agreement for Joint Marine Seismic Undertaking in The Agreement Area in the South China Sea, 14 March 2005, Makati, Philippines, http://www.fmprc.gov.cn/eng/wjb/zwjg/zwbd/ t187333.htm [Accessed on 27 October 2011].

40. The Tripartite Agreement was signed by representatives from China National Offshore Oil Corporation (CNOOC), Vietnam Oil and Gas Corporation (PETROVIETNAM), and the Philippine National Oil Company (PNOC).

41. "China, Vietnam, RP Ink Historic Joint Oil Seismic Research Accord in South China Sea," Republic of the Philippines, Office of the Press Secretary, http://www.news.ops.gov.ph/archives 2005/mar14.htm [Accessed on 27 October 2011].

42. "China, Philippines Issue Joint Statement," *China View,* 25 April 2005, http://news.xinhuanet.com/english/2005-04/28/content_2890712.htm [Accessed on 27 October 2011].

43. Jim Gomez, "Philippine Sends Warplanes Near Disputed Islands," Associated Press, 3 March 2011, http://www.businessweek.com/ap/financialnews /D9LNT87G0.htm [Accessed on 28 April 2011]; Jerome Aning and Norman Bordadora, "China Snubs PH Protest: Aquino to Send 'Spratlys Expert' to Beijing," *Philippine Daily Inquirer*, 3 May 2011.

44. See http://www.un.org/Depts/los/clcs_new/submissions_files/ submission_mysvnm_33_2009.htm [Accessed on 11 January 2012].

45. Republic of the Philippines Note Verbale No. 000228, 5 April 2011.

46. Peoples Republic of China Note Verbale, CML 8/2011, 14 April 2011, http://www.un.org/Depts/los/clcs_new/submissions_files/vnm37_09/chn_2011_re_ phl_e.pdf.

47. Ibid.

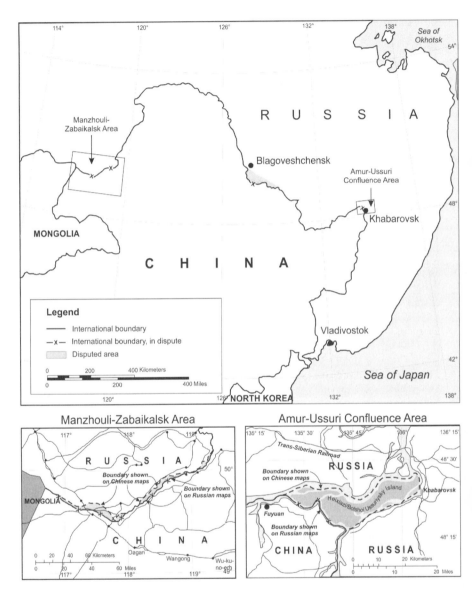

Map 17.1: Russia's Far Eastern Borders with China

17
Sino-Russian Border Resolution

Mark Galeotti

The Sino-Russian border demarcated in 2008 is not just 2,672 miles (4,300 km) long, making it one of the longest in the world, but it stretches back into history and national mythology, as a dividing line between equally imperial but otherwise very different cultures. As well as marking a geopolitical division, it represents a massive economic opportunity to many but also a potential future threat. In 2004, Bobo Lo called "the development of the relationship with China . . . arguably the greatest Russian foreign policy success of the post-Soviet period."[1] Many in Moscow would agree, and the relationship with Beijing remains both a foundation stone of Russia's geopolitical architecture and also a vital economic partnership. This is nonetheless tempered by a deep unease about the border and the rising power that lies beyond it, a concern about the shifting balance of economic and even military power and a sense that Russia remains fundamentally the front line of Europe versus Asia.[2] While selling advanced weapons to China, for example, Russia still retains formidable forces in the Far East and regularly wargames how it would fight a war along the common border.

In sharp contrast to Moscow's wariness, however, to many Russians living in the Russian Far East (RFE) China represents the future, a source of labor, investment, goods, and opportunities that make the border an inconvenience to be bypassed rather than a protective rampart. Even back in 1993, when Boris Yeltsin's tanks were shelling the parliament building in Moscow, there was widespread indifference in the RFE. As the old Russian proverb put it, "God is in his heaven and the Tsar is far away." To people in Vladivostok, Khabarovsk, Blagoveshchensk, and the other border cities increasingly dependent on transborder trade and investment, the coda may be "but China is just next door." For example, the now-divided island of Heixiazi/Bolshoi Ussuriysk looks to become a visa-free tourism destination for both Russians and Chinese, thanks to local initiative along both sides of the border, whereas a few years ago the Russian General Staff regarded it as a key border redoubt.[3] In 1999, Dmitri Trenin urged that "the broadest possible internationalization of the development of the Russian Far East would not only accelerate the process but will prevent the unilateral sinicization of the territories."[4] As of writing, however, this has not happened.

For Beijing there is perhaps less ambivalence about the final resolution of the Sino-Russian border, in part because Moscow is not as important to China as vice versa. So long as Russia's energy and raw material reserves are available to feed China's economic expansion, and so long as Moscow remains a useful counterbalance to Washington, then there is little concern about the country's future. Indeed, arguably Beijing's policy toward Moscow has been strikingly consistent since even before the Soviet collapse.[5] Likewise, Chinese foreign policy analysts have broadly welcomed the more pragmatic and consistent line introduced by Putin and his step away from the Westernizing line adopted during much of the 1990s.[6] Nonetheless, Beijing does not see its relationship with Moscow as more important than that with Washington; talk of a strategic partnership with Russia is minimal in the contemporary Chinese foreign policy debate.

Troubled Sino-Russian Legacies

Russia and China have a long, if sometimes indirect historical relationship dating back to even before the era of the Mongol conquest of the 13th and 14th century, during which time for a while both were dominated by the same nomadic empire. Bobo Lo has observed, that while "Moscow and Beijing are understandably eager to claim that they have consigned past antagonisms to the metaphorical dustbin of history . . . historical memory continues to play a crucial role. Its impact is understated but unmistakable."[7]

To the Russians, that period of often-savage domination and virtual isolation from Europe has left a lasting legacy of pragmatic, patrimonial, and authoritarian rule as well as a deep-seated fear of irresistible invasion from the east. Although Chinese were also victims of the Mongols, China recognizes their rule as the Yuan dynasty. Perhaps for this reason, China tends to be lumped together with the Mongols in Russian popular perception. Likewise, to the Chinese the Mongol experience also may have contributed to a desire to hold back from engagement with "barbarians" to the north and west. All the same, on some level both Russia and China internalize their respective victories over Mongol rulers—the Russians by force of arms, the Chinese as much as anything else by assimilation—and regard themselves as legitimate heirs to the sprawling Eurasian empire of which they had once been part.[8]

Nonetheless, as the Manchu dynasty began a process of engagement with a military and economic penetration of Central Asia from the 17th century, and the Romanov Tsars presided over an often haphazard and informal eastward expansion into and through Siberia, it was inevitable that these two great empires would meet. Intermittent contacts, which could as easily lead to trade as conflict, gave way to more direct competition over the Amur basin, a region claimed by the Manchus but not under their direct control in 1643, when Russian explorer-adventurer Vassily

Polyarkov led a party of Cossacks over the Stanovoy mountains. In 1650, he was replaced by Yerofei Khabarov, who pushed further into the basin, seeing it as a potential bread-basket to support the fur-trapping and fur-trading expeditions which were at the time central to Russia's interests in the region.[9]

Khabarov learned that the native Daurs of the region paid tribute to a foreign lord and bore a letter from Tsar Alexis to one "Prince Bogdoi" demanding submission before the Russian throne, seemingly not fully realizing that the overlord of the Daurs was not just another Siberian chieftain but the Manchu emperor. Perhaps this is not so surprising, since there was no Russian ambassador to the Chinese court and the sole direct contact in living memory had been the visit of Siberian Cossack Ivan Petlin in 1618-1619, who was not an official emissary, failed to get to meet the emperor and produced a rambling, anecdotal, and often simply inaccurate report of his travels. What followed was a messy few decades of clashes and skirmishes that convinced the Russians that the Amur basin offered neither easy conquests nor cheap food, but which also appears to have tied up more resources than the Manchu wanted to spend on this now-ravaged and lawless region.

The result was the 1689 Treaty of Nerchinsk, in which Russia agreed to withdraw from the basin and set their mutual border along the Argun River and Stanovoy mountains. The treaty left the lands west of the Argun undefined because that had recently been conquered by the independent Oirat Khanate, but nonetheless it did what both parties needed it to do. It ended direct conflict, permitted mutually-advantageous trade, and otherwise allowed each nation to attend to its own affairs largely ignoring the others.

The Treaty of Nerchinsk was subsequently confirmed and extended by the 1727 Treaty of Kyakhta that clarified the border and regulated and protected the caravans that traded Chinese tea for Russian furs. To a considerable degree, the impetus came from China, which—as it had pushed the Oirats back—worried about ambiguities in the border and the potential for Russia to support or shelter the Oirats. To this end, the Chinese government had begun to interfere with the caravans, prompting Tsar Peter the Great to seek to conclude a new deal. In an interesting case of asymmetric diplomacy, China used indirect economic pressure to induce a Russia that on paper appeared more advanced, possibly even more powerful, to conclude a border agreement that satisfied Chinese interests.

Balance of Power Shift

If in the 16th to 18th centuries Russia and China seemed relatively evenly matched and to have little reason for sustained interaction, by the 19th century they were becoming increasingly aware of the other. Furthermore, the balance of power had shifted dramatically. Russia may have been a backward power compared with the advanced nations of Europe, but it had railways, modern artillery, and a self-confidence that, when dealing with the Chinese, was buttressed by deep-seated racism. Meanwhile, Manchu China was in terminal decline, mired in corruption, disunity, and willful technological stasis. Whereas before much Russian activity in the Far East had been driven by entrepreneurial individuals and local interests, the state itself increasingly became involved. Tsar Nicholas I instructed Count Nikolai Muraviev-Amursky, the ambitious and energetic Governor General of Eastern Siberia, to push Russia's interests hard. He employed what today would be described as a mix of soft and hard power, encouraging Russian Orthodox missionaries and settlers along the border and also strengthening his military forces.

China, presumably aware that Russia could take what it wanted with relative impunity, signed a series of treaties that together surrendered to St. Petersburg 579,000 square miles (1.5 million km^2) of territory (see Map 17.2). In the midst of the Taiping Rebellion (1850-1864) and the Second Opium War (1856-1860), China was at an evident disadvantage, and the Russians knew it and seized the opportunity to force concessions. The 1858 Treaty of Aigun moved the border to the Amur River and won Russia free access along it to the Pacific. The 1860 Treaty of Beijing handed over yet more of Manchuria. The 1864 Protocol of Chuguchak (Tarbagatai) saw borderlines defined through military posturing. Russian border commissioner Ivan Babkov even wrote: "Eventually, the deployment of our forces on the border clearly demonstrated to the Chinese that we had the means to enforce our demands with an armed hand whenever we wished."[10] The Russian policy was unapologetically to push as hard and as far as they could, and then force the Chinese to accept the *fait accompli.*

Not only did this create a legacy of mistrust and bitterness, the borderlines themselves were often problematic. Drawn up on the basis of topographic convenience instead of ethnicity, they divided Kyrgyz populations in such a way that, for the next century, tribes and individuals would periodically flee across the common border to escape persecution, or sift back to exploit an economic or political opportunity.

The slew of treaties and the humbling of the emperor following the Anglo-French conquest of Beijing in 1860 also forced the Chinese to adopt a more Western approach to borders and sovereignty, one shaped not by notions of a divine mandate to rule and the receipt of tribute from foreign vassals and instead determined by borders, pacts, and the hard-nosed commercial and political interests of rising industrial powers. The tension between the new realities and the old political structures would prove disastrous, though, culminating in the 1899-1901 Boxer Uprising, which again led to foreign intervention.

Map 17.2: Russia's Absorption of Chinese Territory

In 1898, Russia had been granted a renewable lease on Port Arthur (Lüshun), its long-cherished goal of acquiring a warm-water port on the Pacific. Briefly held previously by Japan, which was forced to return it to China in 1895 by the "triple intervention" of Russia, France, and Germany, Port Arthur was a strategic prize the Russians appeared to have no plans to relinquish, and they promptly began its fortification as well as the construction of a spur—called the Chinese Eastern Railway (CER)—to connect it to the Trans-Siberian Railroad.

Following the outbreak of the Boxer Uprising in 1899, Russia expanded its control over Manchuria, ostensibly as a temporary measure. Afterwards, though, the Russians resisted repeated Japanese efforts to induce them to carry out their promised withdrawal, and this proved to be one of the causes of the 1904-1905 Russo-Japanese War that would see them bloodily forced out of Manchuria—which returned to Chinese control—and ceding their lease on Port Arthur and the Liaodong peninsula to Japan.

Sino-Soviet Relations

China had regained certain rights in Manchuria, but only as an incidental boon from a struggle between industrial and imperialist neighbors. The early 20th century would, however, also see the collapse of the imperial dynasties of both China and Russia and the rise of the Soviet Union and first Republican and then Communist China. Their relations would swing between the ostensibly fraternal to the openly hostile, but at all times be informed by an essential pragmatism.

During the 1917 Bolshevik Revolution and the subsequent 1918-1921 civil war, Allied forces, largely from the U.S. and Japan, anti-Bolshevik Whites, opportunists, and the warlord North Chinese Beiyang regime, all challenged Russian authority in the Far East. Even after the Red victory, their control at the furthest extent of the new Soviet state remained at times tenuous, with Mongolia established in 1921 as a client "people's republic." Initially, the Bolshevik government in Moscow supported Sun Yat-sen's Kuomintang—Nationalist—movement and instructed the Chinese Communist Party to support it, but in 1926 its new leader Chiang Kai-shek began to challenge this alliance, expelling Soviet advisers and the next year purging Communists from the United Front's leadership.

The subsequent struggle to power would bubble on until the 1947-1949 civil war would see Mao's Communists ascend to power, but for most of this period Moscow was neither able nor willing to engage itself in Chinese politics. Only when its direct interests were at stake did it intervene, such as in 1929 when it sent troops to rebuff attempts by Chinese warlords to take sole control of the jointly-administered CER. Otherwise, during the early 1930s, the USSR was too consumed by Stalin's campaigns of collectivization and industrialization to spare much thought for its eastern neighbor; in 1935, Moscow sold the CER to Tokyo, which helped Japan secure its hold over all of Manchuria.

In 1945, the Soviet army rolled into Japanese-occupied Manchuria and once again found itself engaged with China. Chiang Kai-shek agreed to recognize Outer Mongolia's independence from China, in return for Stalin's promise only to support his government. Once the Nationalist government carried out its part, however, the Soviets began to back the Chinese Communists, although with a patronizing assumption of superiority. From the first, Mao appears to have resented and resisted this role of the "little brother" and challenged both Leninist-Stalinist orthodoxy as well as Moscow's claim to speak for world communism. Nonetheless, with U.S. forces in neighboring Korea and with the country in ruins, Beijing needed Moscow and was willing to take its aid and support and selectively ignore its advice. A slowly deteriorating relationship improved briefly after Stalin's death in 1953, with the return of Port Arthur to Chinese control, but Soviet leader Nikita Khrushchev's public denunciation of Stalin, his often-abrasive manner, and his attempts to improve relations with the West all served to antagonize Mao, a leader himself increasingly confident in his position. Moscow's refusal to provide Beijing with nuclear weapons seemed to epitomize the asymmetry of their relations.

Tensions led to an open split in 1960. By 1962, Mao was publicly criticizing Khrushchev for capitulating during the Cuban Missile Crisis and for supporting India in the Sino-Indian War. Historical wrongs and border disputes, largely irrelevant in the inter-war era and consciously ignored during the era of fraternal relations suddenly assumed new significance, especially as thousands of Chinese Uyghurs from Xinjiang fled across the border fleeing harsh conditions, a migration Beijing denounced as part of a Soviet plot. Beijing demanded that Moscow acknowledge its imperialist legacy and its 19th-century land grabs. Although at the time the Chinese made no specific territorial claims, Russia's concerns that any recognition of the iniquities of the treaties of Aigun and Beijing would lead in this direction deterred them from any potentially-conciliatory responses. Preliminary negotiations had led to a draft border agreement by 1964. The settlement addressed a Chinese concern about the way that existing border ran along the its bank of the Ussuri River, granting Russia all the islands, and would have seen the disputed Damansky/Zhenbao Island handed to the Chinese. However, when Khrushchev read the text of a provocative speech by Mao to a Japanese delegation that complained about the Soviets occupying "too many places," he refused to sign the agreement, fearing that even these small concession would breed more demands.[11]

In 1969, words gave way to weapons as Chinese troops launched attacks against Soviet border guards on Damansky/Zhenbao and there was also sporadic and inconclusive clashes along the Xinjiang frontier. Ultimately the Soviets repelled the Chinese attacks. The result was a lengthy and bad-natured cold war, which encouraged Beijing to develop its relationship with Washington as a counter-balance; Nixon's highly publicized visit to Beijing in 1972 led to the opening of Sino-U.S. diplomatic relations in 1979.

Following Mao's death in 1976, Sino-Soviet relations became less tense. Even such events as the 1979 Chinese invasion of the Soviet ally Vietnam, and the Soviet invasion of Afghanistan, failed to lead to serious upset. The relationship was hardly friendly, but perhaps best characterized as warily pragmatic, allowing for improved trade and an easier border regime. However, although Beijing had made it clear that it was willing to negotiate on the basis of the modern boundaries and was thus questioning jurisdictions over some 13,514 square miles (35,000 km^2) along Tajikistan's Pamir mountains and the Argun, Amur, and Ussuri rivers, instead of the more than half a million square miles ceded through the 19th-century treaties, no progress was made in resolving the question of the disputed borders until Mikhail Gorbachev began his bid to reshape the USSR's relationship with the world. In

1987, at Moscow's initiative, negotiations were reopened, and they culminated in the 1991 Sino-Soviet Border Agreement.

The 1991 Sino-Russian Treaty

Ironically, the border agreement originally signed between China and the USSR would then be ratified in 1992 by the newly founded Russian Federation, following the collapse of the Soviet Union at the end of 1991. This treaty was then followed by a Complementary Agreement in 2004 that resolved certain outstanding disputes. Other post-Soviet states would likewise assume responsibility for their own border negotiations with Beijing.

The 1991 treaty accepted the thalweg principle, drawing disputed river borders along the midpoints of their main channels. This was easier agreed to than applied, though, as many of the rivers in question are braided, meandering, and divided into multiple streams by the islands that were so often the bones of contention. It thus required both careful survey work as well as patient negotiation to identify the main channel and reach agreement on the precise location of the border and claims to the islands. Some demarcation work continued almost to the 1997 deadline established for the process, on occasion delayed or complicated by local protests, such as over Menkeseli along the Argun. The 6.75 square mile (17.5 km^2) strip of land was to be transferred to China, but locals—who used it for fishing and feared the influx of Chinese farmers—and the Far Eastern Military District command—which claimed that it had strategic significance—raised sufficient opposition that eventually it was agreed in 1996 that while jurisdiction would be transferred to Beijing, local Russian residents would be guaranteed special usage rights. This "joint use" principle proved to be an important step forward in allowing the two sides to resolve similar contentious cases.

Along the Amur, 1,680 islands were in contention, with the status of two at the confluence of the Amur and the Ussuri near Khabarovsk (Bolshoi Ussuriysk and Tarabarov) taking until 2004 to be resolved in an agreement concluded in 2008— China received Tarabarov and about half of Bolshoi Ussuriysk. Overall, 902 of the islands are now Chinese and 708 Russian. Meanwhile, Beijing relinquished its outstanding claims to the 1,390 square mile (3,600 km^2) "Trans-Zeya Region" on the northern bank of the Amur, acquired by Russia in the Treaty of Aigun but with a stipulation that allowed the inhabitants of 64 villages there to "retain their domiciles in perpetuity under the authority of the Manchu government;" in 1900, during the Boxer Uprising, Russian troops ousted the Manchu settlers from their homes by driving them into the Amur, killing many of them in the process. Along the Argun, China now controls 209 islands and Russia 204. Bolshoi Ostrov/Abagaitu, an islet between the Russian city of Zabaykalsk and China's Manzhouli, occupied in 1929, was also returned to the Chinese under the 2004 Complementary Agreement. Of the 320 islands along the Ussuri, 167 ended up in Russian hands and 153 in Chinese: Damansky/Zhenbao, the site of previous bloodshed, was recognized as a Chinese territory while the largest island on the river, Kutuzov, remains Russian.

There were also numerous lesser bones of contention. Two small stretches of land along the Tumen River were transferred to China, reconnecting a hitherto-enclaved region with the mainland. Again, this proved controversial within Russia's Far Eastern elites, not least because of the presence of a war memorial and cemetery. Eventually, at Moscow's suggestion, the disputed land was split such that the memorial remained in Russian hands but China gained access to the Sea of Japan. Likewise, small and essentially symbolic parcels of land around Lake Khanka, on the Suifen delta, and along the Granitnaya River were returned to China.

The 1991 treaty and subsequent clarifications and accords have thus essentially resolved the disputes along the 2,672 mile (4,300 km) long border between Russia and China. Even the complex issue of the triangular border confluence between China, Russia, and North Korea along the Tumen River has since seemingly been settled. North Korea controls the right bank of the Tumen, and the location of the Chinese-Russian border on the left had been the subject of numerous negotiations and back-and-forth movement over the years. Having moved from about 15 miles (24 km) above the mouth of the river in 1860, then from 9.94 miles (16 km), and then again 10.56 miles (17 km) between 1964 and 1991, eventually, the final position—or at least the most recent, final position—was agreed at 11.37 miles (18.3 km) above the mouth. This new boundary was demarcated in 1998 following trilateral negotiations involving Pyongyang.

Common Interests and Rivalries

The territorial border appears at last resolved, barring some unexpected eruption of revanchist nationalism in Moscow, Beijing, or the Russian Far East. All the bones of contention have apparently been buried, all the anomalies tidied up. Until the resolution of the Granitnaya River issue, for example, while officially the border ran along the river, its origins and a small—and indefensible—parcel of land on the other bank was de facto Russian. With the transfer of 3.475 square miles (9 km²) of essentially meaningless territory, this issue has been resolved.

That is not to say, though, that amity rules along this lengthy border. Instead, the border challenges have shifted from the grossly physical questions of demarcation and onto more intangible ones often shaped by the interconnections of politics, economics, and demographics. In broad terms, Beijing and Moscow share many common geopolitical interests—but not all. While prospects for wider "strategic partnerships" are on the wane, they do have a mutual resentment of what they call "monopolarity" or "unipolarity," Washington's perceived global hegemony. Putting aside the question of just how far the U.S. can be considered a global hegemon in any meaningful sense, this has informed a series of Russian and Chinese policy decisions, from military cooperation to their efforts to undermine U.S. policy in the Middle East. Meanwhile, China is a voracious consumer of Siberian energy and raw materials, including timber, as well as a key market for Russian defense exports.

Fulsome diplomatic rhetoric notwithstanding, though, there are serious and arguably growing grounds for mutual suspicion and rivalry between Beijing and Moscow. Instead, cross-border contact and cooperation is shaped now less by the headline initiatives of national leaders and more by a series of entirely practical areas in which there are clear reasons for constructive engagement not just by Moscow and Beijing but by local political and economic actors. Alongside upbeat declaratory political statements with little real content is a range of reactive but intensely practical responses to the needs of the moment. For example, following an incident in 2005, when an explosion at a PetroChina chemical complex in Jilin led to the discharge of around 100 tons of toxic benzene into the Songhua River, contaminating the Amur and water supplies for Russian settlements as far as Khabarovsk, Beijing and Moscow signed a 2008 memorandum on mutual notification and cooperation regarding cross-border ecological emergencies and a 2009 protocol on protecting their 3,500 km of shared waterways.[12]

The practical dimension of the transborder relationship is especially economic. Sino-Russian trade hit a high of $58.8 billion in 2008 before being affected by the global economic downturn and falling by around a third. Nonetheless, by 2010 it had bounced back to its previous high.[13] About half Russia's exports are hydrocarbons and other natural resources and in 2009 Beijing agreed to lend Russian state-owned oil company Rosneft and pipeline monopoly Transneft $25 billion to complete an oil pipeline from Skovorodino in Russia to Daqing in China.

The Kremlin regards its energy supplies as a geopolitical tool, however, and this may help explain its sometimes contradictory policies as it tries to play China and Japan against each other and promises more than it is willing to give. This may prove a serious mistake, however, as it has clearly angered Beijing and raised doubts about Russia's reliability as an energy partner. In 2007, National Development and Reform Commission Vice Chair Zhang Guobao—the country's principal energy strategist—complained that "one moment Russia is saying they have made a decision, the next saying that no decision has been made . . . [while] there have been a lot of promises expressing Russia's interest in exporting natural gas to China, in truth no real progress has been made."[14]

For much of the post-Soviet era, China has also been a crucial market keeping Russia's arms industry afloat. This too is under threat. Anatoly Isaikin, head of

Russia's state-controlled arms exporter Rosoboronexport, has admitted that sales to China, which once accounted for 40 percent of total exports, had by 2008 dropped to some 10 percent.[15] To an extent, this represents a saturation of the Chinese market, but primarily is a result of its increasing sophistication. China's domestic arms production capacity has modernized dramatically and as a result Beijing is now largely interested in only the most advanced Russian designs. Considering that Moscow also regards Beijing as a long-term potential threat, this has created a dilemma, especially once they have come to realize how quickly the Chinese are able to reverse-engineer designs and develop their own analogous equipment. After securing an agreement to produce Sukhoi Su-27SK jets in 1998, for example, China went on to produce its own version in 2005, the Shenyang J-11, without any contract or compensation for the Russians.[16]

Chinese trade and investment is crucially and increasingly important to the local economy in the RFE, but so too are Chinese workers, legal immigrants, and illegal settlers.[17] This huge but thinly-populated region, which has experienced years of outmigration, borders onto China's three Manchurian provinces—Heilongjiang, Jilin, and Liaoning—which together have a total population of 110 million and a disproportionately high unemployment rate.[18] By contrast, Russia's Far Eastern Federal District (DVFO) has an area of 2,393,833 square miles (6,200,000 km^2) but a population of just 6.7 million—and this represents a sharp decline from the 9 million recorded in the 1991 census. Chinese workers have been actively recruited for a range of employment sectors ranging from farming to construction. Over time, inevitably, not only has Chinese investment focused where Chinese settlers cluster, but workers have set up homes, brought their families, established businesses, and formed local relationships.

The result has been a flow across the border of legal and illegal settlers and temporary workers. There has been no authoritative count since a study by the Moscow Carnegie Center, which recorded some 250,000 Chinese living within the region in 1997.[19] Contemporary scholarly estimates suggest figures of up to 400,000-500,000. But it is impossible, barring some extraordinary and unexpected developments, to concede any basis for the alarmist suggestions from some Russian quarters that there were 10-12 million by 2004 and could be 40 million by 2020.[20] Nonetheless, these views are pervasive and say much about Russian attitudes, exemplified in 2009, when Russian television aired far-fetched claims of a secret Chinese master plan to reassimilate the southern RFE through covert demographic means, including sending migrants across the border to settle, intermarry with locals, and take over local businesses.[21]

The issue of illegal migration is intertwined with cooperation against transborder crime and terrorism. While both countries have for years talked about this, through the 1990s and early 2000s this remained an essentially empty exercise. In particular, cross-border crime flourished, with cities such as Khabarovsk and Vladivostok hosting thriving black markets with goods smuggled—often openly, past corrupted border guards—from China. Meanwhile, Siberia's natural resources flood the other way: gold, timber, even livestock and seafood. Originally, these activities were dominated by Russian and Chinese criminals on their respective sides of the border, but as the Chinese population of the Russian Far East expands and settles, so too has this opened the way for Chinese organized crime. Likewise, the value of the Chinese connection is such that Russian gangs are increasingly dependent on their Chinese partners. In the late 1990s, for example, Russian gangs were willing to try and force the Chinese "Big Circle Boys" groups operating in Khabarovsk and Vladivostok to pay tribute. The violent gang war that ensued ended when the Chinese offered concessions, but since around 2007 they have reneged on their side of the deal, without the Russians feeling willing or able to enforce it.[22]

The China-sponsored SCO from the first presented itself as opposed to the "three bads" of terrorism, separatism, and extremism, for example, and its members agreed on an anti-terrorism convention in 2009. It has held regular security exercises and a Regional Antiterrorism Structure was established in 2004, but in the early years this was often of little more than symbolic importance, an excuse for photogenic set-piece exercises in which Russian and Chinese special forces swept onto mock terrorism hide-outs in a hail of stun grenades, smoke, and simulated gunfire. There was no meaningful cross-border sharing of intelligence, and efforts at law-enforcement cooperation were even less effective.

The first glimmerings of Islamist terrorism in China's Xinjiang region and a growing awareness of the political, economic, and social costs of cross-border crime have begun to give substance to these structures and impulses, but Beijing's main interest is in cooperating directly with Kazakhstan, Kyrgyzstan, and Uzbekistan, countries regarded as fighting the same "East Turkestan" movements and potentially harboring transnational insurgents. There appears on the Chinese part to be a belief that the Russians can offer them relatively little on this issue.

Conclusions

At the celebration of 60 years of bilateral diplomatic ties in 2009, Chinese Premier Wen Jiabao grandiloquently proclaimed that "China-Russia relations have reached a historic high and are marching towards a higher level."[23] Russian Prime Minister Vladimir Putin's rhetoric was a little less elevated, but he told the Xinhua news agency that the two countries' cooperation was "one of the most important cornerstones of world stability."[24] Beginning in 2004, border disputes dating back centuries began to be resolved, and on paper and de jure, the Chinese-Russian border is fixed, with the last outstanding areas in dispute resolved in 2008. Furthermore, relations between the two countries appear to be dominated by an awareness on both sides of the advantages in finding practical and mutually-advantageous solutions. China wants Russian energy and raw materials; Russia may be uneasy about the long-term relationship but, in the meantime needs China's money, goods, and markets, and so cannot afford to engage in geopolitical competition with this rising power. The result is less a meeting of minds or even a partnership, but more what Richard Weitz has called "strategic parallelism."[25]

Old concerns, such as the interventions of Russian nationalists or the knock-on effects of specific irritants such as cross-border pollution, have been dealt with or have receded from view. Furthermore, while Moscow and Beijing continue to compete for hegemony in Central Asia, not only are these states proving relatively adept at playing off the would-be hegemons against each other, but it is hard to see this moving beyond conventional political-economic jostling in bilateral links and bodies such as the SCO. However, it is the very asymmetry of the relationship that is most likely to challenge the existing border regime.

Even as matters stand now, some observers see recent economic agreements as evidence "not just of the failure of Russian policy in the RFE, but also China's growing dominance, through its economic power, of Russia's policy toward Asia."[26] If China continues to rise and Russia's attempts to re-establish itself as a viable great power fails, then a new political generation in Beijing may be willing to reopen the question of historical iniquities and the legitimacy of the 19th-century treaties. There remains, after all, a strong strand of Chinese thought, manifest in its historiography of Sino-Russian border relations, that sees territories seized by Russia through the centuries as "'lost' or 'torn' from the Chinese state and therefore as a source of shame for the nation."[27] In doing so they may be motivated not just by nationalism but also a keen awareness that eastern Siberia and the Russian Far East contains 65 percent of Russia's prospective petroleum reserves, 85 percent of its natural gas reserves, almost all its diamonds, 70 percent of its gold, and bountiful coal, timber, and numerous other resources.[28] If Moscow overplays its hand trying to use access to its energy and resources as a lever, Beijing's patience could conceivably wear thin, since Chinese money is eagerly solicited by local economic and political elites desperate to address years of under-investment. No border, after all, is immutable and the logic of history is that over time, borders drift with local and national self-interest.

Notes

1. Bobo Lo, "The long sunset of strategic partnership: Russia's evolving China policy," *International Affairs*, Vol. 80, No. 2 (2004), 296.

2. This is an ambiguity that has deep historical roots; see David van Schimmelpenninck, *Russian Orientalism: Asia in the Russian Mind from Peter the Great to the Emigration* (New Haven, CT: Yale University Press, 2010).

3. *China Daily*, 28 February 2011, http://www.chinadaily.com.cn/world/2011-02/28/content_12091136.htm [Accessed on 16 November 2011].

4. Dmitri Trenin, *Russia's China Problem* (Washington, DC: Carnegie Endowment for International Peace, 1999), 46.

5. Natasha Kuhrt, *Russian Policy Towards China and Japan* (Abingdon: Routledge, 2007), 11-12.

6. Joseph Cheng, "Chinese perceptions of Russian foreign policy under the Putin administration," *Journal of Current Chinese Affairs*, Vol. 38, No. 2 (2009), 150.

7. Bobo Lo, *The Axis of Convenience* (London: Chatham House, 2008), 17.

8. Peter Perdue, *China Marches West: The Qing Conquest of Central Eurasia* (Boston: Harvard University Press, 2005), 82-83.

9. W. Bruce Lincoln, *The Conquest of a Continent* (New York: Random House, 1994) provides an especially elegant overview of Russia's eastward march.

10. Quoted in S.C.M. Paine, *Imperial Rivals: Russia, China and Their Disputed Frontier* (Armonk, NY: M E Sharpe, 1996), 90.

11. Kuhrt, 29.

12. Richard Weitz, *China-Russia Security Relations: Strategic Parallelism without Partnership or Passion?* (Carlisle, PA: Strategic Studies Institute, 2008), 15-16.

13. *China Daily*, 10 December 2010, http://www.chinadaily.com.cn/business/2010-12/10/content_11681821.htm [Accessed on 16 November 2011].

14. Weitz, 21.

15. *Interfax*, 9 March 2011 http://www.interfax.com/newsinf.asp?y=2011&m=3&d=9&pg=8&id=227221 [Accessed on 4 April 2011].

16. *Jane's Defence Weekly*, 20 May 2010.

17. Anatolii Shkurkin, "Chinese in the labor market of the Russian Far East: past, present, future," in Pal Nyiri and Igor Savel'ev, eds., *Globalizing Chinese Migration: Trends in Europe and Asia* (Farnham: Ashgate, 2002).

18. Elizabeth Wishnick, "Chinese migration to the Russian Far East: a human security dilemma," in Melissa Curley and Siu-Iun Wong, eds., *Security and Migration in Asia: The Dynamics of Securitisation* (Abingdon: Routledge, 2009), 155.

19. *ABC News*, 14 July 2000, http://abcnews.go.com/International/story?id=82969&page=1 [Accessed on 16 November 2011].

20. Nataliya Ryzhova and Grigory Ioffe, "Trans-border exchange between Russia and China: The case of Blagoveshchensk and Heihe," *Eurasian Geography*, Vol. 50, No. 3 (2009), 351.

21. *The Observer (UK)*, 2 August 2009, http://www.guardian.co.uk/world/2009/aug/02/china-russia-relationship [Accessed on 16 November 2011].

22. Mark Galeotti, "Eastern Empires: criminals infiltrate Russia's Far East," *Jane's Intelligence Review*, March 2010.

23. *People's Daily Online*, 14 October 2009, http://english.people.com.cn/90001 /90776/90883/6782604.html [Accessed on 16 November 2011].

24. *Xinhua*, 13 October 2009, http://news.xinhuanet.com/english/2009- 10/13/content_12225589.htm [Accessed on 16 November 2011].

25. Weitz.

26. Stephen Blank, "China's Russian Far East," *Jameson Foundation China Brief*, 5 August 2009, http://www.jamestown.org/single/?no_cache= 1&tx_ttnews%5Btt_news%5D=35371 [Accessed on 16 November 2011].

27. Alexei Voskressenski, *The Difficult Border: Current Russian and Chinese Concepts of Sino-Russian Relations and Frontier Problems* (New York: Nova Science Publishers, 1996), 3.

28. Some projections suggest China's net imports of petroleum will more than quadruple by 2035, the balance of risk versus potential benefit in a more assertive policy may begin to shift. *Wall Street Journal Asia*, 4 March 2011, http://online.wsj.com/article/SB10001424052748703559604576175660916870214. html [Accessed on 16 November 2011].

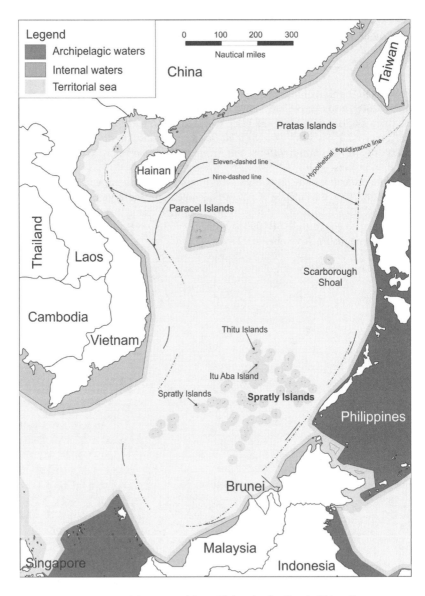

Map 18.1: Chinese Maritime Claims in the South China Sea

18
PRC Disputes with the
ROC on Taiwan

Bruce A. Elleman

The approximately 100 mile (161 km) wide Taiwan Strait separates the People's Republic of China (PRC) from the Republic of China (ROC) on Taiwan. For much of its post-1949 history, the ROC claimed all of mainland China—including Mongolia and many disputed frontier lands—as its sovereign territory. Gradually Taipei's expectation of retaking the mainland diminished, but it still has territorial claims and exerts actual control over a number of small islands off the coast of China, including Jinmen (formerly Quemoy) and Mazu islands, as well as the Pratas islands to the southwest. It also retains control over the largest island in the Spratlys, Itu Aba (Taiping Island in Chinese).

By contrast, the PRC claims not only all of the offshore islands controlled by Taiwan, but all of the islands that make up the ROC proper, comprising the island of Formosa, the Penghu islands (formerly the Pescadores), and many smaller islands like Green (Lü Dao) and Orchid (Lan Yu). The two governments do agree with each other, however, on many South China Sea maritime and territorial claims contested by other Southeast Asian nations. But even though the PRC and the ROC agree that the South China Sea is China's, Beijing disputes Taipei's particular claims to the South China Sea, including Taiwan's physical control over Itu Aba. While the PRC and ROC also agree that the Diaoyu/Senkaku islands located in the southern East China Sea are China's, they disagree on which China.

Interestingly, Beijing and Taipei have cooperated with each when conflicts erupt against another claimant, such as when China fought with Vietnamese troops in the Spratlys during 1988. If the two governments were ever to unify, either in reality or simply on paper—for example, in some form of "United Front"—then Taipei's greater territorial claims might even give Beijing an opportunity to reopen border negotiations with many of China's neighbors. Such an occurrence might allow a newly reunified China one last chance to claim disputed territory that its neighbors may have erroneously assumed were already settled permanently.

Early History of Taiwan and the Defense of the Taiwan Strait

Taiwan is just one of the numerous islands along the so-called first island chain that includes the Japanese and Okinawan islands to the north and the Philippines to the south. Off the coast of the PRC are thousands of smaller offshore islands. Zhejiang Province has an estimated 1,800 islands off its coast. Add to this number the 600 islands off Fujian Province and the 550 islands off Guangdong Province and the total gives China's southeastern coast almost 3,000 islands. Many are too small to be inhabited, while the Mazu islands have about 10,000 and the 60-square mile island of Jinmen had over 60,000 people living there in the 1950s, and it is now closer to 85,000.

The first inhabitants of Taiwan arrived around 6,000 B.C.E. and appear to have been Austronesians, with distinct ethnic ties to the indigenous populations of the Philippines, Malaysia, Indonesia, and the Polynesian islands. While they knew about the island, Han Chinese migrated to Taiwan in large numbers beginning only in the 17th century, spurred by the Manchu domination of northern China in 1644. Zheng Chenggong (1624-1662), in particular, led large numbers of Ming loyalists to Taiwan in 1661, defeating a Dutch stronghold at Anping after a nine-month siege on what the Dutch called Formosa (meaning "Beautiful Island" in Portuguese).

This Han Chinese victory was especially notable because Zheng's forces used a number of offshore islands—including Jinmen and the Penghus—as "stepping stones" to cross the Taiwan Strait. Zheng's successors held out against the Manchus for another twenty years, but Taiwan finally fell to a Qing fleet of 300 warships and 20,000 troops commanded by Admiral Shi Lang (1621-1696) in 1683.[1] At this stage, Taiwan was included in Fujian Province, but became a Chinese province in 1885.

Due to its strategic importance, Taiwan has been fought over many times, including in the 17th century by Ming loyalists opposing the Manchu conquest of China, the Manchus in the 18th century putting down a local rebellion, and during the 1880s Sino-French conflict. As a result of the first Sino-Japanese War, China ceded Taiwan to Japan in the 1895 Treaty of Shimonoseki. Japan maintained sovereignty over Taiwan for fifty years, until Japan's surrender in 1945, at which point—according to the terms of the Cairo and Potsdam agreements—Taiwan was returned to "China." When the San Francisco Peace Treaty was signed in 1951, however, Japan renounced sovereignty to Taiwan without stating whether the PRC or ROC should assume sovereignty.

At the end of World War II, of course, China meant the "Republic of China," or "Nationalist China" since the Chinese government was under the sole authority of Chiang Kai-shek and his Nationalist party. However, the civil war was renewed in China immediately after World War II ended, and by 1949 the Chinese Communists under Mao Zedong were able to push southward into China proper from their base in Manchuria. On 1 October 1949, the Communists created the PRC, while the Nationalist government retreated to the island security of Taiwan. Chiang Kai-shek and his advisers moved completely to Taiwan only in early December 1949.

During the summer and fall 1949, Nationalist forces fought fiercely to defend their control over numerous offshore islands. The Nationalists retained one regiment of marines on the Miao islands north of Shandong peninsula to blockade the Bo Hai Gulf and the northern ports, even while they stationed troops on Zhoushan and the Saddle islands to blockade the Yangzi River. Meanwhile, they fortified the Dachen, Mazu, Jinmen, and the Penghu islands near Taiwan, Lema and Wan Shan islands near Guangzhou, and Hainan Island, fifteen miles off the southern coast of Guangdong Province. During 1949, Nationalist control over these offshore islands, often with the support of local guerrilla groups, allowed them to blockade about two-thirds of China's coastline. This situation began to change during late fall 1949. While a Communist attack on the Nationalist-held base on Jinmen failed during October 1949, the southern city of Guangzhou soon fell to the PLA. Meanwhile, the loss of a number of strategic islands in the north effectively narrowed the Nationalist blockade to central and southern China.[2]

The Nationalists initially also retained control over Hainan, directly off of China's southern coast. From March-May 1950, Communist forces succeeded in pushing the Nationalist forces from Hainan. The key PRC military advantage over the Nationalist defenders proved to be the large size of the PLA, with the Communist junks and troops moving only at night. The PLA's fleets of small boats crossing the Qiongzhou Strait using "riverine tactics," overwhelming the Nationalist air and surface units there. Communist forces, in spite of naval and air inferiority, succeeded in capturing Hainan by early May 1950 and the Zhoushan archipelago by late May 1950, squeezing the Nationalists on Taiwan from both the south and north.

The PLA forces were aided in taking these fortified islands by the fact that they were very close to the Chinese mainland, and so allowed for a mass attack. Naval historians have speculated, however, that such tactics "would be of no use against the primary target, Taiwan, which lay nearly 100 nm from the coast."[3] In fact, for the PRC to invade Taiwan would require a major naval effort on its part, including the gathering of hundreds, perhaps thousands, of ships and the training of tens of thousands of troops. The natural defenses provided by the Taiwan Strait have militated against such an attack.

By the summer of 1950, the Nationalists had lost their crucial island bases in the Bo Hai Gulf, off the mouth of the Yangzi River, and on Hainan Island. These losses cut the Nationalist ability to conduct a blockade against China by over half. The Communists' mass attack on Hainan, which was only 15 miles from the mainland, could not be so easily replicated against Taiwan. As a result, continued Nationalist control of numerous offshore islands in the Taiwan Strait was considered critical to deter the Communists from launching an invasion of Taiwan.

The Importance of Offshore Islands

Traditionally, offshore islands had acted as "stepping stones" to support an invasion of Taiwan. When the PLA halted its spring 1950 offensive, the Nationalists held approximately 30 offshore islands. This gave them the ability to dominate a 400-mile arc of coastal waters from the Dachen islands in the north off Zhejiang Province, to Jinmen in the south off Fujian Province. Taiwan's control over these islands helped stop a PRC cross-strait invasion, while also allowing the Nationalists to conduct a decade-long naval blockade of the mainland.

During early 1950, the Nationalist Navy could dominate the majority of China's southeastern coastline from bases on these strategic offshore islands. But by spring 1950, there was ample evidence that the Communist forces were preparing to attack, as the PLA began to concentrate thousands of motorized junks in the port cities along the Taiwan Strait in preparation for a massive amphibious invasion.[4] According to one U.S. Navy estimate, the Communists could assemble "7,000 merchant steamers and other large vessels" to transport 200,000 troops across the Strait.[5] After the Korean War broke out in June 1950, however, the U.S. Navy formed the Taiwan Patrol Force to help neutralize the Taiwan Strait.[6]

By summer 1953, when the Korean armistice was signed, the Nationalists still controlled about 25 offshore islands. On 30 July 1953, a U.S. Navy report entitled "Security of Offshore islands Presently Held by the Nationalist Government of the Republic of China," divided 20 of these into three categories. In Category I were four offshore islands off Fuzhou, including Mazu, and four islands off Xiamen, including Jinmen, which "could be used to counter Chinese Communist invasion operations." Retaining these eight islands was considered militarily desirable. Category II including two islands in the Dachens, and were not considered important to defend Taiwan and the Penghu islands. Finally, in Category III were ten smaller offshore islands, whose main importance was in defending the ten islands in Categories I and II.[7]

As for the many other offshore islands under Nationalist control, U.S. Navy planners concluded they "are not now being utilized for important operations and are not considered worth the effort necessary to defend them against a determined attack." Still, as this U.S. Navy report was quick to point out, none of the offshore islands could be called "essential" to the defense of Taiwan and the Penghus in the sense of being "absolutely necessary" militarily. Their importance to the Nationalists was mainly for "psychological warfare purposes," as well as for their use in "pre-invasion operations, commando raiding, intelligence gathering, maritime resistance development, sabotage, escape and evasion."[8]

China's southeastern coastline was especially tense during the mid-1950s. Both Communist and Nationalist forces fiercely defended their positions on numerous offshore islands, in the hopes of changing the strategic balance. During early 1955, for example, the People's Liberation Army Navy (PLAN) took Yijiangshan Island as part of the first Taiwan Strait Crisis, forcing the Nationalist troops to retreat from the nearby Dachen islands. This meant that Mazu became their northernmost outpost. Later, in 1958, during the second "Taiwan Strait Crisis," the PRC tried to force the Nationalists to retreat from Jinmen Island. However, with U.S. assistance and training, the Nationalist Navy successfully broke the PRC blockade of Jinmen to bring in essential supplies.

After the two Taiwan Strait crises in the 1950s, the PRC-ROC division of offshore islands remained substantially unchanged down until the present. Taiwan continued to control almost twenty offshore islands, including the island of Jinmen, which includes two other islands, Lesser Jinmen, or in Chinese Xiao Jinmen, and Dadan Island. Nearby were the islands of Wuqiu, Daqiu, and Xiaoqiu. Meanwhile, the Mazu islands included a number of smaller islands, including Beigan (北竿) and Gaodeng. Taiwan also controls a number of small islands off its own shores, including Green Island, or Lü Dao, Orchid Island, or Lan Yu, and Lesser Orchid Island, or Xiao Lan Yu.

In sharp contrast to these disputes in or near the Taiwan Strait, the PRC and ROC tend to agree that the Japanese-claimed Senkaku islands (Diaoyutai in Chinese) should be China's, although they disagree which China, plus some ultra-nationalists claim that all of the Ryūkyū islands (Liuqiu islands in Chinese), including Okinawa, were traditionally part of China's tributary system, and so should be considered Chinese. The two governments also have overlapping maritime and territorial claims in the South China Sea and elsewhere.

Overlapping PRC-ROC Maritime and Territorial Claims

Since 1949, the PRC and the ROC have each considered themselves to be the only legitimate government of China. While both Beijing and Taipei agree that Xinjiang, Tibet, and Inner Mongolia are part of China, for most of this time Taiwan also claimed Mongolia (formerly called Outer Mongolia). The Taiwanese government recognized Mongolia as a separate country on 3 October 2002, even though the official borders of the Republic of China have apparently not yet been changed nor have official ROC maps that include Mongolia as part of China been replaced. Meanwhile, the PRC claims not only the offshore islands garrisoned by Taiwan, but all of the Penghu islands, formerly called the Pescadores, as well as Taiwan Island, also known as Formosa, and the much smaller Green Island, Orchid Island, and Lesser Orchid Island, right off Taiwan's east coast.

Moreover, China and Taiwan both claim disputed territories in the South China Sea, which are likewise claimed in part or wholly by Brunei, Malaysia, the Philippines, and Vietnam. Additionally, while Indonesia holds uncontested sovereignty over the Natuna islands, overlapping maritime claims may exist between Indonesia on behalf of these islands and China (and possibly other claimant states) generated from the disputed Spratly islands. Chinese historical records dating back to the 2nd century B.C.E. pre-date any other historical claims. This does not mean that the islands were never explored or used by Vietnamese or Filipino fishermen, however, but that the Chinese were the first to document their early presence. One academic has concluded that, "it is true that the weight of the evidence appears in the present case to be on the Chinese side, although this may reflect mainly the greater industry of traditional Chinese authors in keeping geographical and historical records."[9]

Beginning in the 1880s, France, Japan, and China became interested in dominating the South China Sea. As a result of the Sino-French conflict in 1884-1885, France made Annam (Vietnam) a protectorate and later a colony, and then during the first Sino-Japanese War of 1894-1895, Japan annexed Taiwan. Faced with what China considered to be illegal Japanese mining operations on several phosphorus and guano-rich islands in the Pratas and Spratly islands, in 1907 Qing Admiral Sa Zhenbing led a naval expedition to reclaim these islands for China. During September 1909 the Qing government renamed the Naval Reorganization Council into the Ministry of the Navy. China's newly modernized navy then conducted several naval operations in the South China Sea, and in 1909 and 1910 China formally annexed many of these islands—including the Paracel and Pratas islands—to Guangdong Province and also sent a ship every year to the South China Sea "to maintain contact with overseas Chinese on these islands."[10]

Following the collapse of the Qing dynasty in 1911, China was in turmoil for many years. In 1926, the recently established Nationalist Navy built a radio station on the Pratas islands. Taking advantage of China's comparative weakness, however, French Indochina occupied the Paracel islands in 1932. But with Japan's invasion of China in 1937 the Japanese began to make their own claims to the Pratas, Paracel, and Spratly islands. During 1937, for example, as part of their occupation of China, Japan seized Pratas Island and captured and interrogated 29 Nationalist soldiers. France, in response to the threat from Japan, sent an expedition to the Paracels, officially claiming it as part of Annam (Vietnam) on 4 July 1938. Immediately, the Nationalist government-in-exile in Chongqing and the Japanese government protested France's action; Japan even stated in its own 8 July 1938 protest that France was violating Chinese sovereignty when it occupied the Paracel islands.

France next claimed the Paracel islands as part of the French Union in 1939. In response, on 31 March 1939, Japan made a parallel claim on behalf of the Governor General of Taiwan, which was at that point an integral part of the Japanese empire. When France withdrew its forces the next year, however, Japan occupied the Paracels, but this time not on behalf of Taiwan but as Japanese territory based on an earlier territorial claim dating to 1917.

Japan also specified that its claim to the Spratly islands included all of the islands 7° 00' and 12° 00' north and 111° 30' and 117° 00' east. From 1939-1945, the Japanese occupied Itu Aba, building a fuel depot, submarine base, and a radio station there. Near the end of the war, the Japanese were forced to withdraw. According to one view, only with the Japanese occupation of the islands in the late 1930s could valid claims of sovereignty through effective occupation even be made. While Chinese historical interaction with these islands could establish the basis for a claim to sovereignty, therefore, such a right must be followed up with de facto occupation of the territory to establish legal sovereignty. This occupation was not attempted by China until after World War II.

Post-World War II South China Sea Claims

Soon after World War II ended, the Nationalist government sent two destroyers to the South China Sea during November-December 1946 to establish a garrison on Itu Aba. Taiwan claims the Spratly islands based on the fact that Nationalist troops were the first to occupy one of the Spratly islands after the Japanese withdrawal in 1945. Beijing's parallel claim to the Spratlys agrees with this, plus is based directly on the 1947 eleven-dashed map issued by the ROC, since Beijing claims to have inherited all ROC territory when the Chinese Communist Party took power in 1949. Accordingly, the PRC has claimed a nine-dashed line from the early 1950s.[11]

However, there is disagreement over whether this Nationalist garrison was later removed, with some sources stating that all Chinese military forces left the Spratly islands in May 1950 due to the ongoing civil war in China and that they only returned in July 1956, possibly in response to exploratory activity in the area by Philippine nationals. During an interview in Taipei in March 1993, this absence of a Chinese military presence in the island for several years was apparently confirmed by retired ROC Navy Vice Admiral Liu Dacai. But other scholars argue that a "small contingent of Taiwanese troops remained on the largest island Itu Aba (Taipingdao) in the Spratly group" during this period.[12]

Either way, on 29 May 1956, the PRC Foreign Ministry stated that "Taiping [Itu Aba] and Nanwei [Storm/Spratly] Island in the South China Sea, together with the small islands in their vicinity, are known in aggregate as the Nansha islands. These islands have always been a part of Chinese territory. The People's Republic of China has indisputable, legitimate sovereignty over these islands."[13] On 2 June 1956, the American Ambassador to Taipei reassured the ROC Foreign Minister that the United States had no intention of getting involved in the Spratly dispute. After receiving this assurance, the ROC also officially reclaimed Itu Aba (see Map 18.2).

On 5 June 1956, the South Vietnamese (ROV) Minister Cao Bai stated that the Spratly and Paracel islands had been under the jurisdiction of the French colonial government and that Vietnam subsequently had jurisdiction by virtue of grant of sovereignty by France; soon afterward, South Vietnam landed naval units in the Spratlys. In response, Beijing insisted that an 1887 treaty with France, the Sino-French Convention, ceded to China the Paracel and Spratly groups. But other scholars argued that despite the historical claims of the Chinese and Vietnamese, "only those events that took place since the 1930s are relevant to the analysis of the present dispute," which would make the 1887 treaty largely moot.[14]

From that time on, all subsequent claims and counterclaims to the Paracels and the Spratlys became even more complex. On 4 September 1958, the PRC issued its own "Declaration on Territorial Waters," which specifically stated that the Paracel (Xisha) and Spratly (Nansha) islands were Chinese territory.[15] The Communist government of North Vietnam, which sought aid from Communist China, appears to have accepted Chinese sovereignty over the Paracel and Spratly islands ten days later. On 14 September 1958, in a note to Chinese Premier Zhou Enlai, North Vietnamese Premier Pham Van Dong expressed his government's support for China's Declaration, stating "the Government of the Democratic Republic of Viet Nam recognizes and supports the Declaration of the Government of the People's Republic of China on China's territorial sea made on September 4, 1958."[16] These statements by the then North Vietnamese government were later cited by the PRC as Vietnamese acceptance of China's sovereignty over the islands.[17]

With regard to the Paracels, both China and Taiwan agree that they are Chinese. In January 1974, the PLAN occupied these islands by force, taking them away from South Vietnam. The Chinese name for this expedition is *Xisha Ziwei Fanjizhan,* or "Counterattack in Self-Defense in the Paracel Islands."[18] Following Vietnam's reunification during 1975, Hanoi disputed China's possession, even though Hanoi had apparently recognized the PRC claim in 1958. On 1 July 1976, Vietnam restated its position that the Paracels were Vietnamese territory.

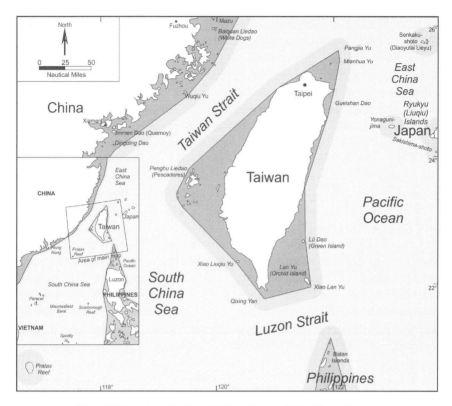

Map 18.2: Taiwan's Straight Baseline and Maritime Claims

Recent PRC-ROC Tensions in the South China Sea

In 1988, the PRC incorporated the Paracels and the Spratlys into a new Chinese province called Hainan Province. Then, on 4 December 2007, China unilaterally announced it had created a new "city," called Sansha, in Hainan Province to administer the Paracels, Macclesfield Bank, and the Spratlys, even though China's sovereignty over these islands remains in dispute. According to news reports, "Shock waves were felt immediately throughout the region: both Vietnam and Indonesia formally protested China's unilateral and preemptive move."[19] In response to China's action, during February 2008 Taiwanese President Chen Shui-bian flew to Itu Aba for an official visit. Chen's trip not only proved that the recently lengthened runway could handle C-130 cargo planes, but was also perceived as reinforcing Taiwan's claim to these disputed territories.[20]

There is really no conflict between the sovereignty claims of the China and Taiwan over the South China Sea. Both the PRC and the ROC feel that they are representing Chinese claims, and "historically, there is no question that the Paracels and Spratlys belong to China."[21] Other scholars disagree that they are of equal weight, however, arguing instead that the PRC's legal position on the islands, based on applicable international law, "is not only weak de jure, but also de facto," principally because China had done nothing to exercise their jurisdiction over the Spratlys prior to establishing its own outposts in the area in 1988. By contrast, Taiwan has a more valid claim to Itu Aba, in particular since they have effectively held and developed it. However, "Taiwan cannot deduce from this any claim to the whole archipelago (which is, after all, an arbitrary definition in regard to insular affiliation and dimension) just because it occupies one feature of the group."[22]

Even though they dispute each other's claims, Taiwan's near continuous occupation of Itu Aba since the end of World War II, which is arguably the "main island" in the Spratlys group, could be considered as underpinning the claims made by mainland China. Thus, any assertion that Beijing has the ability to alone settle the territorial disputes in the South China Sea is debatable, since complete resolution of sovereignty, and delimitation of maritime boundaries, over these disputed territories really hinges on the final resolution of the PRC-ROC political dispute.

Potential PRC-ROC Cooperation

Beginning in 1992, the PRC and ROC conducted a series of informal talks designed to clarify their positions on a wide range of issues, including Taiwan's support for the "one China" principle. These talks broke down in 1998, due to the increasing strength of the Taiwanese pro-independence movement, as indicated by Chen Shui-bian's presidential victories in 2000 and 2004, but resumed again during June 2008 following the Nationalist return to power. Since that time, PRC-ROC relations have improved dramatically, including increased travel, cross-strait investment, and direct shipping. Taiwanese investment in the PRC rose sharply, hitting $13.3 billion in 2010 alone.[23]

While the ROC and the PRC disagree over the ownership of particular islands in the Spratlys, they would appear to back a single Chinese claim against any other. For example, the PRC and Taiwan dispute Vietnam's claim to sovereignty over the Paracels. In the Spratlys, the PRC, Taiwan, and Vietnam all claim the entire group, while the Philippines, Brunei, and Malaysia have more limited claims. Except for Brunei, all these nations have at one time or another supported military actions, and there were almost a dozen reported incidents during the 1990s alone. However, of all the countries that have an interest in these waters, the PRC has arguably spent the most time and money building a comprehensive military support infrastructure in the South China Sea that might allow it to one day obtain its strategic goals through force.[24]

In the past, the PRC and ROC have shown a willingness to cooperate against other claimants in the South China Sea dispute. For example, when Sino-Vietnamese tensions led to conflict during 1988, Taiwan appears to have supported the PRC. Taiwan's Defense Minister Cheng Wei-yuan reportedly stated that if Taiwan was asked, it would help defend PLA forces in the Spratlys against a third party. Although this did not happen, there have been credible claims "that PRC garrisons received freshwater supplies from the ROC troops on Itu Aba in that year."[25]

The 20 May 2008 election of the Nationalist candidate Ma Ying-jeou could presage greater ROC-PRC cooperation in the South China Sea, and perhaps other disputed areas as well, such as over the Diaoyu/Senkaku islands, where the PRC and Taiwan agree that the islands should be China's. While there is still relatively little support on Taiwan for reunifying with the PRC, fully half of Taiwanese agree with continuing economic integration. But the possibility that the Taiwanese government will back down before PRC pressure already concerns some scholars, who fear that "Ma may wittingly sell Taiwan out or inadvertently give away too much, with results that will be harmful to the U.S. and potentially ruinous for Taiwan."[26]

Deepening PRC-ROC cooperation could result in unexpected benefits for Beijing. It is often overlooked that the Nationalist government on Taiwan still claims territory from its neighbors that equals, and in many cases, exceeds those lands claimed by the PRC. For example, the ROC constitution apparently still lists all of Mongolia as being part of China, and perhaps all of Tuva (formerly Tannu Tuva), which was annexed by the USSR outright during World War II. Taiwan also potentially has a large number of outstanding territorial disputes with countries that do not currently recognize it, including Afghanistan, Bhutan, Myanmar, India, North Korea, Pakistan, Russia, and Tajikistan.[27]

In 1927, the Nationalist government even published a map (see Map 18.3) showing the largest extent of China's former borders.[28] During May 2012, the PRC government appeared to support these Nationalist borders when Foreign Ministry officials stated that Beijing's claim to the South China Sea could be dated to a 1279 survey "commissioned by Emperor Kublai Khan," a Mongol leader during China's Yuan dynasty, who controlled most of Eurasia at that time.[29] Notably, Beijing announced on 26 July 2012 that Senior Colonel Cai Xihong would command a newly created Sansha garrison, located on Woody island in the disputed Paracel chain, to help defend China's South China Sea claims.

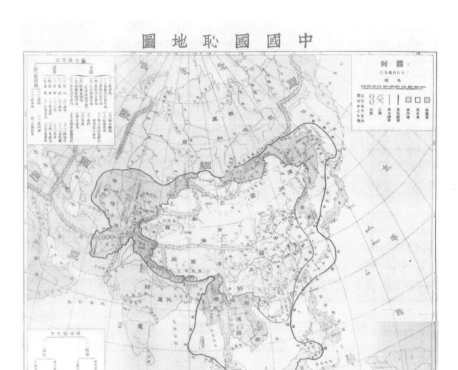

Map 18.3: 1927 Nationalist Map with "Former Borders" Outer Black Line

This raises the possibility that should China and Taiwan ever unify peacefully, then a whole host of border disputes that appear to be settled today could be re-opened for further discussion and negotiation. This situation has happened before. For example, during negotiations leading to the unification of East and West Germany, Poland was very concerned when German Chancellor Helmut Kohl indicated that the border with Poland might need to be renegotiated. During the two plus four talks, only the intervention of the United States, France, Great Britain, and the USSR convinced Germany to declare that the current borders would be maintained unchanged: "The treaty which finally came out of these talks, and paved the way for reuniting Germany, calls for the current borders to be maintained."[30] Unlike Kohl's decision to respect the status quo, it is highly doubtful that a newly unified China would back down so quickly before foreign pressure.

Conclusions

Beijing's and Taipei's opposing territorial claims make the PRC-ROC situation one of the most complex of any of the ongoing maritime and territorial disputes between neighbors. Both governments agree on their territorial claims against Japan, including the Diaoyu/Senkaku dispute, and they also agree that China's sovereign territory includes the South China Sea. But Taiwan currently occupies some of the largest islands there, including the Pratas islands and Itu Aba, or Taiping Island, even while the PRC occupies the Paracels and ten small islands in the Spratlys. In general, Taiwan supports the PLAN activities against all other South China Sea claimants, even though the PRC's official policy is that only Beijing has the right to claim sovereignty over the entire South China Sea, including all Taiwan-controlled islands.

Meanwhile, the PRC has repeatedly stated that it will not interfere with freedom of navigation in the South China Sea, but it refuses to clarify exactly what areas it claims. Beijing's submission of the infamous nine-dashed map of the South China Sea to the CLCS in May 2009 suggests that the PRC continues to treat this entire region as "historic waters." In the unlikely event that the PRC was able to persuade the international community as to the validity of its historic waters claim, this could exempt all or part of the South China Sea from freedom of navigation and over-flight principles. According to one scholar, "Beijing could be intent on transferring large areas of the South China Sea from a regime in which warships have immunity from its jurisdiction, to one in which permission is required for entry. Of course, China cannot now enforce such a regime. But when it is strong enough, it may try to do so."[31]

Taking into account the historical examples of the PRC's maritime disputes, including over the Pratas, Paracel, and Spratly islands, repeated assertions by Beijing beginning in 2002 that it will work with the ASEAN countries to limit frictions over these islands and to resolve their differences peacefully should be met with healthy skepticism. Such doubts are supported by the minimal progress that has been made in the implementation of the confidence building measures outlined in the 2002 China-ASEAN Declaration on the Conduct of Parties in the South China Sea. In particular, Taiwan is excluded from this agreement, even though Taipei is a major claimant of these disputed territories and actually occupies several of the larger disputed islands in the South China Sea. Conversely, if the PRC and ROC were to one day unify, then new border claims could perhaps be made based on Taiwanese maps; this might gave Beijing a golden opportunity to renegotiate borders that it was already not completely satisfied with.

Notes

The thoughts and opinions expressed in this publication are those of the author and are not necessarily those of the U.S. government, the U.S. Navy Department, or the Naval War College.

1. Andrew Erickson and Andrew Wilson, "China's Aircraft Carrier Dilemma," in Andrew Erickson, Lyle Goldstein, William Murray, and Andrew Wilson, eds., *China's Future Nuclear Submarine Force* (Annapolis, MD: Naval Institute Press, 2007), 260.

2. Bruce A. Elleman, "The Nationalists' Blockade of the PRC, 1949-58," in Bruce A. Elleman and S.C.M. Paine, eds., *Naval Blockade and Seapower: Strategies and Counter-strategies, 1805-2005* (London: Routledge, 2006), 133-144; Bruce A. Elleman, *High Sea's Buffer: The Taiwan Patrol Force, 1950-1979* (Newport, RI: NWC Press, 2012), 3-16.

3. David Muller, *China as a Maritime Power* (Boulder: Westview Press, 1983), 16.

4. He Di, "The Last Campaign to Unify China," in Mark A. Ryan, David M. Finkelstein, and Michael A. McDevitt, eds., *Chinese Warfighting: The PLA Experience Since 1949* (Armonk, NY: M.E. Sharpe, 2003),73-90.

5. Edward J. Marolda, "The U.S. Navy and the Chinese Civil War, 1945-1952," Ph.D. Dissertation, The George Washington University, 1990, 159.

6. Elleman, *High Sea's Buffer*, 17-30.

7. Appendix to "Security of the Offshore Islands Presently Held by the Nationalist Government of the Republic of China," Memorandum from CNO, ADM Robert B. Carney, to Join Chiefs of Staff (Top Secret), 30 July 1953, Strategic Plans Division, NHHC Archives, Box 289; cited in Elleman, *High Sea's Buffer*, 13-14.

8. Ibid.

9. John K. T. Chao, "South China Sea: Boundary Problems Relating to the Nansha and Hsisha Islands," Volume 9 (1989-1990), *Chinese Yearbook of International Law and Affairs* (Taipei: Chinese Society of International Law, 1991), 113.

10. Bruce Swanson, *Eighth Voyage of the Dragon: A History of China's Quest for Seapower* (Annapolis, MD: Naval Institute Press, 1982), 117-120.

11. The eleven-dashed line map, called *The Location Map of the South China Sea Islands* or *Nanhai zhudao weizhi tu* in Chinese, was originally published by Geography Department of the Republic of China's Ministry of Internal Affairs in 1947. See, Li Jinming and Li Dexia, "The Dotted Line on the Chinese Map of the South China Sea: A Note," *Ocean Development & International Law*, No. 34 (2003), 287; See also Hsiung Wang, "The ROC's Maritime Claims and Practices with Special Reference to the South China Sea," *Ocean Development and International Law*, No. 41 (2010), 237-252.

12. Pao-Min Chang, *Sino-Vietnamese Territorial Dispute* (New York: Praeger, 1986), 18.

13. Jianming Shen, "China's Sovereignty over the South China Sea Islands: A Historical Perspective," *Chinese JIL* (2002), 146.

14. Hungdah Chiu and Choon-Ho Park, "Legal Status of the Paracel and Spratly Islands," *Ocean Development and International Law*, No. 3 (1975), 19.

15. "Declaration on China's Territorial Sea," *Beijing Review*, No. 1 (9 September 1958), 21.

16. Ibid. A photographic image of this letter: http://en.wikipedia.org/wiki/File:1958_diplomatic_note_from_phamvandong_to_zhouenlai.jpg [Accessed on 11 January 2012].

17. "China's Indisputable Sovereignty Over the Xisha and Nansha islands," *Beijing Review*, No. 23 (18 February 1980), 21.

18. 杨志本 [Yang Zhiben, ed.], 中国海军百科全书 [China Navy Encyclopedia], Vol. 2 (Beijing: 海潮出版社 [Sea Tide Press], 1998), 1,747.

19. Vu Duc Vuong, "Between a Sea and a Hard Rock," *Asian Week*, 8 January 2008.

20. Brian McCartan, "Roiling the Waters in the Spratlys," *Asia Sentinel*, 4 February 2008.

21. Peter Kien-hong Yu, *The Four Archipelagoes in the South China Sea* (Taipei: Council for Advanced Policy Studies, 1991), 10-18.

22. R. Haller-Trost, *Occasional Paper No. 14—The Spratly Islands: A Study on the Limitations of International Law* (Canterbury: University of Kent Centre of South-East Asian Studies, 1990), 61.

23. "Taiwan investment in China Rises Sharply in 2010," *The Strait Times*, 31 December 2010.

24. Jim Bussert and Bruce A. Elleman, *People's Liberation Army Navy (PLAN) Combat Systems Technology 1949-2010* (Annapolis, MD: Naval Institute Press, 2011), 140-151.

25. Kristen Nordhaug, "Taiwan and the South China Sea Conflict: the 'China Connection' Revisited," http://www.southchinasea.org/docs/Nordhaug.pdf; Mark Valencia, personal communication with the author, 29 March 1999.

26. Jacques deLisle, "Taiwan under President Ma Ying-jeou," June 2008 http://www.fpri.org/enotes/200806.delisle.taiwanmayingjeou.html [Accessed on 27 October 2011].

27. For a copy of a map showing the ROC claims, see http://en.wikipedia.org/wiki/File:ROC_Administrative_and_Claims.svg [Accessed on 9 April 2012].

28. "Zhonghua guochi ditu, zaiban" ("Map of China's National Humiliation, Reprint") (Shanghai:Zhonghua Shuju, 1927); reprinted with permission from William A. Callahan, "The Cartography of National Humiliation and the Emergence of China's Geobody," in *Public Culture*, Vol. 21, No. 1 (2009), 154-155.

29. Jane Perlez, "Beijing Exhibiting New Assertiveness in South China Sea," *New York Times*, 31 May 2012.

30. David Petina, "Unified Germany: Friend or Foe?" *Res Publica*, Vol. 2, No. 1 (January 1991), http://www.ashbrook.org/publicat/respub/v2n1/petina1.html [Accessed on 27 October 2011].

31. Mark J. Valencia, "Tension Increasing In South China Sea," *Honolulu Advertiser*, 5 April 2001.

Map 19: Tajikistan's Border with China

19

Tajikistan-China Border Normalization

Gregory Gleason

When the Tajikistan legislature in January 2011 ratified an agreement with China concerning the roughly 250 mile (400 km) border separating the two states in the heart of Asia it brought an end to more than a decade of negotiation and well over a century of dispute. The normalization of the Tajik-China border in 1999 specified that Tajikistan cede to China 77 square miles (200 km^2) of territory, and in 2002 a second agreement increased this to 433 square miles (1,122 km^2) of the country's most remote and underdeveloped region in the Pamir mountains. Tajikistan's chief negotiator, Foreign Minister Hamrokhon Zarifi, heralded it as a great success, explaining that it was far less territory (only about 5 percent) than the 10,811 square miles (28,000 km^2) that had previously been in dispute.[1] The Tajikistan government's political opponents saw it differently, since this equaled .78 percent of Tajikistan's entire territory of 55,212 square miles (143,100 km^2). A major Tajik opposition leader challenged that abandoning "Tajik land" violated the country's constitution.[2]

The "disputed territory" dates back to Tsarist Russia's expansion into Central Asia. In recent years, this issue became a continual irritant in Sino-Tajik diplomatic relations. Beginning in 1987, bilateral talks to solve these tensions began, with a final ratification 24 years later in January 2011. Territory is always important to a nation-state, regardless of whether it is unitary or federal, multi-ethnic or mono-ethnic, large or small.[3] But the land in question in the Tajik-China case was not hotly contested. It concerns a remote and sparsely populated region, not a vital portion of Tajik territory. Nor is it inherently an important area for strategic or commercial purposes for China.

The Tajik Ministry of Foreign Affairs submitted the agreement to the lower house of the country's parliament, but there was no serious deliberation over the outcome. Approval was a foregone conclusion. Similarly, Chinese negotiators were confident of the outcome long before the public announcements were made. China's media reports of the penultimate rounds of diplomatic negotiations in April and November 2010 did not even bother to mention the border issue, simply underscoring that the Tajik partners pledged to combat the "three evils"—separatism, extremism and terrorism.[4] Chinese media did, however, explicitly make reference to the "longstanding border dispute" as resolved once the Tajik parliament ratified the agreement.

Tajikistan plays a critically important role for China's relations with Central Asia in general. Tajikistan has a long history of being seen as having "pivotal" importance, since it occupies Central Asia's "high ground." Tajikistan has also historically been at the epicenter of 19th-century competition over Asian "heartlands." It has continued to play an important role in the foreign policy calculations of Russia, the U.S., and the European Union.[5] Western military engagement in Afghanistan following September 11, 2001, greatly magnified Tajikistan's importance in the foreign policy calculations of certain states, especially given Tajikistan's territorial position and the large and influential ethnic Tajik population in Afghanistan.

The Tajik-China Border

The border between Tajikistan and China separates an Autonomous Province in Tajikistan from an Autonomous County and an Autonomous Province in China. Tajikistan is a small, impoverished country adjoining one of the most sparsely populated regions of China. The Tajikistan population, as estimated by the Population Reference Bureau, in mid-2010 was 7,600,000. The World Bank estimated the adjusted (Atlas method) per capita income in Tajikistan as $700 in 2010.[6] Tajikistan has a total area of 55,212 square miles (143,000 km^2), but its rugged, mountainous terrain leaves only about 7 percent of its territory suitable for agriculture. While it potentially has great mineral resource reserves, Tajikistan's landlocked position and lack of effective transportation networks hinder economic development. Problems of public administration, governance, and civil rights slow the country's political and social development. Tajikistan is bordered to the north and west by Kyrgyzstan and Uzbekistan and on the south by Afghanistan. Tajikistan had no foreign partners prepared to argue or negotiate on its behalf in this highly contentious border dispute with China.

By contrast, China is divided into twenty-two provinces and five autonomous regions. The Xinjiang Uyghur Autonomous Region (XUAR) is the largest of China's administrative divisions, which forms China's western border with the Central Asian states of Kazakhstan, Kyrgyzstan, and Tajikistan. To the north, the XUAR shares an external border with Russia and to the south the XUAR shares external borders with Afghanistan and Pakistan. The XUAR is further divided into seven prefectures and five autonomous prefectures. Tajikistan shares a border with the Akto County of the Kizilsu Kyrgyz Autonomous Prefecture in the northern portion and, in the southern portion, with the Taxkorgan (Tashkurgan) Tajik Autonomous County of the Kashi (Kashgar) Prefecture. The Kizilsu Kyrgyz

Autonomous Prefecture is sparsely populated, mainly by Uyghur speakers. The Taxkorgan Autonomous County is also sparsely populated, but mainly by Tajik speakers.

Tajikistan's eastern border with China is all within the Kuhistoni-Badakshan— also known as Gorno-Badakshan Autonomous Province—which is large but remote and sparsely populated. Kuhistoni-Badakshan occupies nearly 45 percent of Tajikistan's land area, but only accounts for about 4 percent of the country's population. Khurough, the capital, is located in the west, and its other major city is Murghob. The disputed territory with China in this region is basically unpopulated. It has no major towns or population centers. However, it could have strategic value, in particular if it gives China control over the highest points on the Pamir mountains.

During the 19th-century territorial competition between Russia and China, boundary divisions in remote and sparsely populated regions tended to be associated with an area's drainage divide or to control strategic mountain passes. Eastern Turkestan came under the control of the Qing dynasty in the mid-18th century, but Russian advances into Central Asia accelerated during the mid-19th century. The British and the Russian empires met in Central Asia, and the great powers clashed in what is referred to as the "Great Game."[7]

As Russian territorial expansion into Central Asia increased from the north, British expansion responded from the south. Russia and China disagreed over the western border of Eastern Turkestan, but at the same time Russia and Britain were competing over the border between their mutual spheres of influence. Russian diplomats negotiated a frontier between the British and Russian spheres along what is today the northern border of Afghanistan. At the same time, Britain accepted the Pamir region's eastern boundary at the Sarikol divide. In this way, present day Badakshan, now in Tajikistan, fell to Russian control rather than to Chinese, even though China was not a party to the Anglo-Russian agreement of 1895. As a result, China has considered the agreement that is the foundation for the southern Xinjiang boundary to be an "unequal treaty."[8]

In Russia's Treaty of Beijing in 1860 the two sides resolved the delineation of mid-Asia's border mainly according to the water divide principle. In diplomatic theory a continental divide may seem to be easily associated with an international boundary line. But in practice, rugged and serrated mountain ranges with crisscrossing valleys and meandering ridges do not lend themselves to easy territorial divisions between countries. The disputed territory lies along the Sarikol ridge within the Pamir Knot, the intersection of several radiating mountain ranges including the Hindu Kush, the Karakoram Range, the Kunlun mountains, and the Tien Shan. The eastern slope of the Pamir mountain range generally supplies snowmelt and runoff that feeds into the east-flowing into the Tarim River of the Taklamakan desert basin. Southwest sloping valleys flow into the west-flowing Pyandzh River.

The physical geography of this region of the world is an important framework for relationships. Political relations are equally important. In addition to its highly sensitive relations with China, Tajikistan has very distinct political relationships within the region, most importantly with its neighbor Uzbekistan, with Afghanistan, and also with Iran.

Tajikistan's Foreign Policy: Four Points of the Compass

Tajikistan, in a manner that is similar to all the countries of Central Asia, pursues what is viewed as a "multi-vector" foreign policy. The goal of a multi-vector foreign policy is to maintain independence when interacting with multiple and often more powerful neighbors and foreign influences. In the words of the Tajik Minister of Foreign Affairs Hamrokhon Zarifi, "energy independence and releasing the country from communication isolation is a vital necessity for Tajikistan."[9] The essence of Tajikistan's multi-vectoral policy is to leverage the weight and influence of others for the purposes of the country's goals. In Tajikistan's foreign policies there are four distinct dimensions to external relations. Besides the PRC, these other dimensions concern: 1) Uzbekistan; 2) the complex Afghanistan situation; and 3) Iran.

The Uzbekistan-Tajikistan relationship is the defining framework of Tajikistan's foreign policies, influencing every one of its foreign connections. The large Tajik-speaking population currently residing in Uzbekistan is testimony to the reality that Persian-speaking peoples in ages past were spread throughout the larger Central Asian region. When the borders of the Soviet constituent republics were created in Central Asia beginning in 1924, they were basically open among the republics and the peoples were not divided by administrative separations.

However, after the collapse of the USSR in 1991, the borders increasingly became separators rather than connectors; during the 1990s, the political and economic competition among the Central Asian states has progressively led to the tightening of border constraints on cross-border transit and trade. The border between Uzbekistan and Tajikistan grew to be the most problematic in Central Asia, cutting off trade and communication. Many commercial organizations in both Uzbekistan and Tajikistan were prevented from enjoying the most basic trade relationships. Closed borders divided many extended families residing in the two countries. The Uzbek-Tajik relationship has been so troubled that Uzbekistan, given its physical location and the lie of the land in Central Asia giving it control over virtually all rail, freight, and traffic into and out of Tajikistan, has allowed Uzbekistan to block Tajikistan's connections with the west and north.

Tajikistan has a distinct set of foreign policy relationships with respect to its southern neighbor, Afghanistan. The Tajikistan's "southern connection" includes the complex of relationships that have emerged from the travail of Afghanistan's instability and war. The Afghanistan situation played an especially important role between Tajikistan and Uzbekistan. A large and politically influential Persian-speaking (Dari) population in the northern and eastern regions of Afghanistan formed a natural linkage with Tajikistan. The Afghanistan-Tajikistan relationship further acted as a corridor for the infiltration of criminal and terrorist influences into Central Asia and into Uzbekistan during the 1990s.

Uzbekistan's counter-insurgency efforts were specifically focused on opposing what it viewed as Tajikistan's toleration if not promotion of the insurgent efforts of the "Islamic Movement of Uzbekistan" and other al-Qaeda-affiliated political extremist movements dedicated to overthrowing the government of Islam Karimov in Uzbekistan. But Tajikistan's relations with Afghanistan involved a much more complex set of relationships throughout the region, including the shifting political influences within Afghanistan and also the outside influences of Russia during the early 1990s and, increasingly during the mid-1990s, the rise of Taliban control in Afghanistan.

After the events of September 11, 2001 and the beginning of the U.S. military operations (Operation Enduring Freedom) to eliminate international terrorist threats emanating from Afghanistan and then sweep the Taliban government from power for harboring and protecting international terrorists, the situation in Afghanistan changed dramatically. The growing role of multinational forces in Afghanistan after the 2003 assumption of military responsibilities by the NATO-led military consortium, the International Security Assistance Forces (ISAF), brought greater international attention to the Afghanistan stabilization, normalization, and reconstruction efforts.

Reconstruction requires regional cooperation, including a stable and secure physical infrastructure throughout the region based on transport, communication, and energy relations. Rapidly growing demand for energy in Pakistan and India offer a greater opportunity for Tajikistan's substantial, albeit unrealized hydroelectric power potential, if only electricity markets could be linked to Tajikistan hydroelectric stations. Afghanistan and Pakistan are natural conduits for Tajikistan's links to the south. But this also involved an increased array of foreign actors, particularly Russia and Turkey, acting as brokers of an anticipated post-conflict political equilibrium in Afghanistan. Tajikistan, as one of the "front-line" states, was seen by all foreign powers as playing a crucial role in this political equilibrium.

Relations with Iran also constitute a major vector of Tajikistan's foreign policy. Tajikistan is primarily a Persian-speaking country with deep historical roots in Persian culture and tradition. While the Tajik language is somewhat different from modern day Farsi spoken in Iran, day-to-day interaction between Iranians and Tajiks is relatively easy. Day-to-day interaction between Tajikistan and Iran on diplomatic, trade, and cultural levels is by far the easiest for Tajik diplomats, businessmen, and individuals.

But Iran's relationship with Tajikistan is complicated by its physical distance from Tajikistan and by the isolated role Iran plays in the international diplomatic and business communities. Teheran has been subject for two decades to international sanctions because of its state support of terrorist organizations. More recently, Iran has become subject to UN Security Council sanctions because of its government's intransigence regarding compliance with International Atomic Energy Agency (IAEA) demands that it submit to oversight of its uranium enrichment facilities.

Despite Iran's international reputation as a pariah state, Tajik diplomats and businessmen typically welcome their Iranian counterparts as brethren. But there is yet another level of complication in this relationship. The attitude that emerges from Teheran frequently is that the Persian-speaking populations beyond the borders of present-day Iran are external appendages of Persian culture and thus part of "Greater Persia." The perspective from Dushanbe is somewhat different. Tajik diplomats rankle at the suggestion that Dushanbe represents the "younger brother" of Teheran.

Tajikistan's border disputes with its large eastern neighbor, China, have necessarily been framed in the context of these relations with the west, north, and south. Tajikistan throughout its history has been protected from Chinese influence by its geographical location. Close, intimate relations with China have never previously been established by Tajikistan. Prior to the collapse of the USSR, there was no substantial Chinese population in Tajikistan and no natural population that would lobby for Chinese interests. This situation has now changed, and Tajikistan is no longer isolated.

Resolving China's Western Border

The peoples of the Central Asian highlands historically enjoyed elastic conceptions of territoriality. Influenced by transhumance practices of seasonal movement of people with their livestock over relatively short distances for seasonal pasturage, the Central Asian peoples were dispersed by linguistic and ethnic groups throughout the region. West Asian political borders, consequently, tended to be defined principally in relation to the expansion and contraction of external political influences in the region.[10] During the Soviet period, differences emerged between the USSR and China over the legacy of the previous "imperialist" conceptions. China took the position that with respect to the Sarikol divide, the Sino-Soviet border was not legitimate.[11] The USSR and China carried out military fortification of their borders until, by the early 1980s, the Sino-Soviet border grew to be one of the most heavily militarized borders in the world.[12]

The tide turned with the Mikhail Gorbachev, who tried to improve Sino-Soviet diplomatic relations. By the late 1980s, negotiations between China and the USSR were devoted to de-militarizing border areas. Following the disintegration of the USSR in 1991, China initiated an effort among Russia, Kazakhstan, Kyrgyzstan, and Tajikistan to re-open talks on the border issues. In January 1996, the five border countries exchanged topographical maps, a first step in agreement on actual demarcation of the boundaries.[13] On 26 April 1996, the presidents of the five border countries met in Shanghai to sign a package of agreements on border issues. The "Shanghai Accord" constituted a breakthrough in establishing a framework for border normalization in the west Asian region.[14]

Negotiations continued on both multilateral and bilateral bases with the Shanghai Accord countries, with notable progress in Kyrgyzstan and Kazakhstan. The Tajikistan civil war (1992-1997) disrupted normal diplomatic relations. After the war the Tajik government made a turn to the East, emphasizing eastern connections by road to develop an alternative route that could link Murgab in Badakshan with Taxkorgan in westernmost China.[15] Tajikistan President Emomali Rahmon called for opening a customs point in the far eastern part of Tajikistan.[16]

During August 1999, President Rahmon and Chinese President Jiang Zemin signed an agreement on the demarcation of one section of their disputed common border, but did not resolve Chinese territorial claims on parts of Tajikistan's Gorno-Badashkhan Autonomous Oblast.[17] However, on 17 May 2002, Jiang Zemin and Tajikistan's new president Emomali Rahmon co-signed the "Complementary Agreement between the People's Republic of China and the Republic of Tajikistan on the China-Tajikistan Boundary." This was one of the first of what soon became a spate of border agreements that emerged in 2002, following the implementation of the directives of the Central Committee policy of "Neighboring Friendliness and Stability."[18]

As mentioned above, Tajikistan agreed to hand over about 433 square miles (1,122 km^2) of the country's territory, while retaining 10,378 square miles (27,000 km^2) of the disputed lands. Critics point out, however, that the land that was transferred to China is .78 percent of Tajikistan's entire territory, as compared to what Beijing gave up equaling only about .28 percent of China's territory; in percentage terms, therefore, Tajikistan lost almost three times more than China. The Tajikistan parliament implemented this agreement during January 2011 only after more than a decade of debate and discussion.

Conclusions

Tajikistan is important for China, not so much because of the relatively minor addition to the PRC's western border, but because of China's rapidly and significantly extended influence beyond the border. From the Chinese side, the role of the XUAR was partly economic and partly political. China's interaction with the former Soviet countries in Central Asia was to a large extent shaped by preventative security toward internal threats. As one observer has claimed: "The territorial concessions it [China] made to Kazakhstan, Kyrgyzstan, and Tajikistan in order to reach border agreements with them was prompted by a sharp surge in separatist violence in Xinjiang province in the early 1990s."[19] Over the past decade the XUAR grew to play an equally important parallel role as a pathway to the minerals and markets of Eurasia.

It could be argued that the PRC had little choice but to negotiate with Tajikistan. During the mid-1990s, imbalances in the Chinese economy grew more apparent, when the PRC for the first time became a net importer of energy resources. This led to a realization that to sustain its former high growth rates China would require a reliable source of minerals and energy. Beijing began to see the XUAR as a province that could provide this.[20] This gave rise to China's "Go West" strategy announced in June 1999 to spur development of the country's central and western regions. This strategy made possible a gradual rise in China's efforts to promote its commercial interests in Tajikistan and other Central Asian countries.[21]

The negotiation of the Sino-Tajik border agreement was trumpeted as a breakthrough. In fact, the annexation of additional territory to China's westernmost Autonomous Prefecture was mainly symbolic. No population dislocation took place; No distinctly valuable natural resources were transferred; No critical thoroughfares changed hands; No strategic advantages were exchanged. Negotiation over control of the territory in this case was mainly *pro forma*, quite different from the contentious diplomacy over China's more consequential border disputes.[22] More importantly, the negotiations were asymmetrical, since tiny Tajikistan was an "uneven partner" for territorial negotiations with giant China. However, in recent years what began as a gradually increasing stream of bilateral projects, investment, and expertise has turned into a virtual torrent. If current trends continue, the resolution of the Tajik-China border will prove to be of comparatively small significance in comparison with the ever-growing importance of Chinese political and economic influence. For better or worse, Tajikistan's "isolation" from East Asia would appear to be at an end.

Notes

1. Roman Kozhevnikov, "Tajikistan says ends century-old China Border Row," Reuters, 12 January 2011.

2. Muhiddin Kabiri, the head of the Islamic Revival Party (IRPT) as quoted in Alexander Sodiqov, "Tajikistan Cedes Disputed Land to China," *Eurasia Daily Monitor*, Vol. 8, No. 16 (24 January 2011).

3. Conventional international relations theory emphasizes state power and associates influence with the control of territory. The rise of influence is often expressed most directly by the extension of influence beyond the state's borders. Economic development makes possible the growth of military capacity, particularly beyond the state's borders. The rise of state influence, in one form or another, is often associated with expansionist tendencies which are, in turn, often expressed in terms of territorial expansion and, accordingly, with territorial disputes. See for instance Nazli Choucri and Robert C. North, *Nations in Conflict: National Growth and International Violence* (San Francisco: W.H. Freeman, 1975); Robert Gilpin, *War and Change in World Politics* (New York: Cambridge University Press, 1981); John J. Mearsheimer, *The Tragedy of Great Power Politics* (New York: W.W. Norton. 2003).

4. News media announcements detailed the meetings and noted the Tajik Foreign Minister's commitment to crackdown on "Eastern Turkistan" forces, but made no mention regarding the territorial agreement. See the report "Chinese Vice President vows to boost ties with Tajikistan," 29 April 2010, http://au.china-embassy.org/eng/xw/t688557.htm [Accessed on 31 October 2011].
Also see the 26 November 2010 report "China, Tajikistan Sign Joint Communiqué to Promote Ties, Cooperation": "As the three evil forces of terrorism, separatism and extremism are posing grave threats to regional peace and stability, China and Tajikistan will further their coordination and cooperation, take forceful measures within the framework of the SCO, jointly combat terrorism in all forms including the "East Turkistan" terrorist forces, in a bid to guarantee the peace and tranquility in the two countries and in the region at large," http://english.people daily.com.cn/90001/90776/90883/7211643.html [Accessed on 31 October 2011]. Also "Chinese Vice President vows to boost ties with Tajikistan," 29 April 2010, http://au.china-embassy.org/eng/xw/t688557.htm [Accessed on 31 October 2011].

5. Regarding Russia's policy, see Gregory Gleason, "Why Russia Is in Tajikistan," *Comparative Strategy*, Vol. 20, No. 1 (2001): 77-89. For a survey of U.S. policy, see Jim Nichol, "Tajikistan: Recent Developments and U.S. Interests." CRS Report for Congress, Congressional Research Service # 98-594 (10 February 2011).

6. World Bank webpage country data, Tajikistan, http://data.worldbank.org/country/tajikistan [Accessed 20 April 2011].

7. The name for the Central Asian competition has been attributed to Arthur Conolly (1807-1842), an intelligence officer of the British East India Company's Sixth Bengal Light Cavalry. However, this idea was first introduced into mainstream consciousness by British novelist Rudyard Kipling in his novel *Kim* (1901). Peter Hopkirk, *The Great Game: The Struggle for Empire in Central Asia* (New York: Kodansha International, 1992); Patrick French, *Younghusband: The Last Great Imperial Adventurer* (London: HarperCollins, 1994); Parshotam Mehra, *The Younghusband Expedition* (New York: Asia Publishing House, 1968); Karl E. Meyer and Shareen Blair Brysac, *Tournament of Shadows: The Great Game and the Race for Empire in Central Asia* (Washington, DC: Counterpoint, 1999).

8. Ying Cheng Kiang, *China's Boundaries* (Chicago: Institute of Chinese Studies, 1984). Also see Owen Lattimore, *Pivot of Asia: Sinkiang and the Inner Asian Frontiers of China and Russia* (Boston: Little, Brown, 1950).

9. Hamrokhon Zarifi's widely circulated address, "The Message from the Roof of the World," http://www.neurope.eu/articles/The-Message-from-the-Roof-of-the-World/104018.php [Accessed on], http://www.botschaft-tadschikistan.de/PDF/makolai%20Sarifi%20dar%20New%20Europe%20ENG.pdf

10. Lattimore, 32.

11. Alexei D. Voskressenski, *The Difficult Border: Current Russian and Chinese Concepts of Sino-Russian Relations and Frontier Problems* (Commack, NY: Nova Science Publishers, 1996).

12. Jing-dong Yuan, "Sino-Russian Confidence-Building Measures: A Preliminary Analysis," *Asian Perspective*, Vol. 22, No. 1 (1998), 75.

13. Xinhua News Agency, 12 January 1996.

14. Gregory Gleason, "Policy Dimensions of West Asian Borders." *Asian Perspective*, Vol. 25, No. 1 (2001): 107-131.

15. The road leads east from Murgab over the Kulma Pass (4362 meters) into the PRC to connect with the north-south running Karakoram Highway. From Taxkorgan, China the road leads south for 120 kilometers to the border with Pakistan. The road then turns west, climbing over the ridge above the Yorkant River and leads through the Khunjerab Pass at the Pakistan frontier before turning south 300 kilometers through the mountains to Abbotabad and then Rawalpindi. From Rawalpindi, a well-developed road and railroad network leads to the ocean port of Karachi.

16. Tajik Radio, Dushanbe, 18 February 1997.

17. *China Daily*, 14 August 1999.

18. China's Ministry of Foreign Affairs "China's Territorial and Boundary Affairs," http://www.mfa.gov.cn/eng/wjb/zzjg/tyfls/tyfl/2626/t22820.htm [Accessed on 20 April 2011].

19. Sudha Ramachandran, "China Plays Long Game on Border Disputes," *Asia Times* (27 January 2011), http://www.atimes.com/atimes/China/MA2702.html [Accessed on 31 October 2011].

20. Felix K. Chang, "China's Central Asian Power and Problems," *Orbis*, Vol. 41, No. 3 (1997), 403.

21. "China Unveils 225 Western Development Projects," *People's Daily,* 23 June 2000.

22. M. Taylor Fravel, *Strong Borders, Strong Borders, Secure Nation: Cooperation and Conflict in China's Territorial Disputes* (Princeton University Press, 2008).

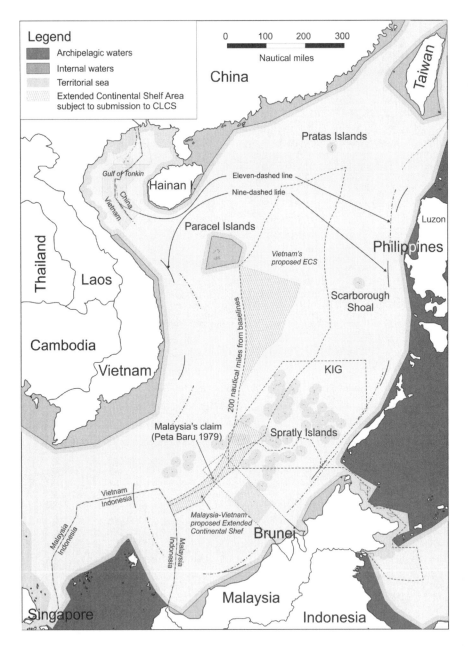

Map 20.1: Competing Maritime Claims in the South China Sea

20
Sino-Vietnamese Border Disputes

Ramses Amer

This chapter on the Sino-Vietnamese border disputes deals with events since 1975 with a special focus on developments since full normalization of bilateral relations in late 1991.[1] The Sino-Vietnamese border disputes encompass both land and maritime issues. The major land dispute along the two countries' 840 mile (1,350 km) long border encompassed approximately 88 square miles (227 km^2) of territory. In 1999, the two countries agreed to split these areas, with Vietnam receiving just under 44 square miles (113 km^2) and the PRC just over 44 square miles (114 km^2).

The maritime disputes encompass or, where resolved, encompassed both maritime areas in the Gulf of Tonkin (Beibu Gulf to China and Bac Bo Gulf to Vietnam) and competing sovereignty claims over the Paracel and Spratly archipelagos. While an agreement dividing the Gulf of Tonkin was reached, the disputes related to the South China Sea proper remained unresolved. Furthermore, China's claim within the so-called nine-dashed lines in the South China Sea overlap with Vietnam's claims to exclusive economic zone (EEZ) and continental shelf areas to the east of Vietnam's coastline.

The disputes in the South China Sea have caused periodic increases in the level of tension, as exemplified in late May and early June 2011 when Vietnam's exploration activities and China's action against these activities prompted accusations and counter-accusations. The two sides have also devoted considerable energy to managing tensions and to seek ways to settle their disputes. The most recent examples are the "Agreement on basic principles guiding the settlement of sea-related issues," signed in Beijing on 11 October 2011, and the Joint Statement, issued in connection with the most recent high-level summit between the two countries in October 2011.

Sino-Vietnamese Border Disputes 1975 to 1991

Following the end of the war in Vietnam in late April 1975, and the formal unification of North and South Vietnam on 2 July 1976, relations between China and Vietnam went through dramatic changes, from seemingly normal relations in the mid-1970s to outright war in early 1979.[2] The boundary disputes between the two countries along their mutual land border, in the Gulf of Tonkin, and in the South China Sea caused tensions. In particular, the disputes in the South China Sea and in the Tonkin Gulf contributed to the deterioration of bilateral relations by adding yet another contentious issue to the growing rift between the two sides. In many ways these border conflicts reflected divergent policies with regard to other Cold War issues, such as their security connections with the USSR, and of the overall deterioration of Communist relations in the post-1975 period.[3]

Relations between the PRC and the recently unified Vietnam had been soured by China's 19 January 1974 attack against South Vietnamese forces stationed on the Paracel islands. Called a "counterattack" in the Chinese sources, this date was in fact the 24th anniversary of Beijing's recognition of Hanoi. When Hanoi disputed China's claim to the Paracels, Beijing reminded them of a 14 September 1958 note from North Vietnamese Premier Pham Van Dong that appeared to support PRC sovereignty. The Sino-Vietnamese territorial dispute over the Paracels became increasingly bitter during the late 1970s, and helped push Hanoi closer to Moscow.[4]

The overall deterioration of Sino-Vietnamese relations led to a militarized conflict that escalated into the PRC's attack on Vietnam in February-March 1979. China's announcement on 5 March 1979, the 26th anniversary of Stalin's death, that it would withdraw from Vietnam, was followed by attempts at negotiations between China and Vietnam from April 1979 through March 1980. However, the two parties did not manage to reach an understanding. Bilateral relations remained tense during these talks and for most of the 1980s. Frictions were most visible along the common border, with mutual accusations about military incursions.

Prior to 1988, the PRC had never established a permanent base in the Spratlys. Early during that year, Chinese forces began to build what was called an "oceanic observation station" on Fiery Cross Reef (Yungshujiao), located near the middle of the Spratly islands. During March 1988, Chinese personnel also landed on Johnson Reef, approximately 80 nm to the east. At this point, Chinese naval forces clashed with Vietnamese naval vessels supplying their outposts in the Spratlys, resulting in the destruction of one Vietnamese ship and damage to two others, with 75 Vietnamese reported killed or missing.[5] The PRC has subsequently managed to gain control over a number of small features in the archipelago and currently controls ten features while Vietnam has likewise moved to expand the number of features under its control in the Spratlys to over twenty.

The normalization process between the PRC and Vietnam began with low-level contacts in the mid-1980s, expanded to high-level meetings from early 1989, and became even more pronounced with the fall of the Berlin Wall and the end of the Cold War. In early September 1990 a high-level—at that point secret—meeting was held in China. In mid-1991 the process gained momentum and the increased diplomatic interaction paved the way for a high-level summit on 5-10 November 1991 during which bilateral relations were fully normalized.[6]

During this initial process, the most important border disputes remained unresolved. If a resolution of the border disputes had been a precondition for full normalization of bilateral relations then the latter would not have been possible in 1991. Only by putting the border disputes to one side, and aiming for a resolution in the longer-term perspective, was full Sino-Vietnamese normalization made a reality in 1991.[7] Following the normalization of diplomatic relations, discussions were opened to try to solve all outstanding disputes relating to both land and maritime disputes.

The Border Issues since Full Normalization of Relations in Late 1991

Tension in Sino-Vietnamese bilateral relations has primarily been caused by differences relating to border disputes.[8] Sharp differences relating to all of the border disputes—to areas along the land border, overlapping claims to the Paracel and Spratly islands, and to water and continental shelf areas in the South China Sea and in the Gulf of Tonkin—were prevalent from May-November 1992. Differences relating to oil exploration in the South China Sea and the signing of contracts with foreign companies for exploration became more pronounced during the periods April-June 1994, April-May 1996, and March-April 1997.

In order to manage their land border disputes, China and Vietnam have initiated a system of talks and discussions that are both highly structured and extensive. From bottom to top it looked as follows: expert-level talks; government-level talks, that is Deputy/Vice-Minister; Foreign Minister-level talks; and, high-level talks, that is Presidents, Prime Ministers, and Secretary-Generals of the respective parties.

The talks at the expert- and government-levels deserve special attention. Talks at the expert-level were initiated in October 1992. Through late 1995, they focused on the land border and the Gulf of Tonkin issues, respectively. The talks at the government-level began in August 1993 and the 13th round was held in January 2007. Since then additional meetings have been held, with the most recent taking place in April 2011.[9]

The first achievement was the signing of an agreement on 19 October 1993 on the principles for handling the land border and Gulf of Tonkin disputes. It was further agreed to set up joint working groups at the expert-level to deal with the two issues, and sixteen rounds of talks were held from February 1994 through December 1999.

Similarly, the joint working group on the Gulf of Tonkin met seventeen times from March 1994 through until December 2000. Talks at the expert-level on the disputes in the South China Sea proper, the so-called "sea issues," were initiated in November 1995 and the 11th round of talks was held in July 2006.

In 1998, there were frictions in January along the land border, and in the South China Sea in April, May, July, and September, amid ongoing negotiations. In 1999, however, the two sides focused on reaching a settlement of the land border dispute and this resulted in the signing of a Land Border Treaty on 30 December 1999. In 2000, the main focus was on settling to Gulf of Tonkin disputes. This resulted in the signing of an Agreement on the Delimitation of Waters, EEZ and Continental Shelves in the Gulf of Tonkin (Delimitation Agreement) on 25 December 2000.

The negotiation process resulting in the signing of Land Border Treaty reflected the substantially higher degree of progress made in negotiations on the land border as compared with talks on maritime border disputes up to the end of 1999. In 2000, the negotiations on the Gulf of Tonkin issue were stepped up with a view of reaching an agreement within that year. This goal was reached on 25 December 2000. Thus, the deadlines for resolving the land border and the Gulf of Tonkin issues were both met in 1999 and 2000, respectively.

Far less progress has been achieved with regard to the disputes in the South China Sea proper, including resolving competing sovereignty claims to the Paracel and Spratly islands, as well as the overlapping claims to waters and continental shelf areas to the east of the Vietnamese coast. Talks have been initiated, but the parties have yet to agree on which disputes to include on the agenda. Vietnam wants to include the Paracel dispute alongside that of the Spratlys. China does not want to discuss sovereignty over the Paracels on the grounds that there is no dispute to discuss, a tactic that closely parallels Indonesia's reticence to open talks with China with respect to waters associated with the Natuna islands. To further complicate matters, China views the disputes over water and continental shelf areas immediately to the east of mainland Vietnam as part of the Spratly dispute whereas Vietnam views them as separate. It appears that Vietnam does not want to initiate talks relating to those areas since it might be interpreted as giving legitimacy to China's claims within the so-called nine dashed lines.

Thus, of the three South China Sea issues to be addressed by the two countries there is only agreement on putting one on the agenda for talks, namely sovereignty over the Spratly archipelago, which is a multilateral conflict situation involving other claimants, including Brunei, Malaysia, the Philippines, and Taiwan. Despite these differences, the two sides managed to sign an "Agreement on basic principles guiding the settlement of sea-related issues" in Beijing on 11 October 2011.[10]

Map 20.2: Vietnam's Land Border with China

The Land Border Treaty of 1999

The Land Border Treaty was the first major achievement in the overall process of managing and eventually resolving the land border dispute between China and Vietnam (see Map 20.2). The negotiation process included regular talks of the joint working group on the land border through 1998. During 1999, the joint working group on the land border met on four occasions, that is four rounds of talks, and the duration of each round was no shorter than two weeks on any of these occasions. This increase in the number and in the duration of the discussions can be attributed to the political pressure to reach a common understanding and to provide political leaders with the basis on which to sign a treaty relating to the land border issue.

Reaching an agreement was by no means a simple task, especially given the geographical characteristics of the border areas that encompass both mountainous terrains, which are not easily accessible, and other parts are made up of rivers, which present their own sets of issues to be settled. Adding to the natural difficulties were the movements of border markers over the decades and activities carried out by the population and local authorities in the border area that had impinged on the borderline. Further, the military clashes along the border in the late 1970s and into the 1980s—in particular in connection with the Chinese attack on Vietnam in February-March 1979—had left some border areas still in dispute.

The Land Border Treaty was ratified in 2000. First, the Standing Committee of the National People's Congress in China ratified the treaty on 29 April and then Vietnam did likewise on 9 June, through a decision by the National Assembly. This was followed by the exchange of letters of ratification in Beijing. The Land Border Treaty took effect on 6 July 2000.

The demarcation process came next, as the two countries subsequently established a Joint Committee for the demarcation of the land border. It held its first meeting in Beijing between 19 November and 1 December 2000. It was determined that the Joint Committee would work on demarcating the border and with the planting of "landmarks." The demarcation process was initiated and the first "double markers" along the border were "planted" on 27 December 2001 and the first "single marker" was "planted" on 4 January 2003. This process was officially concluded at the end of 2008.[11]

Of considerable interest in the context of the Land Border Treaty is that during August 2002 Vietnam published the text of the treaty, although it did not include any of the accompanying maps.[12] In September 2002, one of Vietnam's vice-foreign ministers, Le Cong Phung, provided information about the treaty. He outlined the background to the negotiation process, the process itself, and the mechanisms and principles used in settling disputed areas along the border. The core disputed areas—referred to as "Areas C"—encompassed 164 areas covering 88 square miles (227 km^2). Of these areas, just under 44 square miles (113 km^2) were defined as belonging to Vietnam and just over 44 square miles (114 km^2) as belonging to China.[13] In addition, on 10 October 2006, China, Laos, and Vietnam signed a treaty defining the trijunction of their land boundaries.[14]

Discussion on Delimiting the Gulf of Tonkin

The process of delimiting the Gulf of Tonkin was similar to the land negotiations, with regular rounds of talks of the joint working group occurring on a yearly basis up to 1999.[15] The developments that took place during 2000 showed that an increase occurred with five rounds of expert-level talks held during that year, in March, May, June, September, late October-early November, and late November, respectively, as compared to only one round of talks during the whole of 1999. The Delimitation Agreement signed on 25 December 2000 differs from the Land Border Treaty in that it did stipulate the coordinates for the tracing of the maritime boundary between the two countries in the Gulf of Tonkin.[16]

The core issue to be settled in the Gulf of Tonkin dispute was which principle should be used in order to divide the gulf (see Map 20.3). In this context, the impact of islands was of crucial importance and in particular the Vietnamese island of Bach Long Vi. The first question was whether or not it was capable of generating an EEZ or continental shelf rights according to the provisions of the 1982 United Nations Convention on the Law of the Seas (UNCLOS). If this was the case, as argued by Vietnam, then not only would it be entitled to full maritime zones but, more importantly, it would have an impact on the construction of a line of equidistance if this principle was applied in the Gulf of Tonkin.

Logically, Vietnam took the position that Bach Long Vi Island should be fully included in any agreement on how to divide the Gulf. On the other hand, China had an interest in minimizing the impact that the island would have on any agreed delimitation. This could be done by either arguing that Bach Long Vi was not an island in accordance with the provisions of UNCLOS or by arguing that its impact should be minimized and possibly even be disregarded.[17] For China to argue that it was only a "rock" and so was incapable of generating EEZ and continental shelf claims would have been counterproductive, as China had earlier controlled the island and had claimed that the island was inhabited before it was handed-over to Vietnam in the late 1950s.[18] An analysis of the agreed boundary line show that Bach Long Vi was given only a reduced effect on the course of the delimitation process. Bach Long Vi was eventually given rights over 15 nm from the island. In terms of division of the whole Gulf of Tonkin, Vietnam obtained 53.23 percent while China obtained 46.77 percent.[19]

Another potentially complicating factor in the negotiations was the status of the Sino-French Agreement of 1887. Vietnam favored using it to delimit the Gulf of Tonkin, since it would generally be to its advantage. China opposed using this treaty and argued that the 1887 agreement was only intended to determine administrative control over the islands and did not apply either to the water or to the seabed in the gulf.[20] The compromise they reached suggests that, assuming the status of the Sino-French Agreement of 1887 was brought up during the negotiations, both sides eventually agreed that it would not have an impact on the delimitation of maritime zones in the Gulf of Tonkin.

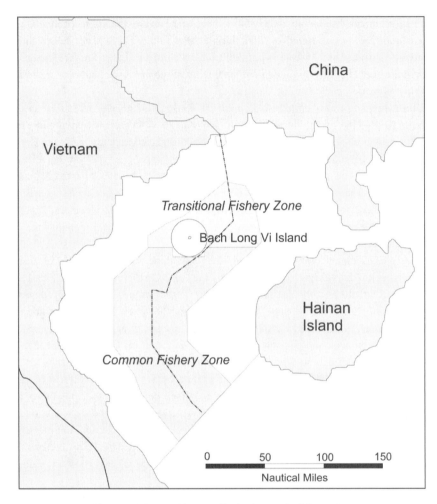

Map 20.3: Gulf of Tonkin Maritime Delimitation and Fishery Arrangements

The increased number or rounds of expert-level talks and indeed of government level talks in 2000 is evidence of the complexities involved in reaching a mutually acceptable compromise in order to sign the delimitation agreement by the end of 2000. Political pressure to reach an agreement before the end of the year did generate increased activity to reach this goal. The agreed coordinates indicate that the two sides ended up with an agreement on a line of equidistance, albeit modified, having sorted out their differences relating to the question of how islands should impact on the delimitation, in particular Bach Long Vi Island.

Although the issue of fishing in the Gulf of Tonkin is not directly linked to the question of border disputes, it is still relevant. The two countries held six rounds of talks between April-December 2000 on the issue of fishing. An Agreement on Fishing Cooperation in the Gulf of Tonkin (hereafter Fishing Agreement) signed on 25 December 2000 included regulations for the establishment of joint fishing areas, cooperation in preserving and "sustainably" exploiting the aquatic resources in the gulf, and regulations for furthering fishing cooperation and scientific research.[21]

In order for the two agreements to enter into force it was necessary to complete talks on a Supplementary Protocol to the Fishery Agreement. The agreement on the additional protocol was eventually signed in Beijing on 29 April 2004. This paved the way for the ratification of the Delimitation Agreement. It was ratified by the National Assembly of Vietnam on 15 June 2004 and by the 10th Standing Committee of the National People's Congress of China at its meeting held from 21 to 25 June 2004. Both the Delimitation Agreement and the Fishery Agreement entered into force on 30 June 2004.

The completion of the ratification process was followed by the initiation of expert-level talks on the delimitation of the area outside the entrance—also referred to as the "mouth"—of the Gulf of Tonkin. The first meeting of the expert-level working group was held in January 2006 in Hanoi. At the time of writing, the fifth, and most recent, meeting took place in Hanoi in January 2009. Thus far, the two sides have not reached an agreement on delimitation.

The South China Sea

If attention is turned to the situation in the South China Sea proper it should first be noted that talks were initiated at a later stage than on the land border and Gulf of Tonkin, respectively. Much still remains to be achieved before the disputes in the South China Sea can be resolved. In view of the reoccurring periods of friction relating to actions carried out in the South China Sea during the 1990s, the two parties need to strive for the establishment of mechanisms and principles regulating their behavior in the South China Sea that would prevent the reoccurrence of conflict. A closer look at this ongoing process is informative.

The initiation of expert-level talks in 1995 was the first obvious move toward an institutionalized form of conflict management of the Sino-Vietnamese disputes in the South China Sea. The noticeable shift in how to deal with actions taken by the other party came in relation to a dispute in May 1998 connected to the activities of a Chinese exploration ship in areas of the South China Sea claimed by Vietnam. This issue was settled without leading to the deep tensions that characterized an incident that was also caused by the activities of a Chinese exploration ships in March-April

1997.[22] Since public statements were fewer in connection with the May 1998 incident, it is difficult to assess fully how the more successful management of this incident was brought about. Obviously less public rhetoric and more restraint by the two parties were contributing factors.[23]

An additional observation that can be drawn from the developments in 1998 is that both China and Vietnam were more reluctant to engage in longer periods of accusations and counter-accusations in connection with incidents in the South China Sea that caused friction in bilateral relations. However, this did not imply that either side refrained from publicizing their discontent or from protesting against actions carried out by the other party. The difference in 1998 as compared to earlier years was that the official complaint or accusation was used on a limited number of occasions and then no further public statement on the incident in question was made. This prevented an escalation in accusations and counter-accusations from taking place and thus tension did not appear to have been as deep as for the 1997 incident.

The developments in 1999 were further indications of the progress made in the management of the disputes between the PRC and Vietnam in the South China Sea. The only public protest was made by Vietnam in late March in response to a Chinese decision to ban fishing temporarily in the South China Sea. This state of affairs could be explained in two ways. First, the two sides respected the status quo and refrained from actions that could have led to protest by the other side, and consequently there was virtually no friction. Second, actions were carried out which may have caused tensions, but both sides opted to deal with the incidents without resorting to public protest or criticism against the other side.

During 2000 no incidents relating to the South China Sea undermined bilateral relations. In fact, the two countries moved to put greater emphasis on conflict management in the South China Sea through continued talks, by exploring potential cooperation in certain fields, and by exercising mutual self-restraint. This was most evidently displayed in the Joint Statement for comprehensive cooperation signed on 25 December 2000 by the two Foreign Ministers. Section IX is devoted to the South China Sea and the two sides agreed to "maintain the existing negotiation mechanisms on marine issues and to persist in seeking a fundamental and everlasting solution acceptable to both sides through peaceful negotiations." Pending a permanent solution the two sides would actively explore possibilities of cooperating in "environmental protection, meteorology, hydrology, disaster prevention and mitigation." They agreed not to take "actions to complicate or aggravate disputes" and not to resort to force or its threat. Finally, they would consult each other in a timely manner if a dispute occurs and adopt a constructive attitude when handling disputes in order to prevent them from impeding the development of bilateral relations.[24]

During 2001-2008, limited friction was caused mainly by legislative decisions relating to the disputed archipelagos, to oil exploration and agreements, and to fishing bans.[25] At the multilateral level both countries are parties to the "Declaration on the conduct of parties in the South China Sea" (DOC) adopted by the member-states of the Association of Southeast Asian Nations (ASEAN) and China on 4 November 2002.[26] During the period 2009-2011 there have been periodic increases in the level of tensions. One reason was Vietnam's submissions to the Commission on the Limits of the Continental Shelf (CLCS) in May 2009—both individual and jointly with Malaysia—which prompted Chinese officials to protest and oppose the submissions. The period from June 2009 to September 2010 was also marked by several arrests of Vietnamese fishermen by China leading to Vietnamese protests.[27]

In response to the heightened tensions the two prime ministers held talks in Hanoi in late October 2010 and agreed to seek satisfactory solutions to existing issues relating to the South China Sea. The arrests of Vietnamese fishermen appear to have stopped. However, deep tension emerged again in late May and early June 2011 linked to Vietnam's exploration activities and China's action against these activities prompting accusations and counter-accusations.[28] Tension was eventually brought under control in late June.[29] Talks had earlier been initiated with the goal of agreeing on basic principles for the settlement of "sea-related issues," eventually this led to the signing of an "Agreement on basic principles guiding the settlement of sea-related issues" in Beijing on 11 October 2011.[30]

The signing took place in connection with the first high-level summit since October 2008, when the Secretary-General of the CPV, Nguyen Phu Trong, visited China for talks with his Chinese counterpart and other Chinese leaders. In the Joint Statement issued in connection with the summit both sides stated their "political will and determination to settle disputes via friendship negotiation and talks in order to maintain peace and stability" in the South China Sea.[31]

Although the two countries have not agreed on a formal bilateral code of conduct, it is evident that fundamental principles that are essential parts of such a scheme had been agreed upon and are being implemented by China and Vietnam. In fact the October 2011 "Agreement on basic principles guiding the settlement of sea-related issues" can be considered a de facto "code of conduct." Also the provisions relating to the South China Sea in Joint Communiqués, in Joint Declarations, and in the Joint Statements from high-level meetings since the late 1990s indicate that China and Vietnam have gradually agreed on an increasingly sophisticated and detailed conflict management scheme to be applied and observed in the South China Sea. The decrease in tension was evident for a decade from the late 1990s, indicating that the agreements and the mechanisms therein had been implemented and respected by the two sides. Thus, despite the lack of progress in the bilateral expert-level talks on "maritime issues," the two sides have made some progress in terms of conflict management of their disputes in the South China Sea.

Conclusions

From the end of the Vietnam War in 1975 through until the 1990s, the fluctuating level of Sino-Vietnamese tensions related to their land and maritime border disputes, and in particular to those in the South China Sea, proved to be a major stumbling block. However, since the late 1990s, major progress has been made in terms of managing the land and maritime border disputes. This led to the formal settlement of the land border issue in 1999, of the Gulf of Tonkin issue in 2000, and to the establishment of more efficient mechanisms to contain friction in the South China Sea. This trend has continued into the 2000s, although the disputes in the South China Sea remain unresolved.

The demarcation of the land border has been completed. This is an essential component for the long-term stability in bilateral relations, as well as for the continued expansion of multifaceted cooperation between the border provinces of both countries. In the Gulf of Tonkin, for example, the successful completion of the delimitating of the so-called mouth of the gulf remains important. The continued implementation of the Fishery Agreement is also essential. Talks and discussions on the remaining border disputes in the South China Sea is a further indication of the importance placed on managing and avoiding tension. However, continued efforts are needed and it is essential to avoid future confrontation in the area, not only for bilateral relations but also for the stability in the region.

The potential for conflict in the South China Sea during the early 1990s was high. Similar disputes were considerably reduced and better managed by the late 1990s, a trend that continued to prevail with constant dialogue and only limited periods of tension up to 2008. Unfortunately, in the period 2009-2011 tensions periodically increased due to actions in and relating to the South China Sea. But the more efficient management of the border disputes from the late 1990s contributed to enhanced bilateral relations and, despite the increased tension in 2009-2011, this progress, in combination with the recent "Agreement on basic principles guiding the settlement of sea-related issues," has created more favorable conditions for managing the remaining disputes and augur well for the long-term stability of the Sino-Vietnamese relationship.

Notes

1. This study is partly derived from Ramses Amer, *The Sino-Vietnamese Approach to Managing Boundary Disputes*, Maritime Briefing 3, no. 5 (Durham:

International Boundaries Research Unit, University of Durham, 2002), and Ramses Amer, "The Sino-Vietnamese Approach to Managing Border Disputes–Lessons, Relevance and Implications for the South China Sea Situation," in Tran Truong Thuy, ed., *The South China Sea: Cooperation For Regional Security and Developments, Proceedings of the International Workshop, Co-organized by the Diplomatic Academy of Vietnam and the Vietnam Lawyers' Association, 26-27 November 2009, Hanoi, Vietnam* (Hanoi: The Gioi and Diplomatic Academy of Vietnam, 2010), 251-271. For studies on Sino-Vietnamese relations with border issues as one of the main factors in the relationship, see Ramses Amer, "Sino-Vietnamese Normalization in the Light of the Crisis of the Late 1970s," *Pacific Affairs*, Vol. 67, No. 3 (1994), 357-383; Ramses Amer, "Sino-Vietnamese Relations: Past, Present and Future," in Carlyle A. Thayer and Ramses Amer, eds., *Vietnamese Foreign Policy in Transition* (Singapore: Institute for Southeast Asian Studies; and, New York: St. Martin's Press, 1999), 68-130; and Ramses Amer, "Assessing Sino-Vietnamese Relations through the Management of Contentious Issues," *Contemporary Southeast Asia*, Vol. 26, No. 2 (2004): 320-345. In addition, see Nguyen Hong Thao and Ramses Amer, "The Management of Vietnam's Maritime Boundary Disputes," *Ocean Development and International Law*, Vol. 38, No. 3 (2007), 305-324.

2. The information in this section is derived from Amer, "Sino-Vietnamese Normalization," 358-366, Amer, "Sino-Vietnamese Relations," 69-102, and Amer, "Assessing Sino-Vietnamese," 320-321.

3. For details on the border disputes during the second half of the 1970s, see Amer, *The Sino-Vietnamese Approach*, 6-8.

4. Bruce A. Elleman, "China's 1974 Naval Expedition to the Paracel Islands," in Bruce A. Elleman and S.C.M. Paine, eds., *Naval Power and Expeditionary Warfare: Peripheral Campaigns and New Theatres of Naval Warfare* (London and New York: Routledge, 2011), 141-151.

5. Beijing's and Hanoi's conflicting claims on this incident are in Chang Pao-Min, "A New Scramble for the South China Sea Islands," *Contemporary Southeast Asia*, Vol. 12, No. 1 (1990), 20-21. For the 1998 clash, see Daniel J. Dzurek, *The Spratly Islands Dispute: Who's On First?* Maritime Briefing, Vol. 2, No. 1 (Durham: International Boundaries Research Unit, University of Durham, 1996), 23-25.

6. For a detailed analysis of the normalization process in the context of relations since 1975, see Amer, "Sino-Vietnamese Normalization," 357-383.

7. For details on the border disputes during the normalization process see Amer, *The Sino-Vietnamese Approach*, 7-8.

8. The information presented in this section is derived from Amer, "Sino-Vietnamese Relations," 108-114, and Amer, "Assessing Sino-Vietnamese," 328-337. For analysis up to 2000, see Amer, *The Sino-Vietnamese Approach*, 8-35 and 49-58. For the 2000s, see Amer, "The Sino-Vietnamese Approach," 251-271.

9. "Viet Nam, China Talk Border-related Issues," *Viet Nam Ministry of Foreign Affairs*, http://www.mofa.gov.vn/en/nr040807104143/nr040807105001 /ns110419090108/newsitem_print_preview [Accessed on 20 April 2011].

10. "Vietnam, China sign agreement on basic principles guiding settlement of sea issues," *Nhan Dan*, http://www.nhandan.com.vn/cmlink/nhandan-online/homepage/politics/external-relations/vietnam-china-sign-agreement-on-basic-principles-guiding-settlement-of-sea-issues-1.315961?mode =print#4UZPByDBT3pU [Accessed on 9 November 2011].

11. "Joint Statement: On the Completion of the Demarcation and Markers Placement on the Entire Land Border Line between Vietnam and China," *Viet Nam Ministry of Foreign Affairs*, http://www.mofa.gov.vn/en/cn_vakv/ca_tbd/nr040818094447/ ns090106100042/newsitem_print_preview [Accessed on 8 January 2009].

12. The full text of the Land Border Treaty without maps has been published as "The Land Border Agreement between the Socialist Republic of Vietnam and the People's Republic of China," in *Công Báo/Official Gazette of the Socialist Republic of Vietnam*, No. 41 (25 August 2002), 3-16.

13. "Vice-foreign Minister on Vietnam-China Land Border Treaty," *Vietnam Law & Legal Forum*, Vol. 9, No. 97 (2002), 21-23.

14. Ramses Amer and Nguyen Hong Thao, "Regional Conflict Management: Challenges of the Border Disputes of Cambodia, Laos, and Vietnam," *Austrian Journal of South-East Asian Studies*, Vol. 2, No. 2 (2009), 56.

15. On the management of the Gulf of Tonkin dispute and related developments in the context of Vietnam's other maritime disputes, see Nguyen and Amer, "The Management of Vietnam's," 305-324. See also Nguyen Hong Thao, "Vietnam and Maritime Delimitation," in Ramses Amer and Keyuan Zou, eds., *Conflict Management and Dispute Settlement in East Asia* (Farnham and Burlington: Ashgate, 2011), 171-199. For an analysis of the Gulf of Tonkin dispute in the context of China's maritime disputes and management, see Zou Keyuan, "China and Maritime Boundary Delimitation: Past, Present and Future," in Ibid., 149-169.

16. The text of the Delimitation Agreement has been reproduced in Nguyen Hong Thao, "Maritime Delimitation and Fishery Cooperation in the Tonkin Gulf," *Ocean Development and International Law*, Vol. 34, No. 1 (2005), 41-44, and in Zou Keyuan, "The Sino-Vietnamese Agreement on Maritime Boundary Delimitation in the Gulf of Tonkin," *Ocean Development and International Law*, Vol. 34, No. 1 (2005), 22-24.

17. The legal terminology used in this context is derived from Zou Keyuan, "Maritime Boundary Delimitation in the Gulf of Tonkin," *Ocean Development and International Law*, Vol. 30, No. 3 (1999), 246. Information pertaining to possible impact of Bach Long Vi Island on boundary delimitation is also derived from Ibid., 245-247.

18. Ibid., 245-246 and 253.

19. Nguyen, "Vietnam," 179; Zou, "China," 156.

20. For an argument along similar lines with a parallel to the "Breviée Line" drawn in 1939 in the Gulf of Thailand, see Zou, "Maritime Boundary," 238-240.

21. The text of the Fishery Agreement has been reproduced in Nguyen, "Maritime Delimitation," 36-41. See also Zou Keyuan, "Sino-Vietnamese Fishery Agreement for the Gulf of Tonkin," *International Journal of Marine and Coastal Law*, Vol. 17, No. 1 (2002), 127-148.

22. For details see Amer, *The Sino-Vietnamese Approach*, 19-21.

23. Ibid., 24-25.

24. "Joint Statement on All-round Cooperation in the New Century between the People's Republic of China and the Socialist Republic of Vietnam," *Ministry of Foreign Affairs of the People's Republic of China*, http://www.fmprc.gov.cn /eng/wjb/zzjg/yzs/gjlb/2792/2793/t16248.htm [Accessed on 24 February 2011].

25. For details see Amer, "The Sino-Vietnamese Approach," 265-267.

26. The full text of the "Declaration on the Conduct of Parties in the South China Sea" can be found on the website of the *Association of Southeast Asian Nations (ASEAN)*, http//www.aseansec.org/13163.htm [Accessed on 28 October 2008].

27. For incidents in 2009, see Ramses Amer, "Vietnam in 2009–Facing the Global Recession," *Asian Survey*, Vol. 50, No. 1 (2010), 215-216. For incidents in 2010 see Ramses Amer, "Vietnam in 2010–Regional Leadership," *Asian Survey*, Vol. 51, No. 1 (2011), 200-201.

28. For China's case see "Foreign Ministry Spokesperson Jiang Yu's Remarks on China's Maritime Law Enforcement and Surveillance on the South China Sea," *Ministry of Foreign Affairs of the People's Republic of China*, http://www.fmprc. gov.cn /eng/xwfw/s2510/2535/t826601.htm [Accessed on 13 July 2011], and "Foreign Ministry Spokesperson Hong Lei's Remarks on Vietnamese Ships Chasing away Chinese Fishing Boats in the Waters off the Nansha Islands," *Ministry of Foreign Affairs of the People's Republic of China*, http://www.fmprc. gov.cn/eng/xwfw/s2510 /2535/t829427.htm [Accessed 13 July 2011]. For Vietnam's case see "Press Conference on Chinese maritime surveillance vessel's cutting exploration cable of PetroViet Nam Seismic Vessel," *Viet Nam Ministry of Foreign Affairs*, http://www.mofa.gov.vn/en/tt_baochi/pbnfn/ns110530220030/ newsitem_print_preview [Accessed on 13 July 2011], and "Foreign Ministry Spokesperson Nguyen Phuong Nga answers question from the media at the Press Conference on June 9th 2011 concerning the Viking II incident," *Viet Nam Ministry of Foreign Affairs*, http://www.mofa.gov.vn/en/tt_baochi/pbnfn/ns 110610100618/newsitem_print_preview [Accessed on 13 July 2011].

29. "Viet Nam-China joint press release." From the website of *Viet Nam Ministry of Foreign Affairs*, http://www.mofa.gov.vn/en/nr040807104143/nr040807105001/ ns110626164203/newsitem_print_preview [Accessed on 13 July 2011].

30. "Vietnam, China sign agreement on basic principles guiding settlement of sea issues," *Nhan Dan*, http://www.nhandan.com.vn/cmlink/ nhandan-online/ homepage/politics/external-relations/vietnam-china-sign-agreement-on-basic-principles-guiding-settlement-of-sea-issues-1.315961?mode= print#4UZPByDBT3pU [Accessed on 9 November 2011].

31. "Vietnam China joint statement," *Nhan Dan*, http://www.nhandan.com.vn /cmlink/nhandan-online/homepage/politics/external-relations/vietnam-china-joint-statement-1.316664?mode=print#qOaZldsqLw5 n [Accessed on 9 November 2011].

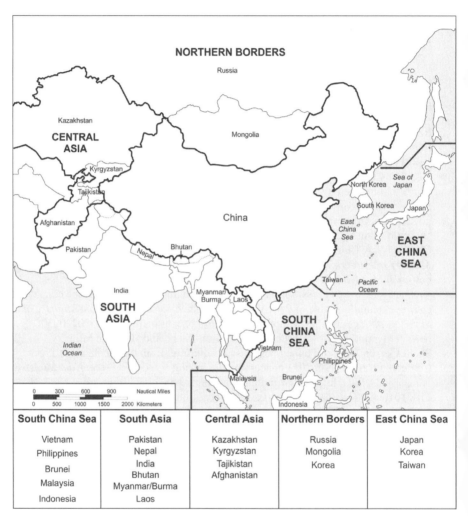

China and Its Neighbors (by Region)

Conclusions

Bruce A. Elleman, Stephen Kotkin, and Clive Schofield

China has more neighbors, and thus boundary treaties with more countries, than any other state, a situation that is rich with opportunities for conflict as well as mutually beneficial exchange. Geography has positioned China's neighbors at the "front line" of Beijing's rising power. This book examines China, and particularly its rise, through the lens of its interactions with its immediate, and in some cases not so obviously immediate, neighbors.

A challenging geography and complex geopolitics are not unique to China. Other large countries often placed in the same category, the so-called BRICs—Brazil, Russia, India, and China—have sprawling territories and multiple international boundaries. Russia, like China, has fourteen land neighbors, though it has fewer maritime neighbors (four, rather than China's six). India has eleven neighbors. Brazil has ten. By contrast, the mainland of the United States has just two land neighbors, even while its islands in the Pacific border on many more.[1] A distinction can, however, be drawn as China's economy is far larger than that of Russia, India, or Brazil, and Beijing's impact on its neighbors, indeed on the world, continues to be significantly greater.[2] Ongoing border claims and counter-claims can be expected to have a major impact on the extent and durability of China's power, both in its region and on the world stage.

Today's tensions should not obscure that over the past several decades, Beijing took great strides in establishing diplomatic and, particularly, economic relations with the majority of its neighbors. Such relations were notable by their absence in the past. Indeed, the ideologically-inspired foreign policy of the PRC featured rhetorical and material support for communist insurgencies bent on the overthrow of the governments of non-communist neighboring states. Consequently, these frequently unsettled borders posed a clear and direct threat, including that of armed cross-border intervention. Francis Watson, writing in 1966, observed that the Chinese government did not view its frontiers as fixed, but had a "tendency to avoid definition" leaving Chinese claims "almost mystically extensive," so that, "[w]ith the prospect of a vague but general intention to call her existing frontiers in question, China has been able to hold all of her neighbours under some degree of suspended sentence."[3]

The gradual erosion in Beijing's ideologically based foreign policy, coupled with its economic reforms, has transformed this picture. China's engagement with its

311

neighbors in diplomatic, social, cultural and, critically, economic terms has strengthened significantly over recent decades. Meanwhile, its neighbors have frequently sought to take advantage of its economic rise for their own ends. These increasingly important ties have led to ever more complex and significant cross-border interactions. While these ties necessarily represent a two-way street, the huge asymmetries of scale involved give China leverage over its many small neighbors. China's economic growth coupled with rising military spending have amplified the underlying asymmetry and arguably made it increasingly difficult for China's neighbors not to accommodate its wishes. Certainly, that is their perception.

Accompanying this significant transformation in cross-border relations, particularly on the diplomatic and economic fronts, has been the settlement, formally at least, of several major border disputes. Nonetheless, significant challenges remain.

As of 2012, the PRC had successfully negotiated borders with nine of its neighbors. Unresolved land and sea border disputes with eleven neighbors persist, however. Additionally, for three others—Afghanistan, North Korea, and Pakistan—borders have been settled by secret treaty, meaning that future governments could well question the terms. Despite their privileged position of boundary treaties in international law with a view to ensuring their permanence and inviolability, borders do shift over time.[4]

Even for those neighbors that appear to have settled their borders with China, problems remain. For example, during negotiations where Beijing has been said to have compromised—such as with Kazakhstan, Kyrgyzstan, and Tajikistan—it acquired territory from each. These apparent concessions have proved to be deeply unpopular in those countries once made public, thereby calling into question the long-term legitimacy and durability of the official border agreements. Bloody demonstrations have taken place, for instance in Kyrgyzstan, where treaty ratification helped provoke the fall of the government that signed the agreement.

Even larger countries feel unease. Despite the formal settlement of the Sino-Russian border, Russian fears of Chinese irredentism over territories lost under "unequal" treaties of 19th-century vintage remain. Additionally, certain river islands disputed by the two countries were divided down the middle, which could offer a potential flashpoint should either side seek to build settlements there. The history of more prominent disputed islands in East Asia—such as Sakhalin, once divided between Russia and Japan—would not appear to be reassuring.

Many chapters in this volume discuss the delimitation and, in the case of land borders, demarcation of international boundaries. International boundaries are fundamental to the definition of sovereign states, which, in turn, remain the basis for the prevailing international political and legal order. They determine the extent of each state's territory and maritime spaces, and therefore its internationally recognized sovereignty and jurisdiction. Furthermore, border and territorial disputes remain significant sources of inter-state friction and conflict, often heightened by nationalism. Such nationalism has become a crucial factor underpinning and sustaining the legitimacy of the Beijing government and this demands that China's interests, including its sovereignty and international boundaries, be resolutely safeguarded.

A number of contributions contained herein do, however, go beyond borders to examine cross and trans-boundary interactions. Borders offer opportunities for cooperation and exchange as well as competition and dispute, even where the position of the boundary line itself has been mutually agreed. We do not mean to downplay that cooperation. We do, however, want to underscore that border frictions continue in relation to breakaway provinces (Myanmar), local jurisdiction problems (Laos), or leasing agreements (Kazakhstan). In fact, virtually every one of China's neighbors has border-related problems with Beijing. This book, therefore, challenges the notion that China has more or less solved most of its border disputes through diplomacy and compromise.[5]

Problems are most acute concerning China's maritime boundaries. For example, although China and Vietnam have delimited and demarcated their land borders, as well as delimited a maritime boundary and associated joint fishing zone within the Gulf of Tonkin, it nonetheless seems too early to say the China-Vietnam border is "permanently settled." In fact, their maritime boundary agreement only extends as far as the "mouth" of the Gulf. The far more expansive territory in dispute—encompassing virtually the entire South China Sea and the vast majority of the islands therein—remains unresolved.

In what follows, we offer a summary of the 20 neighbors grouped into five regions: South China Sea, South Asia, Central Asia, Northern Borders, and East China Sea. We summarize which parts of China's boundaries seem relatively stable, and which seem potentially poised to undergo further changes in the short to medium term.

South China Sea: Brunei, Indonesia, Malaysia, the Philippines, Vietnam

Of the regions surrounding China, the South China Sea remains the tensest. All five neighbors have outstanding maritime boundary disputes with Beijing. This should, however, be set against the backdrop of ever-stronger Chinese trade and investment in Southeast Asia, especially with members of the Association of Southeast Asian Nations (ASEAN).

Brunei and China's maritime claims remain ambiguous and open to interpretation, largely because the PRC refuses to clarify its maritime claims. Nevertheless it is apparent that both countries claim sovereignty over Louisa Reef in the Spratly islands. For the foreseeable future, Brunei—a country of 400,000 people—has no option but diplomatic mechanisms to better manage the dispute. As the 2009 Exchange of Letters between Brunei and Malaysia demonstrated, diplomatic resolution of conflicting maritime claims is possible despite significant hurdles. Brunei is, however, largely dependent on Beijing's goodwill, and on the extent to which it can draw upon solidarity with China's other South China Sea neighbors.

Indonesia's official position is that it does not have a maritime boundary with China in the South China Sea. This view is supported by the fact that Indonesia's maritime activities, including continental shelf delimitation with Malaysia in 1969 and Vietnam in 2003 in the South China Sea, have not been publicly protested by Beijing. It remains to be seen whether Jakarta's position can be maintained, however. Repeated fishing incidents involving Chinese boats operating in Indonesian claimed waters northeast of the Natuna islands indicate that there are conflicting claims to resolve. While Jakarta has made its position explicit, Beijing has yet to do so. Without further clarification from Beijing on the true meaning of its nine-dashed line map, it is impossible to tell whether or not Indonesia and China truly have a maritime boundary to delimit. Further, while it seems likely that overlapping maritime claims do exist, their resolution will necessarily involve Malaysia and Vietnam with which Indonesia has already delimited seabed boundaries in the same area. Amid this uncertainty, Indonesia and China have struggled to manage marine resources that are susceptible to overexploitation.

The PRC and Malaysia have conflicting sovereignty over small South China Sea islands as well as overlapping maritime claims. China claims all of the features making up the disputed Spratly archipelago, numbering well over 100 widely-scattered islets, atolls, and reefs, but only a handful rising above water at high tide. Malaysia claims sovereignty over 11 marine features. Inevitably, these conflicting claims have a maritime dimension. While Malaysia has published an official map indicating the limits of its maritime claims, China's claims remain obscure.[6] Malaysian governments have demonstrated great reluctance to engage in discussions on joint development of the Spratly islands. Instead, Malaysia is actively exploiting these resources on its own, even while trying to enhance its claims through further military occupation and commercial development. These actions have been repeatedly denounced by Beijing. Similarly, Malaysia's 2009 decision to submit with Vietnam a joint submission to the UN Commission on the Limits of the Continental Shelf led to robust protests from Beijing.

The resolution of the territorial and maritime disputes between the Philippines and the PRC, on the one hand, and the Philippines and Taiwan, on the other hand, are likely to prove highly problematic. First and foremost, China/Taiwan and the Philippines dispute ownership over numerous islands and other small insular features in the South China Sea. These sovereignty disputes will need to be addressed, if not resolved, prior to the any treaty on maritime delimitation. Additionally, for its part the Philippines must settle once and for all its confusion over its Treaty Limits, even as the PRC finally clarifies its position regarding its opaque nine-dashed line claim. The absence of jurisdictional clarity will not only prevent access to, and the effective management of, potentially valuable marine resources, but also continues to serve as a source of Sino-Philippine friction and potential confrontation. Indeed, relations between China and the Philippines (as well as other claimant states) on South China Sea issues showed every indication of becoming more fraught, as illustrated by increasingly harshly worded "diplomatic" exchanges and repeated incidents at sea, especially related to marine resource issues, both in terms of fisheries and oil prospecting efforts.

Sino-Vietnamese border disputes have been a major preoccupation since the full normalization of relations in 1991. The two sides settled the land border issue in 1999 and of the Gulf of Tonkin issue in 2000, but key South China Sea disputes remain unresolved. Better management of the border disputes from the late 1990s did contribute to enhanced bilateral relations. Nonetheless, tension periodically flared in the South China Sea during 2009-2011. An October 2011 "Agreement on basic principles guiding the settlement of sea-related issues" created more favorable conditions for managing these disputes, and to some observers the agreement augurs well for the long-term stability of the Sino-Vietnamese relationship.

Others are less sanguine. Looming energy security concerns, access to seabed hydrocarbon reserves, as well as national power and prestige, motivate Beijing. In May 2009, Beijing reiterated its expansive claims to Southeast Asia's maritime area in a protest directed to UN Secretary-General Ban Ki-Moon, in response to a joint UN submission by Vietnam and Malaysia. "China has indisputable sovereignty over the islands in the South China Sea and the adjacent waters," the note verbale stated, "and enjoys sovereign rights and jurisdiction over the relevant waters as well as the seabed and subsoil thereof."[7] The implications for the oil, gas, and minerals suspected to exist on the continental shelf below the South China Sea was clear. In keeping with these views, in 2011 Chinese vessels interfered with Vietnamese oil exploration activities, going so far as to cut seismic survey cables.

In the context of these heightened tensions, the United States saw an opening. On 16 November 2011, U.S. Secretary of State Hillary Clinton urged all claimants to the South China Sea not to resort to intimidation: "The United States does not take a position on any territorial claim, because any nation with a claim has a right to assert it . . . But they do not have a right to pursue it through intimidation or coercion. They should be following international law, the rule of law, the U.N. Convention on the Law of the Sea."[8]

America's insertion between China and its neighbors, partly in response to lobbying by Vietnam and others, angered Beijing, not least because it has long sought to exclude "outsiders." Clinton's warning almost exactly coincided with U.S. President Barack Obama's announcement during a visit to Australia that 2,500 U.S. marines would be stationed in Darwin, Australia—militarily insignificant perhaps, but perceived as symbolically important. Several high-level U.S. officials, including the secretary of defense, emphasized a U.S. "commitment" to protecting security and sea lanes in the Pacific. Observers characterized U.S. actions as a response to China. Huang Jing, a foreign affairs analyst and visiting professor at the National University of Singapore, noted: "The US needs to show the Chinese that they still have the power to overwhelm them, that they still can prevail if something really wrong happens."[9]

Beijing has favored bilateral over multilateral negotiations. Although in 2002 China and ASEAN agreed on a Declaration on the Conduct of Parties in the South China Sea (DoC), there has been scant progress in implementing its terms and signing a legally binding Code of Conduct. This failure to implement the DoC increases the chances of minor incidents escalating into conflict.

Media accounts on all sides have emphasized the resulting tensions. *Global Times*, a Chinese Communist organ, ominously warned in October 2011 that the other claimants should "mentally prepare for the sounds of cannons" if they remain at loggerheads with Beijing.[10] On 9 April 2012 Chinese Major-General Luo Yuan even warned Manila that "The biggest miscalculation of the Philippines is that it has miscalculated the strength and willpower of China to defend its territorial integrity."[11] The International Institute for Strategic Studies published an issue of *Survival* aptly entitled "The Return of Gunboat Diplomacy," which concluded that "China has become increasingly active in the naval sphere as its capabilities improve and its desire to either trial or showcase them expands," and cited PLA Chief of Staff Chen Bingde as cautioning that "preparations for potential military conflicts" in the South China Sea "must be . . . taken."[12]

Such heated rhetoric may be no more than saber-rattling. Still, given the scale of world trade that transits the South China Sea, much is at stake in these territorial and maritime disputes. China's military may be trying to alter the balance of power with the United States, as evidenced by incidents during the spring of 2009 when Chinese vessels harassed USNS *Impeccable* and USNS *Victorious*. China may envision denying U.S. Navy access to the Taiwan Strait.[13]

Such events illustrate Beijing's desire to challenge the "package deal" represented by the UN Convention on the Law of the Sea (UNCLOS), with the goal of keeping extra-regional players, such as the United States, out of what China regards as its "back yard." Undoubtedly China, whose economy is becoming thoroughly globalized, wishes to avoid being vulnerable to blockade by the U.S. or Japanese navies in the event of crisis. However, given the globalized nature of its economy China is itself necessarily dependent on globe-spanning routes for maritime trade. Indeed, in excess of 80 percent of global maritime trade by volume is carried by sea.

On the bright side, China recently established an agency in its Foreign Ministry dedicated to land and sea border disputes with neighboring countries. Previously, the many disputes had been the prerogatives of several departments within the Foreign Ministry alone. The Department of Boundary and Ocean Affairs has a mandate to formulate and oversee land boundary demarcation and maritime delimitation, manage external boundary cases involving territories, maps, and place names, and engage in negotiations and joint development—all of which suggest the possibility of cooperation rather than confrontation with neighboring countries bordering the South China Sea.

South Asia: India, Nepal, Bhutan, Myanmar, Laos, Pakistan

Second in terms of potential risk, but quite possibly even more dangerous in terms of the overall scope of a conflict, is South Asia. Most of the South Asian neighbors have unresolved borders with China, but the Sino-Indian border conflict is the most significant. Settlement of these bilateral tensions is necessary for resolving many of the other contentious border issues on the subcontinent and its environs.

India, or South Asia broadly, and China have a history of rivalry longer than the existence of most of the world's states. Bilateral trade has recently boomed—in 2008 China became India's largest trading partner—but India's trade imbalance with China is huge, and many observers regard economics as of secondary importance in the relationship. Their territorial dispute encompasses a striking 50,000 square miles—the size of the U.S. state of Alabama and one of the world's largest territorial disputes by area—from Aksai Chin in the west to the Tawang District in the east. Memories remain fresh of the 1962 Sino-Indian War, and the 1967 Chola Incident (a day-long military conflict in Sikkim, which became an Indian state in 1975). Unlike the South China Sea, rival Sino-Indian territorial claims are mostly in remote, often mountainous areas without obvious value for world trade or accessible natural resources. The willingness of both countries to resort to military mobilization in order to assert territorial claims is often said to be linked to pride and prestige. Periodic unrest in Tibet, and the Chinese government's actions there, also divide these two great powers.

Nepal's border with China cannot be resolved fully without India's cooperation. Both the eastern and western trijunctions—where the Nepalese, Chinese, and Indian territories meet—remain unsettled. Since one of the concentrations of Tibetan emigration is located in Dharmashala in India, China suspects New Delhi's role in fomenting troubles by taking advantage of an open Indo-Nepalese border. Consequently, Beijing's pressure on Kathmandu for a special status on a par with New Delhi remained among its primary diplomatic goals in Nepal.

The Sino-Indian conflict also adversely affects Bhutan. After 27 years of border negotiations, Bhutan, China, and India have yet to sit down and determine ownership over the territory where the three neighbors meet. Sino-Bhutan border negotiations reflect the larger geopolitical dynamics of South Asia, which ultimately is driven by Sino-Indian competition. Even if Bhutan and China delimit and demarcate their borders, they would still need to manage their relations within the context of Sino-Indian antagonisms.

Myanmar's "provisional western extremity" also awaits the settlement of the Sino-Indian boundary. The Sino-Burmese boundary as defined in 1960-1961 has proved relatively stable and apparently uncontested for the past 50 years. However, over the past ten years, a rebellion backed by a predominantly Han Chinese militia in the Kokang region of the Shan State, called the Kokang Myanmar National Democratic Alliance Army (MNDAA), has forced as many as 50,000 ethnic Han Chinese to flee to China. There are concerns that Beijing might intervene in the conflict, and Chinese humanitarian assistance may be linked to offers to mediate the conflict in Kokang. More ominously, during February 2010, it was reported that Beijing had stationed additional PLA troops along its border with Myanmar.

Although the PRC and Laos have resolved their border disputes, tensions have arisen from its comparative underdevelopment vis-à-vis China, its weak regulation apparatus, and its desire to use almost any means possible to enrich the country. This leaves Laos vulnerable to outside political and economic pressure. The rapid growth of unregulated Chinese industry in northern Laos along the border is of increasing concern to Lao nationalists.

The Sino-Pakistani border has been stable since its settlement in 1963, which has enabled bilateral relations to prosper. The Sino-Pakistani relations focus on India. Secret nuclear support and missile sales to Pakistan in the 1980s and 1990s allowed the PRC to limit India's rise, even as it publicly switched to neutrality on Kashmir and pursued improved Sino-Indian relations. Over the past half century, Beijing and Islamabad have periodically reinvented the meaning of their ties in the face of diverse challenges, with a contemporary focus on Gwadar and China's strategic corridor via the Karakoram Highway through Pakistan to the Indian Ocean. At present, the greatest risk to bilateral border relations remains the transnational threat of terrorism, especially Islamic fundamentalist influence over the Uyghurs of Xinjiang. Though unlikely to imperil state-to-state relations, trepidation over ethnic unrest at home, in conjunction with China's rise to superpower status, has given way to an increasingly assertive discourse on the need to enhance vigilance at the shared Sino-Pakistani border.

Speculation on the future India-China relationship has increased markedly in recent times.[14] In terms of either total Gross Domestic Product or defense spending, India is simply not a genuine rival to China. In 1990, the Chinese and Indian economies were more or less equivalent in size, but by 2010 the PRC's economy had expanded to more than three times that of India, and the gap has continued to widen. Territorially, with only a few exceptions, China already controls the disputed lands that it values most. Beijing, unlike New Delhi, is more or less satisfied with the status quo in terms of actual control of disputed territory. Above all, China controls the high ground and enjoys easier access thanks to the traversable Tibetan plateau.[15]

However, in the Indian Ocean, India, owing to its superior navy in those waters, can claim the upper hand—though for how long is anybody's guess. In the meantime, India can prevent China from settling its territorial disputes with Nepal, Bhutan, and Myanmar, whose border negotiations with Beijing depend upon New Delhi's active participation.

Central Asia: Afghanistan, Tajikistan, Kyrgyzstan, Kazakhstan

Most of the Central Asian states have delimited and demarcated their borders with China, but their relative weakness arguably makes those settlements uncertain, and could allow Beijing to encroach on them incrementally. The cross border economic and power asymmetries offer Beijing opportunities to extend its influence far beyond the formally agreed international boundary lines.

The 40-mile Sino-Afghan border is not currently in dispute. Still, developments in Afghanistan are of great interest to China, because Afghanistan shares a border with Pakistan and—potentially—with India, as well as with Tajikistan, and because Afghanistan possesses purported mineral wealth. High on Beijing's priority list is avoiding the export of "extremism" to the Uyghurs living in Xinjiang. China has been developing infrastructure on its side of the Afghanistan border, including a 47 mile (75 km) road just 6 miles (10 km) from the Sino-Afghan border, which is funded by the Chinese Ministry of Defense.

Tajikistan is the major trade route linking Afghanistan with China. Beijing's "Go West" strategy announced in June 1999 entailed the promotion its commercial interests in Tajikistan and other Central Asian countries. Asymmetrical negotiations led to China's annexation of Tajik territory. In recent years, what began as a gradually increasing stream of Chinese projects, investment, and expertise has turned into a torrent. If current trends hold, the resolution of the border will be of minor significance compared with the ever-growing importance of Chinese political and economic influence in Tajikistan.

The 1999 Sino-Kyrgyz border agreement appears to have settled all outstanding claims, although this accord was highly controversial, precipitating civil unrest and a change in government as a result. Fears in Kyrgyzstan persist about China's expansionism, although Beijing's economic growth does not yet appear to have translated into direct political influence. In 2012, Bishkek officially joined the Moscow-led Eurasian customs union, which suggests efforts to balance Kyrgyzstan's commercial dependence on China.

China and Kazakhstan have also settled their outstanding border disputes, but China's astonishing economic growth has posed many challenges for the bilateral relationship. In particular, Beijing approached Astana in late 2009 with a request to allow Chinese farmers to use one million hectares of Kazakh land to farm soya beans and rapeseed. Beijing's requests for additional land have aggravated tensions. Resentment about the border and Chinese intentions lies close to the surface. Beijing's activist foreign policy has arguably alienated past and potential future partners throughout Central Asia.

When examining Central Asian border agreements as a whole, it would appear that the size of the country is in inverse proportion to the magnitude of these compromises. For example, Tajikistan, the smallest of these three Central Asian states, ceded 433 square miles to China, which equaled 0.78 percent of its total territory.[16] Kyrgyzstan in 1999 ceded 480 square miles of land to China, equaling just over 0.6 percent of its total territory, or only three-quarters (in percentage terms) of what Tajikistan forfeited, even though Kyrgyzstan is about 40 percent larger than Tajikistan.[17] Finally, when Kazakhstan gave up only 72 square miles to China, this equaled about 0.007 percent of its territory.[18] Again, Kazakhstan is about fifteen times larger than Kyrgyzstan, but gave up much less territory.

When viewed in percentage terms, therefore, the PRC appears to be gaining more in its negotiations with smaller states than with larger ones. This gives the alarming impression that territorial disputes between China and its near neighbors in Central Asia are not necessarily being determined in accordance with, admittedly Western-inspired, international legal norms, for example based on existing treaties, old documents, and maps. Instead, these negotiations appear to be based more on the relative sizes of the countries involved, which give China greater weight vis-à-vis its smaller neighbors.

Northern Borders: Russia, Mongolia, Korea

China's longest land borders lie to the north. During the 19th century, China lost more land to the north than all other regions combined. Accordingly, potential Chinese irredentism focuses on this area.

Beginning in 2004, China and Russia began to resolve border disputes dating back centuries. Formally, this border is now fixed, with the last outstanding areas in dispute settled in 2008. However uneasy Russia may be about their long-term relationship, it needs China's money, goods, and markets, and so cannot afford to engage in geopolitical competition. If China continues its rise and Russia's attempts to re-establish itself as a viable great power fall short, then new political leaders in Beijing could reopen the question of historical legitimacy of the 19th-century "unequal" treaties. Not only nationalism might motivate such an inquiry, but also a keen awareness that eastern Siberia and the Russian Far East contain over half of Russia's prospective petroleum reserves, the majority of its natural gas reserves, almost all its diamonds and gold, as well as coal, timber, and other resources. For its part, Russia remains concerned over any reconsideration of settled territorial issues as well as the seemingly inexorable Chinese penetration of the Russian Far East.

In Mongolia, Beijing has already become a dominant political force. Given China's considerable economic leverage, it does not need to occupy Mongolia physically in order to exert considerable influence, so any attempt to reclaim "Outer Mongolia" via outright annexation appears unlikely. The Sino-Mongolian border, although no longer actively in dispute, has become largely irrelevant as the two economies become ever more integrated. A significant challenge for Mongolia is how to protect its sovereignty, territorial integrity, and economic independence, so as to avert Chinese domination.

Since the founding of North Korea and the PRC, and the resolution of the Sino-Korean border by secret treaty in 1963, boundary and territorial issues in North Korea have been relatively muted. For Beijing, the most serious boundary problem is a negative one: how to keep desperate North Korean refugees out. For the Democratic People's Republic of Korea, a country fiercely jealous of its sovereignty and deeply suspicious of the outside world—even of the PRC, its sole ally—all national boundaries are "hard" and movement across them is kept to a minimum. China's fear of being flooded by refugees in the event of instability in North Korea is an important factor behind its support, and perhaps helps explain Beijing's willingness to overlook the regime's provocative behavior.

In sum, China's expansive borders to the north are relatively quiet. Nevertheless, they remain potentially volatile, even dangerous. Unforeseen changes of government in Russia or Mongolia could destabilize generally good relations with China (and vice versa, of course). Even more significantly, if the North Korean government were to collapse, as Charles Armstrong warns us (see page 122), "the validity of a Sino-Korean border established by Kangxi in 1712, by the Japanese in 1909, and by means of the as-yet secret Sino-DPRK treaty in 1963, might be viewed very differently by the leaders of a newly reunified Korea."

East China Sea: Japan, Korea, Taiwan

The East China Sea shares many of the volatile characteristics of the South China Sea, including problematic baseline claims, sovereignty disputes over islands, and overlapping maritime claims. This semi-enclosed ocean space also has a productive marine environment that is threatened by over-exploitation, in part at least as a consequence of jurisdictional uncertainty from undefined borders. The discovery of much desired seabed energy reserves has raised the stakes for the interested coastal states: China, Japan, and also Korea. There is considerable potential for conflict— especially a naval conflict—as the PRC implements its plan to turn the People's Liberation Army Navy (PLAN) into a world class naval force.

Japan and China hold fundamentally different and opposing views on delimitating maritime and particularly seabed entitlements in the East China Sea, and thus for delimitating maritime boundaries. China bases its claims on "natural prolongation" arguments. As a result of the location of the Okinawa Trough considerably closer to Japan's Ryūkyū islands than to mainland China, this approach would make most of the East China Sea seabed China's, and also Korea's, which adopts a similar approach. By contrast, Japan has favored the construction of median or equidistance lines as the starting point for maritime delimitation. As a result of these contrasting approaches, a broad swathe of the central and eastern parts of the East China Sea is subject to overlapping maritime claims. China's discovery of gas fields, notably the Chunxiao/Shirakaba field, located on the Chinese side of, but very close, to the theoretical median line has also become a focus for dispute.

China and Japan also claim sovereignty over a group of small, barren, and uninhabited islands, the Diaoyu/Senkaku islands, in the southern part of the East China Sea. Additionally, while recognizing Japanese sovereignty over Okinotori, located to the east of the East China Sea, China objects to Japan's expansive maritime claims based on this tiny feature. Sovereignty over the Diaoyu/Senkaku islands could potentially give rise to exclusive economic zone rights to approximately 20,000 nm^2 (68,686 km^2), while the maritime claims associated with Okinotori encompass at least some 116,472 nm^2 (400,000 km^2).

Although Korea and Japan were able in 1978 to agree on a maritime joint development to seek seabed hydrocarbon resources, China and Japan have thus far failed to follow suit. Further, although several joint fishing zones have been established in the East China Sea, notably between China and Japan from 1997, between Japan and Korea from 2000, and between China and Korea from 2001, these cooperative arrangements have notable drawbacks, since these zones cover only limited parts of the East China Sea and in fact overlap each other. In addition, enforcement within each joint zone is on a flag-state basis (for example, only Chinese enforcement authorities can arrest a Chinese-flagged fishing vessel) and there is no provision for enforcement against the fishing vessels of third-parties such as those from Taiwan, which has major fishing fleets operating in these waters.

High hopes for progress toward Sino-Japanese joint development in the disputed zone have not been borne out. The June 2008 "principled consensus" on maritime cooperation in the East China Sea outlined a future maritime joint development with the details to be left for future negotiation. However, it proved impossible to reach consensus, and no recent progress has been made. Indeed, if anything, bilateral relations have deteriorated, as illustrated by numerous incidents at sea, resulting in official protests, and counter-protests. While it may be too early to write off entirely the prospects of joint Sino-Japanese development—for example, Malaysia and Thailand took over a decade to implement their own agreement in principle on joint development through a formal treaty arrangement—nonetheless the prospects appear dim. China's salami tactics—advancing its claims in small, carefully measured increments—have proved difficult for Japan to counter. The long-term advantage appears to be on the PRC's side.

Beijing's and Taipei's differing territorial claims make the PRC-ROC situation one of the most complex of any of the ongoing territorial disputes between. Both governments largely agree on their territorial claims against Japan and the Philippines, and they also agree that China's sovereign territory includes all of the South China Sea, where Taiwan has generally supported the PLAN activities against all other claimants. Nevertheless, the PRC and Taiwan continue to dispute sovereign rights and actual control not only over the nearby offshore islands, but over islands in the South China Sea, where Taiwan controls Itu Aba, the largest island in the Spratly group. Chinese protestations beginning in 2002 that it will work with the ASEAN countries to negotiate these differences peacefully excludes Taiwan's participation, even though Taipei is a major claimant of these disputed territories. Its exclusion virtually guarantees that the negotiations will fail.

Including Taiwan as an equal is essential for creating a multilateral solution to these disputes. Even if the PRC were to resolve each and every one of its borders, the Republic of China on Taiwan has outstanding claims on large territories in East Asia, including—as per the as-yet unamended Nationalist constitution—all of Mongolia, all of the South China Sea, and large swaths of Central Asia.

This peculiar situation—where the two governments making up "One China" have differing territorial claims is a holdover from the Cold War. If the PRC and Taiwan were either to unify outright, or sign some form of document—similar to the Nationalist-Communist United Fronts in the 1920s and 1930s—in which their governments agreed to cooperate on settling China's borders, then this could give Beijing increased leverage over its neighbors. Arguably, the PRC's current borders with many of its neighbors could at some point in the future be proclaimed null and void, and a whole new round of negotiations might ensue regardless of international legal niceties regarding the permanence of international boundary treaties and regarding the succession of states. Such an eventuality could even help to explain why China has apparently been willing to "compromise" on its borders with states in Central Asia and with Russia. Beijing perhaps assumes that it could always use the Taiwanese claims as justification to reopen these border talks in the future, should Taiwan unify with the PRC.

*   *   *

As the above sections show, each region surrounding China has either active disputes or the potential for future land and sea boundary disputes. Within each region, the outbreak of tensions between China and one neighbor could easily pull in others. It will take a delicate balancing act for Beijing to keep all of its neighbors content, particularly as its power and its ability to threaten increase, along with the incentives of its neighbors to seek alliances with outside powers—in particular the United States—and with each other.

Developments could become complex. For example, one PRC diplomat told a Bhutanese official that China is surrounded by "25" countries.[19] What might this mean? Our book is based on a count of 20 neighbors. We treat North and South Korea as one, whereas Beijing might count them as two. Our list also includes Taiwan, which the PRC says is an integral part of China, in which case, these might cancel out, putting the total back to 20. Four of the extra five countries might be Sikkim, Assam, Arunachal Pradesh, and Ladakh, which the rest of the world accepts as integral parts of India but which the PRC has from time to time argued should be separate border states, like Nepal and Bhutan. Beijing's list may also include Okinawa as one of these five "extra" neighbors, since it has long argued that Okinawa was a Chinese tributary long before it was annexed by Japan in the 19th century. If this Chinese statement concerning 25 neighbors is accurate, then China's border challenges might turn out to be even more dangerous than many analysts assume.

As China takes on the mantle of a great power, its external behavior could shift. In 2000, Michael Swaine and Ashley Tellis presciently listed six behavioral changes that Beijing might adopt: 1) "augment its military capabilities," 2) "develop a sphere of influence," 3) "redress past wrongs," 4) "rewrite the prevailing 'rules of the game' to reflect its own interests," and 5) prepare itself to "thwart preventive war or to launch predatory attacks on its foes."[20] The chapters contained in this volume provide ample evidence that these changes are already taking place, but the sixth predicted change is of particular interest in the context of this book: To "acquire new or reclaim old territory for their resources or for symbolic reasons by penalizing, if necessary, any opponents or bystanders who resist such claims."[21]

Arguably, China has already done this with some neighbors, and is perhaps even now trying to do so with others.

* * *

China has made considerable progress in the settlement of some, though by no means all, of its land boundary disputes, but this stands in stark contrast to the situation offshore, where Beijing has made minimal progress in the settlement of its maritime territorial and jurisdictional disputes. There has been an agreement on only one partial maritime boundary delimitation with Vietnam, within the confines of the Gulf of Tonkin.

These two maritime spaces both feature sovereignty disputes over small islands whose resolution is a necessary precursor to settling overlapping claims to maritime jurisdiction. Both of these maritime regions are reputed to be major potential sources of energy resources. While there are good reasons to question the existence of a seabed hydrocarbons bonanza underlying the South China Sea, the perception that this may be the case remains a powerful underlying factor in the calculations of the claimant states, including China.[22] Many countries in the region, including China, are increasingly dependent on imported sources of oil and gas. The prospect of substantial and close-to-hand hydrocarbon reserves in the East China Sea and the South China Sea is therefore an alluring one.

Finally, while there may be doubts over the size of potential oil and gas reserves, there is little doubt that the South China Sea's tropical marine environment represents an area of globally significant biological diversity, which sustains fisheries critical to the food security of hundreds of millions of people living in its coastal states. The protection of this staggeringly rich and productive marine environmental resource should be a high priority for policy-makers, but their chances for success are inevitably hampered by conflicting maritime claims and lack of maritime boundary delimitation.

The fact that the South China Sea is also host to sea lanes that are of critical importance to China and its neighbors to sustain their resource-hungry and export-oriented economies adds to these challenges. Moreover, the complex, semi-enclosed coastal geography of both the East China Sea and the South China Sea serves to accentuate the maritime jurisdictional disputes between the littoral states, since their maritime claims tend to converge and overlap.

To compound matters, although the majority of these states are parties to UNCLOS, and are therefore theoretically at least—bound by its framework, many of the maritime claims advanced by the South China Sea states are either excessive or ambiguous in character. Examples of the former include claims to straight baselines that extend significantly further seaward than they should, such as those of China, Taiwan, and Vietnam. These excessive claims have excited international protests, notably from the United States. Ambiguous maritime claims include the historically-based ones of China and the Philippines. Conflicting interpretations of UNCLOS have also led to broad areas of overlap in the East China Sea.

Beijing's broad maritime claims are perhaps symptomatic not only of its desire to secure the greatest possible share of the potential resources of the South China Sea but also of a longstanding frustration that, despite possessing an extensive coastline, China is to a large extent "hemmed in," with its potential maritime claims curtailed through the proximity of other states, such as in the case of Japan's Ryūkyū islands chain to the east. Consequently, the South China Sea is the only ocean space where China is able to assert a 200 nm maritime claim. China's sovereignty claims to the South China Sea islands, its stated position that these small features are capable of generating extensive maritime claims, and its continuing adherence to the apparently expansive yet unclear nine-dashed line map, can all be seen in this light.

The starting point for any resolution of the South China Sea disputes is clarity, especially with regard to which states claim precisely what territory and maritime areas and on what basis. That said, although recent events, especially in relation to extended continental shelf issue, appear to have clarified matters somewhat, one result of the emerging clarity has been to throw the different positions of the contending parties into starker relief. A similar situation pertains in the East China Sea, where the conflicting positions of coastal states remain far removed.

*   *   *

Finally, this book sheds light on another important issue concerning China's rise— sea power. After World War II, a survey of over four centuries of the European balance of power described how "sea power emerged as the most potent force . . . a phenomenon probably unparalleled in the entire course of world history."[23] Accordingly, there is enormous concern in the United States that China will become a global sea power over time and compete as an equal on the world's oceans to challenge the global order.[24] It is taken as an indication that the PRC does indeed seek to alter the world order in its favor that, especially during recent years, the Chinese government has invested heavily in the PLAN, apparently with the goal of building an ocean-going "blue water" navy.

It was Alfred Thayer Mahan who pointed out that a country's geography and its institutions can either help or impede a country that seeks to become a sea power. Historians have since argued that: "States with long land borders with multiple opportunities for attack, territorial expansion, and defense concerns are unlikely to develop successful sea power."[25] Those continental powers that do achieve status as sea powers—usually, in European history at least, for a relatively short period of time—must become regional hegemons as the first step, only after which can they attempt to "acquire supremacy in the realm of intercontinental, maritime trade."[26]

Arguably, China is even now trying to become a regional hegemon. But any claim that the PRC is already a "great power" overlooks the number and complexity of Beijing's outstanding land and sea boundary disputes. China is potentially hemmed in by the territorial demands of its numerous neighbors. Certainly the territorial and maritime boundary disputes in the South China Sea—which involve seven governments including both the PRC and Taiwan—and on land, the Sino-Indian border conflict—which involves as many as eight, including Myanmar, Bhutan, and Nepal on the east, and Pakistan, Afghanistan, and Tajikistan on the west—could hold China back from achieving the status of a full-fledged sea power.

As a consequence of China's extensive and complex geography, a conflict with one neighbor could give another neighbor an unexpected opportunity to exert pressure or carry out an advance, making the multi-front nature of China's challenge even more complex. Even if these outstanding land and sea disputes were resolved, in any future maritime conflict—for example, in the South China Sea or in the East China Sea—one or more of China's large land neighbors—such as India or Russia—could decide to take advantage of Beijing's naval preoccupation to strike. The possibility of a two-front war is inherent in China's geography.

In short, Beijing may not in fact have the freedom to exert its new-found power on the seas for some time to come. Even were China to achieve the status of a global sea power, its actions on the sea would always have to be closely coordinated with those on the land. This simple fact cannot help but act as a major, and lasting, restraint, whatever Beijing's "rising power" ambitions.

*   *   *

We are left with many questions. As China grows more powerful, will it continue to seek accommodation with its neighbors or will it seek to set the terms? Does the Chinese military pursue its own foreign policy, more aggressive than that of the civilian leadership, and perhaps not fully under the control of the latter? Will Beijing continue its assertive efforts to secure what it perceives to be its fair share of valuable marine resources in its bordering seas and thereby risk embroiling its newly modernized PLAN in a maritime conflict?

The answers to these questions will not depend on China alone. India is also a major stakeholder. Will increasing trade and economic links ground India-China relations in mutual compromise and accommodation? Or will Asia's two rising powers discover that their interests clash fundamentally? As China's presence in

Central Asia and across the Indian Ocean basin expands, how will this affect Sino-Indian rivalry?

On another front: Will the United States seek to accommodate or contain China's continuing rise? Does the Pentagon have a sharper view of Chinese behavior than other agencies of the U.S. government? Do the tensions in the China-U.S. relationship stem from correctable misperceptions, or from a fundamental clash of interests? Will China's neighbors look to the United States to counter-balance Beijing and, if so, would U.S. involvement make China more or less accommodating?

Analysts disagree on the answers to these questions, and therefore on both the prospects for resolving China's territorial and maritime disputes and the consequences of failing to do so. Do we face continuing boundary adjustments under the existing regime of international law or a gathering assault to restore a Sino-centric regional order?

While definitive answers to many of these searching questions remain out of reach, it is clear that China's having numerous neighbors represents a double-edged sword for Beijing. China's borders offer tremendous opportunities, especially in terms of economic opportunities and geopolitical leverage. The counterpoint to this is that these multiple international boundaries, particularly where they are unsettled or actively disputed, also have the potential to act as heavy drag on Beijing's trajectory toward superpower status. Thus, although the essays contained in this volume do not pretend to resolve all outstanding mysteries regarding China and her neighbors, they nonetheless serve to illuminate not just the opportunities but also the limits of Beijing's power. Ultimately, all borders are relationships, and power both derives from and is constrained by these relationships.

Notes

The thoughts and opinions expressed in this publication are those of the authors and are not necessarily those of the U.S. government, the U.S. Navy Department, or the Naval War College.

1. The United States does, however, hold sovereignty over nine islands or groups of "minor outlying" islands in the Pacific Ocean and Caribbean Sea. These include American Samoa, Baker Island, Guam, Howland Island, Jarvis Island, Johnston Atoll, Kingman Reef, Northern Mariana islands, and Wake Island in the Pacific as well as Navassa Island and Palmyra Island in the Caribbean. These widely scattered possessions give rise to multiple potential maritime boundaries between the United States and its maritime neighbors.

2. James Kynge, *China Shakes the World: A Titan's Rise and Troubled Future—and the Challenge for America* (Boston: Houghton Mifflin Harcourt, 2006).

3. Francis Watson, *The Frontiers of China* (London: Chatto & Windus, 1966), quoted in T. S. Murty, *Paths of Peace: Studies on the Sino-Indian Border Dispute* (New Delhi: ABC Publishing House, 1983), 295.

4. In particular, Article 62(2)(a) of the Vienna Convention in the Law of Treaties states that boundary treaties are not subject to change even in the case of "subsequent fundamental change of circumstances."

5. M. Taylor Fravel, *Strong Borders Secure Nation: Cooperation and Conflict in China's Territorial Disputes* (Princeton, NJ: Princeton University Press, 2008), 1-9; Fravel argues that China compromised on 17 out of 23 border conflicts, and was willing to "accept less than half of the contested territory in any final settlement." He does acknowledge on page 9, however, that "When vital interests are at stake, China will use force."

6. It was recently announced that Beijing plans to publish a new map of the South China Sea to "strengthen Beijing's claim on the disputed region." *China Reform Monitor*, No. 959, 17 April 2012.

7. As quoted in Michael Richardson, "Beijing has much to do to clarify its boundary claims," *The Straits Times*, 18 May 2009.

8. *The Economic Times*, "Hillary Clinton Warns against Intimidation in South China Sea dispute," 16 November 2011, http://economictimes.indiatimes.com/news/international-business/hillary-clinton-warns-against-intimidation-in-south-china-sea-dispute/articleshow/10757519.cms [Accessed on 20 November 2011].

9. *Global Post*, "Obama: Darwin, Australia, to host US marines: President Obama announces plans to send US marines to Darwin, Australia," 16 November 2011, http://www.globalpost.com/dispatch/news/regions/asia-pacific/111116/darwin-australia-marines-obama [Accessed on 20 November 2011].

10. Reuters, "China paper warns of 'sound of cannons' in sea disputes," 25 October 2011; http://www.reuters.com/article/2011/10/25/us-china-seas-idUSTRE79O1MV20111025 [Accessed on 20 November 2011].

11. *Wall Street Journal*, "Chinese General: Philippines faces 'last chance'," 9 April 2012, http://blogs.wsj.com/chinarealtime/2012/04/09/chinese-general-philippines-faces-last-chance/ [Accessed on 20 April 2012].

12. Christian Le Miere, "The return of gunboat diplomacy," *Survival*, Vol. 53, No. 5 (October-November 2011), 58.

13. Bruce A. Elleman, *High Seas Buffer: The Taiwan Patrol Force, 1950-1979* (Newport, RI: Naval War College Press, 2012), http://www.usnwc.edu/Publications/Naval-War-College-Press/Newport-Papers/Documents/38.pdf.

14. John W. Garver, *Protracted Contest: Sino-Indian Rivalry in the Twentieth Century* (Seattle: University of Washington Press: 2002); Waheguru Pal Singh Sidhu and Jing-dong Yuan, *China and India: Cooperation or Conflict?* (Boulder: Lynne Rienner, 2003).

15. M. Taylor Fravel, "China's response to a rising India," National Bureau of Asian Research, 4 October 2011, http://www.nbr.org/research/activity.aspx?id=177 [Accessed on 20 April 2012].

16. The PRC's total area is 3,704,427 square miles, while Tajikistan is 55,251 square miles, making the PRC approximately 67 times larger than Tajikistan.

17. Kyrgyzstan is 77,181 square miles, making the PRC about 48 times larger than Kyrgyzstan.

18. Kazakhstan is 1,052,085 square miles, making the PRC about 3.5 times larger than Kazakhstan.

19. In July 2002, Bhutanese Foreign Minister Lyonpo Jigmi Y. Thinley told the National Assembly that in his discussions with China: "When Bhutan asked them to be generous with a small neighbour like Bhutan they said that, as a nation which shared its border with 25 other countries they could not afford to be generous with one particular neighbour." Thierry Mathou, "Bhutan-China relations: Towards a new step in Himalayan politics," www.bhutanstudies.org.bt/pubFiles/19-Spdr&Pglt.pdf.

20. Michael D. Swaine and Ashley J. Tellis, *Interpreting China's Grand Strategy: Past, Present, and Future* (Santa Monica, CA: Rand, 2000), 233.

21. Ibid.

22. Nick Owen and Clive Schofield, "Disputed South China Sea Hydrocarbons in Perspective," *Marine Policy*, Vol. 36, No. 3 (2012), 809-822.

23. Ludwig Dehio, *The Precarious Balance: Four Centuries of the European Power Balance* (New York: Vintage Books, 1962), 270.

24. Abraham M. Denmark, Andrew S. Erickson, and Babriel Collins, "Should we be afraid of China's new aircraft carrier? Not yet," *Foreign Policy*, 27 June 2011, http://www.foreignpolicy.com/articles/2011/06/27/should_we_be_afraid_of_chinas_new_aircraft_carrier [Accessed on 12 April 2012].

25. William R. Thompson, "Some mild and radical observations on desiderata in comparative naval history," in John B. Hattendorf, ed., *Doing Naval History: Essays Toward Improvement* (Newport, RI: NWC Press, 1995), 107.

26. Karen A. Rasler, William R. Thompson, *The Great Powers and Global Struggle, 1490-1990* (Lexington: University Press of Kentucky, 1994), 23.

Selected Bibliography

Akiner, Shirin, ed., *Mongolia Today* (London: Kegan Paul, 1991).

Alagappa, Muthiah, ed., *Asian Security Practice: Material and Ideational Influences* (Stanford, CA: Stanford University Press, 1998).

Ambekar, G.V., and Divekar, V.D., eds., *Documents on China's Relations with South and Southeast Asia, 1949-1962* (Bombay: Allied Publishers, 1964).

Amer, Ramses, *The Sino-Vietnamese Approach to Managing Boundary Disputes*, Maritime Briefing 3, no. 5 (Durham: International Boundaries Research Unit, University of Durham, 2002).

Amer, Ramses, and Zou, Keyuan, eds., *Conflict Management and Dispute Settlement in East Asia* (Farnham and Burlington: Ashgate, 2011).

Arpi, Claude, *Born in Sin: The Panchsheel Agreement—The Sacrifice of Tibet* (New Delhi: Mittal, 2004).

Asia Foundation, *Human Trafficking in Mongolia* (Ulaanbaatar, 2006).

Atlas of the Northern Frontier of India (New Delhi: Ministry of External Affairs, 1960).

Austin, Greg, *China's Ocean Frontier: International Law, Military Force and National Development* (St. Leonards, NSW: Allen & Unwin, 1998).

Bakosurtanal, *Map of the Republic of Indonesia* (Cibinong, 2010).

Barkmann, Udo, *Die Beziehungen zwischen der Mongolei und der VR China (1952-1996)* (Hamburg: Mitteilungen des Instituts für Asienkunde, 2001).

Bartow, Barry, "The Policy of the Mongolian People's Republic Toward China, 1952-1973," Ph.D. Dissertation, West Virginia University, 1974.

Bateman, Sam, and Emmers, Ralph, eds., *The South China Sea: Towards a Cooperative Management Regime*, (London: Routledge, 2009).

Bawden, Charles, *The Modern History of Mongolia* (New York: Frederick Praeger, 1968).

Bhasin, Avtar Singh, *Documents on Nepal's Relations with India and China, 1949-1966* (New Delhi: Academic Books, 1970).

Bhola, L., *Pakistan-China Relations: Search for Politico-Strategic Relations* (Jaipur: R.B.S.A. Publishers, 1986).

Brown, William, and Onon, Urgunge, trans., *History of the Mongolian People's Republic* (Cambridge: Harvard University Press, 1976).

Bruun, Ole, and Odgaard, Ole, eds., *Mongolia in Transition: Old Patterns, New Challenges* (Richmond: Curzon Press, 1996).

Bussert, Jim, and Elleman, Bruce A., *People's Liberation Army Navy (PLAN) Combat Systems Technology 1949-2010* (Annapolis, MD: Naval Institute Press, 2011).

Carey, Peter, ed., *Burma: The Challenge of Change in a Divided Society* (Basingstoke & Oxford: Macmillan Press & St. Anthony's College, 1997).

Carlson, Allen, *Unifying China, Integrating With the World: Securing Chinese Sovereignty in the Reform Era* (Ithaca, NY: Cornell University Press, 2004).

Chang, Pao-Min, *Sino-Vietnamese Territorial Dispute* (New York: Praeger, 1986).

Charney, Jonathan I., and Alexander, Lewis M., eds., *International Maritime Boundaries* (The Netherlands: Martinus Nijhoff Publisher, 1993).

Choucri, Nazli, and North, Robert C., *Nations in Conflict: National Growth and International Violence* (San Francisco: W.H. Freeman, 1975).

Christian, John LeRoy, *Modern Burma: A Survey of Its Political and Economic Development* (New York: International Secretariat, Institute of Pacific Relations, 1942).

Colton, Timothy, Frye, Timothy, and Legvold, Robert, *The Policy World Meets Academia: Designing U.S. Policy toward Russia* (American Academy of Arts and Sciences, 2010).

Conboy, Kenneth, and Morrison, James, *The CIA's Secret War in Tibet* (Lawrence: University Press of Kansas, 2002).

Cooley, John K., *Unholy Wars: Afghanistan, America, and International Terrorism* (London: Pluto Press, 2000).

Craig, Susan L., *Chinese Perceptions of Traditional and Nontraditional Security Threats* (Carlisle Barracks, PA: Strategic Studies Institute, US Army War College, 2007).

Cribb, Robert, and Ford, Michele, *Indonesia beyond the Water's Edge: Managing an Archipelagic State* (Indonesian Update Series, RSPAS Australian National University, ISEAS, Singapore, 2009).

Cumings, Bruce, *The Origins of the Korean War, Volume Two: The Roaring of the Cataract, 1947-1950* (Princeton: Princeton University Press, 1990).

Curley, Melissa, and Wong, Siu-Iun, eds., *Security and Migration in Asia: The Dynamics of Securitisation* (Abingdon: Routledge, 2009).

Dashpurev, D., and Soni, S. K., *Reign of Terror in Mongolia, 1920-1990* (New Delhi: South Asian Publishers, 1992).

David, Matthew, *When Things Get Dark: A Mongolian Winter's Tale* (New York: St. Martin's Press, 2010).

Dehio, Ludwig, *The Precarious Balance: Four Centuries of the European Power Balance* (New York: Vintage Books, 1962).

Diener, Alexander, *One Homeland or Two? The Nationalization and Transnationalization of Mongolia's Kazakhs* (Stanford: Stanford University Press, 2009).

Dillon, Michael, *Xinjiang: China's Muslim Far Northwest* (New York: Routledge Curzon, 2004).

Djalal, D. P., "Geopolitical Concept and Maritime Territorial Behavior in Indonesian Foreign Policy," MA Thesis, University of Simon Fraser University, Canada, 1990.

Duara, Prasenjit, *Sovereignty and Authenticity: Manchukuo and the East Asian Modern* (Lanham, MD: Rowman & Littlefield, 2003).

Dutton, Peter, *Scouting, Signaling, and Gatekeeping: Chinese Naval Operations in Japanese Waters and the International Law Implications* (U.S. Naval War College, China Maritime Studies No. 2, 2009).

Dzurek, Daniel J., *The Spratly Islands Dispute: Who's on First?* Maritime Briefing, 2, no. 1 (Durham: International Boundaries Research Unit, University of Durham, 1996).

Elleman, Bruce A., *High Sea's Buffer: The Taiwan Patrol Force, 1950-1979* (Newport, RI: NWC Press, 2012).

Elleman, Bruce A., and Paine, S.C.M., eds., *Naval Blockade and Seapower: Strategies and Counter-strategies, 1805-2005* (London: Routledge, 2006).

————. *Naval Power and Expeditionary Warfare: Peripheral Campaigns and New Theatres of Naval Warfare* (London and New York: Routledge, 2011).

Engardio, Peter, ed., *Chindia: How China and India Are Revolutionizing Global Business* (New York: McGraw-Hill, 2006).

Erickson, Andrew, Goldstein, Lyle, Murray, William, and Wilson, Andrew, eds., *China's Future Nuclear Submarine Force* (Annapolis, MD: Naval Institute Press, 2007).

Evans, Grant, ed., *Laos: Culture and Society* (Chang Mai, Thailand: Silkworm Books, 1999).

Farmer, Jessica, *Trafficking in Persons and Prostitution at Mine Sites in Mongolia* (Ulaanbaatar: Asia Foundation, 2008).

Finke, Peter, *Nomaden im Transformationsprozess: Kasachen in der post-sozialistischen Mongolei* (Münster: Lit Verlag, 2004).

Fraser-Tytler, W.K., *Afghanistan: A Study of Political Developments in Central and Southern Asia* (London: Oxford University Press, 1953).

Fravel, M. Taylor, *Strong Borders Secure Nation: Cooperation and Conflict in China's Territorial Disputes* (Princeton, NJ: Princeton University Press, 2008).

French, Patrick, *Younghusband: The Last Great Imperial Adventurer* (London: HarperCollins, 1994).

Friters, Gerard, *Outer Mongolia and Its International Position* (London: George Allen & Unwin, 1951).

Fu Lo-shu, *A Documentary Chronicle of Sino-Western Relations (1644-1820)* (Tucson: University of Arizona Press, 1966).

Garver, John W., *Protracted Contest: Sino-Indian Rivalry in the Twentieth Century* (Seattle: University of Washington Press, 2001).

Gill, Bates, *Rising Star: China's New Security Diplomacy* (Washington, DC: Brookings Institution Press, 2007).

Gilpin, Robert, *War and Change in World Politics* (New York: Cambridge University Press, 1981).

Goscha, Christopher E., *Vietnam or Indochina? Contesting Concepts of Space in Vietnamese Nationalism, 1887-1954* (Copenhagen: Nordic Institute of Asia Studies, 1995).

Griffin, Keith, ed., *Poverty and the Transition to a Market Economy in Mongolia* (New York: St. Martin's Press, 1995).

Gunn, Geoffrey C., *Rebellion in Laos: Peasant and Politics in a Colonial Backwater* (Boulder: Westview Press, 1990).

Haller-Trost, R., *Occasional Paper No. 14—The Spratly Islands: A Study on the Limitations of International Law* (Canterbury: University of Kent Centre of South-East Asian Studies, 1990).

Hamzah, Andi, *Laut, Teritorial dan Perairan Indonesia: Himpunan Ordonansi, Undang-Undang dan Peraturan Lainnya, Akademika Presindo* [Sea, territory and waters of Indonesia: Compilation of ordinances, acts, and other regulations], (Jakarta, 1984).

Han Zhenhua, ed., *Woguo nanhai Zhudao Shiliao Huibian* [The compilation of historic materials on the South China Sea Islands] (Beijing: The Oriental Publishing House, 1988).

Hancox, David, and Prescott, J.R.Victor, *A Geographical Description of the Spratly Islands and an Account of Hydrographic Surveys amongst Those Islands*, Maritime Briefing, 1, 6 (Durham: International Boundaries Research Unit, 1995).

Harley, J.R., and Woodward, David, eds., *The History of Cartography, Volume Two, Book Two: Cartography in the Traditional East and Southeast Asian Societies* (Chicago: University of Chicago Press, 1994).

Hattendorf, John B., ed., *Doing Naval History: Essays Toward Improvement* (Newport, RI: NWC Press, 1995).

Hawkins, Charles, and Lowe, Robert R., eds., *The New Great Game: Chinese Views on Central Asia* (Fort Leavenworth, KS: Foreign Military Studies Office, 2006).

Hinton, Harold C., *China's Relations with Burma and Vietnam: A Brief Survey* (New York: Institute of Pacific Relations, 1958).

Ho, Khai Leong, ed., *Connecting and Distancing, Southeast Asia and China* (Singapore: Institute of Southeast Asian studies, 2009).

Hong Xuezhi, *Kang-Mei Yuan-Chao zhanzheng huiyi* [Recollections of the resist-America aid-Korea War] (Beijing: Jiefangjun wenyi chubanshe, 1991).

Hopkirk, Peter, *The Great Game: The Struggle for Empire in Central Asia* (New York: Kodansha International, 1992).

Hou, K.C., and Yeoh, K. K., eds., *Malaysia and Southeast Asia and the Emerging China: Political, Economic and Cultural Perspectives* (Kuala Lumpur: Institute of China Studies, 2005).

Jain, Jagdish, and Jain, Rajendra Kumar, *China, Pakistan, Bangladesh* (New Delhi: Radiant Publishers, 1974).

Johnston, Alastair Iain, and Ross, Robert S., eds., *Engaging China: the Management of an Emerging Power* (New York: Routledge, 1999).

Jung Chang and Halliday, Jon, *Mao: The Unknown Story* (London: Jonathan Cape, 2005).

Karrar, Hassan H., *The New Silk Road Diplomacy: China's Central Asian Foreign Policy since the Cold War* (Vancouver: UBC Press, 2009).

Kiang, Ying Cheng, *China's Boundaries* (Chicago: Institute of Chinese Studies, 1984).

Kroenig, Matthew, *Exporting the Bomb: Technology Transfer and the Spread of Nuclear Weapons* (Ithaca, NY: Cornell University Press, 2010).

Kuhrt, Natasha, *Russian Policy towards China and Japan* (Abingdon: Routledge, 2007).

Kux, Dennis, *The United States and Pakistan, 1947-2000: Disenchanted Allies* (Washington, DC: Woodrow Wilson Center Press, 2001).

Kynge, James, *China Shakes the World: A Titan's Rise and Troubled Future—and the Challenge for America* (Boston: Houghton Mifflin Harcourt, 2006).

Lai Hongyi and Lim Tin Seng, eds., *Harmony and Development ASEAN-China Relations* (Singapore: World Scientific Publishing Co. Pte., 2007).

Lamb, Alastair, *The McMahon Line: A Study in the Relations between India, China and Tibet, 1904 to 1914*, 2 vols. (London: Routledge & Kegan Paul, 1966).

———. *Asian Frontiers: Studies in a Continuing Problem* (Melbourne: F.W. Cheshire for the Australian Institute of International Affairs, 1968).

Laruelle, Marlene, and Peyrouse, Sebastien, *China as a Neighbor: Central Asian Perspectives and Strategies* (Stockholm: Institute for Security, Development and Policy, 2009).

Laruelle, Marlene, Huchet, Jean-Francois, Peyrouse, Sebastien, and Balci, Bayram, eds., *China and India in Central Asia: A New "Great Game"?* (New York and London: Palgrave Macmillan, 2010).

Lattimore, Owen, *Pivot of Asia: Sinkiang and the Inner Asian Frontiers of China and Russia* (Boston: Little, Brown, 1950).

———. *Nomads and Commissars: Mongolia Revisited* (New York: Oxford University Press, 1962).

Lee Kwang-kyu, *Overseas Koreans* (Seoul: Jimoondang, 2000).

Lee, Chae-Jin, *China and Korea: Dynamic Relations* (Stanford: Hoover Institution, 1996).

———. *China's Korean Minority: The Politics of Ethnic Education* (Boulder: Westview Press, 1986).

Lee, Luke T., *China and International Agreements: a study of compliance* (Leyden & Durham NC: A.W. Sijthoff & Rule of Law Press, 1969).

Lensen, George A., *Balance of Intrigue: International Rivalry in Korea and Manchuria, 1884–1899* (Tallahassee: University of Florida Press, 1982).

Levine, Steven, *Anvil of Victory: The Communist Revolution in Manchuria* (New York: Columbia University Press, 1987).

Li Ling, *Xizang Zhi Shui Jiu Zhongguo: Da Xi Xian Zai Zao Zhongguo Zhan Lue Nei Mu Xiang Lu* [Tibet's waters will save China] (Beijing: Zhongguo Chang'an Chubanshe, 2005).

Lincoln, W. Bruce, *The Conquest of a Continent* (New York: Random House, 1994).

Liou, K. T., ed., *Handbook of Economic Development* (New York: Marcel Dekker, 1998).

Lo, Bobo, *The Axis of Convenience* (London: Chatham House, 2008).

Lohmeyer, Martin, "The Diaoyu/Senkaku Islands Dispute: Questions of Sovereignty and Suggestions for Resolving the Dispute," Master of Laws Thesis, Faculty of Laws, University of Canterbury, 2006.

MacFarquhar, Roderick, *The Origins of the Cultural Revolution*, Vol. 3: *The Coming of the Cataclysm 1961-1966* (New York: Oxford University Press, 1997).

Mancall, Mark, *Russia and China: Their Diplomatic Relations to 1728* (Cambridge: Harvard University Press, 1971).

Mangrai, Sao Saimong, *The Shan States and the British Annexation*, Data Paper 57, Southeast Asia Program (Ithaca: Department of Asian Studies, Cornell University, 1965).

Marolda, Edward J., "The U.S. Navy and the Chinese Civil War, 1945-1952," Ph.D. Dissertation, The George Washington University, 1990.

Mearsheimer, John J., *The Tragedy of Great Power Politics* (New York: W.W. Norton. 2003).

Mehra, Parshotam, *The Younghusband Expedition* (New York: Asia Publishing House, 1968).

Meyer, Karl E., and Brysac, Shareen Blair, *Tournament of Shadows: The Great Game and the Race for Empire in Central Asia* (Washington, DC: Counterpoint, 1999).

Milne, Elizabeth, Leimone, John Edward, Rozwadowski, F., and Sukachevin, Padej, *The Mongolian People's Republic: Toward a Market Economy* (Washington, DC: International Monetary Fund, 1991).

Muller, David, *China as a Maritime Power* (Boulder: Westview Press, 1983).

Murty, T.S., *Paths of Peace: Studies on the Sino-Indian Border Dispute* (New Delhi: ABC Publishing House, 1983).

Nie Rongzhen, *Inside the Red Star: The Memoirs of Marshal Nie Rongzhen* (Beijing: New World Press, 1988).

Nu, U, *Speech by Hon'ble Prime Minister Asking for the Approval of the Parliament to the Ratification of the Boundary Treaty between the Union of Burma and the People's Republic of China, 5th December 1960* ([Rangoon]: Sarpay Beikman Press, [1960]).

Nyiri, Pal, and Savel'ev, Igor, eds., *Globalizing Chinese Migration: Trends in Europe and Asia* (Farnham: Ashgate, 2002).

Osborne, Milton, *The Mekong: Turbulent Past, Uncertain Future* (New York: Atlantic Monthly Press, 2000).

Pai, Hyung Il, *Constructing "Korean" Origins: A Critical Review of Archaeology, Historiography, and Racial Myth in Korean State-Formation Theories* (Cambridge: Harvard University Asia Center, 2000).

Paine, S.C.M., *Imperial Rivals: Russia, China and Their Disputed Frontier* (Armonk, NY: M.E. Sharpe, 1996).

Palmer, James, *The Bloody White Baron* (New York: Basic Books, 2009).

Pan Shiying, *Nanshaqundao Shiyou Zhengzhi Guojifa* [Islands of the South China Sea, petropolitics, international law] (Hong Kong: Economic Herald Press, 1996).

Park, Alyssa, "A Borderland Beyond: Korean Migrants and the Creation of a Modern Boundary between Korea and Russia, 1860-1937," Ph.D. Dissertation, Columbia University, 2009.

Parry, Clive, ed., *Consolidated Treaty Series* (Dobbs Ferry, NY: Oceana Publications, 1969-86), vol. 168.

Perdue, Peter, *China Marches West: The Qing Conquest of Central Eurasia* (Cambridge: Harvard University Press, 2005).

Perkovich, George, *India's Nuclear Bomb: The Impact on Global Proliferation* (Berkeley: University of California Press, 1999).

Pettman, Ralph, *China in Burma's Foreign Policy* (Canberra: Australian National University Press, 1973).

Porritt, V.L., *British Colonial Rule in Sarawak 1946-63* (Oxford: Oxford University Press, 1997).

Prasad, H.Y. Sharada, Damodaran, A.K., and Gopal, Sarvepalli, eds., *Selected Works of Jawaharlal Nehru, Second Series, Vol. 29, 1 June—31 August 1955* (New Delhi: Oxford University Press, 2005).

Prescott, J.R.Victor, *Map of Mainland Asia by Treaty* (Melbourne: University of Melbourne Press, 1975).

Prescott, J.R.Victor, Collier, Harold J., and Prescott, Dorothy F., *Frontiers of Asia and Southeast Asia* (Melbourne: University of Melbourne Press, 1977).

Prescott, J.R.Victor, and Schofield, Clive, *The Maritime Political Boundaries of the World* (Leiden and Boston: Martinus Nijhoff, 2005).

Ramesh, Jairam, *Making Sense of Chindia: Reflections on China and India* (New Delhi: India Research Press, 2006).

Ramo, Joshua Cooper, *The Beijing Consensus* (London: The Foreign Policy Centre, 2004).

Rasler, Karen A., and Thompson, William R., eds., *The Great Powers and Global Struggle, 1490-1990* (Lexington: University Press of Kentucky, 1994).

Roberts, John W., II, and Roberts, Elizabeth A., *Freeing Tibet: 50 Years of Struggle, Resilience and Hope* (New York: AMACOM, 2009).

Rose, Leo E., *Nepal: A Strategy for Survival* (Berkeley: University of California Press, 1971).

Rossabi, Mary, and Rossabi, Morris, *Socialist Devotees and Dissenters: Interviews with Three Twentieth-Century Mongolian Leaders* (Osaka: National Museum of Ethnology, 2010).

———, trans. and introduction, *From Herder to Statesman: The Autobiography of Jamsrangiin Sambuu* (Lanham, MD: Rowman and Littlefield, 2010).

Rossabi, Morris, ed. *China Among Equals: The Middle Kingdom and Its neighbors, 10ᵗʰ – 14ᵗʰ Centuries* (Berkeley: University of California Press, 1983).

———. *Modern Mongolia: From Khans to Commissars to Capitalists* (Berkeley: University of California Press, 2005).

Rudelson, Justin Jon, *Oasis Identities: Uyghur Nationalism Along China's Silk Road* (New York: Columbia University Press, 1997).

Rumer, Eugene, Trenin, Dmitri, and Zhao Huasheng, *Central Asia: Views From Washington, Moscow, and Beijing* (Armonk, NY: M.E. Sharpe, 2007).

Rupen, Robert, *The Mongolian People's Republic* (Palo Alto: Hoover Institution Press, 1966).

Ryan, Mark A., Finkelstein, David M., and McDevitt, Michael A., eds., *Chinese Warfighting: The PLA Experience Since 1949* (Armonk, NY: M.E. Sharpe, 2003).

Schmid, Andre, *Korea between Empires, 1895–1919* (New York: Columbia University Press, 2002).

Schofield, C.H., Townsend-Gault, I., Djalal, H., Storey, I., Miller, M. and Cook, T., *From Disputed Waters to Seas of Opportunity: Overcoming Barriers to Maritime Cooperation in East and Southeast Asia* (National Bureau of Asian Research Special Report No.30, July 2011).

Schwartz, Henry G., *The Minorities of Northern China: A Survey* (Bellingham: Western Washington University Press, 1982).

Shaha, Rishikesh, *Nepali Politics: Retrospect and Prospect* (New Delhi: Oxford University Press, 1978).

Shahrani, M. Nazif Mohib, *The Kirghiz and Wakhi of Afghanistan: Adaptation to Closed Frontiers* (Seattle: University of Washington, Press, 1979).

Sheth, Jagdish N., *Chindia Rising: How China and India Will Benefit Your Business* (New York: McGraw-Hill, 2008).

Sidhu, Waheguru Pal Singh, and Yuan, Jing-dong, *China and India: Cooperation or Conflict?* (Boulder, CO: Lynne Rienner Publishers: 2003).

Singh, Swaran, *China-South Asia: Issues, Equations, Policies* (New Delhi: Lancer's Books, 2003).

Smith, Warren W., Jr., *China's Tibet? Autonomy or Assimilation* (Lanham, MD: Rowman and Littlefield, 2008).

Snow, Edgar, *Red Star over China* (New York: Random House, 1938).

Starr, S. Frederick, ed., *Xinjiang: China's Muslim Borderland* (Armonk, NY: M.E. Sharpe, 2004).

Storey, Ian, *Southeast Asia and the Rise of China: The Search for Security* (Abingdon, Oxon: Routledge, 2011).

Stuart-Fox, Martin, *Historical Dictionary of Laos* (Metuchen, NJ: Scarecrow Press, 1992).

Suryadinata, Leo, *China and the ASEAN States: The Ethnic Chinese Dimension* (Singapore: Singapore University Press, 1985).

Swaine, Michael D., and Tellis, Ashley J., *Interpreting China's Grand Strategy: Past, Present, and Future* (Santa Monica, CA: Rand Corporation, 2000).

Swanson, Bruce, *Eighth Voyage of the Dragon: A History of China's Quest for Seapower* (Annapolis, MD: Naval Institute Press, 1982).

Syed, Anwar Hussain, *China & Pakistan: Diplomacy of an Entente Cordiale* (Amherst: University of Massachusetts Press, 1974).

Sykes, Percy, *A History of Afghanistan* (London: Macmillan, 1940).

Tang, Shiping, Li, Mingjiang, and Acharya, Amitav, eds., *Living with China: Regional States and China through Crises and Turning Points* (New York: Palgrave Macmillan, 2009).

Tangsubkul, P., *The Southeast Asian Archipelagic States: Concept, Evolution, and Current Practice* (Honolulu, HI: East-West Environment and Policy Institute, 1984).

Thayer, Carlyle A., and Amer, Ramses, eds., *Vietnamese Foreign Policy in Transition* (Singapore: Institute for Southeast Asian Studies; New York: St. Martin's Press, 1999).

Thuy, Tran Truong, ed., *The South China Sea: Cooperation for Regional Security and Developments, Proceedings of the International Workshop, Co-organized by the Diplomatic Academy of Vietnam and the Vietnam Lawyers' Association, 26-27 November 2009, Hanoi, Vietnam* (Hanoi: The Gioi and Diplomatic Academy of Vietnam, 2010).

Trenin, Dmitri, *Russia's China Problem* (Washington, DC: Carnegie Endowment for International Peace, 1999).

Valencia, Mark J., Van Dyke, Jon M., and Ludwig, Noel A., *Sharing the Resources of the South China Sea* (Honolulu: University of Hawai'i Press, 1997).

van Kemenade, Willem, *China, Hong Kong, Taiwan Inc: The Dynamics of a New Empire* (New York: Alfred A. Knopf, 1997).

van Schimmelpenninck, David, *Russian Orientalism: Asia in the Russian Mind from Peter the Great to the Emigration* (New Haven, CT: Yale University Press, 2010).

Vertzberger, Yaacov, *The Enduring Entente: Sino-Pakistani Relations, 1960-1980* (Washington, DC: Praeger, 1983).

————, *China's Southwestern Strategy: Encirclement and Counterencirclement* (New York: Praeger, 1985).

Victory for the Five Principles of Peaceful Coexistence: Important Documents on the Settlement of the Sino-Burmese Boundary Question through Friendly Negotiations and on the Development of Friendly Relations between China and Burma, A (Peking: Foreign Languages Press, 1960).

Voskressenski, Alexei D., *The Difficult Border: Current Russian and Chinese Concepts of Sino-Russian Relations and Frontier Problems* (Commack, NY: Nova Science Publishers, 1996).

Watson, Francis, *The Frontiers of China* (London: Chatto & Windus, 1966).

Weitz, Richard, *China-Russia Security Relations: Strategic Parallelism without Partnership or Passion?* (Carlisle, PA: Strategic Studies Institute, 2008).

Widmer, Eric, *The Russian Ecclesiastical Mission in Peking During the Eighteenth Century* (Cambridge: Harvard University Press, 1976).

Yu, Peter Kien-hong, *The Four Archipelagoes in the South China Sea* (Taipei: Council for Advanced Policy Studies, 1991).

Zhang, Sheldon, *Chinese Human Smuggling Organization: Families, Social Networks, and Cultural Imperative* (Stanford: Stanford University Press, 2008).

Zhang, Yongjin, and Azizian, Rouben, eds., *Ethnic Challenges Beyond Borders: Chinese and Russian Perspectives of the Central Asian Conundrum* (New York: St. Martin's Press, 1998).

Zhao Lihai, *Haiyang fa wenti yanjiu* [Studies on the law of the sea] (Beijing University Press, 1996).

Zhao, Suisheng, ed., *Chinese Foreign Policy: Pragmatism and Strategic Behavior* (Armonk, NY: M.E. Sharpe, 2004).

Zhonggong zhongyang wenxian yanjiushi bian [Chinese Communist Party Central Documents Research Office, ed.], *Zhou Enlai nianpu, 1949-1976* [A chronicle of Zhou Enlai's life: 1949-1976], (Beijing: Zhongyang Wenxian Chubanshe, 1997), Vol. 2.

Index

9/11. *See* September 11 Attack

Abbotabad, 292*n*.15
Abdullah, Badawi, 40, 158, 159
Achayra, Baburam, 210
Achilles heel, 31
Afghanistan, xi, xiv, 4, 13-21, 99,
    128, 129, 130, 140*n*.7, 225, 226,
    227, 257, 277, 284, 285, 286, 287,
    312, 319, 327
Africa, xiii, 224, 228, 229
Agreement on the Maintenance of
    Peace and Tranquility along the
    Sino-Bhutan Border Areas (1998),
    29, 31, 32
agriculture, 13, 132, 158, 183, 236,
    285
Ahmadinejad, Mahmoud, 128
Airborne Warning and Control
    Systems, 55
aircraft carrier, xiv, 85
AK-56 assault rifle, 57
Akayev, Askar, 6, 127, 128, 138
Akhmolinsk, 98
Aksai Chin, 51, 52, 317
Aksy, 127, 138
Akto County, 284
al-Qaeda, 227, 287
Alabama, 47, 317
Alakol Lake, 106
Alatas, Ali, 68, 72
Alison Reef, 162
aluminum, 181
Amboyan Reef, 162
Amboyna Cay, 163
America-centric, xii
American Samoa, 328*n*.1
Amianan Island, 238
Amu Darya River, 14

Amur Basin, xv, 252, 253
Amur River, 114, 254, 257, 258, 260
Ancient Chosôn. *See* Chosôn
Andijan uprising, 130
Angkor, 144, 146
Anglo-Russian Agreement (1895),
    285
Anglo-Russian Convention (1907),
    98
Anglo-Nepalese War (1814-1816),
    208
Annam, 147, 272
Anping, 268
Anti-Rightist Campaign, 118
Arabian Sea, 228
Ardasier Reef, 39, 162
Argun River, 253, 257, 258
Armenia, 128
Armstrong, Charles, 321
artillery, 25, 225, 254
Arunachal Pradesh, 51, 52, 53, 54,
    55, 57, 324
Asahi, 89, 95*n*.25
ASEAN-China Declaration on the
    Conduct of Parties in the South
    China Sea (DoC), 42, 279, 305, 316
ASEAN-China Free Trade
    Agreement, 244
ASEAN+3 (Japan, Korea, and
    China), 106, 158
ASEAN Ministerial Meeting
    (AMM), 156
Asia Foundation, 182
Asia Pacific Economic Organization,
    183
Asian Development Bank (ADB), 55,
    56, 179
Asian Financial Crisis (1997), 150,
    155

Assam, 27, 53, 55, 57, 194, 324
Association of Southeast Asian
  Nations (ASEAN), 4, 37, 42, 43,
  44*n*.1, 105, 149, 150, 155-159, 161,
  244, 279, 313, 323
Astana, 320
Astana Summit, 134
Atambayev, Almazbek, 133, 136
Atlantic Ocean, xi
Australia, 43, 67, 73*n*.1, 151, 316
Austronesian, 268
Aynak, 18
Ayutthaya, 144

Bac Bo Gulf. *See* Gulf of Tonkin
Bach Long Vi Island, 301, 302
Badakshan Province, 13, 285, 289
Bagabandi, Natsagiin, 180, 183
Baikal Lake, 177
Bajo de Masinloc. *See* Scarborough
  Reef
Baker Island, 328*n*.1
Bakiyev, Kurmanbek, 19, 128, 131,
  134, 135, 136, 138, 139, 140*n*.16
Bakiyev, Maksim, 131
Balochistani, 228
Balochistan Province, 228
Ban Houay, 150
Ban Ki-Moon, 315
Ban-noi, 147
Bandar Seri Bagawan, 37
Bandung Conference, 196, 220
Bangkok, 145
Bangkok Declaration (1967), 156
Bangladesh, xiii, 55, 58, 229
Barque Canada Reef, 162, 163
Bashi Channel, 238
Batmönkh, Jambyn, 177, 178
Batyr, Osman, 174
Bay of Bengal, xiv, xv
Beautiful Island. *See* Formosa
Beibu Gulf. *See* Gulf of Tonkin
Beigan Island, 271
Beijing, xii, xv, 16, 23, 24, 27, 29,
  86, 89, 98, 101, 131, 157, 158, 170,
  172, 176, 182, 205, 209, 210, 211,

Beijing (continued) 212, 220, 222,
  257, 259, 263, 295, 298, 300, 303,
  305. *See also* China.
Beijing Olympics, 129, 214
Beijing Review, 86
Beita Region, 176
Beiyang regime, 256
Beknazarov, Azimbek, 127
Belarus, 127, 128, 136
Benham Rise, 237
Berdimukhamedov, Gurbanguly, 128
Berlin Wall, 296
Bhamo, 192, 193
Bhrikuti Devi, 206
Bhutan, xi, 4, 22-35, 49, 207, 213,
  277, 317-319, 324, 327, 330*n*.19
Bhutto, Zulfikar Ali, 220, 222
Big Circle Boys, 262
Bishkek, 6, 127, 128, 131, 132, 133,
  135, 136, 138, 139, 140*n*.16, 320
Bishkek Declaration, 129
Black Sea, xiv
Blagoveshchensk, 251
Bo Hai Gulf, 269
Bogdo Gegen, 170-171
Bogeda Region, 176
Bogra, Mohammad Ali, 220
Bohai State, 112
Bolkiah, Mohamed, 38
Bolkiah, Sultan Haji Hassanal, 40, 42
Bolshevik Revolution (1917), 172,
  256
Bonin islands. *See* Ogasawara islands
border disputes, *See* China, border
  disputes
Borneo, 37, 66, 73*n*.1, 156, 157
The Borneo Bulletin, 38
Bolshoi Ostrov/Abagaitu Island, 258
Bolshoi Ussuriysk. *See* Heixiazi/
  Bolshoi Ussuriysk Island
Boten, 7, 150, 153*n*.26
Boucher, Richard, 86, 135
Bouillevaux, Emile, 146
Boxer Uprising (1899-1901), 194,
  254, 255, 258
Brazil, 311

BRIC (Brazil, Russia, India, and China), 311
British Broadcast Company (BBC), 150
Brown, Gordon, 18
Brunei, xi, 4, 36-45, 156, 162, 163, 164, 241, 272, 276, 298, 313-317
Brunei Darussalam. *See* Brunei
Buddhism, 173, 183, 206
buffer state, 4, 5, 14, 15, 23, 28, 48, 58, 113
Bukhara, 98
Bulganin, Nikolai Aleksandrovich, 59*n*.5
Burma. *See* Myanmar
Burma Road, 195, 201*n*.21
Bush, George W., 57

C-130 Cargo Plane, 275
Ca Chau Vien. *See* Cuatereon Reef
Cairo Declaration (1943), 84, 268
Cambodia, 44*n*.1, 143, 144, 146, 148-150
camels, 182
Canada, xi, 181
Cao Bai, 274
carpets, 13
Caribbean Sea, 328*n*.1
cashmere, 180, 181
casino, 7, 150-151, 153*n*.26
Caspian Sea, xiv, 229
cement, 131, 181
Central Asia, xiv, 6, 14, 15, 19, 97-107, 127-138, 183, 228, 229, 252, 263, 283-291, 292*n*.7, 313, 319-320, 323, 324, 328
Central Asian Railroad, 132-133
Central Intelligence Agency (CIA), 17, 210, 212
Central London Reef, 162
Central Treaty Organization (CENTO), 220
Chagang-do, 111
challenges, xi, xii, 6, 8, 47, 56, 70-72, 100, 102, 105, 106, 107, 111, 117, 127, 134, 137, 159, 223, 225,

challenges (continued) 226-228, 229, 230-231, 232*n*.20, 243, 256, 259, 263, 283, 312, 313, 318, 320, 321, 324, 325, 326, 327
Cham, 144
Champa, 149
Champasak Kingdom, 145
Champasak Province, 143, 147
Changbai Mountain, 111, 113, 115, 118, 124*n*.32
Changbaishan Biosphere Reserve, 118, 124*n*.32
Chen Bingde, 215, 316
Chen Jian, 131, 134
Chen Shui-bian, 275, 276
Chen Yi, 211, 220
Cheng Wei-yuan, 277
Chiang Kai-shek, 116, 169, 173-174, 256, 268-269
China
  compromise, willingness to, xii, 6, 51, 69, 81, 104, 161, 176, 177, 220, 246, 301, 302, 312, 313, 320, 324, 327-328, 329*n*.5
  land border neighbors
    Afghanistan, xi, xiv, 4, 13-21, 99, 128, 129, 130, 140*n*.7, 225, 226, 227, 257, 277, 284, 285, 286, 287, 312, 319, 327
    Bhutan, xi, 4, 22-35, 49, 207, 213, 277, 317-319, 324, 327, 330*n*.19
    India, xi, xiii, xiv, 4-5, 7-8, 15, 18, 23-29, 31, 33, 34*n*.15, 46-59, 128, 136, 140*n*.7, 176, 191, 195, 196-198, 204-217, 218-233, 257, 277, 287, 311, 317-319, 324, 327, 328
    Kazakhstan, xi, xiii, xiv, 5-6, 96-109, 127, 128, 129, 130, 136, 138, 229, 262, 284, 289, 290, 312, 313, 319-320, 330*n*.18
    Kyrgyzstan, xi, xiv, 6, 19, 97, 98, 104, 126-141, 262, 284, 289, 290, 312, 319-320, 330*n*.17

China
    land border neighbors (continued)
        Laos, xi, 7, 44*n*.1, 142-153, 191,
            196, 197-198, 300, 313, 317-319
        Mongolia, xi, xiv, 7, 9, 98, 100,
            119, 128, 140*n*.7, 168-189, 256,
            267, 271, 277, 320-321, 323
        Myanmar, xi, xiii, xiv-xv, 7-8,
            44*n*.1, 54, 55, 56, 143, 150,
            151, 190-203, 229, 277, 313,
            317-319, 327
        Nepal, xi, 8, 27, 49, 54, 55, 204-
            217, 317-319, 324, 327
        Pakistan, xi, 8, 13, 14, 15-17, 18,
            19, 26, 49, 51, 54, 55, 57, 128,
            140*n*.7, 219-233, 277, 285, 287,
            292*n*.15, 312, 317-319, 327
        Russia, xi, xiii, xiv, xv, 6, 9, 14-
            16, 17, 19, 59*n*.5, 89, 97-99,
            103-104, 106-107, 111, 114-
            115, 119, 124*n*.31, 127, 128,
            129, 130, 133, 134-139, 169-
            172, 175, 180, 182-183, 250-
            265, 277, 283, 284-285, 287,
            289, 311, 312, 320-321, 324, 327
        Tajikistan, xi, xiv, 9-10, 13-14,
            18, 97, 98, 104, 128, 130, 257,
            277, 282-293, 312, 319-320,
            327, 329*n*.16
    land and maritime neighbors
        Korea, xi, xiii, xiv, xv, 6, 48, 50,
            89, 106, 111-125, 158, 181,
            182, 256, 259, 270, 277, 312,
            320-321, 322-324
        Vietnam, xi, 7, 10, 16, 37, 38, 39,
            40, 41, 42, 44*n*.1, 61, 63-64, 66-
            67, 72, 73*n*.1, 76*n*.28, 76*n*.29,
            79*n*.69, 89, 143, 144-145, 146-
            147, 148-150, 162-163, 164,
            165, 167*n*.20, 194, 241, 242,
            244-245, 248*n*.28, 257, 267,
            272-273, 274, 275, 276-277,
            294-309, 313-317, 325, 326
    maritime neighbors
        Brunei, xi, 4, 36-45, 156, 162,
            163, 164, 241, 272, 276, 298, 313-317

China
    maritime neighbors *(continued)*
        Indonesia, xi, 5, 42, 44*n*.1, 60-79,
            156, 165, 241, 245, 268, 272,
            275, 298, 314-317
        Japan, xi, xii, xiii, 5, 18, 52, 58,
            63, 80-95, 106, 112, 114-119,
            122, 148, 153*n*.19, 158, 160,
            165, 171-172, 174, 176, 179,
            181, 182-183, 184, 195, 238,
            241, 255, 256-257, 259, 260,
            268, 271, 272-273, 279, 312,
            316-317, 321, 322-324,
            326
        Malaysia, xi, 7, 37, 38, 39-41, 42,
            43, 44*n*.1, 61, 63, 64, 66-67,
            72, 73*n*.1, 76*n*.28, 76*n*.29,
            79*n*.69, 154-167, 182, 241, 242,
            244-245, 268, 272, 276, 298,
            305, 313-317, 323
        Philippines, xi, 8-9, 42, 44*n*.1, 63,
            73*n*.1, 75*n*.20, 76*n*.31, 153*n*.19,
            156, 162, 163-164, 234-249,
            268, 272, 273, 276, 298, 313-
            317, 323, 326
        Taiwan, xi, xii, 9, 31, 41, 52, 64,
            82, 84, 85, 87-88, 89, 94*n*.3,
            101, 102, 105, 116, 130, 134,
            157, 160, 162, 163, 165, 223,
            232*n*.20, 235, 237-238, 240,
            241, 246, 247*n*.15, 247*n*.16,
            248*n*.29, 248*n*.30, 266-281,
            298, 314, 316, 322-326, 327
    military, xii, xiii, xv, 4, 7, 19, 23,
        26, 30, 31, 42, 48-49, 50, 51-55,
        56, 57, 68, 82, 93, 99, 100, 101,
        102, 103, 105-106, 112,
        114, 116,
        128, 130, 134-135, 137-138, 143,
        144, 147, 155, 156, 160, 162,
        163, 165, 172, 177, 180, 183,
        195-196, 201*n*.24, 208, 210, 212,
        213, 215, 223-224, 227, 229, 230,
        235, 244, 251, 252, 254, 258,
        260, 269, 273, 276-277, 284, 287,
        289, 291*n*.3, 296, 300, 312, 315,
        316, 317, 324, 327

China (continued)
  People's Liberation Army (PLA),
    8, 24, 25, 32, 48, 54-55, 56, 88,
    93, 95*n*.24, 155, 195, 198, 209,
    211, 215, 269, 270, 277, 316, 318
  People's Liberation Army Navy
    (PLAN), 43, 89, 91, 92, 271, 274,
    279, 322, 323, 326, 327
  relations with United States, xi, xii,
    xiii, xiv, xv, 3, 16, 18, 19, 23, 33,
    39, 43, 47, 49, 50, 54, 55, 57, 82,
    83, 84, 85, 86, 87, 88-89, 94*n*.7,
    101, 102, 105, 106, 114, 116,
    117, 127, 134-135, 137, 138, 139,
    148, 151, 178, 182, 183, 195,
    210, 212, 214, 220, 221, 223,
    225-226, 227, 228, 229, 230,
    232*n*.20, 240, 252, 256, 257, 260,
    270-271, 274, 277, 278, 284, 287,
    311, 315, 316, 317, 324, 326, 328
  tributary system, 82, 89, 145, 169,
    170, 192, 207, 208, 253, 254, 262
China Export Import Bank, 215
China Harbor Engineering Company
  Group, 228
China Metallurgical Group
  Corporation, 18
China-Central Asia Railroad. *See*
  Central Asian Railroad
China-centric. *See* Sino-centric
China-Kyrgyzstan-Uzbekistan
  Railroad Construction Agreement,
  132-133
China National Machinery Import
  & Export Corporation, 132
China-Pakistan Joint Declaration
  (2003), 227
chinaware, 13
Chindia concept, 57
Chinese Communist Party (CCP), 51,
  91, 116, 174, 177, 178, 214, 256,
  270, 273, 316
Chinese Eastern Railway (CER),
  255, 256
Chinese People's Volunteer troops
  (CPV), 117

Chinese Turkestan, 15
Chitral, 17
Choibalsan, Khorloogiin, 174
Chola Incident (1967), 317
Chomolungma. *See* Mount Everest
Chonghou, 98
Chongqing, 272
Chosôn dynasty, 113
Chosôn kingdom, 112, 113, 114, 115
Chosŏn ŭiyonggun. See Korean
  Volunteer Army
Christianity, 129, 146
Chulalongkorn, 146
Chumbi Valley, 31
Chunxiao/Shirakaba, 5, 81, 82, 83,
  86-88, 92, 93, 322
civil wars, 115-118, 172, 174, 256,
  268-269, 273, 289
civilization, 47, 48
Cixi, 84
Clinton, Hillary, 315, 316
Clipperton Island, 86
Cloma, Tomas, 242
cloth, 222
coal, 9, 70, 133, 181, 263, 321
coastal defense, xiii
Cold War, 15-17, 121-122, 156, 163,
  209, 219-221, 224, 230, 257, 296,
  323
Collective Security Treaty
  Organization (CSTO), 6, 127, 128,
  134, 137, 138, 139
Commodore Reef, 162, 163, 242
communication, 19, 102, 130, 221,
  286, 287
Communist International
  (Comintern), 173
Complementary Agreement Between
  the People's Republic of China
  and the Republic of Tajikistan on
  the China-Tajikistan Boundary
  (2002), 289
computers, 70
Confidence Building Measures
  (CBM), 42, 51, 66, 104, 279
Confucianism, 129, 160

Conolly, Arthur, 292*n*.7
continental shelf, 7, 10, 37, 38, 39,
    40, 43, 52, 63, 64, 66, 67, 71, 72,
    75*n*.20, 76*n*.28, 76*n*.29, 76*n*.32,
    78*n*.63, 81, 82-83, 87-88, 162, 163-
    164, 165, 167*n*.20, 236-237, 240,
    242, 245, 295, 297, 298, 301, 305,
    314, 315, 326
copper, 18, 180
Cornwallis South Reef, 162
corruption, 134, 139, 174, 179, 181,
    184, 254, 262
cotton, 13, 222
Council for Mutual Economic
    Assistance (COMECON), 175
Counterattack in Self-Defense in the
    Paracel Islands, 274, 296
Cuarteron Reef, 162, 241
Cuban Missile Crisis, 50, 57, 257
Cuban Quarantine, 50
cultural relations, 17, 23, 24, 26, 30,
    46, 48, 105, 117-118, 129, 137,
    139, 145, 156, 159, 177, 183, 191,
    235-236, 251, 288, 312
Cultural Revolution, 117, 118, 157,
    176, 221
cumin seed, 13
Customs Union (CU), 6, 127, 136,
    139, 320

Da Chu Thap. *See* Fiery Cross Reef
Da Gac Ma. *See* Johnson Reef
Da Gaven. *See* Gaven Reef
Da Gri-san, 162
Da Hi Gen, 162
Da Hu-go. *See* Hughes Reef
Da Subi. *See* Subi Reef
Dacca, 221
Dachen islands, 269, 270, 271
Dadan Island, 271
Dagahoy Dugao/Kota. *See* Loaita
    Island
Dalai Lama, 24, 25, 26, 27, 53, 56,
    170, 183, 205-207, 209
Damansky/Zhenbao Island, 257, 259
Dandong, 118, 119

Daqing, 260
Daqiu Island, 271
Dari, 287
Darussalam-class patrol boat, 43
Darwin, 316
Daurs, 253
De Lagreé, Doudant, 146
deer, 181
Democratic People's Republic of
    Korea (DPRK), 6, 117, 118, 119-
    120, 121, 122. *See also* North
    Korea.
Democratic Republic of Afghanistan.
    See Afghanistan
demonstrations, 25, 101, 178, 210,
    211, 214, 215, 312
Deng Xiaoping, 16, 52, 100, 102,
    149, 157, 212, 224
Deora, Murli, 128
Department of Boundary and Ocean
    Affairs (PRC), 317
Deva, King Narendra, 206
Dharmashala, 213, 214, 216, 317
diamonds, 9, 263, 321
Diaoyu/Senkaku islands, xiii, 5, 52,
    81, 82, 83-86, 88-91, 93, 94*n*.3,
    94*n*.7, 267, 271, 277, 279, 322
Diaoyudao Uplift Belt, 83
Dien Bien Phu, 148
Dinggue County, 205
Diphu L'Ka Pass, 194, 197, 198,
    200*n*.14
disaster prevention, 304
Djoeanda Declaration (1957), 62,
    74*n*.6
Doig, Desmond, 27
Doklam, 30, 31
Dongsha islands. *See* Pratas islands
donkey, 182
Dordoi bazaar, 131
Dorje, Jigme, 27
Douglas Reef, 87
Dramana, 30
Drenthang township, 205
drugs, 53, 129, 138, 199, 245
dry fruit, 222

Durand, Sir Mortimer, 14
Durand Line, 15
Dushanbe, 288
Dutch, 119, 268
Dutch East Indies, 62

eagles, 15
earthquake, 93
East Asia, xiv, xv, 5, 13, 82, 132,
  187*n*.36, 244, 291, 312, 323
East China Sea, 5, 41-42, 52, 63, 81-
  93, 121, 165, 237, 267, 313, 322-
  324, 325, 326, 327
  Chunxiao/Shirakaba, 5, 81, 82, 83,
    86-88, 92, 93, 322
  Diaoyu/Senkaku islands, xiii, 5, 52,
    81, 82, 83-86, 88, 89, 90, 91, 93,
    94*n*.3, 94*n*.7, 267, 271, 277, 279,
    322
  Okinotorishima, 5, 81, 87-88, 92,
    93, 322
East London Reef, 162
East Turkestan, 19, 104, 262, 291*n*.4
East Turkestan Independence
  Movement, 227, 262
Economist Intelligence Unit, 179
education, 17, 118, 158, 183
eleven-dashed line map, 9, 64, 160,
  248*n*.30, 273, 280*n*.11
Enkhbayar, Nambaryn, 128
environment, 4, 58, 93, 151, 171,
  183, 322, 325
environmental protection, 304
equidistance principle, 83, 86, 92,
  212, 237, 301, 302, 322, 328
Ereli, Adam, 86
Erenhot. *See* Erlian
Erica Reef, 39
Erlian, 175, 177, 182
Eternal Friendship Treaties, 129-130.
  See also treaties.
ethnicity, xv, 8, 15, 50, 100, 103,
  115, 116, 117, 118, 121, 130, 137,
  139, 144, 146, 147, 152*n*.1,
  153*n*.17, 156, 196, 198, 215, 227,
  254, 268, 283, 284, 288, 318

Europe, xiii, xiv, 9, 13, 48, 114, 132,
  133, 136, 144, 145-146, 175, 251,
  252, 254, 326-327
European Economic Community. *See*
  European Union
European Union, 183, 284
Evans, Grant, 151
Ever-Victorious Army, 99
Exchange of Letters (EoL), 40, 41,
  44, 314
Exclusive Economic Zone (EEZ), 5,
  10, 38, 39, 40, 41, 42, 43, 63-64,
  66-72, 75*n*.20, 76*n*.28, 76*n*.32,
  78*n*.63, 81, 82-83, 87-89, 91, 121,
  235, 236-237, 240, 244, 245, 295,
  298, 301, 322
extremism, 18, 129, 137, 138, 227,
  262, 283, 287, 291*n*.4, 319

F-16 jet fighters, 223
Far Eastern Federal District (DVFO),
  261
Far Eastern Military District, 258
far sea defense, xiii
farm equipment, 222
Fazal-ur-Rahman, 225
Fiery Cross Reef, 162, 241, 296
First Sino-Japanese War (1894-
  1895), 268, 272
fisheries management area, 63, 69,
  72
fishing, 5, 6, 10, 38, 57, 63, 68-70,
  72-73, 89, 90, 92, 93, 94*n*.7, 112,
  121, 122, 181, 184, 215, 238, 240,
  258, 272, 302-303, 304-305, 306,
  313, 314, 315, 322-323, 325
Flat Island, 162, 242
fluorspar, 181
food products, 70, 132, 262, 325
Formosa, 84, 267, 268, 272. *See also*
  Taiwan.
forward policy, 56
France, 88, 143, 145, 146-148, 151,
  152*n*.1, 153*n*.17, 153*n*.19, 162,
  192, 193, 194, 241, 255, 268, 272-
  273, 274, 278, 301

Fravel, M. Taylor, xi, xii, 329*n*.5
Free Laos, 148
Free Tibet Movement, 213, 214
French Indochina, 145, 146, 194, 272
French Union, 148, 273
fundamentalism, 8, 225-228, 230
Fujian Province, 160, 268, 270
furs, 13, 253

Gampo, King Srong-tsen, 206
Gandhi, Indira, 28
Gandhi, Rajiv, 223-224
Gansu Province, 98
Gaodeng Island, 271
Gates, Robert, 135
Gaven Reef, 162, 241
Gawlum, 196
Gelugpa sect, 27
Geneva Conference (1954), 148
geography, xi, 64, 144, 151, 171,
    286, 311, 325, 326, 327
geopolitics, xiv, 5, 47, 230, 311
Germany, 88, 160, 255, 278
Gfoeller, Tatiana C., 135
Gieu, 30
Gilani, Yousuf Raza, 19
Gilgit, 230
Global Times, 162, 316
Global War on Terror (GWOT), 225-
    226
globalization, xii, 5, 47
Go West strategy, 103, 290, 319
gold, 9, 181, 206, 207, 262, 263, 321
Gorbachev, Mikhail, 99, 177-178,
    257, 289
Gordon, Charles, 99
Gorkha, 206, 207
Gorno-Badakshan Autonomous
    Province. *See* Kuhistoni-
    Badakshan
Granitnaya River, 259
Great Britain, 14-16, 18, 23, 26, 27,
    50, 87, 91, 95*n*.29, 123*n*.5, 148,
    157, 191-196, 200*n*.12, 201*n*.21,
    202*n*.38, 208, 209, 248*n*.23, 279,
    285, 292*n*.7

Great Discovery Reef, 162
Great Game, 14, 285
Great Leap Forward, 117, 118
Great Power, xi, 3, 93, 102, 263, 321,
    324, 327
Great Wall, 98, 113
Greater East Asia Co-Prosperity
    Sphere, 82
Greater Mekong Sub-region States,
    149
Greater Persia, 288
Greater Tumen Initiative (GTI), 119,
    122
Green Island, 9, 267, 271, 272
Gross National Happiness (GNH), 30
Group of 77, 182-183
Guam, 87-88, 328*n*.1
Guangdong Province, 268, 269, 272
Guangzhou, 157, 221, 269
Gulf of Tonkin, 10, 295, 296, 297,
    298, 300-303, 306, 308*n*.15, 313,
    315, 325
Gwadar, 8, 219, 228, 229, 230, 318
Gyantse, 49

Haa Dzongkhag, 31, 32
Hainan Island, 5, 37, 61, 162, 269
Hainan Province, 241, 275
Hamgyong Pukto, 111
Han Chinese, 8, 48, 49, 52, 99, 103,
    116, 117-118, 123*n*.5, 181, 191,
    196, 198, 214, 268, 318
Han dynasty, 112, 169
Han-class submarine, 91
Hanoi, 10, 39, 41, 72, 144, 148, 149,
    194, 274, 296, 303
Harbin, xiv
Heaven Lake, 118
heavy water, 222
hegemonism, 89, 177, 260, 263
Heilongjiang Province, 261
Heixiazi/Bolshoi Ussuriysk Island,
    251
herbs, 32, 84, 222
High Conical Peak, 191, 192, 194,
    196, 197, 198

high-speed railway, 151, 229
Hilsa Pass, 205
Himalayan Mountains, 23, 47, 48, 51, 52, 54, 55, 56, 206, 208, 210, 212
Hindi-Chini bhai bhai slogan, 57
Hindu Kush, 14, 285
Hinduism, 129
Hsin Wan Pao, 95*n*.29
Hiu 04, 69-70
Hiu 10, 69-70
Hmong, 151
Ho Chi Minh, 148
Ho Chi Minh City, 145
Ho Chi Minh Trail, 148
Höhhot, 178
Hokkaido Island, 84, 85
Hong Kong, xii, 91, 119, 157, 238
Hongshanzui, 176
Honshū Island, 84
Howland Island, 328*n*.1
Hpimaw Village, 194, 196, 197
Hu, Nien-Tsu Alfred, 73
Hu Jintao, 128, 129, 158, 227, 236, 244
Hu Yaobang, 177
Hu Zhengyue, 32-33
Hua-panh-ha-tang-hoc, 147
Huang Hua, 223
Huang Jing, 316
Huangyan Dao, 161, 238. *See also* Scarborough Shoal.
Huanqiu Shibao, 4, 19
Huaphan Province, 148-149
Hughes Reef, 162, 241
human trafficking, 182, 184
Hungary, 182
Hunza Region, 220
Hussein, Onn, 157
hydroelectric power plants, xv, 387

I-pang, 147
I-wou, 147
Ieodo Rock. *See* Socotra Rock
Ijhtihad-class fast attack boat, 43
Ili Valley, 98, 99

Imperial Russia, xv, 9, 14-16, 19, 97-99, 114-115, 119, 169-171, 251, 252-253, 254, 283
India, xi, xiii, xiv, 4-5, 7-8, 15, 18, 23-29, 31, 33, 34*n*.15, 46-59, 128, 136, 140*n*.7, 176, 191, 195, 196-198, 204-217, 218-233, 257, 277, 287, 311, 317-319, 324, 327, 328
Indian Ocean, xiv-xv, 8, 219, 228, 229, 230, 318, 319, 328
Indo-Pakistan Nuclear Crisis (1998), 225
Indo-Pakistan War (1971), 221
Indochina, xiii, 146, 148, 193
Indonesia, xi, 5, 42, 44*n*.1, 60-79, 156, 165, 241, 245, 268, 272, 275, 298, 314-317
Inner Mongolia, 117, 170, 171, 172, 174, 175, 176, 177, 178, 183, 271
intermestic, 97, 102, 103
International Atomic Energy Agency (IAEA), 228
International Committee of the Red Cross (ICRC), 213
International Court of Justice, 165
international history, xi
International Monetary Fund (IMF), 179
International Security Assistance Forces (ISAF), 18, 19, 287
Investigator Shoal, 39
Iphigenia, 87
Iran, 13, 128, 132, 140*n*.7, 286, 288
Irrawaddy River, xv, 193, 194, 196
Irrawaddy watershed, 191, 192, 194, 196
irredentism, 312, 320
Isaikin, Anatoly, 260-261
Isakov, Ismail, 135
Iselin, Frédéric, 195
Islam, 8, 17, 101, 129, 225, 226, 227, 228, 230, 262, 287
Islamabad, 51, 219, 220, 221, 222, 223, 224, 225, 226, 227, 228, 229, 230
Islamic fundamentalism, 227

Islamic Revival Party (IRPT), 291*n*.2
Israel, 182
Issyk Kul, 128, 132
Isu Razi Pass, 194
Itu Aba Island, 9, 160, 162, 241, 267, 273, 274, 275, 276, 277, 279, 323

Jakarta, 61, 68, 314
Jammu, 51, 52, 54
Japan, xi, xii, xiii, 5, 18, 52, 58, 63, 80-95, 106, 112, 114-119, 122, 148, 153*n*.19, 158, 160, 165, 171-172, 174, 176, 179, 181, 182-183, 184, 195, 238, 241, 255, 256-257, 259, 260, 268, 271, 272-273, 279, 312, 316-317, 321, 322-324, 326
Japan International Cooperation Association, 183
Japanese Self Defense Force, 93
Jarvis Island, 328*n*.1
Jiandao, 114, 115, 116
Jiang Zemin, 103, 180, 289
Jilin, 119, 260
Jilin Province, 104, 111, 115, 117, 119, 261
Jinmen Island, 9, 267, 268, 269, 270, 271
Johnson Reef, 162, 241, 296
Johnston Atoll, 328*n*.1
joint fishing zone, 6, 10, 112, 121, 122, 303, 313, 322
Joint Malaysia-Brunei Darussalam Land Boundary Technical Committee, 41
Joint Marine Seismic Undertaking Tripartite Agreement (JMSU), 243, 244
Jurchen, 113
jurisdiction, 4, 7, 10, 41, 43, 62, 63, 64, 67, 87, 111, 115, 122, 164, 175, 194, 196, 240, 243, 245, 246, 257, 258, 274, 276, 279, 313, 315, 322, 325

K2, 220
Kabul, 14, 16, 17, 18

Kabul University, 16
Kachin State, 197
Kalapani-Limpiyadhuri, 205
Kalayaan Island Group (KIG), 8-9, 162, 235, 239, 242-245
Kalimantan, 69, 156
Kampuchea Krom, 144-145
Kando. *See* Jiandao
Kangfang, 196
Kangmei Yuanchao Zhanzheng. See Resist-America, Aid-Korea War
Kangxi Emperor, 113, 122, 321
Kara-Keche coal factory, 133
Kara-Suu bazaar, 131
Karachi, 220, 229, 292*n*.15
Karakoram Diplomacy, 221-223, 224-225, 228-230
Karakoram Highway (KKH), 8, 219, 221, 222, 223, 226, 227, 228, 229, 230, 292*n*.15, 319
Karakoram Mountain Range, 225, 285
Karakoram passes, 51, 221
Karen rebels, xv
Kargil, 225
Kargil Conflict, 225
Karimov, Islam, 128, 287
Karshi-Khanabad airbase, 138
Kartawidjaja, Ir. H. Djuanda, 74*n*.5
Karzai, Hamid, 19, 128, 129
Kashgar, 13, 15, 227, 229
Kashgar Prefecture. *See* Kashi Prefecture
Kashi Prefecture, 4, 13, 284
Kashmir, 25, 51, 52, 54, 219, 220, 221, 224, 230, 232*n*.25, 318
Kashmiri mujahideen, 225
Kasuri, Khurshid, 128
Kathmandu, 206, 207, 208, 209, 210, 211, 212, 213, 214, 215, 216, 318
Kathmandu Valley, 206, 207
Kazakh Soviet Socialist Republic, 99
Kazakhstan, xi, xiii, xiv, 5-6, 96-109, 127, 128, 129, 130, 136, 138, 229, 262, 284, 289, 290, 312, 313, 319-320, 330*n*.18

Keng-Hung State, 192, 193
Keoboulapha, Khampoui, 143
Kerong, 206, 207, 208
Kerong Pass, 206
Khabarov, Yerofei, 253
Khabarovsk, 124*n*.31, 251, 258, 260, 262
Khampa guerrillas, 210, 212
Khan, Ayub, 221
Khan Quest military exercises, 183
Khan Tengri Peak, 128
Khanh Hoa Province, 162
Khanka Lake, 259
Khik, 13
Khitan, 113
Khiva, 98
Khmer, 144-145
Khmer Rouge, 146, 149, 150
Khokand, 14, 15
Khrushchev, Nikita, 118, 256, 257
Khunjerab Pass, 292*n*.15
Khushab nuclear reactor, 222
Kim dynasty, 6
Kim Il Sung, 116, 117, 118, 124*n*.31
Kim Jong Il, 118, 124*n*.31,
Kingman Reef, 328*n*.1
Kipling, Rudyard, 292*n*.7
Kizilsu Kirghiz Autonomous Prefecture, 284-285
Kochosôn. *See* Chosôn
Kodari Highway, 211
Kodari Pass, 205, 211
Koguryô, 111-113
Koguryô Dispute, 111-112
Kohl, Helmut, 278
Koirala, B.P., 210, 211
Kokang, 8, 191, 198, 199, 318
Kokang Myanmar National Democratic Alliance Army (MNDAA), 198, 318
Konrad Adenauer Foundation, 183
Korea, xi, xiii, xiv, xv, 6, 48, 50, 89, 106, 111-125, 158, 181, 182, 256, 259, 270, 277, 312, 320-321, 322-324. *See also* North Korea, South Korea.

Korean peninsula, xiv, xv, 111, 112-113
Korean People's Army (KPA), 116, 117
Korean Volunteer Army (KVA), 116, 117
Korean War, 48, 50, 116, 117, 118-119, 270
Kota Island, 162, 242
Kremlin, 128, 137, 260
Kreutzmann, Hermann, 17
Kuala Lumpur, 156, 157, 159. *See also* Malaysia.
Kuanshang. *See* Sansi
Kublai Khan, 240-241, 277
Kuensel, 31
Kuhistoni-Badakhshan, 285
Kuldzha Province, 98
Kulma Pass, 292*n*.15
Kunlun Mountains, 51, 285
Kunming, 157, 194, 195, 199
Kuomintang (KMT). *See* Nationalist Party
Kuti, 206, 207, 208
Kutuzov Island, 259
Kwantung Army, 114
Kyaukphyu, 199
Kyôngsông, 113
Kyrgyz, 13-14, 15, 254
Kyrgyzstan, xi, xiv, 6, 19, 97, 98, 104, 126-141, 262, 284, 289, 290, 312, 319-320, 330*n*.17
Kyūshū Island, 84

L'Union d'Incochine. *See* French Indochina
Ladakh, 27, 50, 52, 55, 324
Ladd Reef, 162
Lal Masjid. *See* Red Mosque
Lamkian Cay. *See* Panata Cay
Lan Xang, 143, 145, 151
Lan Xang Hom Khaothe. *See* Lan Xang
Lan Yu Island. *See* Orchid Island
Landsdowne Reef, 162
Lankiam Cay, 242

Lao Issara. *See* Free Laos
Lao People's Democratic Republic
    (Lao PDR). *See* Laos
Laos, xi, 7, 44*n*.1, 142-153, 191, 196,
    197-198, 300, 313, 317-319
Laos-Sino Treaty and Supplementary
    Protocol (1991), 149
Lashio, 195
Latin America, 224
Lavrov, Sergei, 135
Lawak Island. *See* Nanshan Island
Le Cong Phung, 300
League of Nations, 195
leather, 222
lebensraum, 176
Lema and Wan Shan Islands, 269
Lesser Jinmen Island, 271
Lhasa, xiv, 24, 49, 53, 206, 207, 208,
    209, 214
Lhasa Uprising (1959), 26, 209, 212,
    213
Li Mi, 195
Li Peng, 180, 224
Liao dynasty, 113
Liaodong peninsula, xv, 255
Liaodong Province, 111
Liaoning Province, 119, 261
Liberal Democratic Party (LDP), 89
Lifanyuan. *See* Office of Colonial
    Affairs
Likas Island. *See* West York Island
Limbang, 39, 40
line of actual control, 51
line of control, 47, 51, 52, 55, 220,
    225
linguistics, 145, 215, 288
Little Pamir Mountains, 13
Liu Dacai, 273
Liuqiu islands, 271. *See also* Ryūkyū
    islands
livestock, 15, 30, 173, 177, 181, 262,
    288
Lo, Bobo, 251, 252
Loaita Island. *See* Kota Island
*The Location Map of the South China
    Sea Islands*, 64

Long-term Treaty of Good-
    neighborliness, Friendship, and
    Cooperation (2007), 129
Lop Nor, 222-223
Louisa Reef, 4, 37, 38, 39, 41, 43,
    162, 314
Lu Rebellion, 147, 153*n*.17
Lü Dao Island. *See* Green Island
Luang Namtha, 147
Luang Phabang, 145
Lufang Ridge, 195, 197
Lungnai, 197
Luo Yuan, 316
Lüshun. *See* Port Arthur
Luzon, 237, 238, 240

M-11 Short Range Ballistic Missile
    (SRBM), 223
Ma Ying-jeou, 277
Macao, xii, 119
Macapagal-Arroyo, Gloria, 236, 244
MacArthur, Douglas, 153*n*.19
Macclesfield Bank, 64, 238, 241,
    247*n*.15, 275
MacFarquhar, Roderick, 56
machine guns, 89, 90
machinery, 70
madrassas, 226, 227
Mahan, Alfred Thayer, 326
Mahendra, King, 211
Malacca, 66
Malacca Strait, xiv, 66, 229
Malayan Communist Party, 156, 157
Malayan Races Liberation Army,
    156
Malaysia, xi, 7, 37, 38, 39-41, 42, 43,
    44*n*.1, 61, 63, 64, 66-67, 72, 73*n*.1,
    76*n*.28, 76*n*.29, 79*n*.69, 154-167,
    182, 241, 242, 244-245, 268, 272,
    276, 298, 305, 313-317, 323
Malaysian Armed Forces, 163
Malaysian Friendship and Trade
    Centre (MFTC), 157
Malla, King Pratap, 206
Malla Kingdom, 207
Manang Pum. *See* Mulang Pum

Manas airbase, 19, 135
Manchu, 98, 99, 113, 118, 170,
  202*n*.38, 206, 252, 253, 254, 258,
  268
Manchukuo, xii, 115, 116
Manchuria, xi, 84, 98, 112, 113, 114,
  115, 116, 117, 123*n*.6, 124*n*.21,
  124*n*.31, 170, 172, 254, 255, 256,
  261, 269
mandala, 144, 145
Manipur, 57
Manwaing. *See* Manwyne
Manwyne, 193
Manyunjie. *See* Manwyne
Manzhouli, 258
Mao Zedong, 23, 25, 48, 49, 50, 56,
  91, 116, 169, 173, 174-175, 176,
  195, 210, 211, 222, 224, 256, 257,
  269
March 2008 Tibetan Uprising, 56,
  317
Marcos, Ferninand, 242
Marine Science and Technology
  Center, 88
Mariveles Reef, 39, 162
Marxism, 149, 184
Maryland, 23
Massachusetts Institute of
  Technology (MIT), xi
Mazu islands, 9, 267, 268, 269, 270,
  271
McMahon line, 50, 194, 196, 197
Medvedev, Dmitry, 183
Mekong Delta, 147
Mekong River, 143, 146, 147, 150,
  151, 191, 192, 194, 198
Memoranda of Understanding
  (MOU), 158
Memorandum of Understanding on
  the Resumption of Diplomatic
  Relations (1990), 68
Menkeseli, 258
meteorology, 304
Mexico, xi
Middle East, xiii, xiv, 85, 136, 228,
  260

MiG-29 fighter jet, 163
military, xii, xiii, xv, 4, 7, 19, 23, 26,
  30, 31, 42, 48-49, 50, 51-55, 56,
  57, 68, 82, 93, 99, 100, 101, 102,
  103, 105-106, 112, 114, 116, 128,
  130, 134-135, 137-138, 143, 144,
  147, 155, 156, 160, 162, 163, 165,
  172, 177, 180, 183, 195-196,
  201*n*.24, 208, 210, 212, 213, 215,
  223-224, 227, 229, 230, 235, 244,
  251, 252, 254, 258, 260, 269, 273,
  276-277, 284, 287, 289, 291*n*.3,
  296, 300, 312, 315, 316, 317, 324,
  327
minerals, 18, 94*n*.5, 131, 133, 146,
  181, 184, 194, 284, 290, 315, 319
Ming dynasty, 206, 208
Ministry of Marine Affairs and
  Fisheries (MMAF), 63, 75*n*.14
Minquiers and Ecrehos Case, 86
Mir of Wakhan, 13, 15
Mischief Reef, 42, 162, 241
missiles, 16-17, 50, 57, 223, 224,
  225, 230, 232*n*.20, 257, 318
Mohamad, Mahathir, 40, 159
Momein. *See* Tengyue
monastery, 207, 208
Mong Pan State, 195
Mong-wou, 147
Mongkong, King, 146
Mongol Defense White Paper, 180
Mongolia, xi, xiv, 7, 9, 98, 100, 119,
  128, 140*n*.7, 168-189, 256, 267,
  271, 277, 320-321, 323
Mongolian People's Republic
  (MPR), 7, 169, 173, 174, 175, 176,
  177, 178
Mongolian People's Revolutionary
  Party (MPRP), 178
monopolarity, 260
Moscow, xiv, 59*n*.5, 136, 178, 251,
  256, 259. *See also* Russia, Soviet
  Union, Union of Soviet Socialist
  Republics.
Moscow Carnegie Center, 261
Motuo Dam, 52

Mouhout, Henri, 146
Moung-poung, 147
Mount Everest, 8, 205, 210
Muang Sing, 150
Mukedeng, 113, 114
Mukedeng stele, 115
Mulang Pum, 191
multi-vector foreign policy, 286
Muraviev-Amursky, Nikolai, 171, 254
Murgab, 289, 292n.15
Murkushi, 13
Murphy Oil Company, 39, 40, 41
Musharraf, Pervez, 227
mushroom, 32
Muslim Rebellion (1862-78), 98, 99
Myanmar, xi, xiii, xiv-xv, 7-8, 44n.1, 54, 55, 56, 143, 150, 151, 190-203, 229, 277, 313, 317-319, 327

Nagaland, 56
Nagri Prefecture, 205
Najin-Sonbong Special Economic Zone (SEZ), 119
Nam Tha, 150
Nam-la, 147
Nam La River, 198
Nam-wou, 147
Namkhan, 192
Namwan Assigned Tract, 194, 195, 196, 197
Namwan River, 192, 193
Namyit Island, 162
Nan Tong Jiao. *See* Louisa Reef
Nan-nuo-ho, 147
Nan-ouo-ho, 147
Nansha islands. *See* Spratly islands
Nansham Island. *See* Lawak Island
Nanshan Island, 242
Nanwei Island. *See* Spratly Island
narcotics, 129, 149, 151, 180, 181, 182, 184, 199. *See also* drugs.
National Assembly of Bhutan, 30, 330n.19
National Assembly of Vietnam, 300, 303

National People's Congress of China, 300, 303
nationalism, xii, 90, 116, 226, 259, 263, 313
Nationalist Navy, 270, 271, 272, 300
Nationalist Party, 116, 268
Natuna Island Group, 5, 61, 62, 63, 64, 66, 68, 71-73, 272, 298, 314
Natuna Sea, 5, 62, 73
natural gas, 5, 9, 61, 163, 229, 260, 263, 321
natural prolongation principle, 81, 82-83, 86-87, 322
natural resources, 58, 70, 73, 181, 246, 260, 262, 290, 317
Nazarbayev, Nursultan, 97, 102, 104, 128, 129
Nehru, Jawaharlal, 23, 25, 26, 27, 48-49, 50, 57, 59n.5, 220
Nepal, xi, 8, 27, 49, 54, 55, 204-217, 317-319, 324, 327
Nepal Communist Party, 214
Nepal Valley. *See* Kathmandu Valley
Netherlands, 62, 74n.3, 148
New Delhi, 28, 29, 209, 212, 230. *See also* India.
new security concept, 105
Ngum, King Fa, 145
Nguyen Phu Trong, 305
nickel, 70
Nigeria, 53
nine-dashed line map, 9, 10, 41, 62, 64, 66, 67-68, 71, 72, 73, 75n.20, 76n.29, 76n.31, 155, 160, 165, 241-242, 244-245, 246, 248n.30, 273, 279, 295, 314, 315, 326
Ningxia Province, 227
Nixon, Richard, 85, 86, 88, 212, 221, 257
Norbulingka, 25
North America, xiii
North East Cay, 162, 242
North Korea, xiii, xv, 6, 111, 115, 116-117, 118-119, 121, 122, 124n.31, 181, 259, 277, 312, 321. *See also* Korea.

North Vietnam, 149, 274, 296. *See also* Vietnam.
Northern Mariana islands, 328*n*.1
nuclear energy
  accident, 93
  crisis, 225
  free state status, 180
  missiles, 223, 224, 225, 230, 318
  power, 54, 222
  technology transfer, 8, 219, 222, 223, 230, 318
  testing, 90, 222-223
  war, 50
  weapons, 85, 222, 223, 225, 257
Nuclear Suppliers Group (NSG), 54-55
nylon, 222

Obama, Barack, 57, 137, 316
Office of Colonial Affairs, 170
Ogasawara islands, 87
Oirat Khanate, 253
Okinawa, 82, 85, 86, 91, 92, 94*n*.7, 268, 271, 324
Okinawa Prefecture, 84, 85
Okinawa Trough, 82, 83, 322
Okinotorishima, 5, 81, 87-88, 92, 93, 322
Olangchunggola Pass, 205
Olangchunggola Township, 205
One China Policy, 165, 215, 276, 323
Ong Kham, 147, 153*n*.17
Onn, Tun Hussein, 157
opium, 18, 193, 254
opportunities, xii, 3, 9, 51, 57, 70-72, 73, 105, 130, 136, 145, 151, 169, 171-172, 174, 179, 193, 212, 215, 251, 254, 267, 279, 287, 311, 313, 319, 326-327, 328
Oprang Valley, 220
Orchid Island, 9, 267, 271, 272
Oudomxay, 147

P'yongan Pukto, 111
Pacific Ocean, xi, xiii, xv, 114, 132, 254, 255, 311, 316, 328*n*.1

Paektu Mountain. *See* Changbai Mountain
Pag-asa Island. *See* Thitu Island
Pakistan, xi, 8, 13, 14, 15-17, 18, 19, 26, 49, 51, 54, 55, 57, 128, 140*n*.7, 219-233, 277, 285, 287, 292*n*.15, 312, 317-319, 327
Pakistan International Airlines (PIA), 221
Pakistani-occupied Kashmir (PoK), 54
Pakxe, 146
Palau, 73*n*.1
Palauig, 238
Palawan Island, 244
Palawan Province, 162, 242
Palmas Island, 86
Palmyra Island, 328*n*.1
Pamir Boundary Commission, 14
Pamir Mountains, 10, 13, 15, 17, 257, 283, 285
Pamir Region, 14, 285
Pan Guang, 135
Pan Kung, 197
Pan Nawng, 197
Pan Wai, 197
Panata Cay, 162, 242
Panata. *See* Lankiam Cay
Panchsheel Agreement (1954), 49, 50
Pande, Damodar, 207
Panghung, 197
Panglao, 197
Papua New Guinea, 73*n*.1
Paracel islands, 10, 41, 63, 64, 89, 160, 161, 163, 236, 241, 272-274, 275-276, 279, 295, 296, 297, 298
Parkae State. *See* Bohai State
Parola Cay. *See* North East Cay
Pascoe, Lynn, 128
Patag Island. *See* Flat Island
Pathet Lao, 148, 149, 153*n*.21
Peace Mission Exercises (2005), 130, 134
Pearson Reef, 162
Penghu islands, 9, 84, 267, 268, 269, 270, 272

People's Daily, 51, 54
People's Liberation Army (PLA), 8, 24, 25, 32, 48, 54-55, 56, 88, 93, 95*n*.24, 155, 195, 198, 209, 211, 215, 269, 270, 277, 316, 318
People's Liberation Army Navy (PLAN), 43, 89, 91, 92, 271, 274, 279, 322, 323, 326, 327
People's Republic of China (PRC). *See* China
perestroika, 149
Perpetual Peace and Friendship Treaty (1949), 24
Persia, 14, 288
Persian Gulf, 229
Persian language, 286, 288
Pescadores islands. *See* Penghu islands
Peshawar, 228
Peter the Great, 253
Petley Reef, 162
Petlin, Ivan, 253
PetroChina Chemical Complex, 260
petroleum, xv, 5, 9, 39, 40-41, 52, 81, 85, 86-87, 90, 93, 128, 135, 163, 229, 244, 260, 263, 265*n*.28, 297, 304, 315, 321, 325
Petronas Oil Company, 39, 41
Pham Van Dong, 274, 296
Philippine Archipelagic Baselines Law (2009), 237, 240
Philippine Coast Guard, 244
Philippine Treaty Limits, 237, 238, 239, 242
Philippines, xi, 8-9, 42, 44*n*.1, 63, 73*n*.1, 75*n*.20, 76*n*.31, 153*n*.19, 156, 162, 163-164, 234-249, 268, 272, 273, 276, 298, 313-317, 323, 326
Phnom Penh, 144
Phongsaly, 147, 150
Pianma Village. *See* Hpimaw Village
pipeline, xv, 8, 199, 229, 230, 260
plutonium, 222
poaching, 32, 33, 181
Pol Pot regime, 149

Poland, 278
political bridge, 5, 58
pollution, 263
Polyarkov, Vassily, 252-253
Polynesian, 268
population, 4, 13, 17-18, 23, 32, 51, 93, 100, 111, 112, 114, 117-118, 121, 136, 144, 146, 152*n*.1, 152*n*.8, 159, 171, 174, 175, 176-177, 179, 191, 192, 212, 213, 226-227, 254, 261, 262, 268, 284-285, 286, 287, 288, 290, 300
Population Reference Bureau, 284
Port Arthur, 255, 256
Potsdam Declaration (1945), 84, 148, 268
Potuna, 98
Pratas islands, 9, 64, 235, 237, 238, 247*n*.15, 267, 272, 279
Presidential Decree 1596 (1978), 242
Presidential Decree 1599 (1978), 242
Prince Bogdoi, 253
Proekt Budushchego, 136
Protocol of Chuguchak (1864), 254
Provisional Measures Zone (PMZ), 121
Pulau Layang-Layang. *See* Swallow Reef
Pulau Sekatung, 68
Purang County, 205
Putin, Vladimir, 128, 129, 135, 183, 252, 262
Pyandzh River, 286
Pyongyang, xiv, 112, 259

Qian Qichen, 156
Qing dynasty, 15, 99, 113, 114, 115, 117, 119, 169-171, 268, 272, 285
Qinghe, 176
Qiongzhou Strait, 269
Qualified Domestic Institutional Investor (QDII), 159
Quemoy Island. *See* Jinmen Island

Rahman, Abdur, 14
Rahmon, Emomali, 128, 289

railways, xi, xiv, 51, 132-133, 151, 153n.12, 171, 175, 182, 183, 194, 195, 254, 255, 292n.15. *See also* Chinese Eastern Railway, high-speed railway, Trans-Mongol Railroad, Trans-Siberian Railroad.
Rangoon, 195, 196
rapeseed, 6, 106, 320
Rasuwagarhi Pass, 205
Rawalpindi, 292n.15
Razak, Hussein, 157
red fox, 182
Red Guards, 118, 176
Red Mosque, 228
Red River, 147, 194
Reed Bank, 244
refugees, 6, 8, 26, 27, 34n.15, 121, 122, 198, 199, 205, 210, 212, 213, 214, 321
Regional Anti-Terrorism Structure (RATS), 137-138, 228, 262
Regulation 1 (2009), 63
religion, 26, 129, 144
Republic of China (ROC), 9, 64, 84, 85, 89, 94n.3, 116, 160, 162, 235, 248n.30, 266-281, 323. *See also* Taiwan.
Republic of Kazakhstan, 99. *See also* Kazakhstan.
Republic of Korea (ROK), 111. *See also* South Korea.
Republic of Vietnam (ROV), 149, 274. *See also* South Vietnma, Vietnam.
Resist-America, Aid-Korea War, 117
Riau Province, 61
rice, 143, 181, 193
Rifleman Bank, 38, 39, 41
ring magnets, 222
riverine tactics, 269
Rizal Reef. *See* Commodore Reef
road-building, 4, 16, 19, 26, 29, 31-32, 150, 182, 192, 195, 222, 229, 289, 293n.15, 319
Rogers, William, 85
Roman Londinium, 123n.5

Romanov dynasty, 252
Rosneft Oil Company, 260
Rosoboronexport, 261
Royal Brunei Armed Force (RBAF), 43
Royal Brunei Navy (RBN), 43
Royal Charlotte Reef, 163
Russia, xi, xiii, xiv, xv, 6, 9, 14-16, 17, 19, 59n.5, 89, 97-99, 103-104, 106-107, 111, 114-115, 119, 124n.31, 127, 128, 129, 130, 133, 134-139, 169-172, 175, 180, 182-183, 250-265, 277, 283, 284-285, 287, 289, 311, 312, 320-321, 324, 327. *See also* Soviet Union, Union of Soviet Socialist Republics.
Russia-Belarus-Kazakhstan Customs Union, 127, 136
Russian Far East (RFE), xi, 9, 107, 114, 119, 251, 259, 261, 262, 263, 321
Russian Federation, 173, 258
Russian Orthodox Church, 170, 254
Russo-Japanese War (1904-1905), 115, 255
Ryūkyū islands, 84, 271, 322, 326

Sa Zhenbing, 272
Sabah, 156-157
Sagarmatha. *See* Mount Everest
Sakhalin Island, 312
Sakishima islands, 238
salami tactics, 5, 93, 323
Salween, 192, 196
San Francisco Peace Treaty (1951), 84, 268
Sand Cay, 162
Sansha, 275
Sansi, 193
Sarawak, 39, 156, 157, 163
Sard-e Wakhan, 18
Sarikol Divide, 285, 289
Sarikol Range, 15, 285
Sato Eisaku, 85
Saur Revolution, 16
Savanakhet, 149

Scarborough Shoal (or Reef), 9, 162, 235, 237, 238, 240, 243, 248*n*.23
science, 88, 158, 236
SCO Studies Center, 135
sea lanes, xiii, 316, 325
Sea of Japan, 119, 259
sea power, 326, 327
sea routes, 13
seafood, 262
Second Indochina War, 152*n*.9, 153*n*.20
Second Opium War (1856-1860), 254
secret treaty, 4, 13, 312, 321
security, 5, 16, 24, 31, 32, 47, 49, 56, 58, 61, 99, 100, 102, 103, 104, 105-106, 116, 121, 127, 128, 129-130, 134, 137-139, 149-150, 157, 174, 177, 178, 179, 180, 187*n*.36, 219, 224, 226, 227, 228, 236, 262, 269, 270, 287, 288, 290, 296, 315, 316, 325
seismic survey cables, 315
Semenov, Grigori, 172
Semirech'e, 98
separatism, 129, 130, 138, 227, 262, 283, 291*n*.4
September 11 attack, 226, 227, 284, 287, 302, 305
Seventeen Point Agreement for the Peaceful Liberation of Tibet (1951), 24, 25
Shaanxi Province, 98
Shah, King Prithvi Narayan, 207
Shah, King Ram, 206
Shah dynasty, 207
Shahi, Agha, 220
Shanghai, 135, 157, 221
Shanghai Accord, 289
Shanghai Cooperation Organization (SCO), 6, 97, 128, 139, 228, 262, 263
Shanghai Five, 97, 103, 128, 132
Shanghai Spirit, 128, 129
Shaping the Force Today: Defence White Paper Update 2007, 43

Sharpening, 2008 Military Exercises, 183
sheep, 182
Shell Oil Company, 39, 87
Shenyang J-11, 261
Shi Lang, 268
Shigatse, 206, 207
Shigatse Prefecture, 205-206
Shiite Ismailis, 13
Shikoku Island, 84
Short Range Ballistic Missile (SRBM), 223
Shweli River, 192, 197
Shweli Valley, 192, 195
Siberia, xi, 9, 170, 171, 181, 252, 254, 260, 262, 263, 321
Sichuan Province, 192, 195
Sihanouk, King Norodom, 148
Sikh, 14
Sikkim, 26, 27, 55, 207, 317, 324
Siliguri Corridor, 31
silk, 222
Silk Road, xiv, 13, 98, 129
Silla, 112, 113
Simla Agreement, 224
Sin Cowe Island, 162
Sinchulumpa, 30
Singapore, 43, 44*n*.1, 73*n*.1, 156, 165, 316
Singapore Strait, xiv, 63
Singh, Swaran, 222
Sino-centric, 57, 328
Sino-DPRK Treaty (1963), 6, 122, 321
Sino-DPRK Treaty of Friendship, Cooperation and Mutual Assistance (1961), 118
Sino-French Agreement (1887), 274, 301
Sino-French Treaty (1895), 145-147
Sino-French Conflict (1884-1885), 268, 272
Sino-Indian Treaty (1954), 209
Sino-Indian War (1962), 257, 317
Sino-Mongol Treaty of Friendship and Cooperation (1994), 180

Sino-Nepal Agreement on Trade, Intercourse, and Related Questions (1966), 213

Sino-Nepal Boundary Treaty (1961), 205, 209

Sino-Nepal Joint Commission, 209

Sino-Nepal Treaty of Peace and Friendship (1960), 209

Sino-Nepalese Treaty (1792), 208

Sino-Russian Complementary Agreement (2004), 258-259

Sino-Soviet Border Agreement (1991), 258-259

Sino-Soviet border conflict, 97, 176

Sino-Soviet split, 15, 175, 196

Sino-Soviet Treaty of Friendship, Alliance, and Mutual Assistance (1950), 175

Sino-Vietnamese Agreement on Fishing Cooperation in the Gulf of Tonkin (2000), 303

Sino-Vietnamese Agreement on the Delimitation of Waters, EEZ and Continental Shelves in the Gulf of Tonkin (2000), 298, 300-303

Sino-Vietnamese Land Border Treaty (1999), 298, 299-300, 306

Sino-Vietnamese Supplemental Protocol to the Fishing Agreement (2004), 303

Sinuiju, 118, 119, 122

Sipsong Panna, 147

Skovorodino, 260

smuggling, 33, 149, 151, 177, 180, 181, 182, 184

Snow, Edgar, 174

snow leopard, 182

Sochi, 129

Socialist Republic of Vietnam, 149. *See also* Vietnam.

Socotra Rock, 121

Somatash, 14

Sommer, Martin, 153n.26

Songhua River, 98, 99, 260

Soochow University, 150

South America, xiii

South Asian Association for Regional Cooperation (SAARC), 30

South China Sea, xiv, 5, 7, 8, 9, 10, 36, 37-44, 61-73, 75n.20, 95n.24, 143, 146, 154, 155-166, 234, 235-246, 266, 267, 271-277, 279, 294, 295-298, 303-305, 306, 313-317, 322, 323, 325, 326, 327, 329n.6

eleven-dashed line map, 9, 64, 160, 248n.30, 273, 280n.11

nine-dashed line map, 9, 10, 41, 62, 64, 66, 67-68, 71, 72, 73, 75n.20, 76n.29, 76n.31, 155, 160, 165, 241-242, 244-245, 246, 248n.30, 273, 279, 295, 314, 315, 326

Paracel islands, 10, 41, 63, 64, 89, 160, 161, 163, 236, 241, 272-274, 275-276, 279, 295, 296, 297, 298

Pratas islands, 9, 64, 235, 237, 238, 247n.15, 267, 272, 279

Spratly islands, 4, 7, 8, 9, 37, 38, 39, 41, 43, 61, 63, 64, 66, 67, 69, 71, 72, 75n.18, 76n.32, 79n.69, 155, 159, 160, 161-163, 165, 237, 238, 241, 242, 245, 248n.28, 267, 272-273, 274, 275, 276, 277, 279, 296, 297, 298, 314

South Korea, xv, 6, 112, 119, 121, 122, 181, 182, 324. *See also* Korea.

South Reef, 162

South Vietnam, 89, 274, 295. *See also* Vietnam.

South West Cay, 162

Southeast Asia, xii, xv, 4, 37, 42, 43, 69, 94n.7, 106, 143, 144, 145, 146, 149, 151, 156, 163, 184, 220, 267, 305, 313, 315

Southeast Asian Treaty Organization (SEATO), 220

sovereignty, xii, 4, 7, 8, 10, 24, 37, 38, 39, 41, 42, 43, 54, 61, 63, 64, 68, 72, 83, 84-85, 86, 87, 88, 91, 94*n*.3, 100, 105, 106, 111, 113, 117, 122, 134, 145, 151, 155, 157, 159-161, 163-164, 172, 180, 197, 209, 235, 237, 240, 241, 242-243, 245, 246, 254, 268, 272–276, 279, 295, 296, 298, 313, 314-315, 321, 322, 325, 326, 328*n*.1

Soviet Air Force, 48

Soviet bloc, 178, 183

Soviet Union, 5, 16, 17, 50, 89, 97, 99, 119, 130, 149, 163, 169, 172-178, 187*n*.36, 223, 256, 257, 258, 277, 278, 286, 288, 289, 296. *See also* Russia, Union of Soviet Socialist Republics.

Soviet-Afghan War, 16-17, 226

Soviet-Mongol Treaty of Friendship, Cooperation, and Mutual Assistance (1966), 176

soya bean, 6, 106, 320

space technology, 183

Spain, 240

Special Administrative Region (SAR), 119, 122

Special Economic Zone (SEZ), 119, 181

sphere of Influence, 145, 324

spices, 13

Spratly Island, 71, 78*n*.64, 162

Spratly islands, 4, 7, 8, 9, 37, 38, 39, 41, 43, 61, 63, 64, 66, 67, 69, 71, 72, 75*n*.18, 76*n*.32, 79*n*.69, 155, 159, 160, 161-163, 165, 237, 238, 241, 242, 248*n*.28, 267, 272-273, 274, 275, 276, 277, 279, 296, 297, 298, 314

Sri Lanka, 54, 55, 229

St. Petersburg, 98, 99, 254

Stalin, Joseph, 48, 58*n*.2, 99, 117, 169, 173, 174, 256, 296

Stanovoy Mountains, 253

stepping stone strategy, 268, 270

Storm Island. *See* Spratly Island

Straits of Hormuz, 229

Strike Hard campaign, 227, 232*n*.35

String of Pearls, 229

stun grenades, 262

SU-27SK fighter jets, 261

SU-30 MKI bomber, 55

Subi Reef, 162, 241

Subic Bay, 240

Suez Canal, xiv

Suhartono, Agus, 70

Sui dynasty, 82

Suifen Delta, 259

Sultanov, Marat, 135

Sumdorong Chu sector, 55

Sun Yat-sen, 256

Sunni, 13

superpower, xi, 3, 10, 318, 328

Suyan Rock. *See* Socotra Rock

Swaine, Michael, 324

Swallow Reef, 39, 162, 163

Switzerland, 51, 182, 195

Tai Lu, 147

Tai Lue, 147

Taipei, 238, 273, 274. *See also* Taiwan.

Taiping Island. *See* Itu Aba Island

Taiping Rebellion (1850-1864), 99, 208, 254

Taiping River, 192

Taiping Valley, 192

Taiwan, xi, xii, 9, 31, 41, 52, 64, 82, 84, 85, 87-88, 89, 94*n*.3, 101, 102, 105, 116, 130, 134, 157, 160, 162, 163, 165, 223, 232*n*.20, 235, 237-238, 240, 241, 246, 247*n*.15, 247*n*.16, 248*n*.29, 248*n*.30, 266-281, 298, 314, 316, 322-324, 326, 327

Taiwan Patrol Force, 270

Taiwan Strait, 268-269, 270, 271

Tawan Strait Crisis, 271

Tajik language, 286, 288

Tajikistan, xi, xiv, 9-10, 13-14, 18, 97, 98, 104, 128, 130, 257, 277, 282-293, 312, 319-320, 327, 329*n*.16

Tajikistan civil war (1992-1997), 267, 289

Tajiks, 286, 288

Taklamakan desert basin, 286, 289

Taliban, 18, 225, 226-227, 287
Talok Pass. *See* Diphu L'Ka Pass
Tanaka Kakuei, 89
Tang dynasty, 15, 112
Tang Jiaxuan, 158
tanks, 55, 251
Tannu Tuva, 172, 173, 174, 277
Tannu Tuva People's Republic. *See* Tannu Tuva
Tarabarov Island, 258
Tarim River, 286
Taron River, 191, 194, 196, 197, 200*n*.14
Tashilhunpo monastery, 207, 208
Tashkent, 97-98, 132, 133, 137
Tashkurgan Tajik Autonomous County. *See* Taxkorgan Tajik Autonomous County
Tawang District, 53, 317
Tawang Valley, 53
Taxkorgan Tajik Autonomous County, 284-285, 289, 292*n*.15
Tebian electric company, 133
technology, 8, 82, 88, 89, 130, 158, 183, 223, 236
Tellis, Ashley, 324
Tengyue, 193
Tennent Reef, 162
territorial sea, 38, 40-41, 62, 63, 64, 75*n*.20, 78*n*.61, 89, 91, 162, 236-237, 243, 245, 274
Territoriale Zee en Maritime Kringen Ordonnantie 1939, 62
terrorism, 8, 19, 57, 129, 130, 135, 137-138, 219, 225-228, 230, 261-262, 283, 287, 288, 291*n*.4, 318
Terumbu Layang. *See* Swallow Reef
Terumbu Mantanani. *See* Mariveles Reef
Terumbu Semarang Barat Kecil. *See* Louisa Reef
Terumbu Ubi. *See* Ardasier Reef
textiles, 262
Thailand, 7, 44*n*.1, 73*n*.1, 143, 144, 145, 151, 155-156, 195, 201*n*.23, 308*n*.20, 323

That Luang monument, 150
think tanks, 216
Thinley, Lyonpo Jigmi Y., 330*n*.19
Thitu Island. *See* Pag-asa Island
three evils, 129, 138
Three Gorges Dam, 52
Tiananmen Massacre (1989), 101
Tianchi Lake. *See* Heaven Lake
Tibet Autonomous Region (TAR), 130, 213
Tibetan Refugee Reception Center, 213
Tibetan Welfare Office, 213
Tien Shan Mountains, 128, 285
timber, 9, 181, 260, 262, 263, 321
Timor Island, 73*n*.1
Timor Sea, 67
Timor-Leste, 73*n*.1
Tinkar village, 205
Tokdo/Takeshima islands, 112, 123*n*.4
Tokyo, 87. *See also* Japan.
Tokyo High Court, 84
Tongzhi Emperor, 98
Tonkin, 147, 152*n*.1, 248*n*.28
Torrens system, 146
Torsa River, 31
Total Oil Company, 39
tourism, 92, 158, 177, 215, 251
toys, 55, 70
trade, xiii, xiv, 3, 4, 7, 13, 15, 19, 26, 29, 37, 50, 53-54, 55, 58, 70, 90-91, 98, 99, 101, 102, 103, 104, 105-106, 107, 119, 131, 136, 143, 149, 153*n*.15, 155, 156, 157-159, 165, 170-171, 175, 176, 177, 180-183, 184, 185*n*.9, 192, 193, 194, 199, 201*n*.21, 206-207, 208, 213, 215, 222, 228, 229, 235-236, 244, 247*n*.3, 251, 252-253, 257, 260, 261, 286, 288, 313, 316, 317, 319, 327
Trans-Mongol Railroad, 175
Trans-Siberian Railroad, xiv, 133, 171, 175, 255
Trans-Zeya Region, 258

Transitional Zones (TZ), 121
transhumance practices, 288
transnational influences, 3, 8, 130,
    138, 225, 226-228, 230, 236, 261,
    262, 318
Transneft Oil Company, 260
Treaty of Aigun (1858), 254, 258
Treaty of Beijing (1860), 119, 254,
    285
Treaty of Bura (1727), 170
Treaty of Kyakhta (1727), 170, 253
Treaty of Livadia (1879), 98-99
Treaty of Nerchinsk (1689), 170, 253
Treaty of Shimonoseki (1895), 84,
    268
Treaty of Sinchula (1865), 23
Treaty of St. Petersburg (1881), 99
Treaty of Tarbagatai. See Protocol of
    Chuguchak
Trenin, Dmitri, 251
tribute system, 82, 89, 145, 169, 170,
    192, 207, 208, 253, 254, 262
trijunction, 7, 15, 29, 147, 149, 191,
    194, 196-198, 200n.14, 237, 300
Tripartite Agreement for Joint
    Marine Seismic Undertaking in the
    Agreement Area in the South China
    Sea (JMSU Tripartite Agreement),
    243-244, 249n.40
Trishuli River, 215
tritium, 222
Tsar Alexis, 253
Tsar Nicholas I, 254
Tsedenbal, Yumjaagiin, 175, 176,
    177
Tsheetem, Karma, 30
tsunami, 93
Tumen River, 111, 113-114, 115,
    119, 121, 181, 259
Tumen River Area Development
    Project (TRADP). See Greater
    Tumen Initiative (GTI)
Turgai, 98
Turkey, xiv, 99, 132, 136, 182, 287
Turkmenistan, xiv, 130, 136, 140n.7,
    229

Tuva. See Tannu Tuva
Tuvan Autonomous Oblast. See
    Tannu Tuva
Twenty-one Demands (1915), 171
two-front war, 54, 327
Type 86 grenade, 57

Ukraine, xiv
Ulaanbaatar, 172, 175, 180, 182, 183
Umhpa, 197
unequal treaties, xiii, 196, 285, 312,
    321
Ungern-Sternberg, Baron Roman,
    172, 185n.5
Union of Soviet Socialist Republics
    (USSR), 5, 16, 89, 97, 99, 169,
    172-178, 256, 257, 258, 277, 278,
    286, 288, 289, 296. See also
    Russia, Soviet Union.
United Front, 256, 267, 323
United Kingdom, 4, 37. See also
    Great Britain.
United Nations (UN), 18, 23, 28, 30,
    37, 38, 40, 41, 43, 48, 49, 62-63,
    76n.31, 76n.32, 81, 82, 87, 88, 91,
    94n.5, 118, 121, 164, 167n.20, 177,
    181, 212, 213, 224, 235, 236, 237,
    240, 242, 243, 244, 245, 279, 301,
    305, 316, 325, 326
United Nations Commission on the
    Limits of the Continental Shelf
    (UNCLCS), 37, 38, 40, 41, 43,
    167n.20, 242, 244, 279, 305
United Nations Convention on the
    Law of the Sea, 1982
    (UNCLOS), 38, 41, 62, 63,
    76n.32, 81, 82, 87, 88, 91, 164,
    235, 236, 237, 240, 243, 245, 301,
    316, 325, 326
United Nations Development
    Programme, 181
United Nations Educational,
    Scientific and Cultural
    Organization (UNESCO), 118
United Nations General Assembly,
    48, 177

United Nations High Commissioner for Refugees (UNHCR), 121, 213
United Nations Refugee Convention (1951), 213
United States, xi, xii, xiii, xiv, xv, 3, 16, 18, 19, 23, 33, 39, 43, 47, 49, 50, 54, 55, 57, 82, 83, 84, 85, 86, 87, 88-89, 94n.7, 101, 102, 105, 106, 114, 116, 117, 127, 134-135, 137, 138, 139, 148, 151, 178, 182, 183, 195, 210, 212, 214, 220, 221, 223, 225-226, 227, 228, 229, 230, 232n.20, 240, 252, 256, 257, 260, 270-271, 274, 277, 278, 284, 287, 311, 315, 316, 317, 324, 326, 327, 328
Unocal Oil Company, 87
Uralsk, 98
uranium, 183, 222, 288
Urga, 172. *See also* Ulaanbaatar.
U.S. Agency for International Development, 18
U.S.-Japan Treaty of Mutual Cooperation and Security (1960), 85-86
U.S. Navy, xiv, 240, 270, 316
U.S. Peace Corps, 182
U.S. State Department, 85, 86, 135, 315
USNS *Impeccable*, 316
USNS *Victorious*, 316
Ussuri River, 114, 257, 258, 259
utensils, 13
Uyghur, 13, 17-18, 97, 99-104, 130, 176, 225, 226-227, 257, 284-285, 318, 319
Uzbek Khanate, 98
Uzbek Kokand Khanate, 98
Uzbekistan, xiv, 97, 128, 130, 132-133, 136, 138, 262, 284, 286-287
Uzengi-Kush, 128

vegetables, 181
veterinarians, 183
victim mentality, xiii, 252
Vientiane, 144, 145, 150

Vietnam, xi, 7, 10, 16, 37, 38, 39, 40, 41, 42, 44n.1, 61, 63-64, 66-67, 72, 73n.1, 76n.28, 76n.29, 79n.69, 89, 143, 144-145, 146-147, 148-150, 162-163, 164, 165, 167n.20, 194, 241, 242, 244245, 248n.28, 257, 267, 272-273, 274, 275, 276-277, 294-309, 313-317, 325, 326
Vladivostok, xiv, 177, 194, 197, 198, 199, 251, 262
Vo Nguyen Giap, 148

Wa State, 194, 197, 198, 199, 200n.12
Wake Island, 328n.1
Wakhan Corridor, 4, 13, 14, 16, 18, 19
Wakhi, 13
Wakhir Pass, 18
Wakhir River Valley, 13
Wall Street Journal, 19
Wang Di, 212
Wangchuck, King Jigme Dorji, 28
Wangchuck, King Jigme Singye, 30
Wangchuk, Dasho Pema, 32
War on Terror. *See* Global War on Terror
Washington, DC, 230, 257. *See also* United States.
water projects, xiii, xv, 52, 58
Watson, Francis, 311
Weitz, Richard, 263
Wen Jiabao, 42, 53, 54, 158, 182, 262
Wen Wei Pao, 95n.29
West Kalimantan Fishery and Ocean Agency, 69
West London Reef, 162
West York Island, 162
Westphalian state, 144
White Russians, 172
Wikileaks, 135
Wilayah Pengelolaan Perikanan (WPP). *See* Regulation 1 (2009), 63
Winter Olympics (2014), 129

wolves, 182
Wonsan, 113
World Bank, 179, 284
World Trade Organization (WTO), 131, 136, 138, 183
World War II, 83, 84, 87, 90, 116, 124*n*.31, 143, 148, 156, 174, 195, 209, 241, 268, 273, 276, 277, 326
Wou-te, 147
Wu Xinbo, 100
Wuqiu Island, 271

Xiamen, 270
Xiamen University, 160
Xiao Jinmen Island. *See* Lesser Jinmen Island
Xiao Lan Yu. *See* Lesser Orchid Island
Xiaoqiu Island, 271
Xing, Guancheng, 100
Xinhua, 87, 262
Xinjiang, xiv, 4, 13, 17, 18, 19, 50, 51, 97, 98, 99-106, 117, 130, 171, 174, 176, 182, 220, 222, 225, 226-227, 229, 232*n*.34, 257, 262, 272, 285, 290, 318, 319
Xinjiang Uyghur Autonomous Region (XUAR). *See* Xinjiang
Xisha islands. *See* Paracel islands
Xisha Ziwei Fanjizhan. See Counterattack in Self-Defense in the Paracel Islands
Xu Shuzheng, 172
Xuanzhuang, 206

yak, 28, 32
Yakub Beg, 15
Yakub Khan, 222
Yalu River, 111, 112, 113, 114, 118, 119
Yanbian Chaoxianu Zizhizhou. See Yanbian Korean Nationality Autonomous Prefecture

Yanbian Korean Nationality Autonomous Prefecture, 115, 116, 117, 118, 121
Yangang-do, 111
Yangzi River, 269
Yashil Kul, 15
Yasukuni shrine, 90
Yatung, 49
Yawng Hok, 197
Yellow River, 58
Yellow Sea, 6, 111, 112, 118, 120, 121, 122
Yi Hong-gwang detachment, 116
Yijiangshan Island, 271
Yorkant River, 292*n*.15
Yuan dynasty, 113, 240, 252
Yunnan Province, 7, 143, 147, 150, 153*n*.23, 192, 194, 195, 201*n*.21
Yungshujiao. *See* Fiery Cross Reef
Yusgiantoro, Purnomo, 73

Zabaykalsk, 258
Zambales, 238, 240
Zardari, Asif Ali, 227
Zarifi, Hamrokhon, 10, 283, 286, 292*n*.9
Zeng Guofan, 99
Zeng Jize, 99
Zhang Dejiang, 134
Zhang Guobao, 260
Zhang Yannian, 135
Zhang Zuolin, 114, 172
Zhao Ziyang, 223
Zhejiang Province, 91, 268, 270
Zheng Chenggong, 268
Zhou Enlai, 27, 50, 89, 209, 210, 220, 223, 274
Zhoushan islands, 269
Zia, ul-Haq, 223
zinc, 181
Zunghars, 170, 185
Zuo Zongtang, 98, 99

About the Editors and Contributors

Ramses Amer: Associate Professor in Peace and Conflict Research, is Senior Research Fellow, Department of Oriental Languages, Stockholm University, Sweden; Guest Professor, National Institute for South China Sea Studies, Haikou, Hainan, China; and Research Associate, Swedish Institute of International Affairs (SIIA), Stockholm, Sweden. Major areas of research include security issues and conflict resolution in Southeast Asia and the wider Pacific Asia, and the role of the United Nations in the international system. He is the author of *The Sino-Vietnamese Approach to Managing Boundary Disputes*, Maritime Briefing, Vol. 3, No. 5 (Durham: International Boundaries Research Unit, University of Durham, 2002), and of *The Ethnic Chinese in Vietnam and Sino-Vietnamese Relations* (Forum, 1991). He is co-editor, with Carlyle A. Thayer, of *Vietnamese Foreign Policy in Transition* (Institute for Southeast Asian Studies; and St Martin's Press, 1999).

Charles K. Armstrong: The Korea Foundation Professor of Korean Studies in the Social Sciences in the Department of History and the Director of the Center for Korean Research at Columbia University. A specialist in the modern history of Korea and East Asia, he is the author or editor of several books, including *The North Korean Revolution, 1945-1950* (Cornell University Press, 2003), *Korea at the Center: Dynamics of Regionalism in Northeast Asia* (M.E. Sharpe, 2006), *Korean Society: Civil Society, Democracy, and the State* (Routledge, 2006), and *The Koreas* (Routledge, 2007), as well as many journal articles and book chapters. His next book is titled *Tyranny of the Weak: North Korea and the World, 1950–1992* (Cornell University Press, forthcoming 2012). He has taught at Princeton, Seoul National University, and the University of Washington, and has been a member of the Columbia faculty since 1996. Armstrong holds a B.A. in Chinese Studies from Yale University, an M.A. in International Relations from the London School of Economics, and a Ph.D. in History from the University of Chicago.

I Made Andi Arsana: Lecturer and researcher in the Department of Geodetic Engineering, Gadjah Mada University, Indonesia. He is currently an Australian Leadership Awards Scholar (Ph.D. candidate) at the Australian National Centre for Ocean Resources and Security (ANCORS), University of Wollongong. He obtained a Masters degree from the University of New South Wales, Australia, focusing on the maritime delimitation between Indonesia and Timor Leste. Andi is also an alumnus of the UN-Nippon Foundation Fellowship, a research and internship program organized by the UN Division for Ocean Affairs and the Law of the Sea (DOALOS). For the program he spent six months of research at ANCORS and three months at DOALOS in New York. Andi has been focusing his research on technical/geodetic aspects of the law of the sea, especially on maritime boundaries.

He has published several works in the field including journals, books, and popular-scientific articles.

Stephen Blank: Professor of Russian National Security Studies at the Strategic Studies Institute of the U.S. Army War College in Pennsylvania. He has published or edited 15 books focusing on Russian foreign, energy, and military policies and on International Security in Eurasia. His most recent books include *Russo-Chinese Energy Relations: Politics in Command* (Global Markets Briefing, 2006), and *Natural Allies? Regional Security in Asia and Prospects for Indo-American Strategic Cooperation* (Strategic Studies Institute, US Army War College, 2005). Author of a study of the Soviet Commissariat of Nationalities, *The Sorcerer as Apprentice: Stalin's Commissariat of Nationalities* (Greenwood Publishing Group, 1994), and the co-editor of *The Soviet Military and the Future* (Greenwood Publishing Group, 1992). He received a B.A in History from the University of Pennsylvania, and M.A. and Ph.D. in Russian History from the University of Chicago.

Lowell Bautista: Research Fellow at the Australian National Centre for Ocean Resources and Security (ANCORS), Faculty of Law, University of Wollongong, Australia. Lowell Bautista is a practicing lawyer with over ten years of experience in legal and policy research, litigation, and consultancy. He was formerly Senior Legal Researcher, and Head of the Law of the Sea Program at the Institute of International Legal Studies (IILS) of the University of the Philippines Law Center, and Research Assistant at the Marine and Environmental Law Institute, Faculty of Law, Dalhousie University. His areas of research include international environmental law, maritime boundary delimitation, the South China Sea, maritime piracy and terrorism, and Philippine maritime and territorial issues, on which topics he has also published. He holds a Bachelor of Arts in Political Science (cum laude) and Bachelor of Laws degrees from the University of the Philippines and a Master of Laws (Marine and Environmental Law) degree from Dalhousie University, and a Doctor of Philosophy (PhD) in law from the University of Wollongong.

Brahma Chellaney: Professor of Strategic Studies at the Centre for Policy Research. He has served as a member of the Policy Advisory Group headed by the Foreign Minister. Before that, Professor Chellaney was an adviser to India's National Security Council until January 2000, serving as convenor of the External Security Group of the National Security Advisory Board. He has held appointments at Harvard University, the Brookings Institution, Johns Hopkins University's School of Advanced International Studies, and the Australian National University. He is the author of five books.

June Teufel Dreyer: Professor of Political Science at the University of Miami, Coral Gables, Florida. Dr. Dreyer is a Senior Fellow of the Foreign Policy Research Institute, a member of the Board of Scholars of the U.S.-China Research Institute of the University of Southern California, and a member of the Institute for Strategic Studies. She was appointed Commissioner of the U.S.-China Economic and

Security Review Commission by Speaker of the House Dennis Hastert, and served three terms thereon. She also served as Asia adviser to the Chief of Naval Operations. Author of *China's Forty Millions: Minority Nationalities and National Integration in the People's Republic of China* (Harvard University Press, 1976), and *China's Political System: Modernization and Tradition* (Pearson Longman, 2012), now in its eighth edition. Her current project is a book on Sino-Japanese relations, under contract to Oxford University Press, and her most recent journal articles have focused on the effect of the Kosovo conflict on Chinese military strategy, Sino-Japanese, and Taiwan-Japanese relations. She received her B.A. from Wellesley and M.A. and Ph.D. degrees from Harvard University.

Bruce A. Elleman: Research Professor, Maritime History Department, U.S. Naval War College. Recent books include *Diplomacy and Deception: The Secret History of Sino-Soviet Diplomatic Relations, 1917–1927* (M.E. Sharpe, 1997); *Modern Chinese Warfare, 1795–1989* (Routledge, 2001, translated into Chinese); *Wilson and China: A Revised History of the Shandong Question* (M.E. Sharpe, 2002); *Japanese-American Civilian Prisoner Exchanges and Detention Camps, 1941–45* (London: Routledge, 2006); and *Moscow and the Emergence of Communist Power in China, 1925–30: The Nanchang Uprising and the Birth of the Red Army* (Routledge, 2009). He received his B.A. at UC Berkeley, the M.A. and Ph.D. from the History Department, Columbia University; M.S. in international history, London School of Economics; and M.A. in national security and strategic studies, with distinction (2004), from the U.S. Naval War College.

Vivian Louis Forbes: Adjunct Associate Professor, School of Earth and Environment; Map Curator, The Library, The University of Western Australia (Marine Political Geographer, Professional Cartographer, Lecturer). Author with Mohd Nizam Basiron, *Malaysia's Maritime Realm Atlas* (Kuala Lumpur: Maritime Institute of Malaysia, 2009); *Conflict and Cooperation in Managing Maritime Space in Semi-enclosed Seas* (Singapore University Press, 2001); and with Mohd Nizam Basiron, *Malaysia's Maritime Space–Analytical Atlas of Environments and Resources* (Kuala Lumpur: Maritime Institute of Malaysia, 1998). He received his M.A. from Curtin University of Technology, School of Social Sciences (1993), and his Ph.D. from The University of Western Australia, Department of Geography (1998).

Mark Galeotti: Academic chair and clinical professor, Center for Global Affairs. Galeotti is an expert in transnational organized crime, security affairs, and modern Russia, and has had an impressive career which spans teaching, research, the private sector, and government service. He has published widely, with 13 authored and edited books and numerous other pieces, from articles in peer-reviewed academic journals to newspaper op-eds. His most recent edited book is *The Problems of Security in Modern Russia* (Ashgate, 2010). His current projects include a global history of organized crime and an analysis of the Russian mafiya.

Gregory Gleason: Currently serving at the Marshall Center while on leave from the University of New Mexico, where he is a professor of political science. Author of *Federalism and Nationalism: The Struggle for Republican Rights in the USSR* (Westview, 1991), *Central Asian States: Discovering Independence* (Westview, 1997), and *Markets and Politics in Central Asia* (Routledge, 2003), as well as articles in scholarly journals. Gleason has spent considerable time in applied, field-based activities. During 1993-1995 Gleason served as chief-of-party for the first USAID program on legal and governmental reform in Central Asia. In 1996 he worked on a USAID program on market reform and privatization in Kazakhstan. In 1997-1998 he initiated an Asian Development Bank program on regional economic cooperation in Central Asia. During 1998-2000 he was director of the University Partnership Program between the University of New Mexico and Urals State Technical University, sponsored by the U.S. Department of Energy's efforts in nuclear nonproliferation. During 1999-2001 Gleason headed a partnership between the University of New Mexico and Kazakhstan universities sponsored by the U.S. Department of State. During 2005-2007 Gleason worked with the Eurasian National University in Astana, Kazakhstan to develop a new academic program on environmental management and engineering under the sponsorship of the Kazakhstan government and the U.S. government. He holds degrees from the University of California at Irvine and the University of California at Davis.

Artemy M. Kalinovsky: Assistant Professor (Universitair Docent) of East European Studies at the University of Amsterdam. He is the author of *A Long Goodbye: The Soviet Withdrawal from Afghanistan* (Harvard University Press, 2011), and co-editor with Sergey Radchenko, *The End of the Cold War and the Third World* (London: Routledge, 2011). His publications include "Soviet Decision-making during the War in Afghanistan, from Intervention to Withdrawal," *Journal of Cold War Studies* (Fall 2009), and "Politics, Diplomacy and the Soviet Withdrawal from Afghanistan: From National Reconciliation to the Geneva Accords," *Cold War History* (August 2008). He has also written for *Foreign Policy*, *National Journal*, and *Washington Post*. His current project is called The Modernization of Tajikistan and the Making of Modern Central Asia. Artemy has a B.A. from the George Washington University, and his M.A. and Ph.D. from the London School of Economics, International History.

Stephen Kotkin: Rosengarten Professor of Modern and Contemporary History and a professor of international affairs at Princeton University, where he has taught since 1989. His publications include *Uncivil Society: 1989 and the Implosion of the Communist Establishment*, with a contribution by Jan Gross (Random House, 2009); *Armageddon Averted: The Soviet Collapse 1970-2000* (Oxford University Press, 2001; revised edition 2008) and *Magnetic Mountain: Stalinism as a Civilization* (University of California Press, 1995). He has served on and chaired the editorial board of Princeton University Press (2003-2007) and directed Princeton's Russian and Eurasian Studies program (1996-2009). He was the lead book reviewer for the *New York Times* Sunday Business section for nearly three years (2006-2009). He now runs Princeton's Global History initiative. He has been a consultant and investigator in post-communist higher education for the Soros Foundation, Ford Foundation, and U.S. State Department. He completed his M.A. and Ph.D. at University of California Berkeley (1988).

Erica Marat: Expert on security issues in Central Asia, with a specific interest in military, national and regional defense, as well as state-crime relations in Eurasia. Erica has published widely, both in peer review journals and policy-oriented forums. She is a regular contributor to the Central Asia—Caucasus Analyst (http://www.cacianalyst.org/) and to the Eurasia Daily Monitor. Her most recent book is *The Military and the State in Central Asia: From Red Army to Independence* (Routledge, 2009). She holds a B.A. in Sociology from the American University—Central Asia, an M.A. in Political Sociology from the Central European University, and a Ph.D. in Political Science from the University of Bremen.

Morris Rossabi: Professor of History, Queens College and Graduate Center of City University of New York. Author of numerous books on Mongolia, including *Modern and Traditional China and Mongolia: Essays from Morris Rossabi's Career* (Global International, 2010), *Mongolian Empire and World History* (W.W. Norton, 2010), and *Modern Mongolia: From Khans to Commissars to Capitalists* (University of California Press, 2005). He received his B.A. from New York University, his M.A. from Columbia University, and the Ph.D. in East and Central Asian History, Columbia University.

Clive Schofield: Professor and Director of Research at the Australian National Centre for Ocean Resources and Security (ANCORS), University of Wollongong, Australia. He currently holds an Australian Research Council Future Fellowship. Dr Schofield is a political geographer and international legal scholar whose research interests relate to international boundaries and particularly maritime boundary delimitation. He has researched and published primarily on issues related to the delimitation of maritime boundaries, geo-technical issues in the law of the sea, maritime security and regarding maritime boundary disputes and their resolution. He is co-author with Professor Victor Prescott, Emeritus Professor of Geography, University of Melbourne, of the book, *The Maritime Political Boundaries of the World* (M. Nijhoff, 2005). He has been involved in the peaceful settlement of boundary and territory disputes, for example through the provision of technical advice and research support to governments engaged in boundary negotiations and in dispute settlement cases before the International Court of Justice.

Paul J. Smith: Professor, National Security Affairs Department, U.S. Naval War College. Paul is the author of *The Terrorism Ahead: Confronting Transnational Violence in the 21st Century* (M.E. Sharpe, 2007), and editor of *Terrorism and Violence in Southeast Asia: Transnational Challenges to States and Regional Stability* (M.E. Sharpe, 2005), and *Human Smuggling: Chinese Migrant Trafficking and the Challenge to America's Immigration Tradition* (CSIS, 2006). His scholarly articles have appeared in such journals as *Asian Affairs: an American Journal,*

Contemporary Southeast Asia, Dynamics of Asymmetric Conflict, Fletcher Forum of World Affairs, Jane's Intelligence Review, Orbis, Parameters, Studies in Conflict & Terrorism, and *Survival.* His current research centers on nontraditional security issues in East and South Asia. He earned his B.A. from Washington and Lee University, his M.A. from the University of London's School of Oriental and African Studies (SOAS), and his Ph.D. from the University of Hawaii.

Ian Storey: Senior Fellow at the Institute of Southeast Asian Studies (ISEAS), Singapore. He specializes in Asian security issues, with a focus on Southeast Asia. At ISEAS he is the editor of the peer review journal *Contemporary Southeast Asia.* His research interests include Southeast Asia's relations with external countries (specifically China and the United States), maritime security in the Asia Pacific, and China's foreign and defense policies. Ian has published articles in *Asia Policy, Asian Affairs, Contemporary Southeast Asia, Harvard Asia Quarterly, Naval War College Review, Parameters, China Brief, Terrorism Monitor,* and *Jane's Intelligence Review.* His latest books are *Southeast Asia and the Rise of China: The Search for Security* (Routledge, 2011) and *The Five Power Defence Arrangements at Forty* (ISEAS, 2011, co-edited). Prior to joining ISEAS he held academic positions at the US Defense Department's Asia-Pacific Center for Security Studies (APCSS) in Honolulu, Hawaii and at Deakin University, Melbourne, Australia.

Christopher Tang: Ph.D. student at Cornell University, specializing in modern Chinese history. His graduate research has focused on Sino-Pakistani relations, 1962-1972. He has conducted archival research in Canada and at the Foreign Ministry Archives in Beijing. In 2010, he began doctoral studies where he will continue to study China's Cold War foreign relations and domestic politics throughout the 1960s. He completed his B.A. and M.A. at McGill University.

Chitra K. Tiwari: Formerly an Assistant Professor of Political Science and International Affairs at Nepal's Tribhuvan University, he currently lives in Arlington, Virginia, and works as free-lance analyst of international affairs and political analyst and commentator on South Asian Affairs. He has contributed several articles to *The Washington Times* covering Nepal's Maoist insurgency and has been interviewed on BBC, ABC News, National Public Radio, Voice of America, and other venues. He is also the author of "Red Star over the Himalayas," published in the *Current History* (September 2005), and coauthor with Ole Borre and Sushil R. Pandey of *Nepalese Political Behavior* (Aarhus University Press, 1994). Dr. Tiwari holds a Ph.D. from The George Washington University.

Ian Townsend-Gault: Associate Professor of Law and Director, Southeast Asian Legal Studies. He teaches and researches in international law, especially marine resource law, maritime boundaries, terrestrial and maritime transboundary management, maritime cooperation, and the protection of the environment, and now works also on human rights and international justice issues. Co-editor with Heather Nicol, *Holding the Line: Borders in a Borderless World* (University of British Columbia Press, 2004), and co-author with Hasjim Djalal, "Managing Potential

Conflicts in the South China Sea: Informal Diplomacy for Conflict Prevention," in Crocker, Hampson and Aall, eds., *Herding Cats: Multiparty Mediation in a Complex World* (United States Institute of Peace Press, 1999). He has acted as a consultant to the United Nations, the Asian Development Bank, and the international development agencies of Canada, Norway, Sweden, and Finland, and has advised governments in Southeast Asia and Eastern Europe on a variety of international legal issues, domestic law and policy-making, and legal reform. He was co-founder and co-director of the multilateral Track-Two informal diplomacy initiative "Managing Potential Conflicts in the South China Sea." He has close links with a number of government agencies, universities and research institutions in countries such as Cambodia, Indonesia, Laos, Philippines, Thailand, and Vietnam.

Brendan Whyte: Assistant Curator of Maps at the National Library of Australia. An historical and political geographer by training, with interests in enclaves and international boundary disputes, he has held academic posts in Australia, Israel and Thailand. His Ph.D. at the University of Melbourne investigated the history and geography of the enclaves along the Indo-Bangladeshi and Belgo-Dutch borders. He has published books on both sets of enclaves, a railway atlas of Thailand, and articles on topics as diverse as Siam's military contribution to World War I, a global analysis of visa-free travel privileges, and cartographic vexillology.